MICROSOFT Works 4.5
Introductory Concepts and Techniques

Gary B. Shelly
Thomas J. Cashman
Kathleen Shelly

COURSE TECHNOLOGY
ONE MAIN STREET
CAMBRIDGE MA 02142

an International Thomson Publishing company I(T)P

CAMBRIDGE • ALBANY • BONN • CINCINNATI • LONDON • MADRID • MELBOURNE
MEXICO CITY • NEW YORK • PARIS • SAN FRANCISCO • TOKYO • TORONTO • WASHINGTON

© 1998 by Course Technology — I(T)P*

For more information, contact:

Course Technology
One Main Street
Cambridge, Massachusetts 02142, USA

ITP Europe
Berkshire House
168-173 High Holborn
London, WC1V 7AA, United Kingdom

ITP Australia
102 Dodds Street
South Melbourne
Victoria 3205 Australia

ITP Nelson Canada
1120 Birchmount Road
Scarborough, Ontario
Canada M1K 5G4

International Thomson Editores
Saneca, 53
Colonia Polanco
11560 Mexico D.F. Mexico

ITP GmbH
Konigswinterer Strasse 418
53227 Bonn, Germany

ITP Asia
60 Albert Street, #15-01
Albert Complex
Singapore 189969

ITP Japan
Hirakawa-cho Kyowa Building, 3F
2-2-1 Hirakawa-cho, Chiyoda-ku
Tokyo 102, Japan

All rights reserved. This publication is protected by federal copyright laws. No part of this publication may be reproduced, stored in a retrieval system, or transmitted in any form or by any means, electronic, mechanical, photocopying, recording, or otherwise, or be used to make a derivative work (such as translation or adaptation), without prior permission in writing from Course Technology.

TRADEMARKS

Course Technology and the Open Book logo are registered trademarks and CourseKits is a trademark of Course Technology.

I(T)P* The ITP logo is a registered trademark of International Thomson Publishing.

SHELLY CASHMAN SERIES® and **Custom Edition**® are trademarks of International Thomson Publishing. Some of the product names and company names used in this book have been used for identification purposes only and may be trademarks or registered trademarks of their respective manufacturers and sellers. International Thomson Publishing and Course Technology disclaim any affiliation, association, or connection with, or sponsorship or endorsement by, such owners.

DISCLAIMER

Course Technology reserves the right to revise this publication and make changes from time to time in its content without notice.

PHOTO CREDITS: *Project 1, page W 1.4,* Laptop Computer, Scott R. Goodwin Photography; *page W 1.5, TIME* Magazine Cover © 1982 TIME, Inc.; *Project 3, page W 3.3,* Couple playing golf image provided by PhotoDisc Inc. ©1997

ISBN 0-7895-4552-7

2 3 4 5 6 7 8 9 10   BC   02 01 00 99

Microsoft Works 4.5
Introductory Concepts and Techniques

CONTENTS

Microsoft Works 4.5 — W 1.1

▶ PROJECT ONE
CREATING A FORMATTED DOCUMENT WITH CLIP ART

Objectives	W 1.3
Introduction to Microsoft Works for Windows 95	W 1.6
Microsoft Works Accessories	W 1.7
Templates and TaskWizards	W 1.7
Mouse Usage	W 1.7
Project One	W 1.8
Starting Microsoft Works	W 1.8
Starting the Word Processor	W 1.10
Maximizing the Document Window	W 1.12
The Word Processor Window	W 1.13
Title Bar	W 1.13
Menu Bar	W 1.13
Toolbar	W 1.14
Ruler	W 1.15
Scroll Bars	W 1.15
Status Bar	W 1.15
Mouse Pointer	W 1.16
View Modes	W 1.16
Changing View Modes	W 1.16
Page Break Mark, Insertion Point, and End-of-File Mark	W 1.18
Word Processor Defaults	W 1.18
Understanding Fonts, Font Styles, and Font Sizes	W 1.18
Fonts	W 1.19
Font Style	W 1.19
Font Sizes	W 1.19
Formatting Requirements for Project One	W 1.20
Creating a Document	W 1.20
All Characters Command	W 1.21
Entering Text	W 1.22
Paragraph Marks	W 1.23
Using the Wordwrap Feature	W 1.23
Entering Text that Scrolls Through the Document Window	W 1.24
Saving a Document	W 1.26
Formatting the Document	W 1.28
Highlighting Characters, Words, Lines, and Paragraphs	W 1.29
Centering Paragraphs	W 1.29
Changing Fonts	W 1.31
Changing Font Size	W 1.32
Formatting the Remaining Heading Lines	W 1.33
Formatting Additional Text	W 1.34
Creating a Bulleted List	W 1.35
Displaying Text in Italics	W 1.39
Displaying Text in Color	W 1.40
Bold Style	W 1.42
Using Clip Art in a Document	W 1.44
Inserting Clip Art in a Word Processing Document	W 1.44
Changing the Size of Clip Art	W 1.47
Saving an Existing Document with the Same Filename	W 1.49
Print Preview	W 1.50
Printing a Document	W 1.52
Closing a Document	W 1.54
Closing Works	W 1.55
Opening an Existing Document	W 1.56
Moving Around in a Word Processor Document	W 1.59
Deleting and Inserting Text in a Document	W 1.59
Inserting Text	W 1.60
Overtyping Existing Text	W 1.60
Replacing Text with New Text	W 1.60
Undo Command	W 1.60
Undo Paragraph Formatting	W 1.61
Undo Font Styles	W 1.61
Online Help	W 1.61
Viewing Introduction to Works	W 1.64
Project Summary	W 1.65
What You Should Know	W 1.65
Test Your Knowledge	W 1.66
Use Help	W 1.68
Apply Your Knowledge	W 1.70
In the Lab	W 1.71
Cases and Places	W 1.75

▶ PROJECT TWO
BUILDING A SPREADSHEET AND CHARTING DATA

Objectives	W 2.1
The Works Spreadsheet Tool	W 2.4
Project Two	W 2.5
Spreadsheet Preparation Steps	W 2.6
Starting the Works Spreadsheet	W 2.6
The Spreadsheet	W 2.8
Cell, Highlighted Cell, and Mouse Pointer	W 2.8
Spreadsheet Window	W 2.9
Menu Bar, Toolbar, Entry Bar, and Status Bar	W 2.10
Highlighting a Cell	W 2.11
Entering Text in a Spreadsheet	W 2.11
Entering the Spreadsheet Title	W 2.12
Correcting a Mistake While Typing	W 2.13
Entering Column Titles	W 2.14
Entering Row Titles	W 2.15
Entering Numbers	W 2.16
Calculating a Sum	W 2.18
Copying a Cell to Adjacent Cells	W 2.20
Summing a Row Total	W 2.21
Copying Adjacent Cells in a Column	W 2.23
Formatting the Spreadsheet	W 2.24
Formatting Text and Changing the Color of Cells	W 2.24
Using the AutoFormat Command	W 2.30
Comma Format	W 2.31
Changing Column Widths	W 2.33
Checking the Spelling on the Spreadsheet	W 2.35
Saving a Spreadsheet	W 2.35
Printing a Spreadsheet	W 2.37
Charting a Spreadsheet	W 2.38
Printing the Chart	W 2.41
Viewing the Spreadsheet	W 2.43
Saving the Spreadsheet and Chart	W 2.45
Closing a Spreadsheet	W 2.45
Closing Works	W 2.45
Opening an Existing Spreadsheet File	W 2.46
Correcting Errors	W 2.48
Correcting Errors Prior to Entering Data into a Cell	W 2.49
Editing Data in a Cell	W 2.49
Clearing a Cell or Range of Cells	W 2.50
Clearing the Entire Spreadsheet	W 2.51
Project Summary	W 2.51
What You Should Know	W 2.51
Test Your Knowledge	W 2.52
Use Help	W 2.54
Apply Your Knowledge	W 2.55
In the Lab	W 2.56
Cases and Places	W 2.60

▶ PROJECT THREE
USING FORM DESIGN TO CREATE A DATABASE

Objectives	W 3.1
Introduction	W 3.4
Project Three	W 3.4
Creating the Database	W 3.6
Starting Microsoft Works	W 3.6
Creating a Database	W 3.7
Saving the Database	W 3.12
Form Design View	W 3.12
Formatting the Database Form in Form Design View	W 3.13
Displaying the Database in Form Design View	W 3.14
Changing Form Margins	W 3.16
Setting Field Widths	W 3.17
Positioning Fields on the Form	W 3.19
Moving the Field Names as a Unit	W 3.22
Importing Clip Art from Microsoft Clip Gallery Live on the World Wide Web	W 3.23
Quitting a Web Session	W 3.28
Entering and Formatting a Title on a Database Form Using WordArt	W 3.28
Inserting a Rectangular Bar Below the Title	W 3.33
Adding Color to the Rectangle	W 3.35
Formatting Field Names	W 3.36
Adding a Border on Fields	W 3.37
Adding Text Labels to the Database Form	W 3.39
Adding an Underline and Bold to the Text Labels	W 3.40
Entering Data into the Database in Form View	W 3.41
Changing to Form View	W 3.41
Entering Data into the Database	W 3.42
List View	W 3.46
Formatting the Database in List View	W 3.48
Setting Field Widths	W 3.50
Printing the Database	W 3.52
Printing the Database in Form View	W 3.52
Printing a Single Record in Form View	W 3.55
Printing the Database in List View	W 3.57
Exiting Works	W 3.60
Project Summary	W 3.60
What You Should Know	W 3.60
Test Your Knowledge	W 3.61
Use Help	W 3.64
Apply Your Knowledge	W 3.65
In the Lab	W 3.65
Cases and Places	W 3.68

Preface

The Shelly Cashman Series® offers the finest textbooks in computer education. The Microsoft Works books continue with the innovation, quality, and reliability that you have come to expect from this series. We are proud that both our previous Microsoft Works books were best-sellers, and we are confident that this book will join its predecessors.

Microsoft Works 4.5 is identical to Microsoft Works 4 in the way it looks and operates. The updated Microsoft Works 4.5 version includes extensive new clip art images, more than 100 additional templates, and a companion copy of Microsoft Internet Explorer, which you optionally can install. As well as the numerous clip art images available with the Works update, you also have access to the Microsoft Clip Gallery Live Web site via a button in the Microsoft Clip Gallery dialog box. The button connects you to the World Wide Web where you can browse a comprehensive gallery and then download the desired images into the Microsoft Clip Gallery dialog box.

In our Microsoft Works books, you will find an educationally sound and easy-to-follow pedagogy that combines a step-by-step approach with corresponding screens. The projects and exercises in the books are designed to take full advantage of the Microsoft Works features. The popular Other Ways and More About features offer in-depth knowledge of Microsoft Works. The project openers provide a fascinating perspective on the subject covered in the project. The Shelly Cashman Series Microsoft Works books will make your computer applications class exciting and dynamic and one that your students will remember as one of their better educational experiences.

Objectives of This Textbook

Microsoft Works 4.5: Introductory Concepts and Techniques is intended for a course that covers a brief introduction to Microsoft Works. No expreience with a computer is assumed and no mathematics beyond the high school freshman level is required. The objectives of this book are:

- To teach the fundamentals of Microsoft Works
- To give students an overview of how to use the Word Processor, Spreadsheet, and Database tools
- To provide a knowledge base of Microsoft Works on which students can build
- To expose students to examples of the computer as a useful tool
- To help students who are working on their own

When students complete the course using this textbook, they will have a basic knowledge and understanding of Microsoft Works.

The Shelly Cashman Approach

Features of the Shelly Cashman Series Windows applications books include:

- **Project Orientation:** Each project in the book uses the unique Shelly Cashman Series screen-by-screen, step-by-step approach.
- **Screen-by-Screen, Step-by-Step Instructions:** Each of the tasks required to complete a project is identified throughout the development of the project and is shown screen by screen, step by step.
- **Multiple Ways to Use the Book:** The book can be used in a variety of ways, including: (a) Lecture and textbook approach; (b) Tutorial approach; (c) Many teachers lecture on the material and then require their students to perform each step in the project, reinforcing the material lectured. The students then complete one or more of the In the

> **More About Microsoft Clip Gallery**
>
> Approximately 7,000 additional clip art images are on the Microsoft Works CD-ROM. To see previews of these images in Microsoft Clip Gallery, insert the CD-ROM into your CD-ROM drive before starting Microsoft Clip Gallery.

vi • Preface

> **OtherWays**
> 1. Click field entry, click top right handle and drag to desired width

Lab exercises; and (d) Reference: Each task in a project is clearly identified. Therefore, the material serves as a complete reference.

- **Other Ways Boxes for Reference:** Microsoft Works provides a wide variety of ways to carry out a given task. The Other Ways boxes displayed at the end of most of the step-by-step sequences specify the other ways to do the task completed in the steps.

Organization of This Textbook

Microsoft Works 4.5: Introductory Concepts and Techniques consists of three projects. A short description of each follows.

Project 1 – Creating a Formatted Document with Clip Art In Project 1, students are introduced to the Works Word Processor tool. Topics include starting and closing Works; entering and correcting text; centering text; creating a bulleted list; changing font, font size, and font style; inserting clip art; using print preview; opening and editing a word processing document; and using Works online Help.

Project 2 – Building a Spreadsheet and Charting Data In Project 2, students are introduced to the Works Spreadsheet tool. Topics include entering text and numeric values; summing columns and rows using the AutoSum button; copying cells using the fill handle; centering text across columns; coloring text; using the AutoFormat feature; changing column widths; saving a spreadsheet; printing a spreadsheet; charting the data in the spreadsheet using a 3-D Bar chart; opening a spreadsheet file; and correcting errors.

Project 3 – Using Form Design to Create a Database In Project 3, students are introduced to the Works Database tool. Topics include an explanation of form design view; creating a form design view title using WordArt, entering fields and labels on the form; saving; formatting the database title; inserting clip art from the Microsoft Clip Gallery Live Web site; positioning the fields on the form by dragging; and formatting fields and labels. The form view of the database is described; data is entered into the database; list view is explained; and the data is formatted in list view. Finally, the database is saved, printed in form view, and then printed in list view using landscape orientation.

End-of-Project Student Activities

A notable strength of the Shelly Cashman Series Windows applications books is the extensive student activities at the end of each project. Well-structured student activities can make the difference between students merely participating in a class and students retaining the information they learn. These activities include:

- **What You Should Know** A listing of the tasks completed within a project together with the pages where the step-by-step, screen-by-screen explanations appear. This section provides a perfect study review for students.

- **Test Your Knowledge** Four activities designed to determine students' understanding of the material in the project. Included are true/false questions, multiple-choice questions, and two short-answer activities.

- **Use Help** Any user of Windows applications must know how to use Help. Therefore, this book contains extensive exercises that require students to use Help. These exercises alone distinguish the Shelly Cashman Series from any other set of Windows instructional materials.

- **Apply Your Knowledge** This exercise requires students to open and manipulate a file from the Student Floppy Disk (Data Disk) that no longer accompanies this book. Instructions for obtaining the Data Disk are listed on the inside back cover of this textbook.

- **In the Lab** Three in-depth assignments require students to apply the knowledge gained in the project to solve problems on a computer.
- **Cases and Places** Seven unique case studies allow students to apply their knowledge to real-world situations.

Instructor's Resource Kit

A comprehensive Instructor's Resource Kit (IRK) accompanies this textbook in the form of a CD-ROM. The CD-ROM includes an electronic Instructor's Manual (called ElecMan) and teaching and testing aids. The CD-ROM (ISBN 0-7895-4554-3) is available through your Course Technology representative or by calling one of the following telephone numbers: Colleges and Universities, 1-800-648-7450; High Schools, 1-800-824-5179; and Career Colleges, 1-800-477-3692. The contents of the CD-ROM are listed below.

- **ElecMan (*Electronic Instructor's Manual*)** ElecMan is made up of Microsoft Word files. The files include lecture notes, solutions to laboratory assignments, and a large test bank. The files allow you to modify the lecture notes or generate quizzes and exams from the test bank using your own word processor. Where appropriate, solutions to laboratory assignments are embedded as icons in the files. When an icon appears, double-click it and the application will start and the solution will display on the screen. ElecMan includes the following for each project: project objectives; project overview; detailed lesson plans with page number references; teacher notes and activities; answers to the end-of-project exercises; test bank of 110 questions for every project (50 true/false, 25 multiple-choice, and 35 fill-in-the blank) with page number references; and transparency references. The transparencies are available through the Figures on CD-ROM described below. The test bank questions are numbered the same as in Course Test Manager. Thus, you can print a copy of the project and use the printed test bank to select your questions in Course Test Manager.

- **Figures on CD-ROM** Illustrations for every figure in the textbook are available. Use this ancillary to create a slide show from the illustrations for lecture or to print transparencies for use in lecture with an overhead projector.

- **Course Test Manager** Course Test Manager is a powerful testing and assessment package that enables instructors to create and print tests from the large test bank. Instructors with access to a networked computer lab (LAN) can administer, grade, and track tests online. Students also can take online practice tests, which generate customized study guides that indicate where in the textbook students can fine more information for each question.

- **Lecture Success System** Lecture Success System files are for use with the application software, a personal computer, and projection device to explain and illustrate the step-by-step, screen-by-screen development of a project in the textbook without entering large amounts of data.

- **Lab Tests** Tests that parallel the In the Lab assignments are supplied for the purpose of testing students in the laboratory on the material covered in the project. You also can use these assignments as supplementary exercises.

- **Instructor's Lab Solutions** Solutions and required files for all the In the Lab assignments at the end of each project are available.

- **Student Files** All the files that are required by students to complete the Apply Your Knowledge exercises are included.

- **Interactive Labs** Eighteen hands-on interactive labs take students from ten to fifteen minutes to step through to help solidify and reinforce computer concepts. Student assessment is available in each interactive lab by means of a Print button. The assessment requires students to answer questions about the contents of the interactive lab.

Shelly Cashman Online

Shelly Cashman Online is a World Wide Web service available to instructors and students of computer education. Visit Shelly Cashman Online at www.scseries.com. Shelly Cashman Online is divided into four areas:

- **Series Information** Information on the Shelly Cashman Series products.
- **Teaching Resources** This area includes password-protected data, course outlines, teaching tips, and ancillaries such as ElecMan.
- **Student Center** Dedicated to students learning about computers with Shelly Cashman Series textbooks and software. This area includes cool links and much more.
- **Community** Opportunities to discuss your course and your ideas with instructors in your field and with the Shelly Cashman Series team.

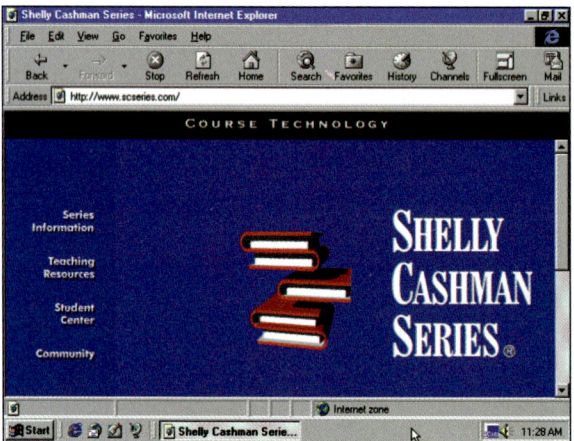

Acknowledgments

The Shelly Cashman Series would not be the leading computer education series without the contributions of outstanding publishing professionals. First, and foremost, among them is Becky Herrington, director of production and designer. She is the heart and soul of the Shelly Cashman Series, and it is only through her leadership, dedication, and tireless efforts that superior products are made possible. Becky created and produced the award-winning Windows 95 series of books.

Under Becky's direction, the following individuals made significant contributions to this book: Ginny Harvey, series specialist and developmental editor; Ken Russo, senior graphic designer/Web developer; Mike Bodnar and Stephanie Nance, graphic artists; Mark Norton, graphic artist and cover designer; Jeanne Black, Quark expert; Sarah Evertson of Image Quest, photo researcher; and Cristina Haley, indexer. Special thanks go to Jim Quasney, our dedicated series editor; Lisa Strite, senior editor; Lora Wade, associate product manager; Tonia Grafakos, editorial assistant; Jon Langdale, online developer; and Kathryn Coyne, project marketing manager. Special mention must go to Suzanne Biron, Becky Herrington, and Michael Gregson for the outstanding book design.

Gary B. Shelly
Thomas J. Cashman
Kathleen Shelly

Microsoft **Works 4** Windows 95

▸ PROJECT ONE

CREATING A FORMATTED DOCUMENT WITH CLIP ART

Objectives W 1.3
Case Perspective W 1.6
Introduction to Microsoft Works for Windows 95 W 1.6
Project One W 1.8
Starting Microsoft Works W 1.8
The Word Processor Window W 1.13
View Modes W 1.16
Word Processor Defaults W 1.18
Understanding Fonts, Font Styles, and Font Sizes W 1.18
Formatting Requirements for Project One W 1.20
Creating a Document W 1.20
Saving a Document W 1.26
Formatting the Document W 1.28
Using Clip Art in a Document W 1.44
Saving an Existing Document with the Same Filename W 1.49
Print Preview W 1.50
Printing a Document W 1.52
Closing a Document W 1.54
Closing Works W 1.55
Opening an Existing Document W 1.56
Deleting and Inserting Text in a Document W 1.59
Online Help W 1.61
Project Summary W 1.65
What You Should Know W 1.65
Test Your Knowledge W 1.66
Use Help W 1.68
Apply Your Knowledge W 1.70
In the Lab W 1.71
Cases and Places W 1.74

▸ PROJECT TWO

BUILDING A SPREADSHEET AND CHARTING DATA

Objectives W 2.1
Case Perspective W 2.4
The Works Spreadsheet Tool W 2.4
Project Two W 2.5
Starting the Works Spreadsheet W 2.6
The Spreadsheet W 2.8
Highlighting a Cell W 2.11
Entering Text in a Spreadsheet W 2.11
Entering Numbers W 2.16
Calculating a Sum W 2.18
Copying a Cell to Adjacent Cells W 2.20
Summing a Row Total W 2.21
Copying Adjacent Cells in a Column W 2.23
Formatting the Spreadsheet W 2.24
Formatting Text and Changing the Color of Cells W 2.24
Using the AutoFormat Command W 2.30
Checking the Spelling on the Spreadsheet W 2.35
Saving a Sspreadsheet W 2.35
Printing a Spreadsheet W 2.37
Charting a Spreadsheet W 2.38
Printing the Chart W 2.41
Saving the Spreadsheet and Chart W 2.45
Closing a Spreadsheet W 2.45
Closing Works W 2.45
Opening an Existing Spreadsheet File W 2.46
Correcting Errors W 2.48
Project Summary W 2.51
What You Should Know W 2.51
Test Your Knowledge W 2.52
Use Help W 2.54
Apply Your Knowledge W 2.55
In the Lab W 2.56
Cases and Places W 2.60

▸ PROJECT THREE

USING FORM DESIGN TO CREATE A DATABASE

Objectives W 3.1
Case Perspective W 3.4
Introduction W 3.4
Project Seven W 3.4
Starting Microsoft Works W 3.6
Creating a Database W 3.7
Saving the Database W 3.12
Form Design View W 3.12
Formatting the Database Form in Form Design View W 3.13
Entering Data into the Database in Form View W 3.41
List View W 3.46
Formatting the Database in List View W 3.48
Printing the Database W 3.52
Exiting Works W 3.60
Project Summary W 3.60
What You Should Know W 3.60
Test Your Knowledge W 3.61
Use Help W 3.64
Apply Your Knowledge W 3.65
In the Lab W 3.65
Cases and Places W 3.68

Microsoft Works 4.5 Windows 95

Microsoft Works 4

Windows 95

Creating a Formatted Document with Clip Art

Objectives:

You will have mastered the material in this project when you can:

◗ Start Microsoft Works
◗ Start the Word Processor tool
◗ Identify the features of the Works word processing window
◗ Enter text
◗ Highlight a character, word, line, or paragraph
◗ Center one or more words
◗ Change fonts, font sizes, and font styles
◗ Create a bulleted list
◗ Change the color of text
◗ Insert clip art in a document
◗ Use the Print Preview feature
◗ Save a document
◗ Print a document
◗ Close a document
◗ Close Works
◗ Open an existing document
◗ Delete and insert data
◗ Use online Help

Project 1

Four Score and Seven Years Ago...

How did Abe ever get by without a Word Processor?

What if Abraham Lincoln had owned a laptop computer? While he might not have improved the Gettysburg Address, he could have saved himself a case of writer's cramps from handwriting the multiple copies requested by friends and historians.

Today, writers are more fortunate than Mr. Lincoln. Whether facing a term paper for Poly Sci or writing home for more money, the Works Word Processor, with its built-in TaskWizards for letters, resumés, and other documents, gives anyone a running start.

In college and in virtually any career thereafter— engineer, scientist, movie writer, journalist, or U.S. President—it is essential that you present the ideas and products of your work in clear, accurate written form. In fact, just getting a start in a chosen profession may depend on how well you are represented by your stand-in: a well-prepared resumé. Making a favorable first impression is not only important, it is vital.

Once you have a job, you are likely to find that companies no longer provide secretarial assistance for creating and revising documents. Now employers expect professionals to come to the workplace armed with these skills.

Fortunately, technology has risen to the challenge. In the days of typewriters, every change and every mistake meant retyping a page or sometimes the whole document. Today's tools permit words, sentences, pages, and even whole sections of text to be added, deleted, or reordered with the click of a mouse before using a single page of printer paper. With the built-in spelling checker and thesaurus, capabilities are included for searching out spelling errors and finding those elusive synonyms.

Why the emphasis on accuracy? Because errors are expensive. Consider *TIME* magazine's $100,000 missing "r." The presses had already begun rolling out the covers for the March 21, 1983 issue when someone discovered the letter r missing from the word "Control" in the headline: "A New Plan for Arms Contol." This mistake cost the publication $100,000 and a day's delay to add back the letter r. Spelling checker would have spotted this.

In the same manner, written errors can become legend. In 1631, an authorized edition of the *Holy Bible* came off the presses in London with the "not" missing from the seventh of the Ten Commandments. The result: "Thou shalt commit adultery." The book's publishers were fined 3,000 English pounds and went down in history as the creators of the *Wicked Bible*. This illustrates that even the best tools cannot replace careful proofreading.

Though the Works Word Processor is not a substitute for original thought and careful review, it can remove many of the artificial barriers to completing a quality education and later on, getting a quality job.

In the Beginning...¶

Microsoft **Works 4** Windows

Project 1

Microsoft Works 4
Windows 95

Creating a Formatted Document with Clip Art

Case Perspective

The National Business Training Seminars has grown rapidly in the last four years — primarily as a provider of continuing business education on leadership skills. The management feels that by the year 2000, more than one million companies will be disseminating information and services on the Internet. To instruct businesses how to effectively use the Internet as a business tool, the management has designed a new workshop. They have asked you to design and create an announcement advertising the company's new comprehensive, one-day seminar on how businesses can gain desktop access to the world. In addition, Victor Lebar, marketing director, has asked you to insert an illustration in the announcement to make it more visually appealing and draw attention to the global opportunities of using the Internet.

You are to create an attractive, informative advertisement that will convey the importance of attending the seminar. You are to enter the text and format the document with color and clip art so it is suitable for mailing to businesses.

Introduction to Microsoft Works for Windows 95

Microsoft Works for Windows 95 is application software that provides word processing, spreadsheet, database, and communications capabilities in a single package.

The applications within Microsoft Works for Windows 95, called **tools**, work together to help you create your documents. These tools are briefly described in the following paragraphs.

1. **Word Processor Tool** — Use the Word Processor tool to prepare all forms of personal and business communications, including letters, business and academic reports, and other types of written documents.
2. **Spreadsheet Tool** — Use the Spreadsheet tool for applications that require you to enter, calculate, manipulate, and analyze data. You can also use the Spreadsheet tool to display data graphically in the form of charts, such as bar charts and pie charts.
3. **Database Tool** — Use the Database tool for creating, sorting, retrieving, displaying, and printing data such as names and addresses of friends or customers, company inventories, employee payroll records, or other types of business or personal data. You can use the Database tool for virtually any type of record keeping activity that requires you to create, sort, display, retrieve, and print data.

4. **Communications Tool** — Use the Communications tool with a modem to communicate computer to computer with other computer users, information services, and special-interest bulletin board services. You can use the Communications tool to send and receive messages through electronic mail or fax.

Microsoft Works Accessories

Additional software features, called **accessories**, are a part of the software package that helps you work more effectively with the various tools. These accessories include Spelling Checker, which allows you to check the spelling in documents; Microsoft Clip Gallery 3.0, which contains illustrations you can insert in documents; a WordArt feature, which allows you to change plain text into artistically designed text; Note-It, which allows you to insert pop-up notes in a document, and Microsoft Draw, which allows you to create and modify drawings that can be inserted into a Word Processor document or a Database form. These accessories will be explained in detail as they are used throughout the book.

Templates and TaskWizards

In addition to the Microsoft Works tools and accessories, Works includes templates and TaskWizards to help you create professional looking documents. **Templates** are documents that contain all the settings, text, and formats that you can reuse. For example, when you create a thank you letter for a job interview, you can save it as a template and reuse it as a basis for writing other thank you letters for interviews.

TaskWizards permit you to create a letter, design a database, create a newsletter, and similar activities by asking you what you want to do. Based on your responses, TaskWizard performs the task. For example, when creating a resume, Works will ask if you want to add a letterhead to the resume, what type of professionally designed layout you want to use, or what category headings you want to include in the resume. Based on your responses, Works inserts the elements you specify and designs the resume automatically for you. When the TaskWizard is finished, you can add or remove text and make any changes you want.

Mouse Usage

In this book, the mouse is used as the primary way to communicate with Microsoft Works. You can perform five operations with a mouse: point, click, right-click, double-click, and drag.

Point means you move the mouse across a flat surface until the mouse pointer rests on the item of choice on the screen. As you move the mouse, the mouse pointer moves across the screen in the same direction. **Click** means you press and release the left mouse button. The terminology used in this book to direct you to point to a particular item and then click is, Click the particular item. For example, Click the Bold button, means point to the Bold button and then click.

More *About* Microsoft Works for Windows 95

Microsoft Works for Windows 95 combines four of the more popular types of PC programs in one package – a word processor, a spreadsheet program, a database management program, and a communications program. Each of the four tools is not as refined as the larger and more sophisticated stand-alone products such as Microsoft Word or Lotus 1-2-3. Works' big advantage is that it offers a package that includes the most important features of the stand-alone products at a fraction of the cost.

Right-click means you press and release the right mouse button. As with the left mouse button, you normally will point to an item on the screen prior to right-clicking. When you right-click in Microsoft Works, a context-sensitive menu displays. The **context-sensitive menu** contains frequently used commands you can use with the current selection.

Double-click means you quickly press and release the left mouse button twice without moving the mouse. In most cases, you must point to an item before double-clicking. **Drag** means you point to an item, hold down the left mouse button, move the item to the desired location on the screen, and then release the left mouse button.

The use of the mouse is an important skill when working with Microsoft Works.

Project One

Because word processing is widely used in both the academic and business world, the Word Processor is the first of the Works tools presented. To illustrate the use and power of the Word Processor, the steps necessary to create the document shown in Figure 1-1 are explained on the following pages. This announcement advertises a one-day seminar, Doing Business on the Internet.

To create the announcement, you must type the text, center selected lines, use several different fonts and font styles, enlarge the fonts, change the font styles to bold, add bullets to the list, insert an illustration into the document, and display the last three lines in red. You can accomplish these tasks easily using the Microsoft Works Word Processor.

DOING BUSINESS ON THE INTERNET

A ONE-DAY SEMINAR

Discover how you can tap into the Internet marketplace to successfully promote your company's products and services. Ride the information superhighway to greater profits.

Learn to:

- **Identify business opportunities on the Internet**
- **Use the Internet's tools to attract customers**
- **Publish Home Pages that introduce your business to potential prospects**
- **Safeguard information and ensure confidentiality for your company and your clients**

Register Now

CALL (714) 555-3567
FAX (714) 555-2468
E-MAIL seminar@email.com

FIGURE 1-1

Starting Microsoft Works

To start Works, Windows must be running and Microsoft Works must be installed on your computer. Perform the following steps to start Works.

Microsoft **Works 4** Windows 95
Starting Microsoft Works • W 1.9

Steps To Start Microsoft Works

1 **Click the Start button on the taskbar, point to Programs, point to the Microsoft Works folder on the Programs submenu, and then point to Microsoft Works on the Microsoft Works submenu.**

The Start menu displays (Figure 1-2). The right-pointing arrow to the right of Programs indicates a submenu is associated with the menu. When you point to Programs, the Programs submenu displays. When you point to the Microsoft Works folder on the Programs submenu, the Microsoft Works submenu displays.

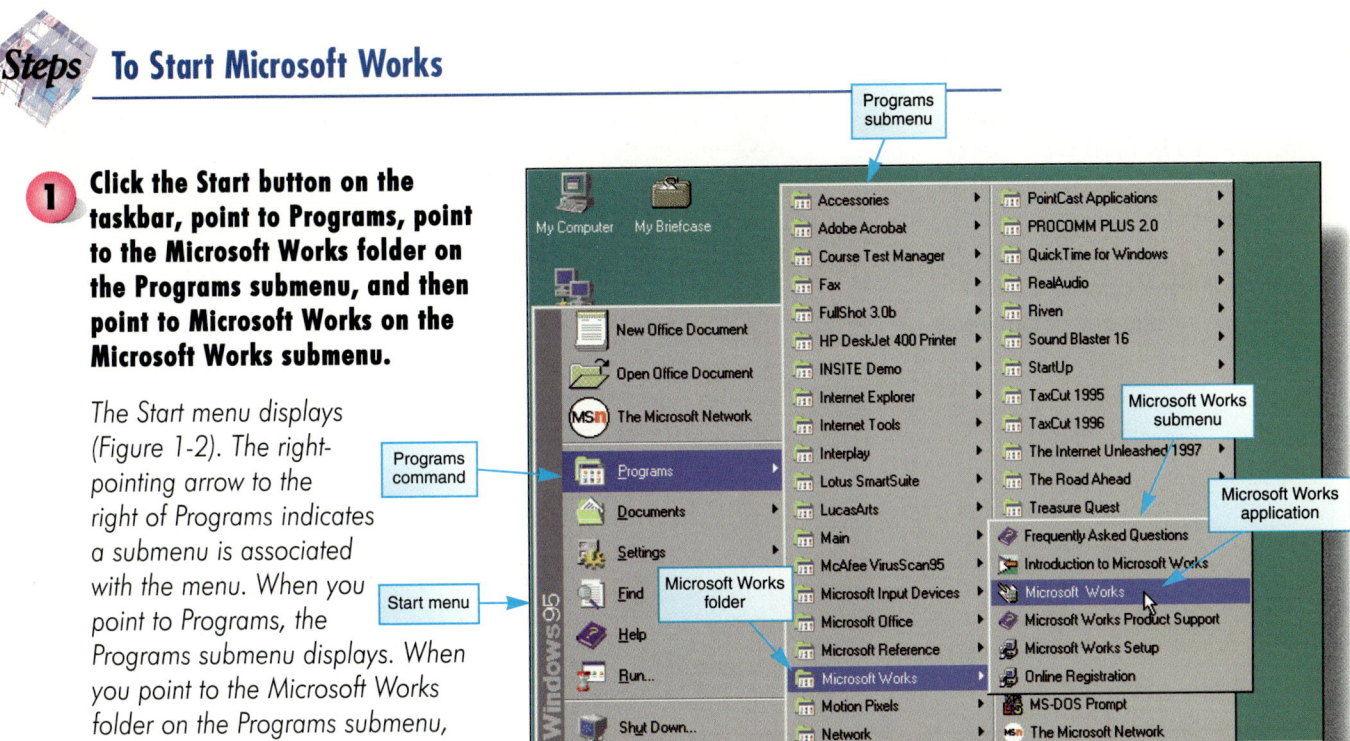

FIGURE 1-2

2 **Click Microsoft Works. When the Works Task Launcher dialog box displays, point to the Works Tools tab.**

The Microsoft Works application window containing a dialog box with the title, **Works Task Launcher**, displays (Figure 1-3). The Works Task Launcher dialog box contains three tabbed sheets; TaskWizards, Existing Documents, and Works Tools. The **TaskWizards sheet** currently displays on the screen. A list of wizard categories displays in the list box. The **Common Tasks category** displays six TaskWizards you can use to quickly create a document. The **List categories in different order button** rearranges the TaskWizards list. The **Exit Works button** closes all open Works documents and closes Works. A brief description of the TaskWizard sheet displays below the Works Task Launcher dialog box. The **Microsoft Works button** displays on the taskbar.

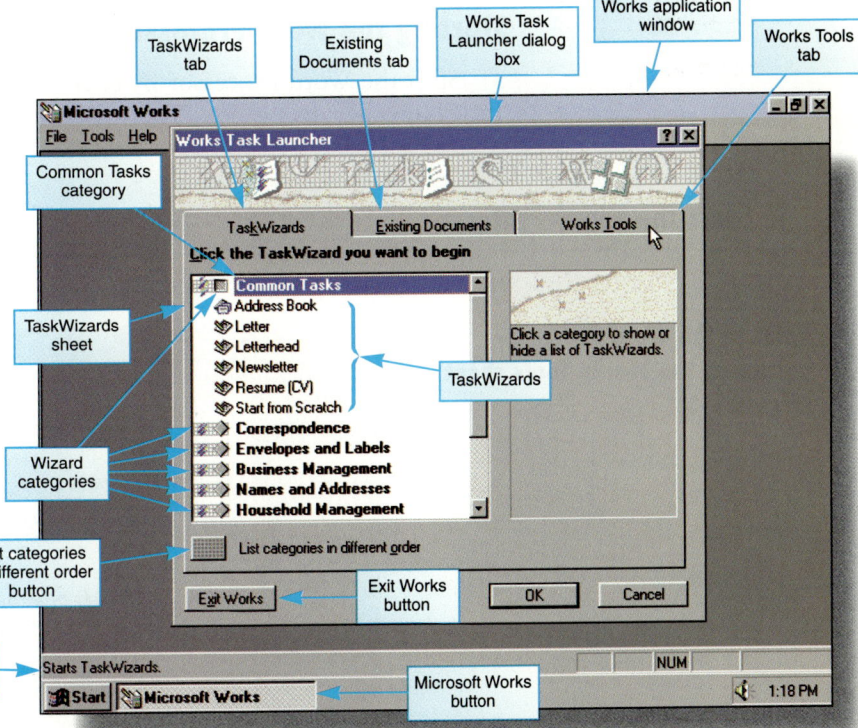

FIGURE 1-3

W 1.10 • Project 1 • Creating a Formatted Document with Clip Art

3) Click the Works Tools tab.

When you click the Works Tools tab, the **Works Tools sheet** moves forward and the TaskWizards sheet that was on top moves behind the Works Tools sheet (Figure 1-4). The buttons in the Works Tools sheet allow you to start any of the Works tools.

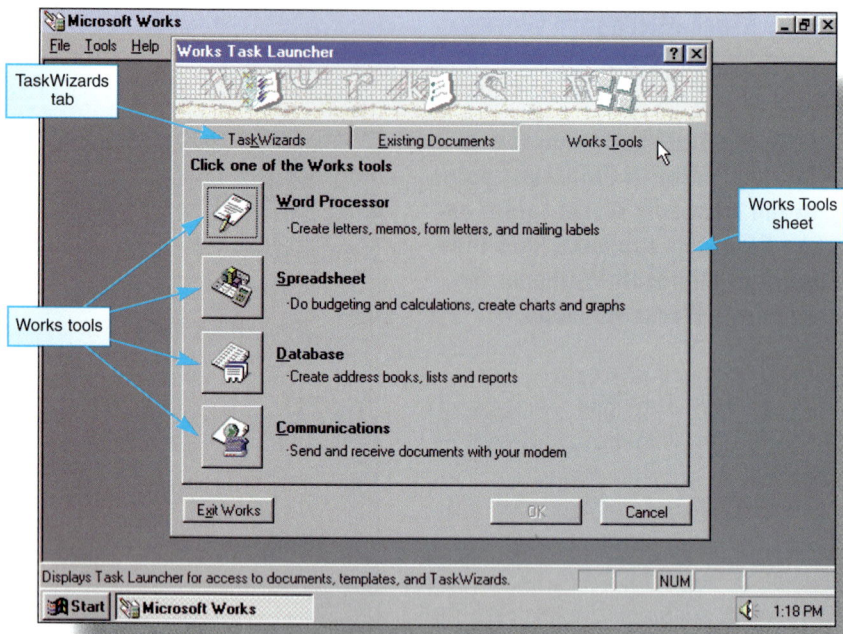

FIGURE 1-4

You have now started Works and are ready to choose the tool you want to use. To create the document in Figure 1-1 on page W 1.8, use the Word Processor tool.

Starting the Word Processor

Start the Word Processor by clicking the appropriate button in the Works Task Launcher dialog box. The following steps explain this process.

Steps To Start the Word Processor

1) Point to the Word Processor button on the Works Tools sheet (Figure 1-5).

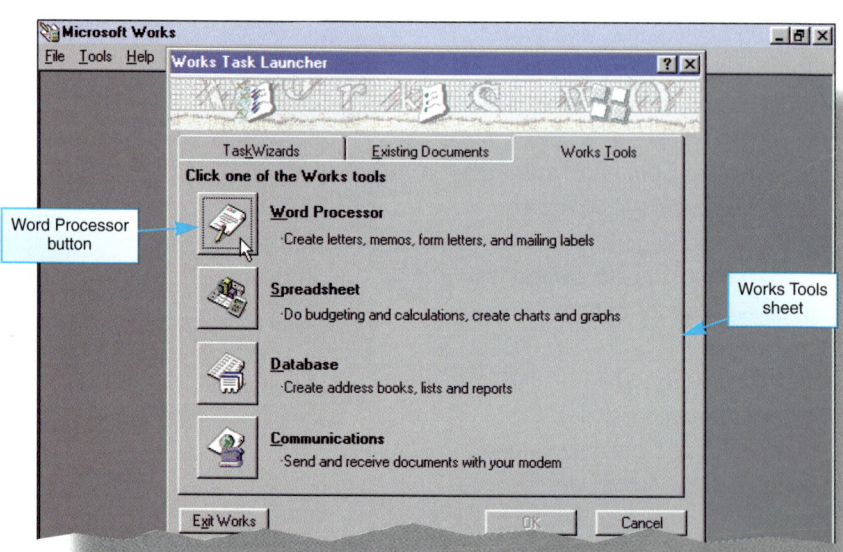

FIGURE 1-5

Microsoft **Works 4** Windows 95

Starting Microsoft Works • W 1.11

2 **Click the Word Processor button.**

Works displays the Word Processor document window containing the document name, Unsaved Document 1, within the Microsoft Works application window (Figure 1-6). The Help window displays next to the document window. The Word Processor Menu displays in the Help window because the Word Processor tool was chosen. Be aware the Help window may or may not display to the right of the document. The display of the Help window depends on the status of the Help window the last time the Word Processor was used.

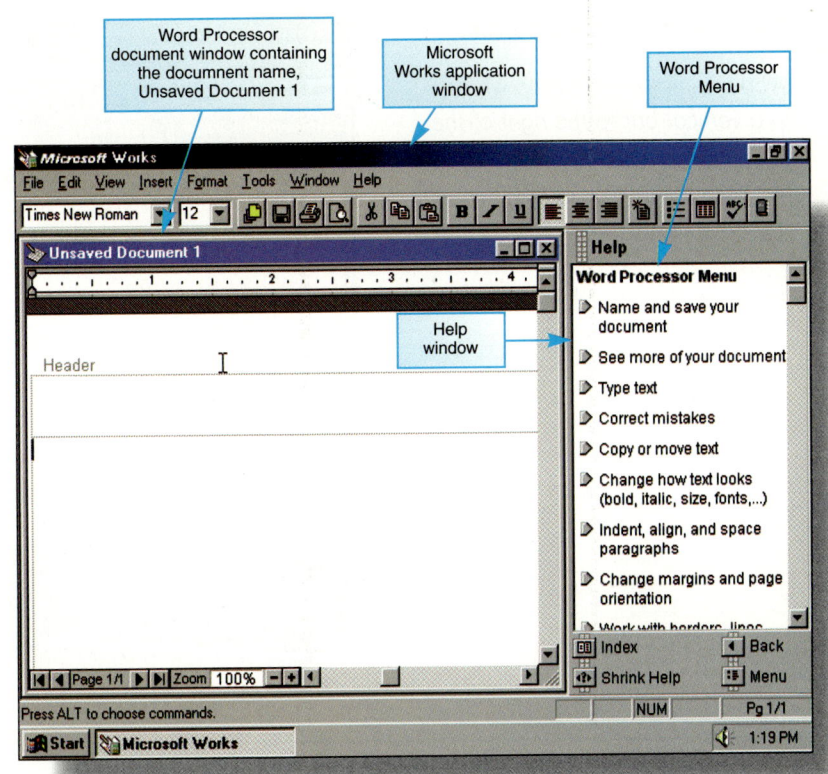

FIGURE 1-6

3 **Point to the Shrink Help button located below the Word Processor Menu in the Help window (Figure 1-7).**

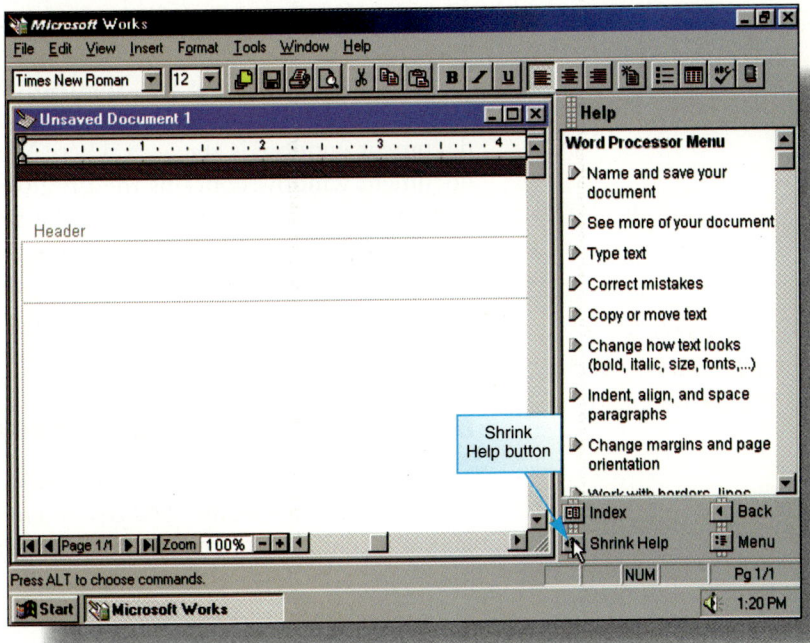

FIGURE 1-7

W 1.12 • Project 1 • Creating a Formatted Document with Clip Art

 Click the Shrink Help button.

Works minimizes the Help window in a vertical bar to the right of the document window and increases the working space of the document window (Figure 1-8).

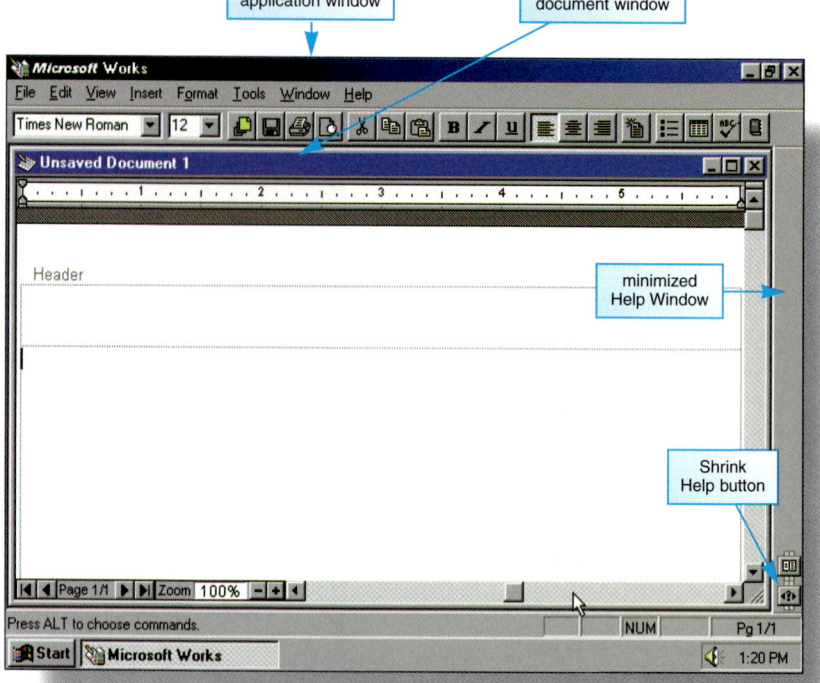

FIGURE 1-8

When you minimize the Help window (Figure 1-8), you can see more of your document. To display the Help window to the right of the document window, click the Shrink Help button located at the bottom right corner of the Works window.

The large window is the Microsoft Works application window, and the smaller window is the Word Processor document window. The blank area in the document window is the area where Works displays the text as you type. The document window contains the title, Unsaved Document 1. Unsaved Document 1 is the name assigned by Works to the first word processing document you create. Works uses this name until you name the document and save it on disk.

Each window has its own border, title bar, Minimize, Maximize or Restore, and Close buttons. It is recommended that both the application window and the document window be maximized when you use the Word Processor tool.

Maximizing the Document Window

When you start the Word Processor, the Microsoft Works application window is maximized by default. The document window, however, is not maximized. To maximize the document window, complete the following steps.

Microsoft **Works 4** Windows 95

The Word Processor Window • W 1.13

 **Steps** **To Maximize the Document Window**

1 Point to the Maximize button in the document window (Figure 1-9).

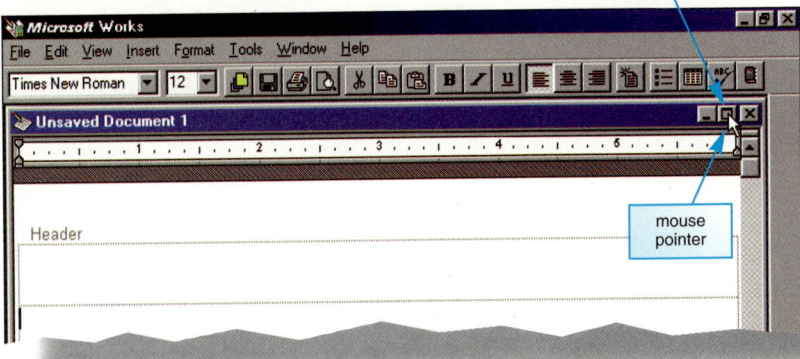

FIGURE 1-9

2 Click the Maximize button.

The document window is maximized (Figure 1-10). The document name, Unsaved Document 1, now displays in the application window title bar at the top of the screen.

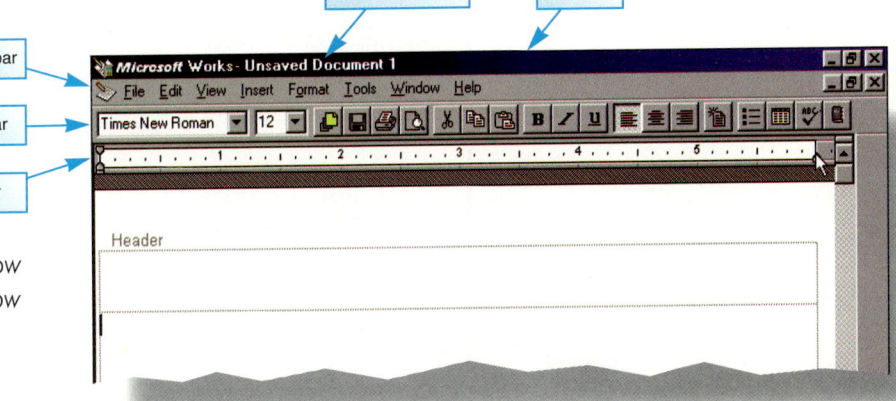

FIGURE 1-10

The Word Processor Window

The Word Processor window has many of the features common to all window screens. The following section describes these features.

Title Bar

The **title bar** (see Figure 1-10) contains the title of the application window, Microsoft Works, and the document name, Unsaved Document 1.

Menu Bar

The **menu bar** displays menu names. Each menu name represents a menu that contains commands you choose when you open, close, save, or print documents, or otherwise manipulate data in the document you are creating.

Toolbar

The **toolbar** contains buttons that allow you to perform frequently required tasks more rapidly than when using the commands in the menus. Each button on the toolbar has a pictorial representation in a small square box that helps you identify its function. Figure 1-11 illustrates the toolbar and describes the function of each of the buttons. The use of the toolbar is explained in more detail as you use the buttons in the projects in this book.

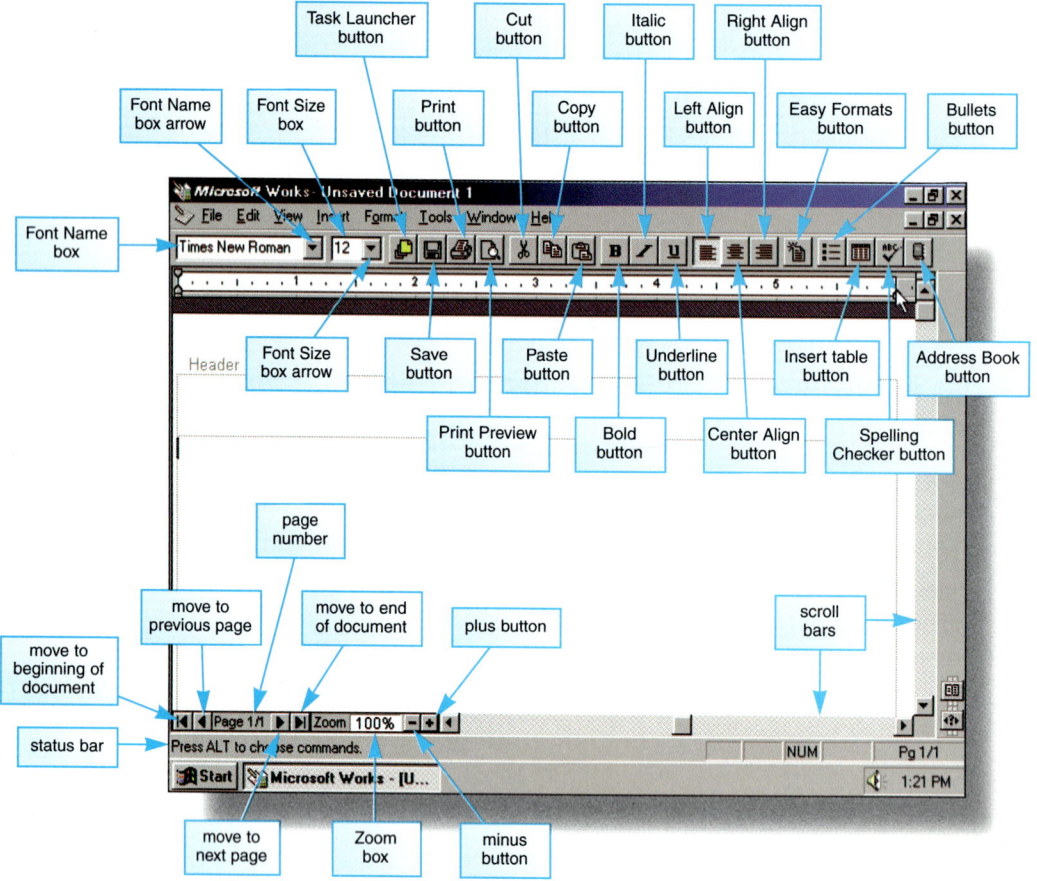

FIGURE 1-11

To choose any of these buttons, position the mouse pointer on the button and click. Any button you choose appears recessed or light gray. When you position the mouse pointer on a button on the toolbar, a ToolTip displays. A **ToolTip** is a small rectangular box that contains a word or words describing the purpose of the button. A more complete description of the button function displays in the status bar. You can control when the toolbar displays by clicking the Toolbar command on the View menu. You can also control the display of the ToolTip. On the Tools menu, click the Customize Toolbar command, and then click Enable ToolTips. Works displays a check mark in the box. Removing the check mark from the Enable ToolTips check box prevents a ToolTip from displaying when the mouse pointer is positioned on a button on the toolbar.

Ruler

In the area below the toolbar is a numbered bar called the **ruler** (Figure 1-10 on page W 1.13). The zero point is at the left edge of the ruler and it indicates the left edge of your text. Toward the right side of the ruler is the 6-inch mark that indicates the right edge of your text. The numbers in between show the distance in inches on the document. Thus, a line approximately six inches in length is represented on the screen. As you type characters on the screen, the characters display in the blank area below the ruler. By comparing the characters typed to the ruler, it is easy to see the number of inches occupied by the typed characters. If the ruler does not display on your screen, click Ruler on the View menu.

You can use the small triangles on the left and right sides of the ruler to control paragraph indents. When the ruler is displayed, you can change paragraph indents by dragging the small triangles. Tab stops are set by default at each half inch on the ruler and are denoted by the small vertical line on the ruler line.

Scroll Bars

When the text you enter occupies a length or width greater than the size of the display screen, you can use the **scroll bars** to move through the document (Figure 1-11). The left side of the scroll bar contains page arrows that assist you in moving through a document that consists of more than a single page. Clicking the left-pointing page arrow that is preceded by a vertical line will move the insertion point to the beginning of the document. Click the left-pointing page arrow without a vertical line to move the insertion point to the beginning of the previous page. Clicking the right-pointing page arrow without the vertical line will move the insertion point forward to the beginning of the next page in the document. When you click the right-pointing page arrow with a vertical line, the insertion point will move to the end of the document. The page number and total number of pages in a document display between the page arrows.

The **Zoom box** is located to the right of the page arrows. The Zoom box controls how much of a page displays at one time in the document window. Clicking the Zoom box displays a list of available zoom percentages to magnify or reduce your document on the screen. You can also use the plus or minus buttons next to the Zoom box to control the document display. To magnify your document, click the plus button. To reduce your document, click the minus button.

Status Bar

The **status bar** is located at the bottom of the Works window (Figure 1-11). The left side of the status bar displays comments that assist you in using Works. Keyboard indicators such as NUM display on the right side of the status bar. NUM indicates that Works will display numbers if you press the keys on the numeric keypad that is located to the right of the standard keyboard. The page number and total number of pages in a document display in the lower right corner of the status bar.

W 1.16 • Project 1 • Creating a Formatted Document with Clip Art

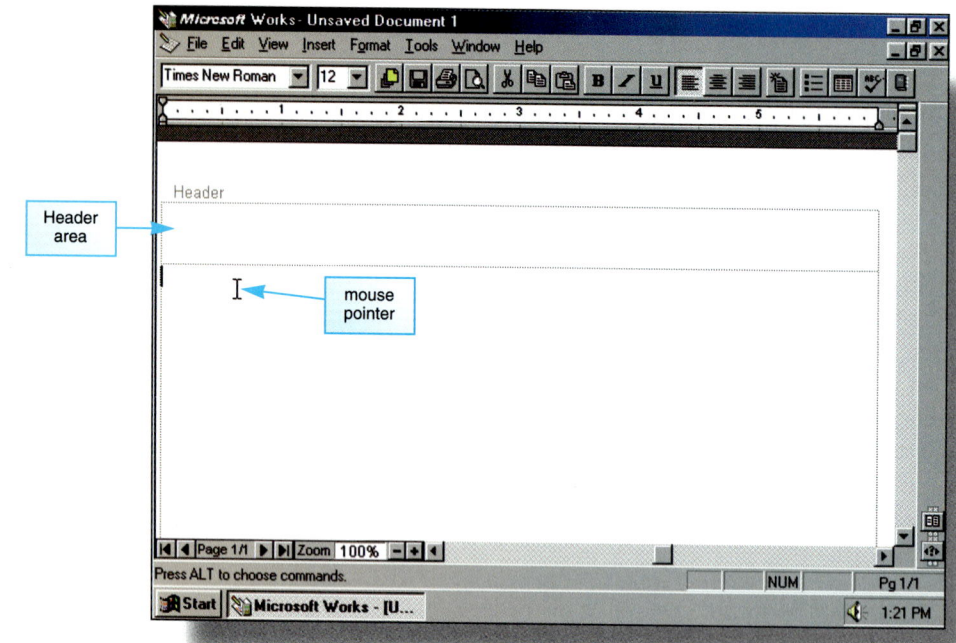

FIGURE 1-12

Mouse Pointer

The **mouse pointer** is used to point to various parts of the screen and indicates which area of the screen will be affected when you click or right-click (Figure 1-12). The mouse pointer changes shape in different parts of the screen. Within the blank area of the screen, called the **document workspace**, the mouse pointer takes the shape of an I-beam. An **I-beam** is a vertical line with short crossbars on the top and bottom.

On the menu bar, the ruler, and the scroll bar areas, the mouse pointer takes the shape of a block arrow. Other forms and uses of the mouse pointer are explained as required in the development of various documents.

> **More About Views**
>
> The more document formatting, features, and special effects you choose to display on-screen, the more computer resources Works requires. Page layout view requires the most computer resources and may cause slow response on a computer lacking adequate memory. Normal view requires less computer resources and is the best view to use on a low-memory computer.

View Modes

You can work with a Word Processor document in one of two **view modes**; page layout view or normal view. **Page layout view** displays each page of your document as it will look when printed. Figure 1-12 displays a blank document in page layout view. The **header area** displays at the top of the document. Any text typed in this area will appear at the top of every page.

Normal view displays your document close to the way it looks when it is printed. In normal view, however, more of your document displays on the screen at one time. When you first start the Works Word Processor, the initial view mode setting is page layout view.

Changing View Modes

Project 1 uses the normal view to create the document in Figure 1-1 on page W1.8. To change the view from page layout to normal view, click the **Normal command** on the **View menu**. Complete the following steps to change views in the Word Processor.

Microsoft **Works 4** Windows 95
View Modes • W 1.17

Steps  To Change Views in the Word Processor

1 **Point to View on the menu bar.**

The mouse pointer points to the View menu name (Figure 1-13).

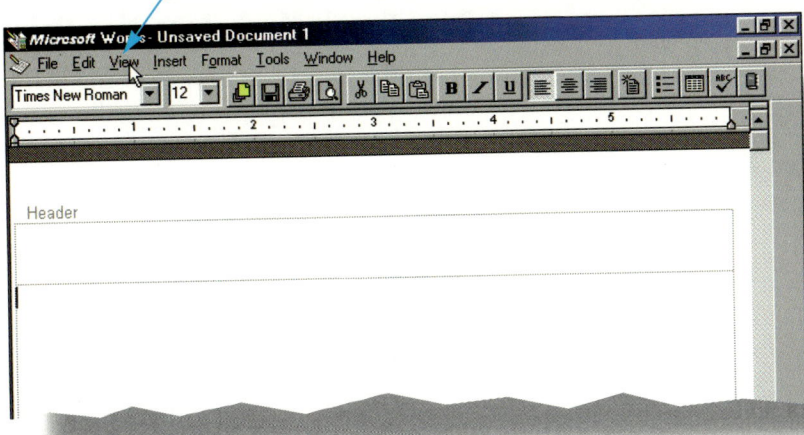

FIGURE 1-13

2 **Click View on the menu bar. When the View menu displays, point to Normal.**

The View menu displays and the Normal command is highlighted (Figure 1-14). A check mark displays to the left of the Page Layout command indicating the command is in effect.

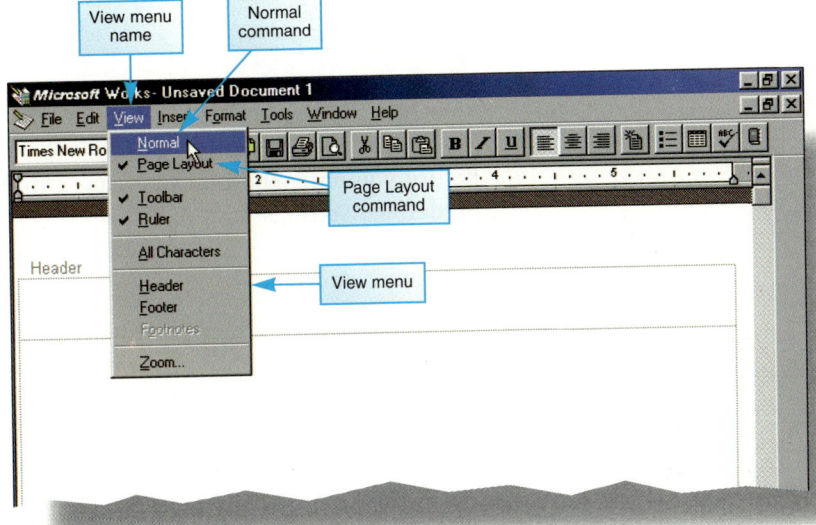

FIGURE 1-14

3 **Click Normal.**

Works displays the document in normal view (Figure 1-15).

FIGURE 1-15

After you click Normal, a check mark appears to the left of this command the next time you display the View menu, indicating the command is in effect.

Page Break Mark, Insertion Point, and End-of-File Mark

In the upper left corner of the blank workspace in normal view (Figure 1-15 on the previous page), two small arrows, called a **chevron character**, point to the right. The chevron character is the **page break mark** that appears on the first line of a new document. The mark also appears in the left margin of the screen when a page break occurs after you have entered a full page of text.

The **insertion point** is a blinking vertical bar that indicates where the next character you type will appear on the screen. The insertion point also indicates the beginning position in a document where you can insert text, delete text, or change the appearance of text. The insertion point is controlled by the movement of the mouse.

The short horizontal line below the insertion point in Figure 1-15 is the **end-of-file** mark. This mark displays as the last character in every document and indicates where the document ends. You can move the insertion point throughout the document you create, but you cannot move it beyond the end-of-file mark.

Word Processor Defaults

Before you enter the text to create a document, you should know about the predefined settings for the Word Processor, called **defaults**, that affect the way your screen displays and the way a document prints. Consider the following important defaults.

1. Margins – When printing a document, Works places a one-inch top margin and a one-inch bottom margin on each page. The right and left margins are 1.25 inches each.
2. Spacing – Text is single-spaced.
3. Line width – Line width is six inches, based on a paper size of 8.5 inches by 11 inches.
4. Tab stops – Tab stops are set along the ruler at one-half inch intervals.
5. Default drive – Drive C, the hard disk, is the default drive for saving and retrieving documents.

You can change these defaults by using the commands from various Works menus.

Understanding Fonts, Font Styles, and Font Sizes

To create the announcement in Figure 1-1 on page W1.8, you must format the page. **Formatting** refers to the process of controlling the appearance of the characters that appear on the screen and in the printed document. With Works you can specify the font, font size, font style, and color of one or more characters, words, sentences, or paragraphs in a document.

Fonts

A **font** is a set of characters with a specific design. Each font is identified by a name. Some of the commonly used fonts are **Times New Roman, Courier New,** and **Arial** (Figure 1-16).

Each of the fonts in Figure 1-16 has a unique design. When using Windows, a variety of fonts become available that you can use with Works.

Most fonts fall into one of two major categories: (1) serif, or (2) sans serif. **Serif** fonts have small curved finishing strokes in the characters. The Times New Roman and Courier New fonts are examples of a serif font. Serif fonts are considered easy to read when large blocks of text are involved and normally are used in books and magazines for the main text material.

Sans serif fonts are relatively plain, straight letter forms. The Arial font in Figure 1-16 is a sans serif font. Sans serif fonts are commonly used in headlines and short titles.

FIGURE 1-16

Font Style

In Works, **font style** is the term used to describe the special appearance of text and numbers. Widely used font styles include bold, italic, and underlined (Figure 1-17). You can choose bold, italic, and underlined font styles using toolbar buttons. All three styles can be applied to a set of characters.

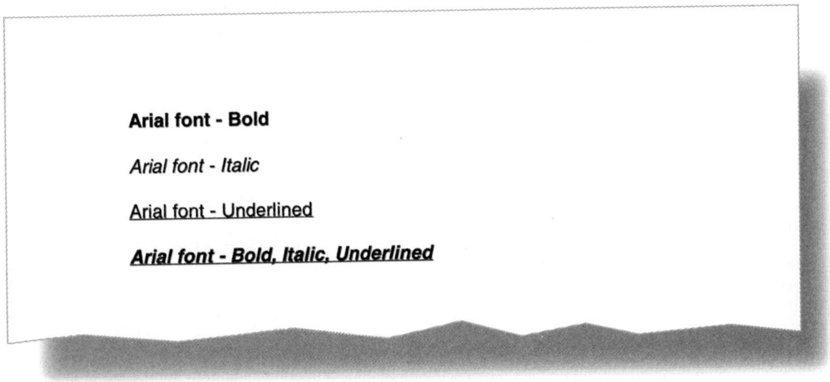

FIGURE 1-17

Font Sizes

Font sizes are measured in **points**. One inch consists of seventy-two points. Thus, a font size of thirty-six points is approximately one-half inch in height. The measurement is based on measuring from the top of the tallest character in a font (such as a lowercase l) to the bottom of the lowest character (such as a lowercase g, which extends below a line). Figure 1-18 illustrates the Arial font in various sizes.

The fonts and font sizes you choose sometimes depend on the printer you are using and the fonts available within your software. Available fonts can vary from system to system. In the Works Word Processor, the default font is 12-point Times New Roman.

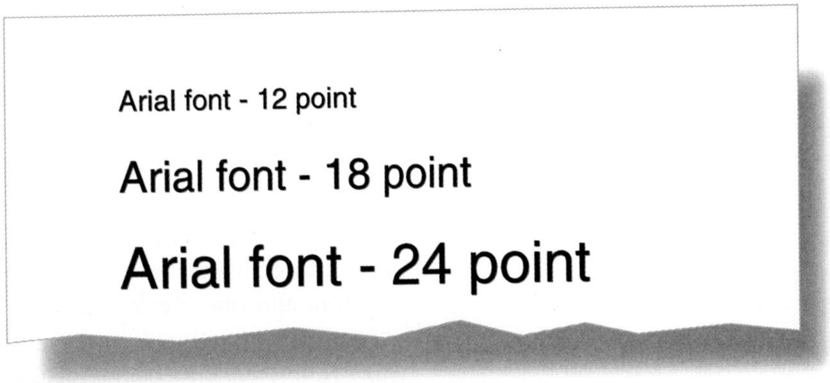

FIGURE 1-18

Formatting Requirements for Project One

The announcement used in this project is again illustrated in Figure 1-19. Before typing the text, you must understand the fonts, font styles, font sizes, and colors you will use in creating the announcement.

In this document, the first heading displays on the first two lines of the document, is centered on the page, and displays in 36-point Book Antiqua font. The second heading is centered on the page and displays using 16-point Book Antiqua font. An illustration from the Microsoft Clip Gallery is placed after the second heading. The next three lines are single-spaced and display in 12-point Times New Roman font. These lines are followed by a blank space and then another line displays in 16-point Times New Roman. The next four entries are indented one-half inch, contain a bullet (solid diamond) before the beginning of each entry, and display in 16-point Times New Roman. The line following the bulleted list is centered on the page and displays in 16-point Arial italic font. The last three lines in the document are centered and display in red using 16-point Arial font. The entire document displays in bold.

When you understand the format of the document, you are ready to use the word processing software to create the document.

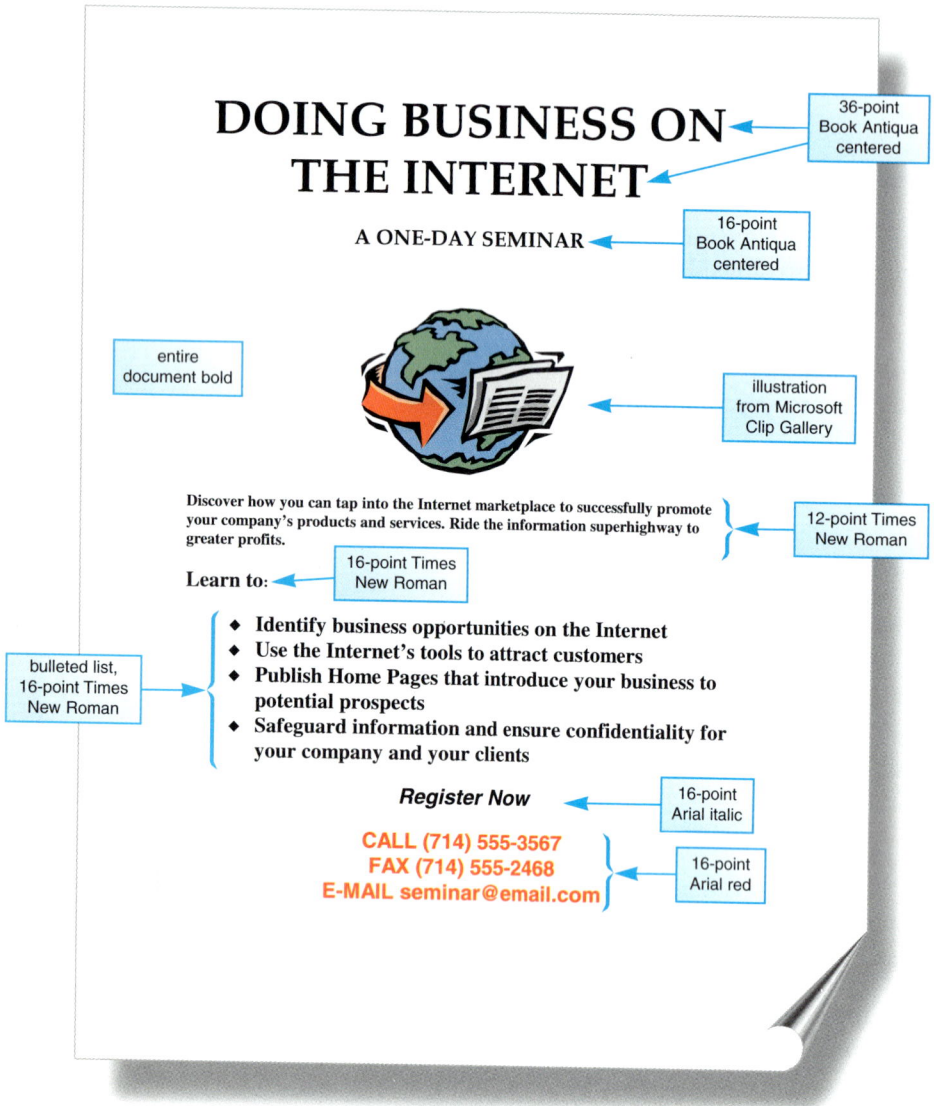

FIGURE 1-19

Creating a Document

The following tasks will be completed in this project.

1. Type the text line by line.
2. Begin each line at the left margin.
3. Leave three blank lines before the illustration, one blank line for the illustration, and one blank line after the illustration.
4. Format the document; that is, center lines, change fonts, font sizes, font styles, and color as required to produce the document.

5. Insert the clip art illustration.
6. Save the document.
7. Print the document.

The following pages contain a detailed explanation of these tasks.

All Characters Command

When using the Works Word Processor, each time you press a key on the keyboard a character is entered, and each character becomes part of the document. For example, pressing the SPACEBAR between words creates a small black dot, called a **space mark**, in the space between the words. Pressing the ENTER key creates a character called the **paragraph mark**. These characters do not print, but it is recommended that you display these special characters as you type. The following steps explain how to display on the screen all the characters you type.

Steps **To Display All Characters**

1 Click View on the menu bar. Point to All Characters.

Works displays the View menu and the mouse pointer is positioned on the All Characters command (Figure 1-20).

2 Click All Characters.

A paragraph mark now appears after the insertion point (Figure 1-21).

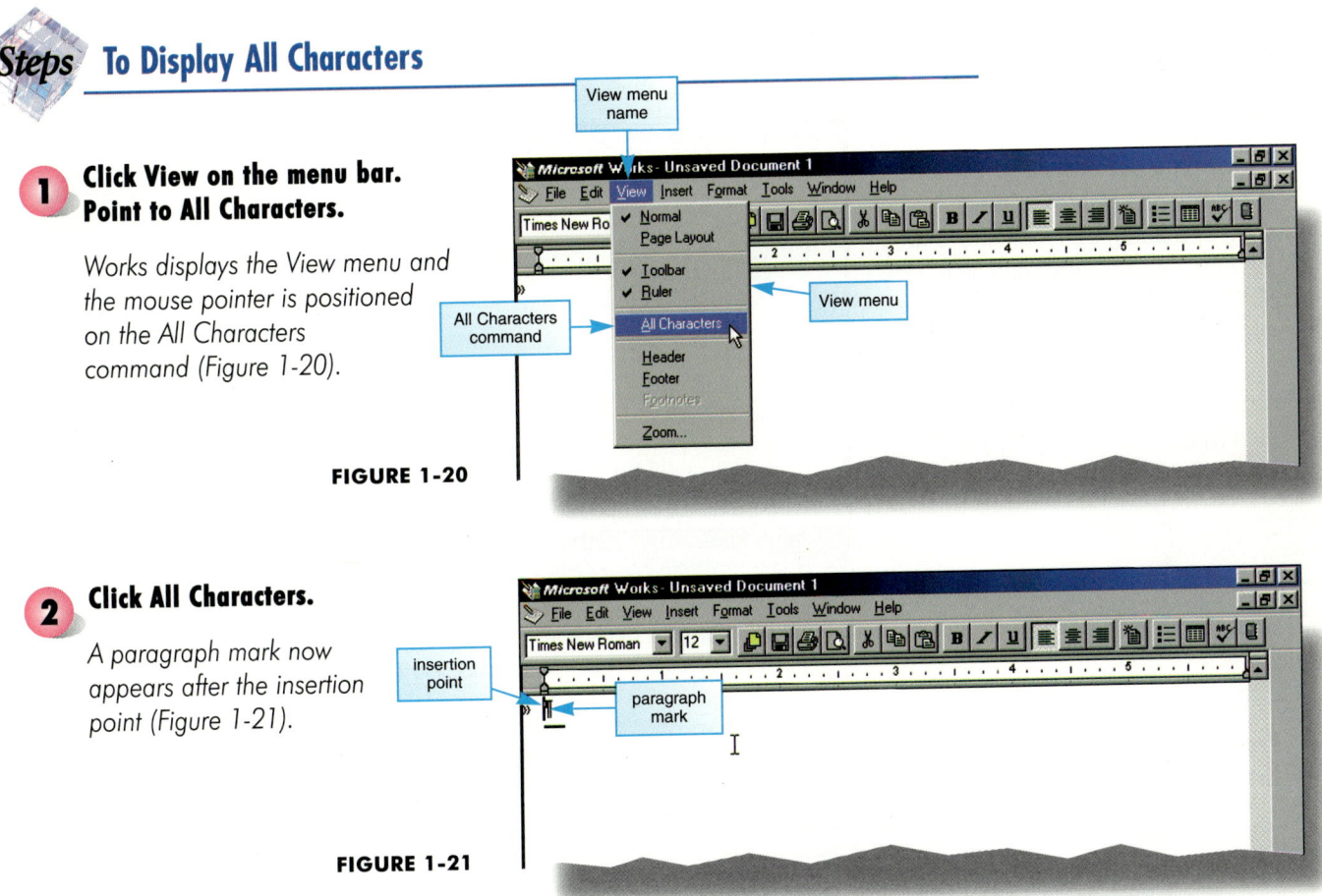

FIGURE 1-20

FIGURE 1-21

Works automatically inserts a paragraph mark at the end of every document. Because you have not yet entered text, a paragraph mark appears after the insertion point because it is the end of the document at this time. As you type, a small dot appears when you press the SPACEBAR, and a paragraph mark will appear whenever you press the ENTER key.

W 1.22 • Project 1 • Creating a Formatted Document with Clip Art

More About Entering Text

Oftentimes when you first enter a heading in a document, you have no idea how the formatting of the text will affect the display of the text. When increasing the font size at a later time, the one-line heading may display on multiple lines.

After you click the All Characters command, a check mark appears to the left of this command the next time you display the View menu, indicating the command is in effect. Clicking the left mouse button again when pointing to this command will turn off the All Characters command and remove the check mark.

You are now ready to enter the text to create the document.

Entering Text

Perform the following steps to enter the text of the document.

Steps To Enter Text

1 **Press the CAPS LOCK key on the keyboard and type** DOING BUSINESS ON THE INTERNET **as the first line of text.**

As you type, the characters display in capital letters and the insertion point and paragraph mark move to the right one character at a time (Figure 1-22). If you make an error while typing, press the BACKSPACE key to delete the character or characters you have just typed and then type the characters correctly.

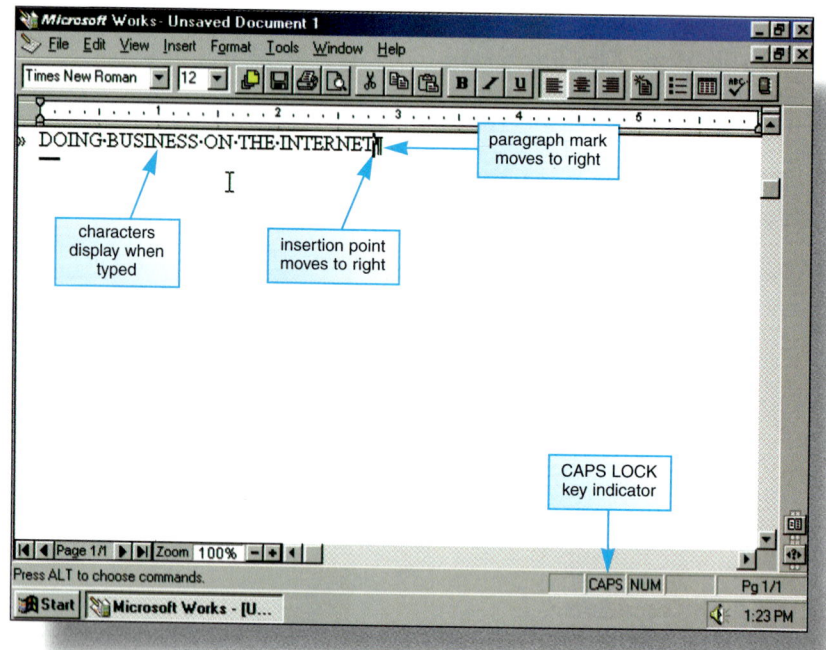

FIGURE 1-22

2 **Press the ENTER key to end the first line.**

When you press the ENTER key, Works inserts a paragraph mark immediately after the last character typed (Figure 1-23). The insertion point moves to the beginning of the next line followed by a paragraph mark, and the end-of-file mark moves down one line.

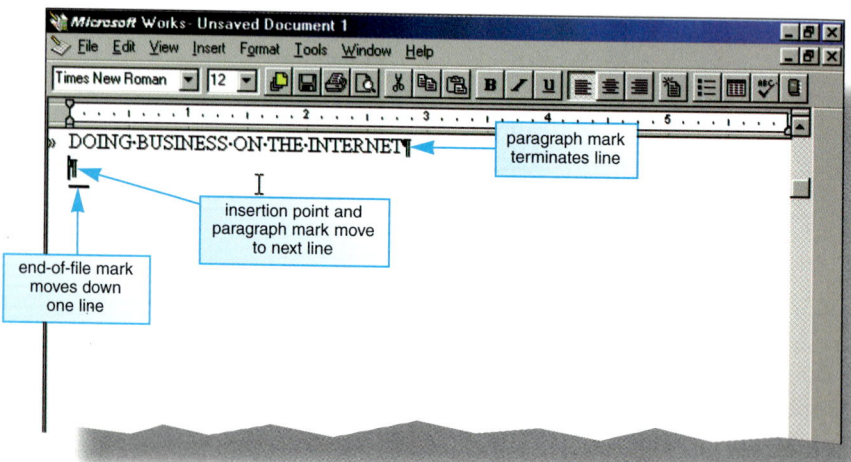

FIGURE 1-23

③ **Press the ENTER key to create a blank line.** Type A ONE-DAY SEMINAR **as the second line of text, and then press the ENTER key once to end the second line of text. Press the ENTER key five more times to create three blank lines before the clip art illustration, a line for the illustration, and a blank line following the illustration. The insertion point now displays on the line where you will type the next line of text.**

Only one line needs to be allowed for the clip art illustration (Figure 1-24). When Works inserts the clip art in the document, the space is expanded to allow the clip art to be placed between the lines of text.

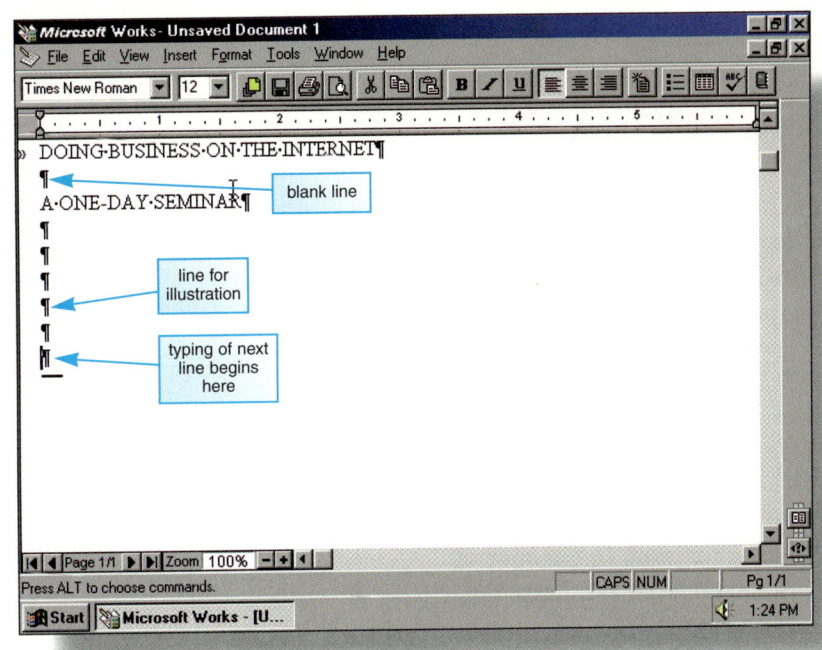

FIGURE 1-24

Paragraph Marks

It is important to understand the purpose of the paragraph mark. The term **paragraph**, when using the Works Word Processor, can mean a blank line, a single character, a word, a single line, or many sentences. You create a paragraph by pressing the ENTER key. When you are typing and then press the ENTER key, Works inserts a paragraph mark after the last character typed.

A paragraph is a section of text treated as a unified group of characters to which various types of formatting can be applied. Once you have established the characteristics of a paragraph, text you add to the paragraph will take on the characteristics of that paragraph.

Using the Wordwrap Feature

Wordwrap allows you to type multiple lines without pressing the ENTER key at the end of each line. When typing text that requires more than one line, the insertion point continues to the right margin and then automatically drops down to the beginning of the next line. In addition, when you type a line and a word extends beyond the right margin, the word is automatically placed on the next line. Thus, as you enter text, do not press the ENTER key when the insertion point reaches the right margin.

W 1.24 • Project 1 • Creating a Formatted Document with Clip Art

Perform the following step to use the wordwrap feature.

 **Steps** To Use Wordwrap

1. **Press the CAPS LOCK key to remove this feature. Type** Discover how you can tap into the Internet marketplace to successfully promote your company's products and services. Ride the information superhighway to greater profits. **as the first paragraph in the body of the announcement. Press the ENTER key.**

   The CAPS LOCK indicator on the status bar is turned off (Figure 1-25). Works automatically wraps the word, company's, to the beginning of the next line because it is too long to fit on the first line. Your document may wordwrap on a different word, depending on the type of printer you are using.

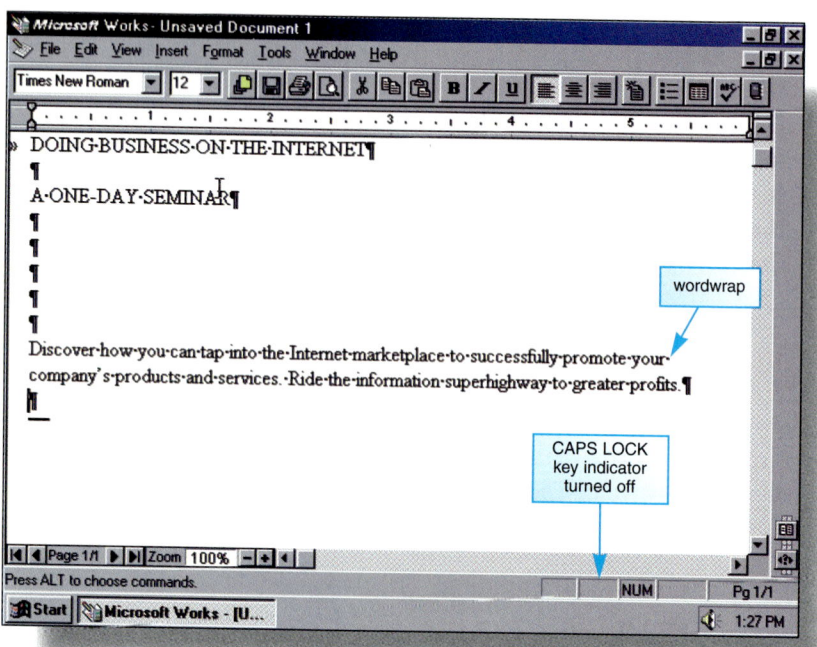

FIGURE 1-25

Wordwrap is an important feature of the Word Processor because it facilitates rapid entry of data and allows Works to easily rearrange characters, words, and sentences within a paragraph when you make changes.

Entering Text that Scrolls Through the Document Window

As you type more lines of text than Works can display in the text area, Works **scrolls** the top portion of the document upward off of the screen. Although you cannot see the text once it scrolls off the screen, it still remains in the document.

Perform the following steps to enter text that scrolls through the document window.

Steps To Enter Text that Scrolls Through the Document Window

1 Press the ENTER key to enter a blank line. Type the text paragraph in the announcement: `Learn to:` and then press the ENTER key twice (Figure 1-26).

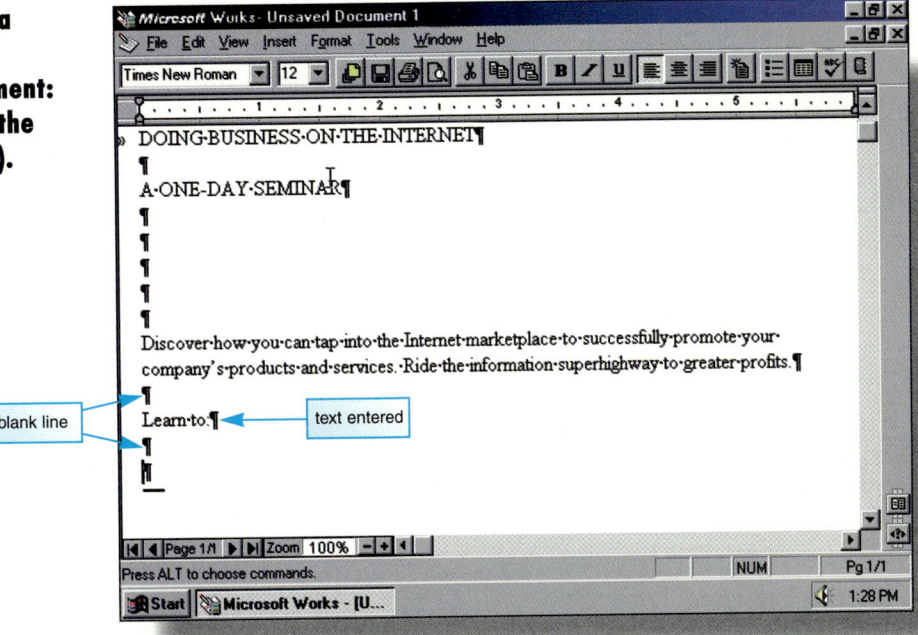

FIGURE 1-26

2 Type the remaining lines of text. Press the ENTER key to end each paragraph.

As you type the paragraph beginning, Safeguard, Works scrolls the beginning of the announcement off the screen (Figure 1-27). All the text in the announcement has been entered.

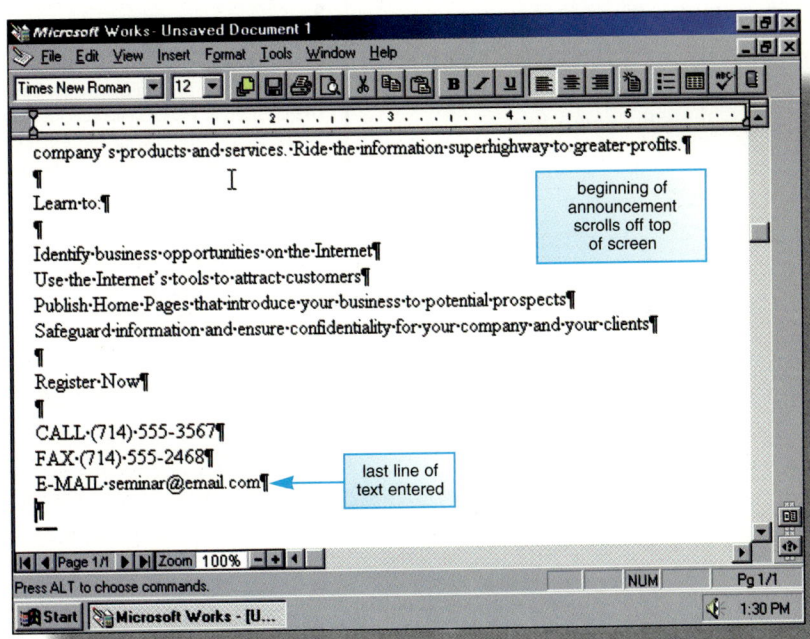

FIGURE 1-27

W 1.26 • Project 1 • Creating a Formatted Document with Clip Art

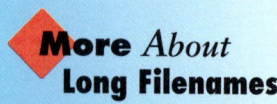

More About
Long Filenames

One of Works new features is the ability to support long filenames. Using long filenames can save you time because you can give your files names that mean something even months after they have been created.

Saving a Document

When you create a document, the document is stored only in your computer's random access memory. If the computer is turned off or a power loss occurs before you save a document, your work will be lost. You should save all documents either on the hard disk or on a floppy disk. When saving a document, you must select a filename. The filename is the name that is used to reference the file (document) when it is stored on a hard disk or floppy disk. The complete path to the file, including drive letter and filename, can contain up to 255 characters. Filenames cannot include any of the following characters: forward slash (/), backslash (\), greater-than sign (>), less-than sign (<), asterisk (*), question mark (?), quotation mark ("), pipe symbol (|), colon (:), or semicolon (;). To save the document created in Project 1 on a floppy disk in drive A using the filename, Business on the Internet Seminar, perform the following steps.

 To Save a New Document

1 **Insert a formatted floppy disk into drive A. Point to the Save button on the toolbar.**

The mouse pointer points to the Save button (Figure 1-28). Works displays the ToolTip for the button. The description of the Save button displays on the status bar.

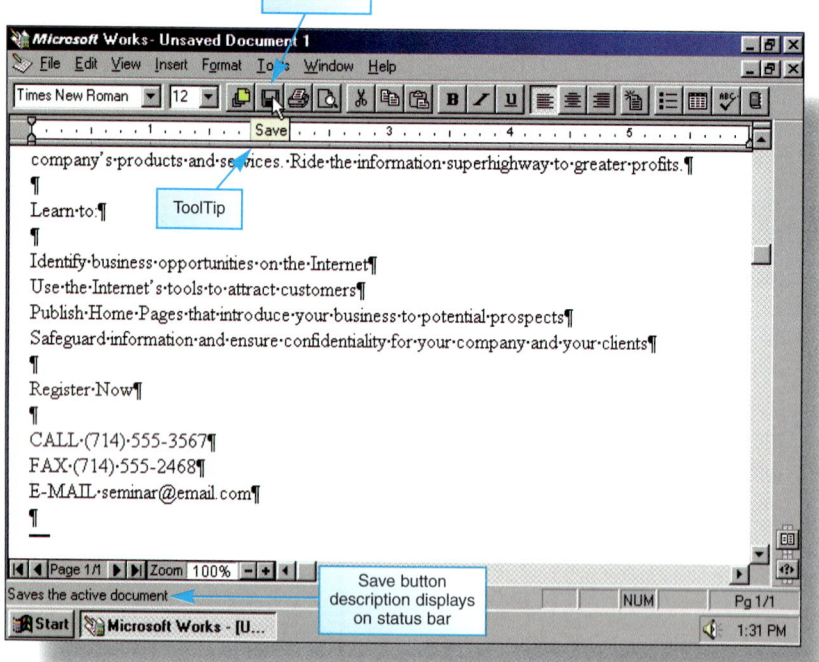

FIGURE 1-28

② **Click the Save button on the toolbar. When the Save As dialog box displays, type** Business on the Internet Seminar **in the File name text box. Point to the Save in box arrow.**

The Save As dialog box displays on the screen (Figure 1-29). A blinking insertion point displays in the File name text box when the Save As dialog box first displays on screen. The filename you typed displays in the File name text box.

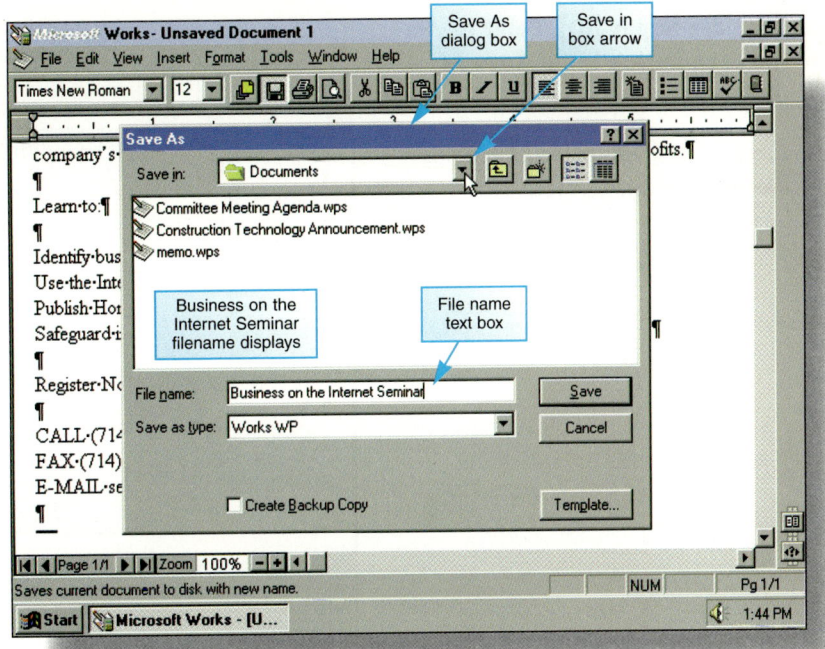

FIGURE 1-29

③ **Click the Save in box arrow and then point to the 3½ floppy [A:] icon. (If necessary, scroll up to bring 3½ floppy [A:] into view.)**

The Save in drop-down list box displays a list of available drives and folders (Figure 1-30). The list of available drives may be different on your system.

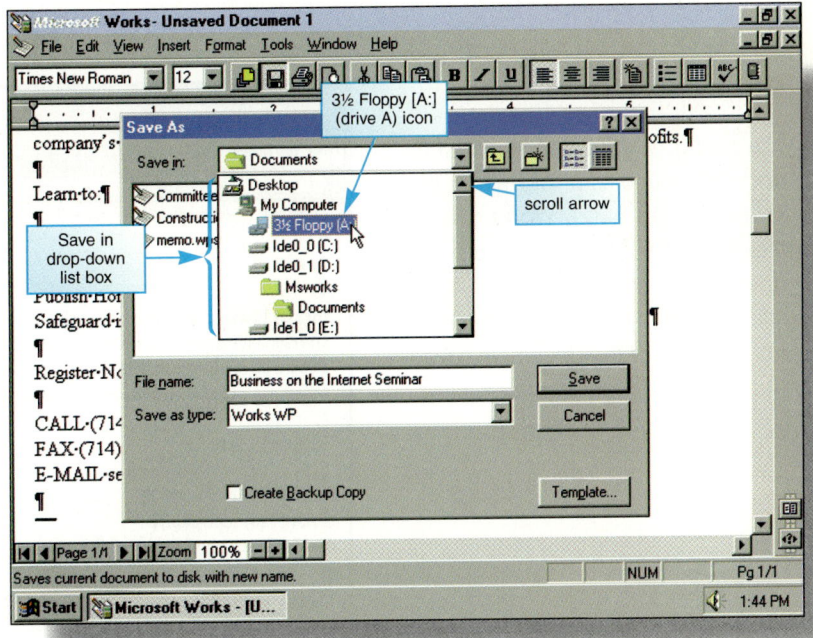

FIGURE 1-30

W 1.28 • Project 1 • Creating a Formatted Document with Clip Art

4 **Click 3½ floppy [A:]. Point to the Save button in the Save As dialog box.**

Drive A (3½ Floppy [A:]) becomes the selected drive (Figure 1-31).

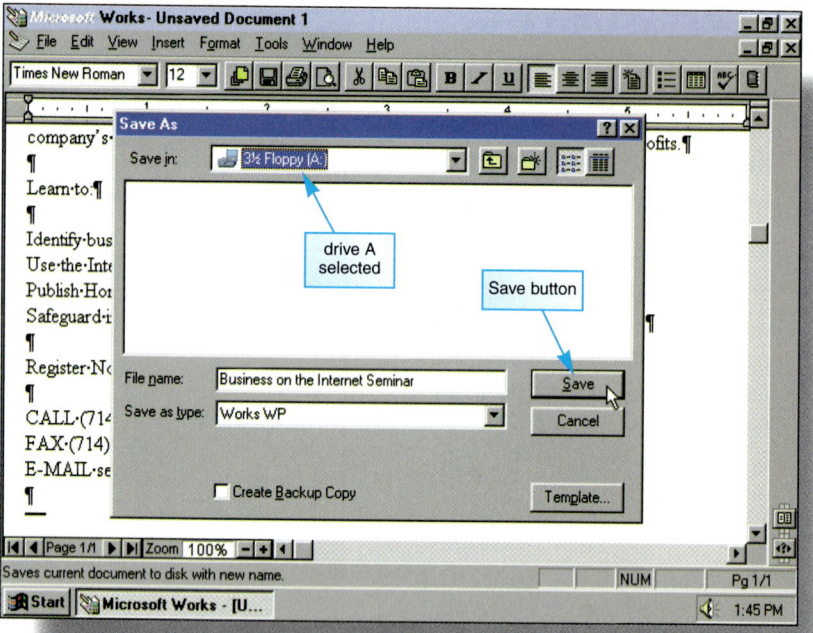

FIGURE 1-31

5 **Click the Save button.**

The dialog box disappears and the document remains displayed on the screen (Figure 1-32). Works saves the document on the floppy disk in drive A. The name changes in the title bar from Unsaved Document 1 to the name of the document saved (Business on the Internet Seminar).

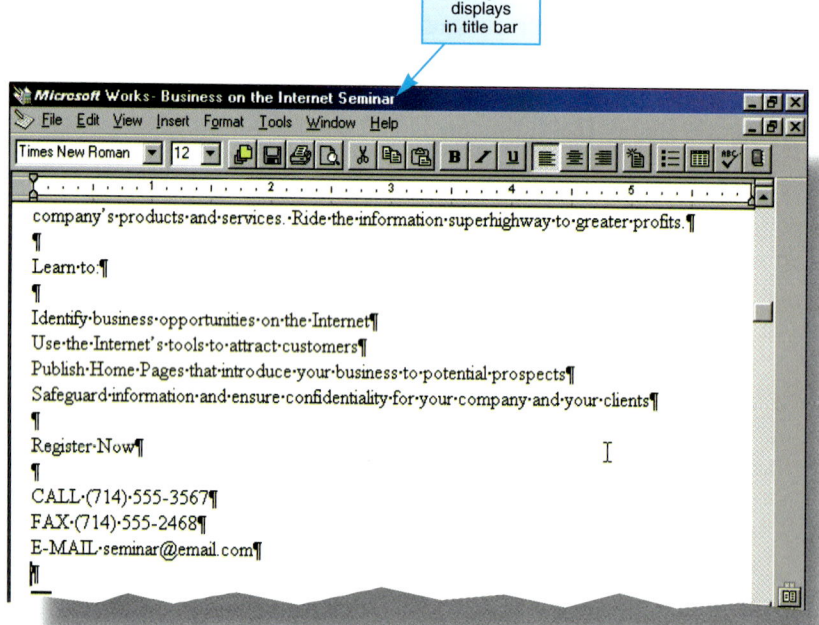

FIGURE 1-32

OtherWays

1. On File menu click Save As, enter filename, click OK button
2. Press CTRL+S

Formatting the Document

The next step in preparing the announcement is to format the document, which involves centering selected lines, specifying the font and font size for each of the lines, and applying the proper font style and color to the lines.

Highlighting Characters, Words, Lines, and Paragraphs

Before you can change the format of a document, you must **highlight** the text you want to change. Highlighted text displays as white text on a black background on the screen. Figure 1-33 illustrates a highlighted word in a sentence.

Works provides a variety of ways to highlight text. One method of highlighting is to move the mouse pointer to the first character of the text to format and then drag the mouse pointer through the text you want to highlight.

Table 1-1 explains other techniques you can use to highlight text.

When highlighting more than one word, Works automatically highlights all of the next word as you drag through that word. If you prefer to highlight character by character, you can turn off the Automatic word selection feature by removing the check mark from the Automatic word selection check box on the Editing sheet in the Options dialog box. The Options dialog box can be displayed by clicking Options on the Tools menu.

If you have highlighted text and want to remove the highlighting for any reason, click anywhere within the workspace area of the screen. The highlighting will be removed. You also may press any arrow key to remove highlighting.

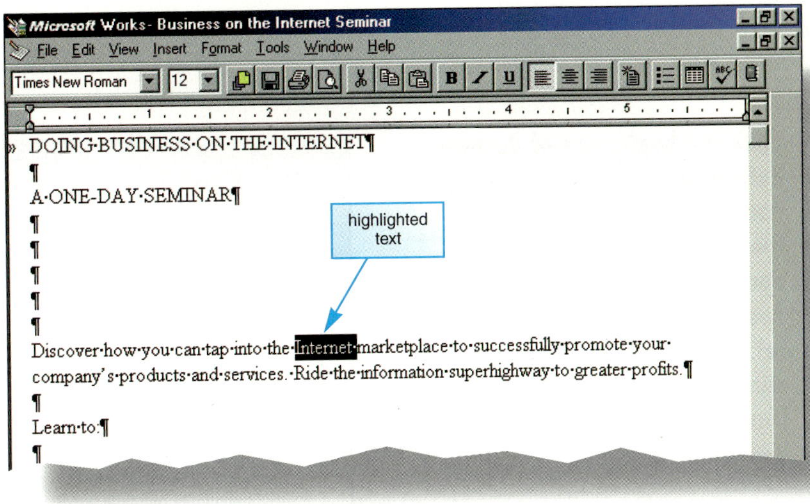

FIGURE 1-33

TABLE 1–1	
TO HIGHLIGHT	ACTION TO BE PERFORMED
A word	Double-click when the mouse pointer is located anywhere within the word.
A line	Click in the left margin of the document window beside the line. The I-beam pointer changes to a block arrow in this area.
A sentence	Drag the mouse pointer through the sentence, or press the CTRL key and click with the mouse pointer located anywhere within the sentence.
A paragraph	Double-click in the left margin of the document window beside the paragraph.
Several lines	Position the mouse pointer in the left margin of the document window and drag the pointer up or down.
An entire document	Hold down the CTRL key and click in the left margin of the document window or click the Select All command on the Edit menu.

Centering Paragraphs

The first two heading lines of the announcement are centered within the margins of the document. Several approaches can be taken when centering these two lines. You can center one line at a time, or by highlighting both lines, you can center both lines at once with a single click of the mouse button. It is more efficient to center both lines at once, so this approach is illustrated in the following steps.

Perform the steps on the next page to center the paragraphs.

More *About* Formatting

Be cautious when using multiple fonts, font styles, and colors in a document. Beginning designers usually use too many special features that make reading a document difficult. Most experts advise using no more than three fonts in a document so you do not overtax and confuse the reader. Use color to draw attention to an important fact in the document.

W 1.30 • Project 1 • Creating a Formatted Document with Clip Art

Steps: To Center Paragraphs

1 **Click the beginning of document button at the lower left of the document window to display the top portion of the document on the screen. Position the mouse pointer in the left margin of the document window next to the first line of the paragraphs you want to center.**

The insertion point is moved to the beginning of the document (Figure 1-34). The mouse pointer becomes a block arrow pointing to the right.

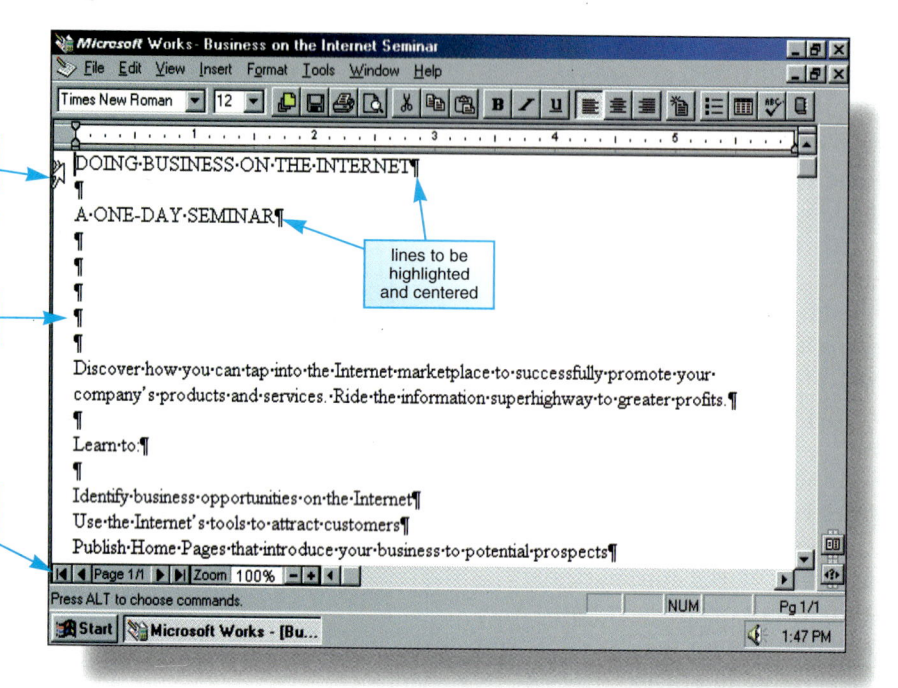

FIGURE 1-34

2 **Drag the mouse pointer down the left margin of the document window until the lines you want to center are highlighted. Release the left mouse button.**

The lines are highlighted (Figure 1-35).

FIGURE 1-35

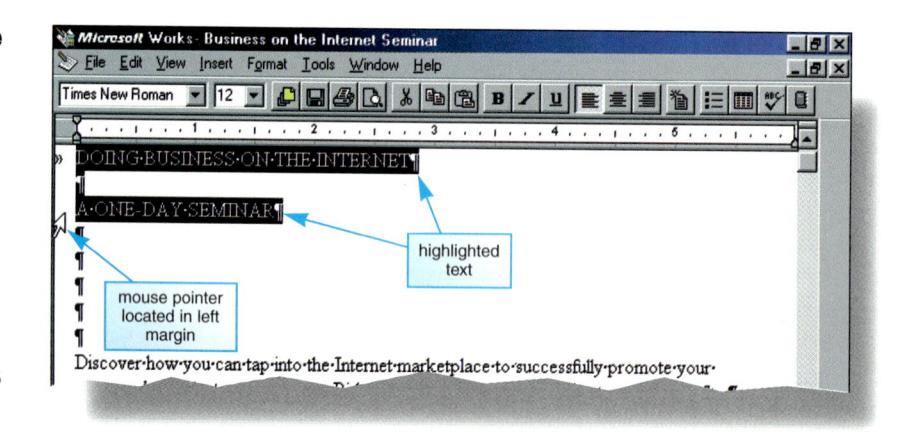

3 **Click the Center Align button on the toolbar.**

Works centers the two heading lines between the page margins (Figure 1-36). Notice the Center Align button on the toolbar is recessed, indicating the paragraphs are centered.

FIGURE 1-36

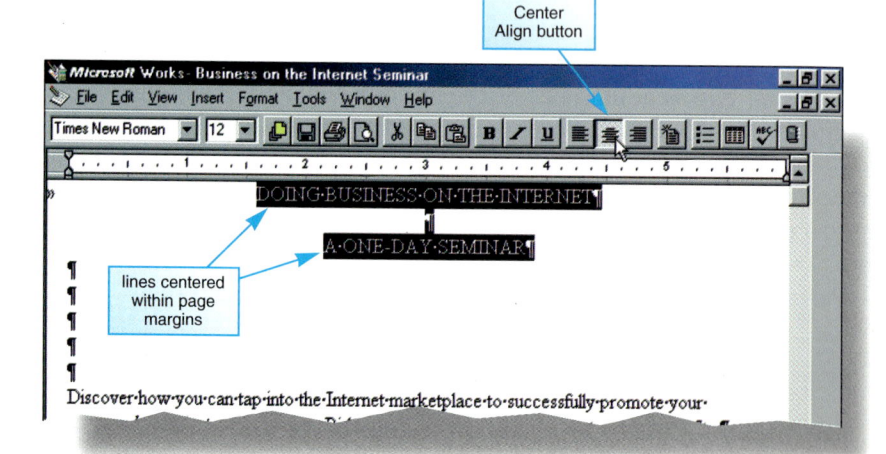

Changing Fonts

When Works is started, the default font is Times New Roman and the default font size is 12 points. Works displays this information on the left side of the toolbar.

The text in the announcement now displays in 12-point Times New Roman font. The first two heading lines should display in Book Antiqua font. To change from Times New Roman font to Book Antiqua font, perform the following steps.

> **OtherWays**
>
> 1. Right-click selected text, click Paragraph on context-sensitive menu, click Indents and Alignment tab, click Center, click OK button
> 2. On Format menu click Paragraph, click Indents and Alignment tab, click Center, click OK button
> 3. Press CTRL+E

Steps: To Change Fonts

1 **Highlight the paragraphs you want to change to Book Antiqua font. Click the Font Name box arrow.**

Works displays the Font Name drop-down list box containing a list of font names (Figure 1-37). The font list displays the fonts the way they will look on screen. The font names on your computer may be different from the font names shown in Figure 1-37.

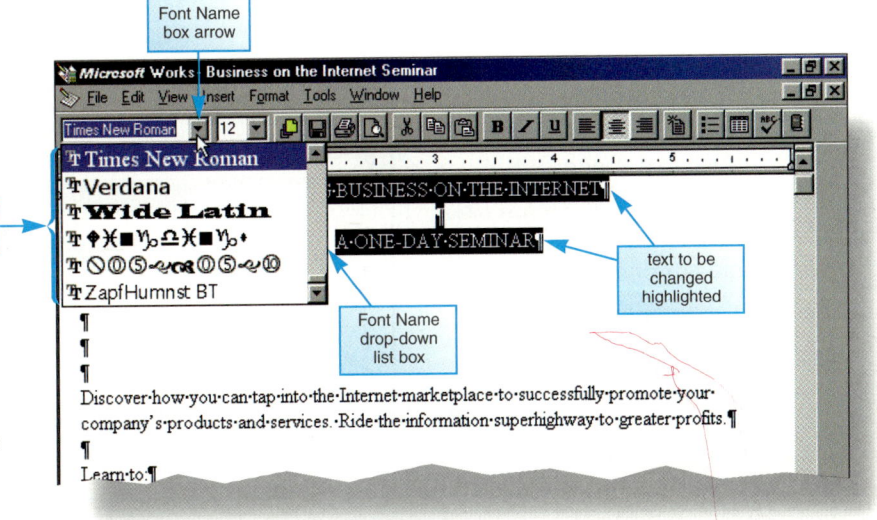

FIGURE 1-37

2 **Position the mouse pointer on the up scroll arrow and scroll to display additional names until the Book Antiqua font name appears in the Font Name drop-down list.**

Additional font names display as you scroll through the Font Name drop-down list (Figure 1-38). The Book Antiqua font name displays near the top of the list.

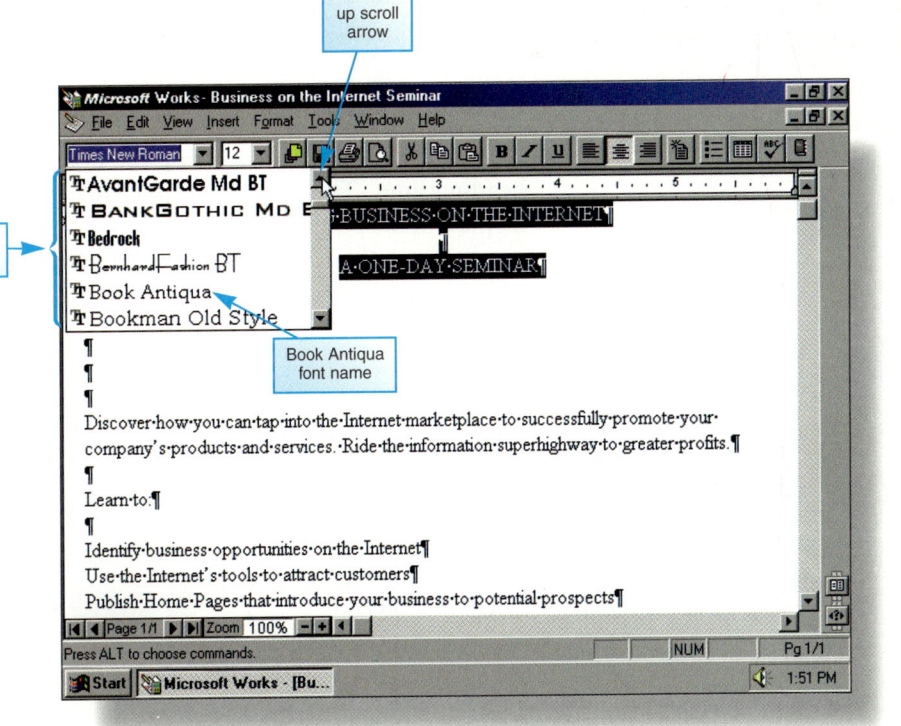

FIGURE 1-38

W 1.32 • Project 1 • Creating a Formatted Document with Clip Art

3 **Point to the Book Antiqua font name in the Font Name drop-down list.**

The Book Antiqua font name is highlighted in the list of font names and displays highlighted in the Font Name box on the toolbar (Figure 1-39).

Book Antiqua font name displays highlighted in Font Name box

Book Antiqua font name

mouse pointer

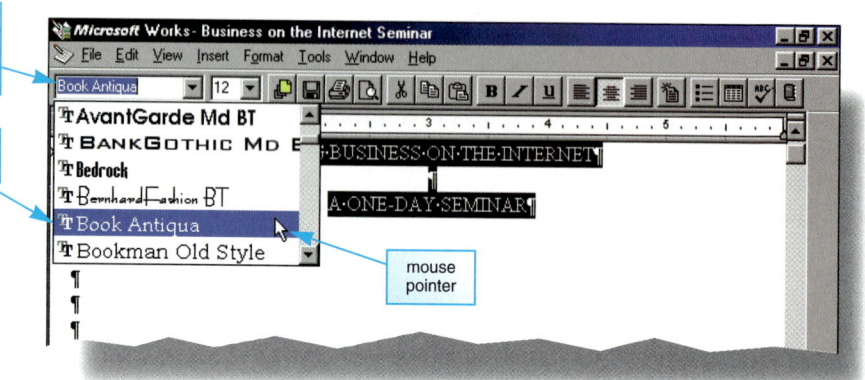

FIGURE 1-39

4 **Click Book Antiqua.**

The two heading lines display in Book Antiqua font (Figure 1-40). The Book Antiqua font name appears in the Font Name box on the toolbar.

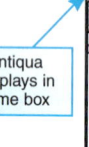

Book Antiqua name displays in Font Name box

highlighted text displays in Book Antiqua font

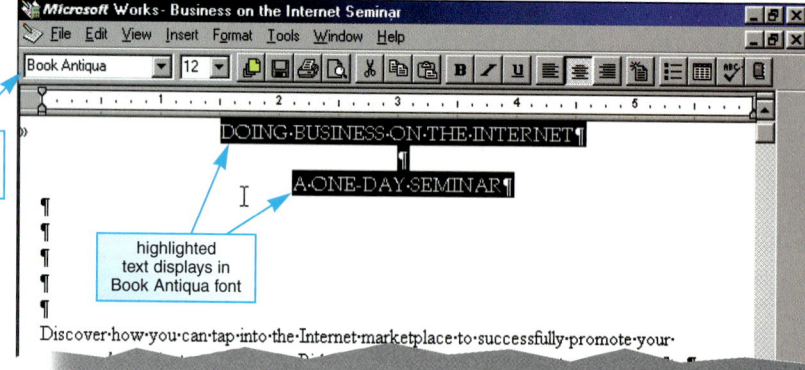

FIGURE 1-40

OtherWays

1. Right-click selected text, click Font and Style on context-sensitive menu, click desired font name in Font list, click OK button
2. On Format menu click Font and Style, click desired font name in Font list, click OK button
3. Press CTRL+SHIFT+F

After choosing the font, the changed lines remain highlighted. To remove the highlighting, click anywhere in the workspace area of the screen.

Changing Font Size

The next step in formatting the document is to change the font size of the heading lines. The words, DOING BUSINESS ON THE INTERNET, should display in 36-point font size.

Perform the following steps to change the font size.

Steps   To Change Font Size

1 **Highlight the line of text to enlarge (DOING BUSINESS ON THE INTERNET) by clicking in the left margin of the document window on the same line as the text.**

Works highlights the words, DOING BUSINESS ON THE INTERNET (Figure 1-41).

mouse pointer in left margin

text to be enlarged highlighted

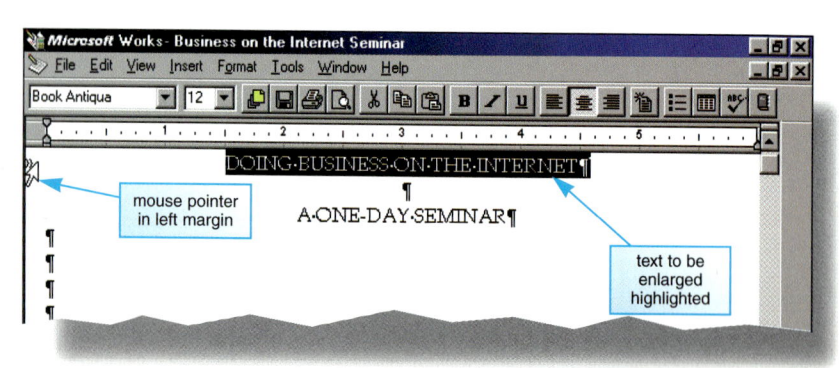

FIGURE 1-41

Microsoft **Works 4** Windows 95

Formatting the Document • **W 1.33**

2 **Click the Font Size box arrow on the toolbar.**

A list of font sizes displays (Figure 1-42). The current font size (12) is highlighted in the list.

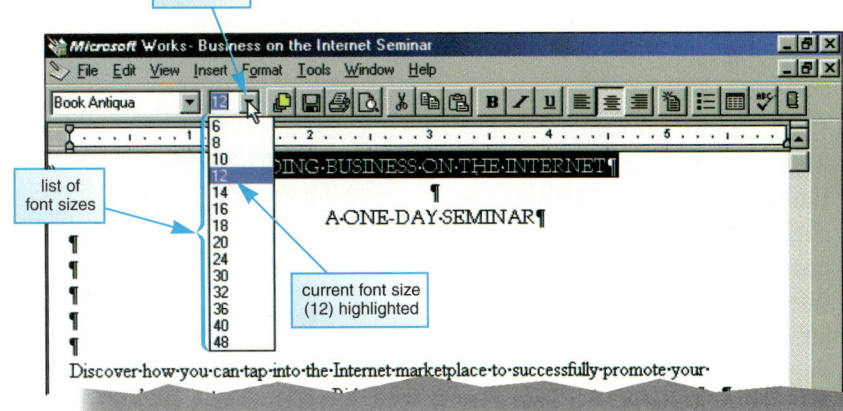

FIGURE 1-42

3 **Point to the number 36, which indicates 36-point font size (Figure 1-43).**

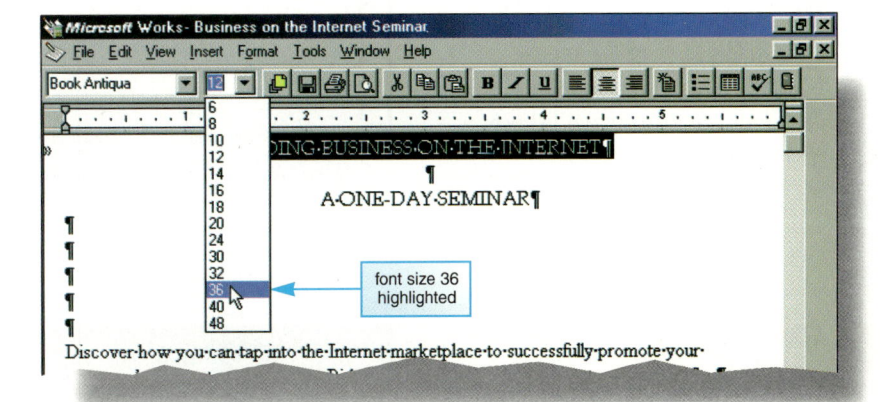

FIGURE 1-43

4 **Click 36.**

Works changes the first heading line to 36-point Book Antiqua font (Figure 1-44). The number 36 displays in the Font Size box on the toolbar. Because the heading line is increased to 36 points, Works automatically wraps the word, THE, to the beginning of the next line and centers the text.

FIGURE 1-44

Formatting the Remaining Heading Lines

The heading line, A ONE-DAY SEMINAR, should display in 16-point Book Antiqua font. Perform the steps on the next page to accomplish this formatting.

OtherWays

1. Right-click selected text, click Font and Style on context-sensitive menu, click desired font size in Size list, click OK button
2. On Format menu click Font and Style, click desired font size in Size list, click OK button
3. Press CTRL+SHIFT+P

Steps To Change Font Size

1 **Highlight the line of text to change (A ONE-DAY SEMINAR) by clicking the left margin of the document window on the same line as the text. Click the Font Size box arrow on the toolbar. Point to the number 16, which indicates 16-point font size.**

Works highlights the words, A ONE-DAY SEMINAR, a list of font sizes displays, and the mouse pointer points to the number 16 in the Font Size drop-down list box (Figure 1-45).

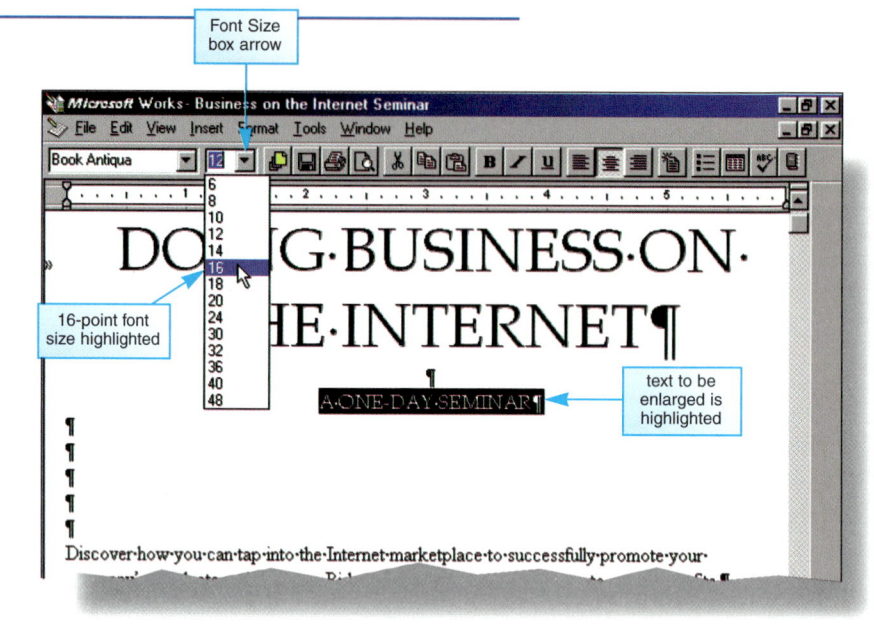

FIGURE 1-45

2 **Click 16.**

Works changes the second heading line to 16-point Book Antiqua font (Figure 1-46). The number 16 displays in the Font Size box on the toolbar.

FIGURE 1-46

The heading lines are now formatted in the proper font and font size.

Formatting Additional Text

The three lines following the heading lines display in 12-point Times New Roman. Because the default font and font size are 12-point Times New Roman, no additional steps are necessary. The five lines following the body of the announcement beginning with the words, Learn to:, are to display in 16-point Times New Roman. Because the default font and font size are 12-point Times New Roman, the only step necessary is to change the font size for the lines to 16-point. To accomplish this formatting, perform the following steps.

Microsoft **Works 4** Windows 95

Formatting the Document • W 1.35

Steps: To Change Font Size

1 **Scroll the document to view the line containing the words, Learn to:. Highlight the five lines of text to be formatted by dragging down in the left margin of the document window from the words, Learn to:. Click the Font Size box arrow on the toolbar. Point to the number 16, which indicates 16-point font size.**

Works highlights the five lines, a list of font sizes appears, and the mouse pointer points to the number 16 in the drop-down list box (Figure 1-47).

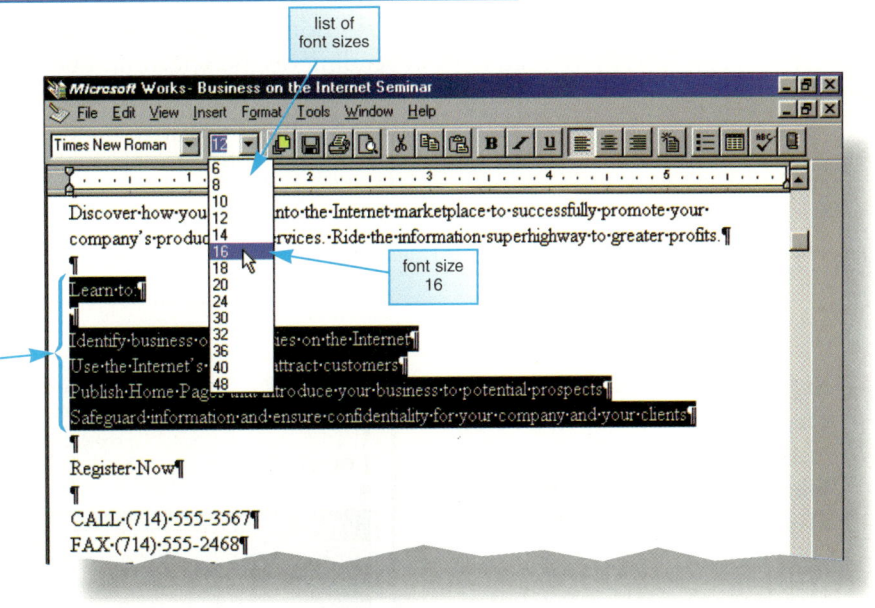

FIGURE 1-47

2 **Click 16.**

Works changes the five lines to 16-point font size. The number 16 displays in the Font Size box on the toolbar (Figure 1-48). When Works increases the font size of the highlighted lines, the last two lines automatically wrap to the next line down.

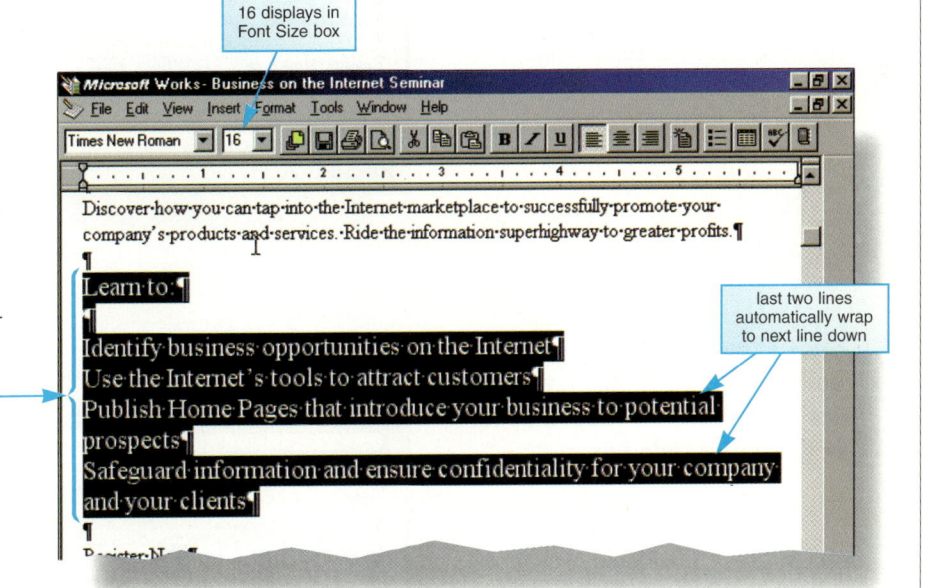

FIGURE 1-48

The first part of the announcement is now formatted with the proper fonts and font sizes.

Creating a Bulleted List

The four paragraphs following the words, Learn to:, are indented one-half inch from the left margin and appear as a bulleted list. A **bulleted list** consists of a word or words on one or more lines that are preceded by a special character at the beginning of the line. The purpose is to have the list stand out from the rest of the text.

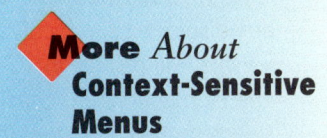

More *About*
Context-Sensitive Menus

Right-clicking any selection causes Works to display a context-sensitive menu with commands you can use. In addition to clicking any command on the context-sensitive menu, you can also right-click any command to carry out a task.

W 1.36 • Project 1 • Creating a Formatted Document with Clip Art

You can create a bulleted list by clicking **Bullets** on the context-sensitive menu. The context-sensitive menu contains frequently used commands you can use with the current selection. The commands available on the context-sensitive menu change, depending on the selection. For example, the list of commands available when text is selected is different from the list available when an object is selected. You activate the context-sensitive menu by right-clicking the selection. To create a bulleted list using the context-sensitive menu, complete the following steps.

Steps   To Create a Bulleted List

1 **Highlight the lines that are to comprise the bulleted list. Point to the selection and right-click. When the context-sensitive menu displays, point to Bullets.**

Works highlights the lines and displays the context-sensitive menu (Figure 1-49). The mouse pointer points to the Bullets command. The context-sensitive menu contains the most frequently used commands you can use with the current selection.

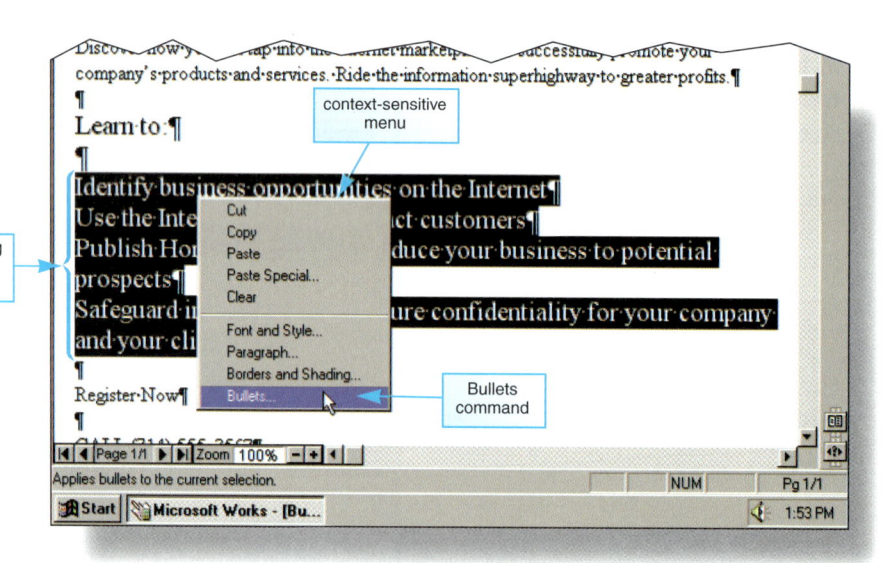

FIGURE 1-49

2 **Click Bullets. When the Format Bullets dialog box displays, click the solid diamond-shaped bullet in the Bullet style box.**

Works displays the Format Bullets dialog box (Figure 1-50). Twenty-four different styles of bullets display in the Bullet style box. The solid diamond-shaped bullet in the Bullet Style box is highlighted, indicating it is selected. The Bullet size box displays 12, indicating the bullet style will display in 12-point size. The Hanging indent check box is selected, indicating that the first line of each highlighted paragraph will begin farther to the left than the rest of the lines in the paragraph. The Sample box shows how the bulleted list will display.

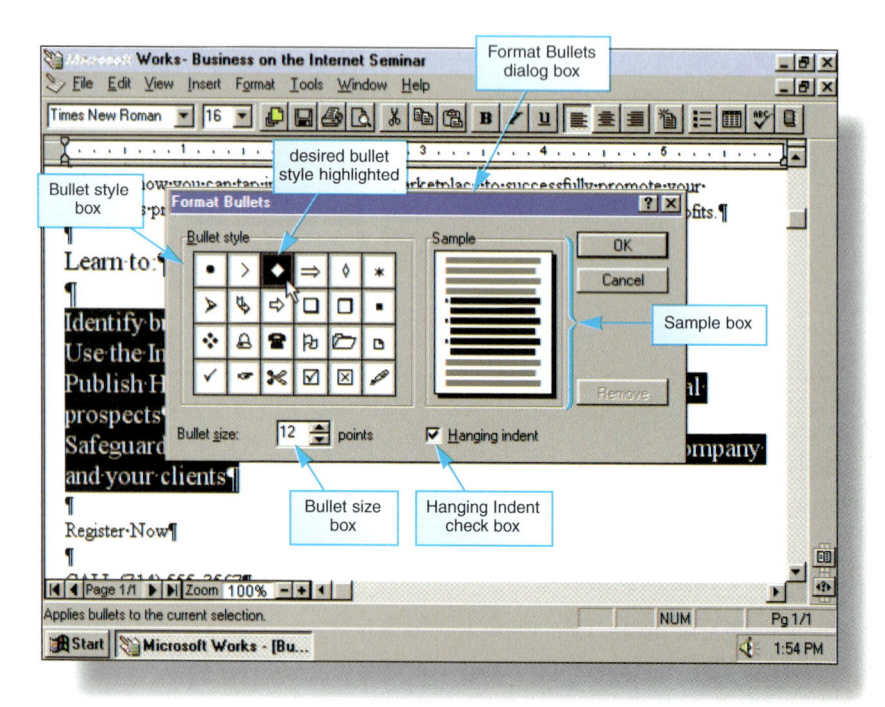

FIGURE 1-50

Microsoft **Works 4** Windows 95

Formatting the Document • W 1.37

3 **Point to the Bullet size box up arrow and click four times until 16 displays in the Bullet size box. Point to the OK button.**

The Bullet size box displays 16, indicating the bullet style will display in 16-point size (Figure 1-51).

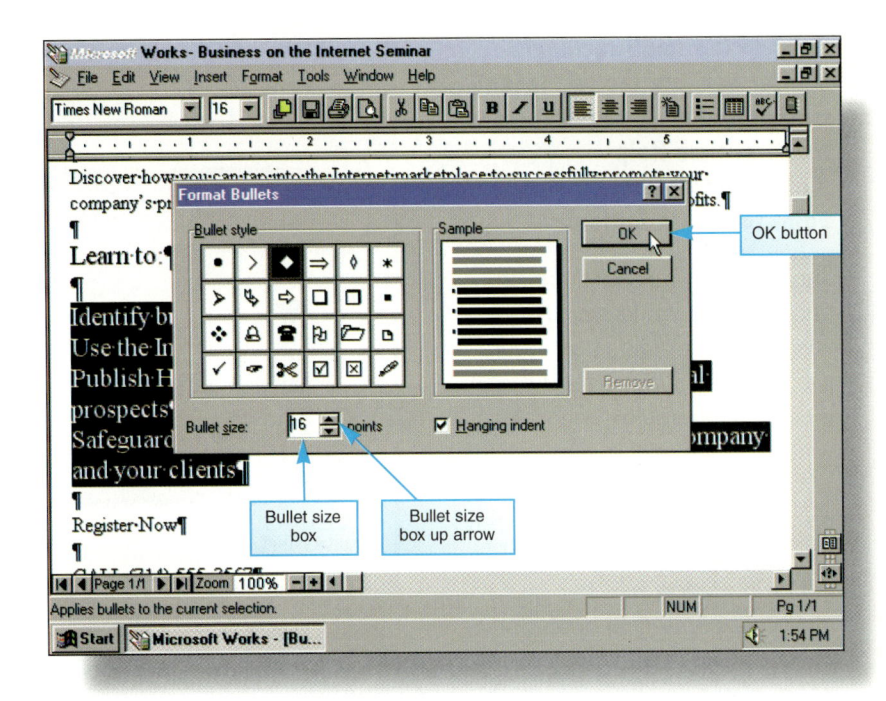

FIGURE 1-51

4 **Click the OK button.**

A 16-point solid black diamond shaped bullet displays in front of the text (Figure 1-52). The text moves to the right one-quarter of an inch. The bottom triangle on the left side of the ruler, called the **left indent marker**, *moves to the right one-quarter of an inch. The Bullets button on the toolbar is recessed, indicating the highlighted text contains bullets.*

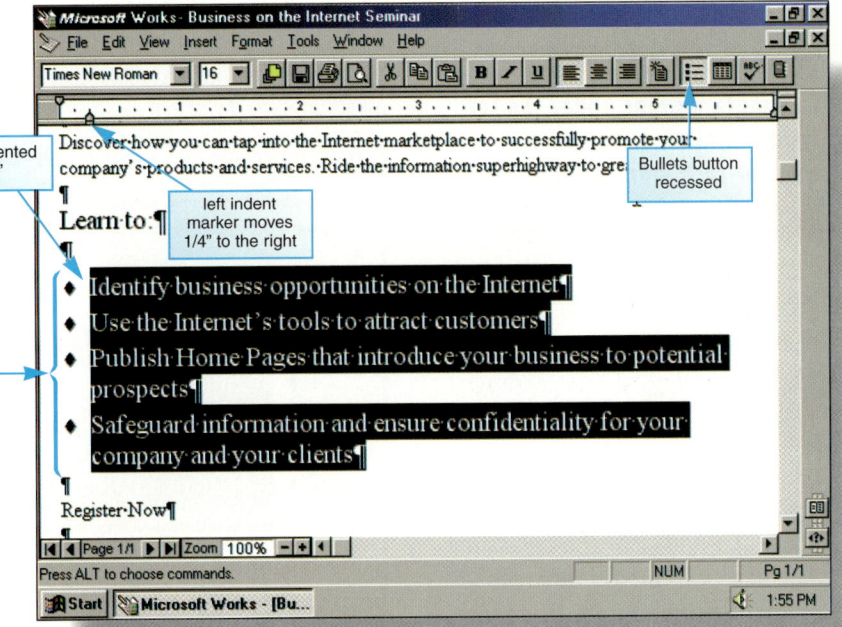

FIGURE 1-52

W 1.38 • Project 1 • Creating a Formatted Document with Clip Art

5 **Point to the small rectangle marker beneath the left indent marker and click. When the First-time Help dialog box displays, point to the OK button.**

The first time you click the ruler in each session, Works displays the First-time Help dialog box (Figure 1-53). Clicking the To set a custom indent button displays the Help window to the right of the document screen with step-by-step instructions on setting a custom indent. Clicking the To set a tab stop button displays the Help window with step-by-step instructions on setting a tab stop. The First-time Help dialog box will not display if you have previously clicked the Don't display this message in the future check box.

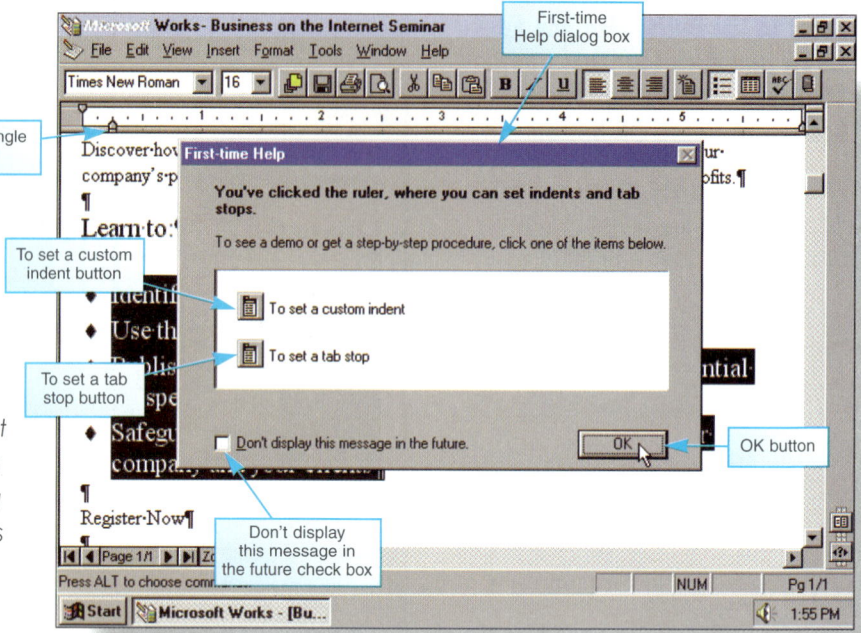

FIGURE 1-53

6 **Click the OK button. Drag the rectangle marker under the left indent marker to the three-quarter inch mark on the ruler.**

*The First-time Help dialog box closes. The bullets and related text indent an additional one-half inch (Figure 1-54). The top triangle on the left side of the ruler, called the **first-line indent marker**, moves to the right one-half inch, and the left indent marker moves to the right an additional one-half inch. The bullets are indented one-half inch from the left margin. The text begins three-quarters of an inch from the left margin.*

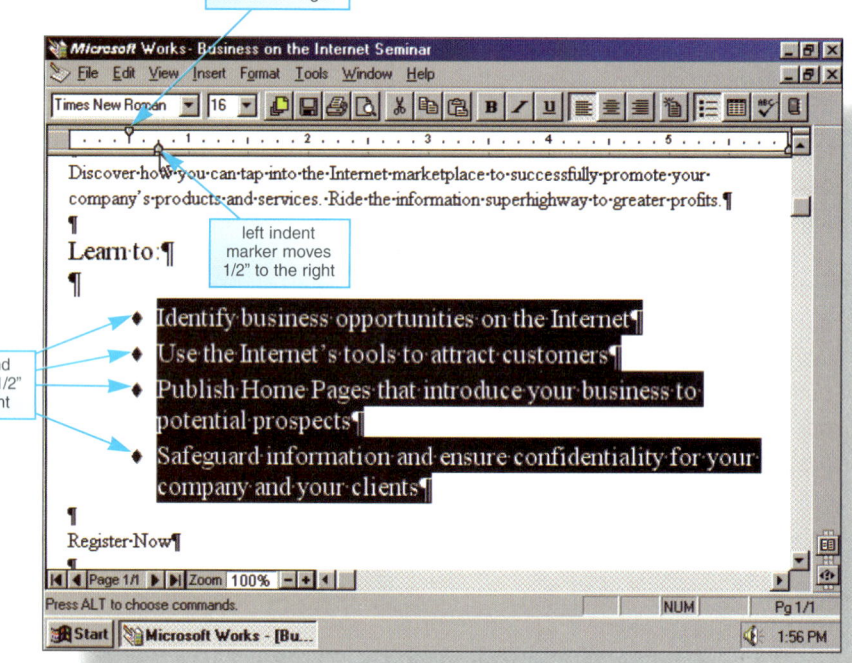

FIGURE 1-54

OtherWays

1. On Format menu click Paragraph, click Indents and Alignment tab, click Bulleted, click OK button
2. On Format menu click Bullets, click desired bullet style, click OK button
3. Click Bullets button on toolbar

Microsoft **Works 4** Windows 95

Formatting the Document • W 1.39

on or the Paragraph command creates a
hat was last chosen in the Format Bullets

the mouse pointer anywhere in the

ted list, highlight the bulleted list and
f you want to change the bulleted list to
t the bulleted list and press the CTRL+Q

h the proper font and font sizes except
g the bulleted list should be centered
display in 16-point Arial. To center the
to Arial and the font size to 16, complete

ND FONT SIZE

in the document.
on the toolbar.
row to display the list of fonts. Scroll the
ame into view.

w to display the list of font sizes.

Step 6: Click 16.

More *About* First-time Help Feature

The first time you try to do a new task such as Print a document or change the paragraph indent on the ruler in a Works session, Works opens the First-time Help dialog box where you can display additional information to help you complete the task. You can view the Help screen or just click the OK button to close the dialog box and continue with the original task. To turn the First-time Help feature off, click Options on the Tools menu and clear the Show first-time Help check box on the View sheet.

The last four lines are centered and display in 16-point Arial font (Figure 1-55)

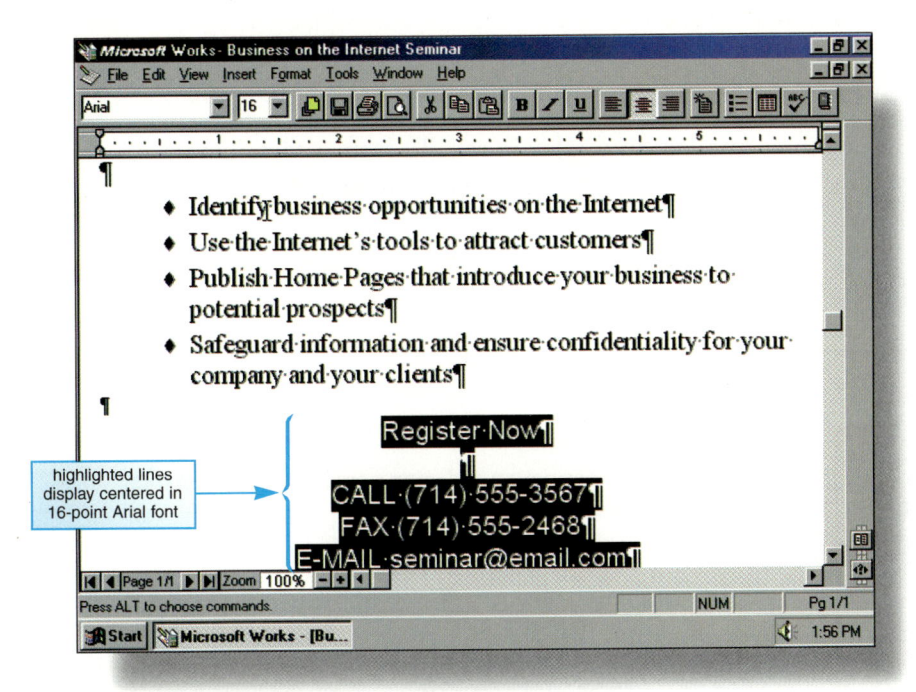

FIGURE 1-55

highlighted lines display centered in 16-point Arial font

Displaying Text in Italics

The next step is to select the first line after the bulleted list and italicize the characters in it. Perform the step on the next page to italicize text.

W 1.40 • Project 1 • Creating a Formatted Document with Clip Art

Steps: To Italicize Text

1 **Highlight the line to be italicized. Click the Italic button on the toolbar.**

The first line after the bulleted list displays in italics (Figure 1-56).

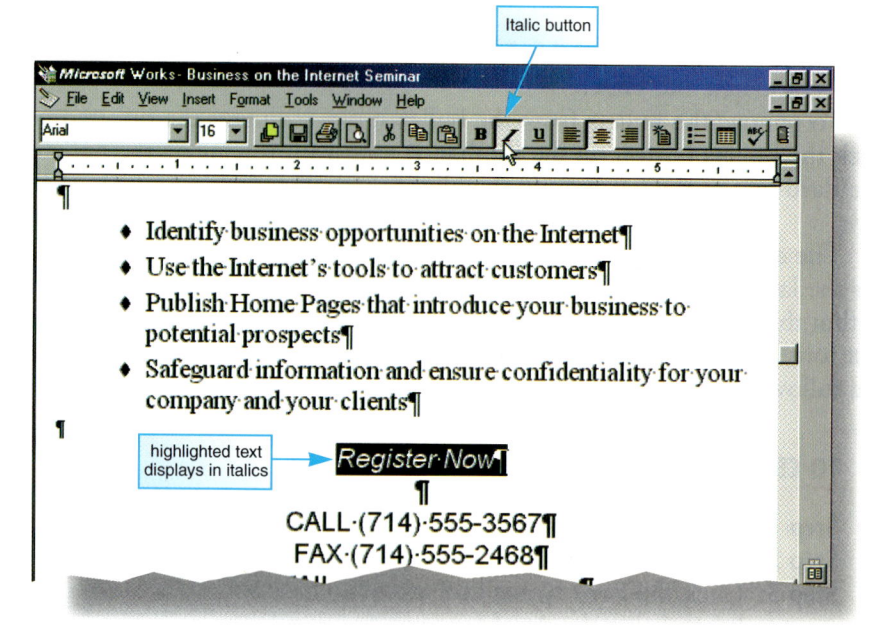

FIGURE 1-56

> **OtherWays**
> 1. Right-click selected text, click Font and Style on context-sensitive menu, click Italic, click OK button
> 2. On Format menu click Font and Style, click Italic, click OK button
> 3. Press CTRL+I

When the selected text is italicized, the Italic button on the toolbar is recessed. If you want to remove the italic format from the selected text, click the Italic button a second time.

Displaying Text in Color

The last three lines are to display in red. To format these lines, use the Font and Style command on the context-sensitive menu as shown in the following steps.

Steps: To Display Text In Color

1 **Highlight the last three lines in the document. Point to the highlighted lines and right-click. Then, point to Font and Style on the context-sensitive menu.**

The last three lines in the document are highlighted (Figure 1-57). Works displays the context-sensitive menu and the mouse pointer is positioned on Font and Style.

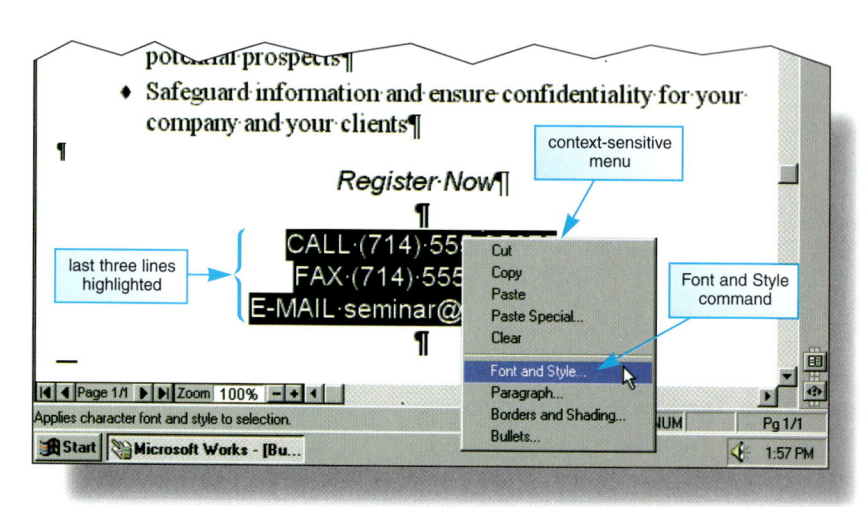

FIGURE 1-57

Microsoft **Works 4** Windows 95
Formatting the Document • W 1.41

2 **Click Font and Style on the context-sensitive menu. When the Format Font and Style dialog box displays, click the Color box, scroll through the list until the Red color box displays, and then point to the Red color box.**

Works displays the Format Font and Style dialog box (Figure 1-58). In the Format Font and Style dialog box, Arial displays in the Font box, 16 displays in the Size box, indicating the font for the highlighted text is 16-point Arial. The mouse pointer points to the red rectangle in the Color drop-down list box.

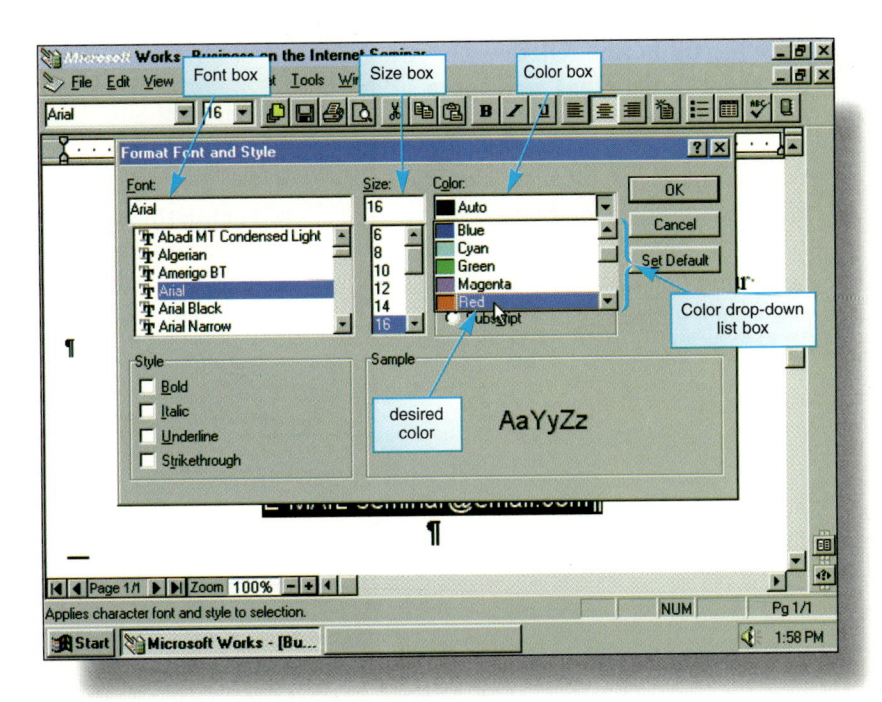

FIGURE 1-58

3 **Click Red and then point to the OK button.**

Text in the Sample box displays in red 16-point Arial font (Figure 1-59). The mouse pointer points to the OK button.

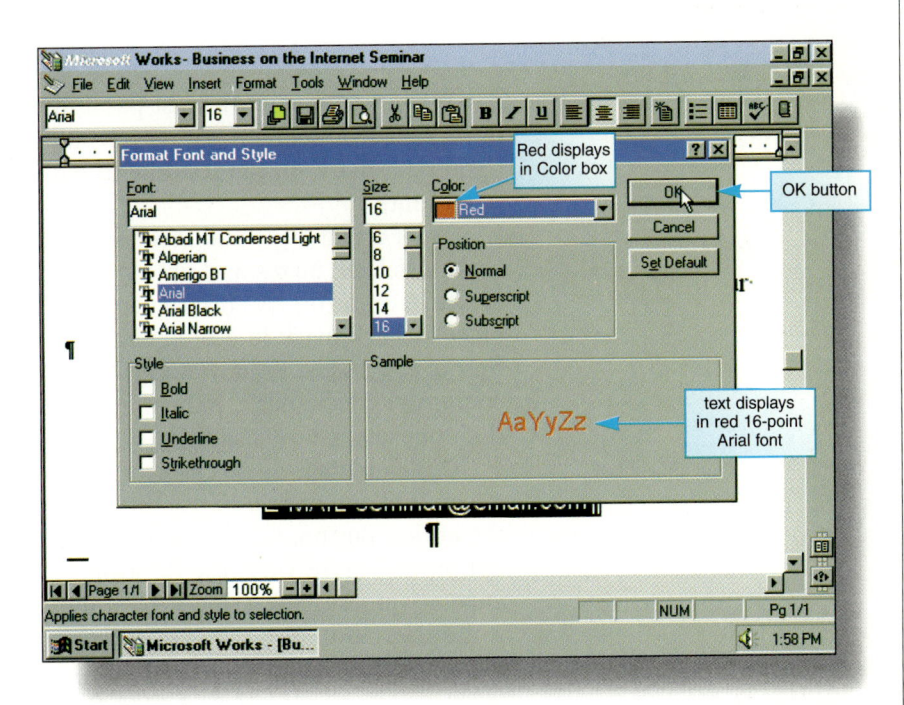

FIGURE 1-59

4 **Click the OK button. Click anywhere in the blank workspace area to remove the highlighting.**

Works displays the last three lines in red 16-point Arial font (Figure 1-60). The paragraph mark for the next paragraph retains the formatting from the previous paragraph.

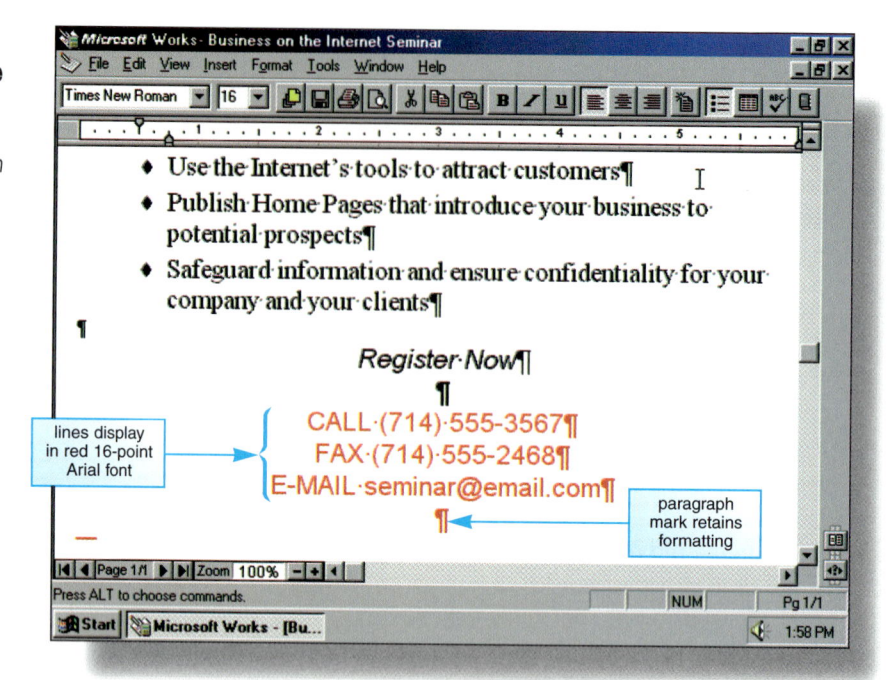

FIGURE 1-60

OtherWays

1. On Format menu click Font and Style, click desired color in Color drop-down list box, click OK button

When you format the last paragraph in a document, the formatting remains in place for subsequent paragraphs unless you change it. That is the reason the paragraph mark on the last line in Figure 1-60 displays centered in red 16-point Arial font.

The Format Font and Style dialog box in Figure 1-59 on the previous page contains check boxes and option buttons. A **check box** represents options that you can turn on or off. A check in a check box indicates the option is turned on. To place a check mark in a box, click the box. In Figure 1-59, the Style box contains four check boxes; Bold, Italic, Underline, and Strikethrough. None of the boxes contains a check mark, indicating the options are turned off. You can select more than one check box at a time.

Option buttons also represent options that you can turn on or off. You can select only one option button at a time, however. To select an option button, click the option button. Choosing a new option automatically turns off the previous option. In Figure 1-59, the Position box contains three option buttons; Normal, Superscript, and Subscript. The option button containing the black dot, (Normal), is the selected button. The **Normal option** positions highlighted characters on the line with other text.

Bold Style

To further emphasize the contents of the announcement, the entire document should display in bold. To do this, you must first highlight the entire document, and then click the Bold button on the toolbar. To display the document in bold, perform the following steps.

Steps **To Display an Entire Document in Bold**

1 **Hold down the CTRL key and then click in the left margin.**

The entire document is highlighted (Figure 1-61).

FIGURE 1-61

2 **Click the Bold button on the toolbar.**

Works changes all text to bold (Figure 1-62).

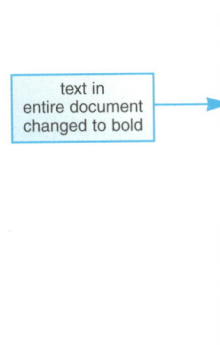

FIGURE 1-62

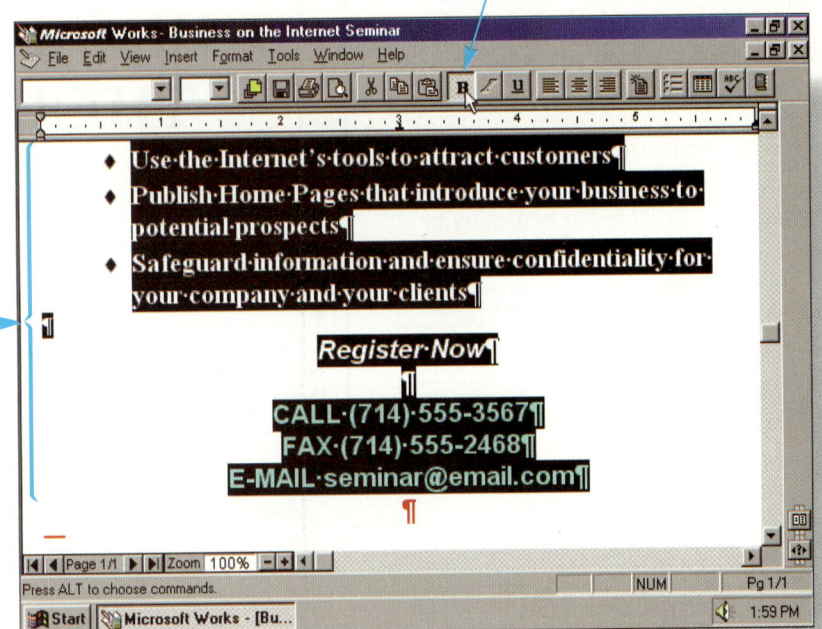

The document is now formatted except for the illustration that must be inserted in the document.

OtherWays

1. Right-click selected text, click Font and Style on context-sensitive menu, click Bold, click OK button
2. On Format menu click Font and Style, click Bold, click OK button
3. Press CTRL+B

More About
Microsoft Works Clip Art

Many software applications include clip art with their package. Microsoft Clip Gallery can contain clip art from Microsoft Word, Microsoft PowerPoint, and Microsoft Works, as well as any additional software vendor. If this is the case on your computer, you may find duplicate pictures in the gallery.

Using Clip Art in a Document

The next step in preparing the announcement is to insert an illustration related to the seminar in the document (see Figure 1-1 on page W1.8). To accomplish this, you must use the Microsoft **clip art** (predrawn illustrations) that is available for use as a part of the Word Processor.

Inserting Clip Art in a Word Processing Document

You insert clip art into a document by clicking **ClipArt** on the **Insert menu**. The steps to insert clip art into the announcement are explained below and on the next three pages.

Steps To Insert Clip Art into a Document

1 **Click the beginning of document button at the lower left of the document window to display the top portion of the document on the screen. Click the line in the document where you want to place the clip art.**

When you click the beginning of document button, Works moves the insertion point to the beginning of the document and displays the first lines of the document on the screen. The insertion point is positioned on the line where you will insert the clip art (Figure 1-63).

FIGURE 1-63

Using Clip Art in a Document • **W 1.45**

2 **Because you want to center the clip art, click the Center Align button on the toolbar.**

Works centers the insertion point and the paragraph mark on the screen (Figure 1-64).

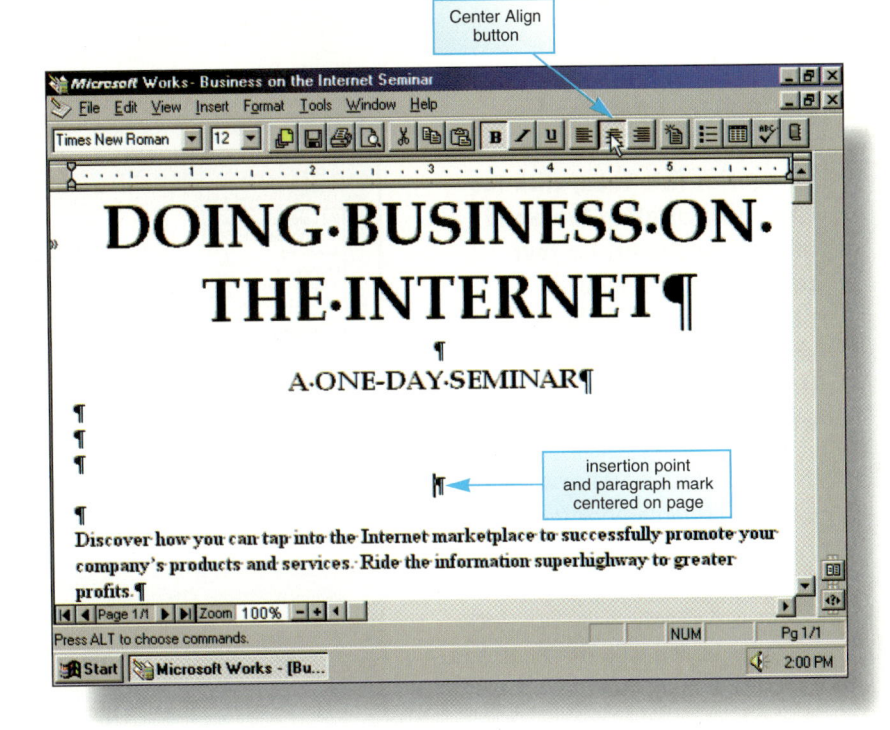

FIGURE 1-64

3 **Click Insert on the menu bar and then point to ClipArt.**

Works displays the **Insert menu** (Figure 1-65). The mouse pointer points to ClipArt.

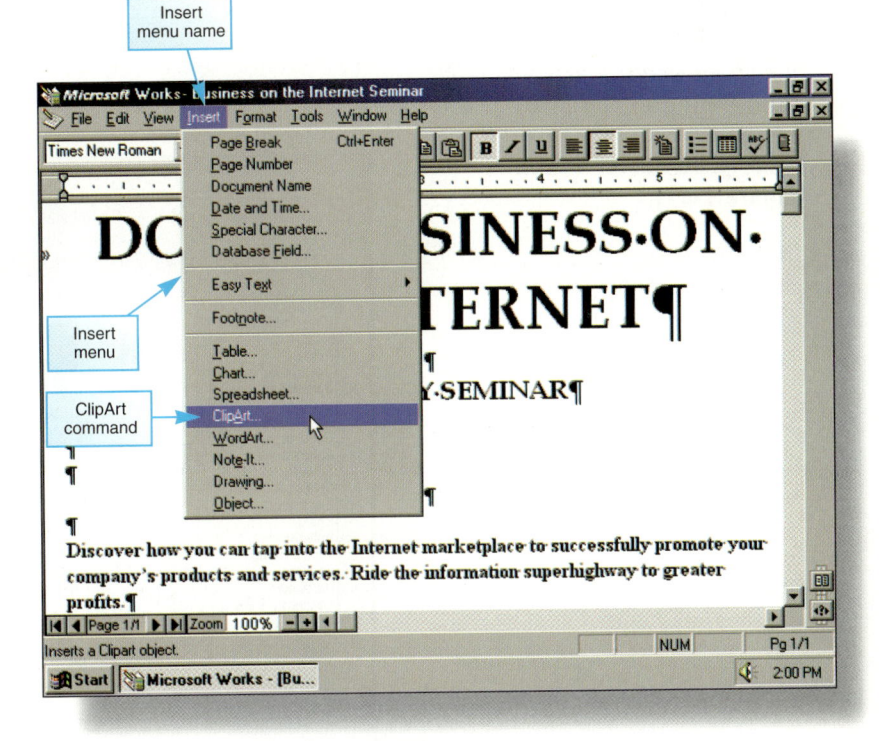

FIGURE 1-65

W 1.46 • Project 1 • Creating a Formatted Document with Clip Art

4 Click ClipArt. When the Microsoft Clip Gallery 3.0 dialog box displays, click Business in the Categories list. Then, click the clip art illustrating the world globe. The clip art on your computer may appear in a different sequence than shown in Figure 1-66. If so, scroll until the world globe displays.

Works displays the *Microsoft Clip Gallery 3.0 dialog box* (Figure 1-66). The Clip Art list box displays clip art images by category. The Business category is the selected category on the Clip Art sheet. You can click a different category name to display a particular type of clip art. The clip art with the illustration of the world globe is selected as indicated by the blue outline around the image.

FIGURE 1-66

5 Point to the Insert button (Figure 1-67).

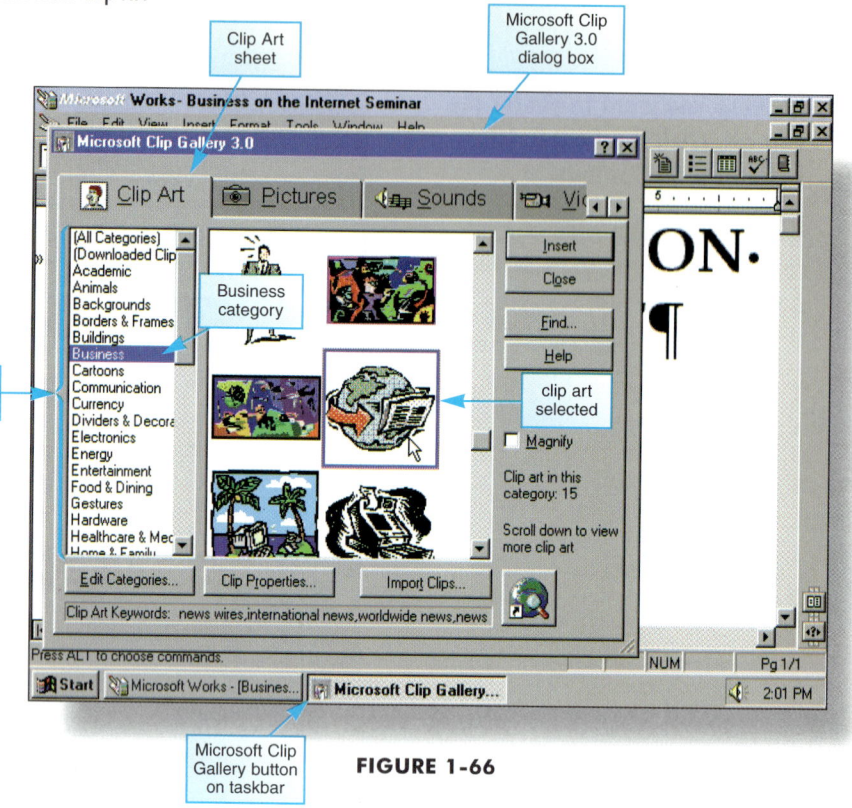

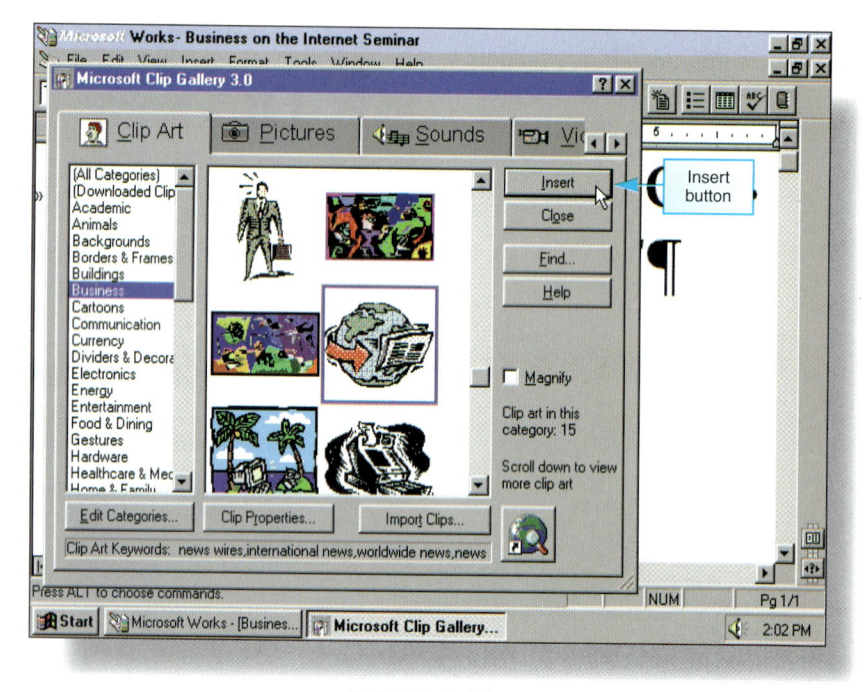

FIGURE 1-67

Microsoft Works 4 Windows 95

Using Clip Art in a Document • W 1.47

6 **Click the Insert button.**

Works inserts the clip art in the word processing document at the location of the insertion point (Figure 1-68). A rectangular border that contains small dark squares, called **resize handles**, displays around the border of the clip art. This border indicates the clip art is selected.

FIGURE 1-68

To remove the border around the clip art, click anywhere outside the clip art.

The Microsoft Clip Gallery 3.0 dialog box that displays on your computer may contain additional images. Many different clip art images may be purchased and added to Works.

The clip art that is placed in the word processing document is called an **object**. Once in the word processing document, the object may be resized, that is, made larger or smaller, as required.

Changing the Size of Clip Art

After adding the clip art to the document, the size of the clip art must be changed to correspond to Figure 1-1 on page W1.8. To change the size of the clip art, complete the steps on the next two pages.

W 1.48 • Project 1 • Creating a Formatted Document with Clip Art

Steps To Resize Clip Art

1 **If the clip art is not selected, click the clip art object. Position the mouse pointer over the resize handle in the upper right corner of the border that surrounds the clip art.**

When the mouse pointer is positioned inside a selected object, it changes to a block arrow with the word DRAG beneath it. This indicates you can drag the clip art to any position within the document. A border surrounds the clip art indicating the object is selected (Figure 1-69). Positioning the mouse pointer on a resize handle causes the mouse pointer to change to a small square with a two-headed arrow intersecting the square. The word RESIZE displays beneath the square.

mouse pointer changes shape when positioned over resize handle

FIGURE 1-69

2 **With the mouse pointer pointing to the resize handle in the upper right corner of the clip art, drag downward and to the left until the scaling percentage displayed on the status bar is 46% high and 46% wide.**

As you drag downward and to the left, the entire rectangular border around the clip art reduces (Figure 1-70). As you drag the resize handle downward and to the left, Works displays the percentage of the object's original width and height on the status bar.

rectangular border reduces

percentage of object's original width and height

FIGURE 1-70

3 **Release the mouse button.**

The illustration reduces in size to 46% of the original size (Figure 1-71). Works also recenters the reduced illustration.

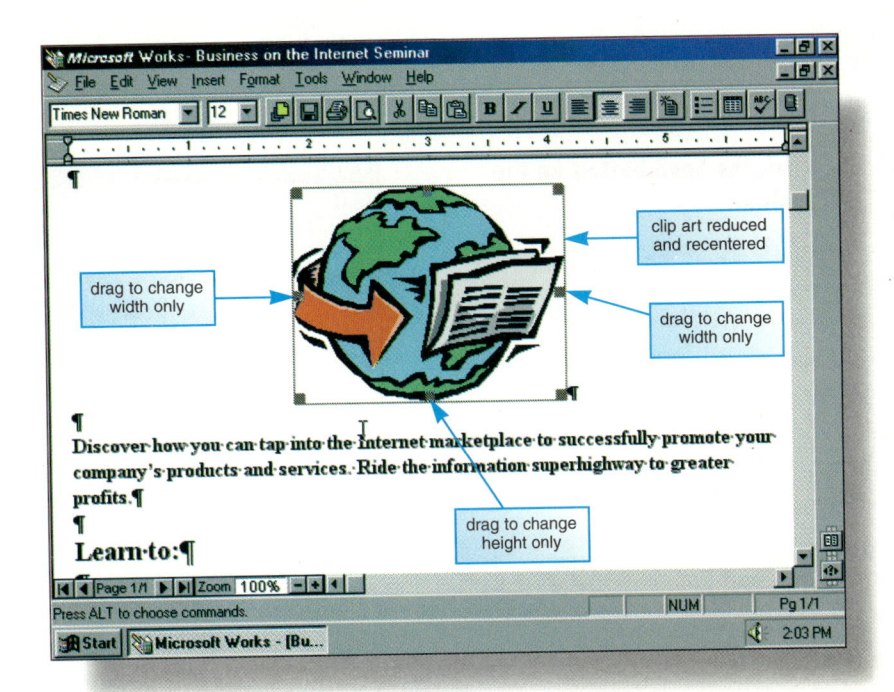

FIGURE 1-71

For objects in a Word Processor document, when you drag one of the corner resize handles, the entire rectangular border increases or decreases proportionately in size. If you drag a resize handle in the middle of a vertical border, only the width of the illustration changes. Similarly, if you drag a resize handle in the middle of a horizontal border, only the height of the illustration changes. Be aware that dragging a resize handle in the middle of a vertical or horizontal border will change the original proportions of the object.

If you ever need to clear a clip art image from a Microsoft Works Word Processor document, select the image and then press the DELETE key. You also can select the image and then click Clear on the context-sensitive menu or the Edit menu.

If an object has been previously selected, clicking anywhere in the document workspace except the selected object will remove the rectangular border.

Saving an Existing Document with the Same Filename

The announcement for Project 1 is now complete. To save the formatting changes and clip art to your floppy disk in drive A, you must save the document again. When you saved the document the first time, you assigned a filename to it (Business on the Internet Seminar). When you make changes to an already saved document and want to save the modified document without changing the filename, use the **Save button** on the toolbar. Works will save the modified document without displaying the Save As dialog box and asking you for a new filename. Perform the step on the next page to save the existing document with the same filename.

> **OtherWays**
>
> 1. Right-click selected object, click Format Picture on the context-sensitive menu, click Size tab, type exact size or scaling percentages, click OK button
> 2. On Format menu click Picture, click Size tab, type exact size or scaling percentages, click OK button

> **More *About***
> **Saving a Document**
>
> You have struggled so hard to create the perfect paper on the computer for an English class. Suddenly, a student trips over your power cord and your monitor goes blank. It has been 30 minutes since you last saved your work. Horror stories such as this have happened to most people who have used a computer. There is no such thing as saving too often to protect the work you have completed.

W 1.50 • Project 1 • Creating a Formatted Document with Clip Art

Steps: To Save an Existing Document with the Same Filename

1 **Click the Save button on the toolbar.**

Works saves the document on a floppy disk inserted in drive A using the currently assigned filename, Business on the Internet Seminar. When the save is finished, the document remains in main memory and displays on the screen (Figure 1-72).

FIGURE 1-72

> **OtherWays**
> 1. On File menu click Save
> 2. Press CTRL+S

If you want to save the modified document using a filename different from the name under which the file is currently saved, then you must use the **Save As command** on the File menu. When you use the Save As command, Works will display the Save As dialog box, and then you must enter the new filename, drive, and location. Works will save the document using the new filename in the location you specify. Note, however, that the file saved using the old filename still resides on disk. The file using the new name does not replace the file with the old name.

Print Preview

After you create and save a Word Processor document, you often will want to print the document. To view the document in reduced size on the screen, use the **print preview** feature of the Word Processor. To use print preview, perform the following steps.

Steps: To Use Print Preview

1 **Point to the Print Preview button on the toolbar (Figure 1-73).**

FIGURE 1-73

② Click the Print Preview button.

Works opens the print preview window, and you can see the entire document as it will print (Figure 1-74).

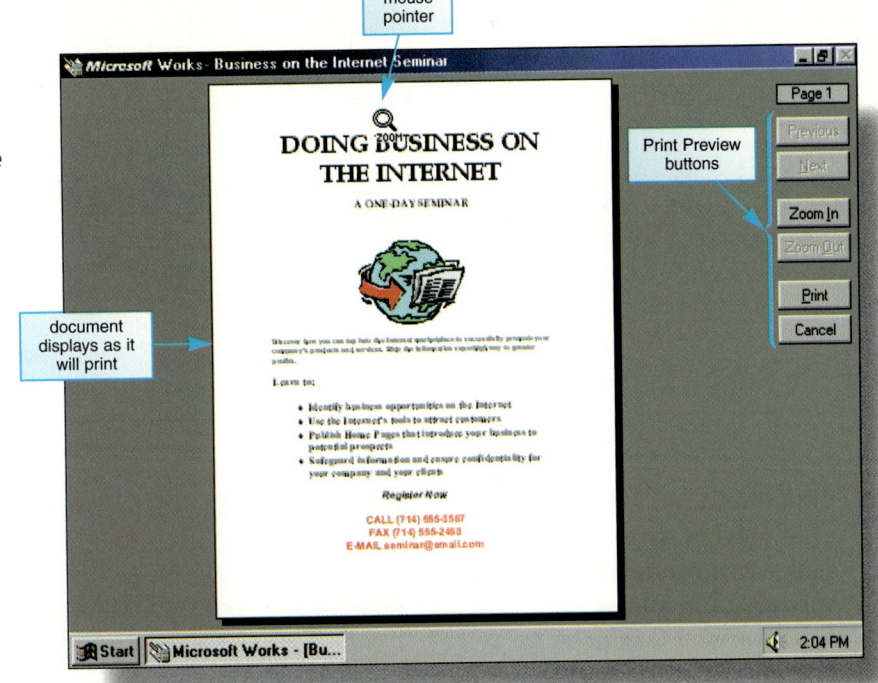

FIGURE 1-74

> **OtherWays**
> 1. On File menu click Print Preview
> 2. Press CTRL+F+V

At the top right side of the print preview window, a box contains the page number of the page displayed. Below the page number box is a series of buttons, called **Print Preview buttons,** you can use to control what you want to display. Clicking the **Previous button** will display a previous page, if there is one. Clicking the **Next button** will display the next page, if there is one.

The document image that Works displays is reduced in size. It is possible to enlarge the image. Clicking the **Zoom In button** once will enlarge the image approximately one-half the size displayed in the document window where you enter text. Clicking the Zoom In button twice will enlarge the image to the full size displayed in the document window where you enter text. Use the **Zoom Out button** to reduce the size of the image after you have enlarged it.

Clicking the **Print button** will cause Works to print the document. Clicking the **Cancel button** returns you to the document window where you can enter text.

If you position the mouse pointer in the print preview image area, the mouse pointer shape changes to a magnifying glass and you can use the mouse to enlarge the print preview image. Clicking the print preview image area one time will enlarge the image one-half its normal screen size. Clicking a second time will enlarge the image to approximately full-size. Clicking a third time will reduce the image to its original size as shown in Figure 1-74.

If you have a color printer, the document will display as illustrated in Figure 1-74. If you do not have a color printer, the document will display in black and white and the clip art appears in black and green.

Printing a Document

The following steps explain how to print a document that displays in the document window by clicking the **Print command** on the File menu. The Print command available on the File menu should be used the first time you print a document on a given computer to ensure the print options are properly selected.

Steps: To Print a Document

1 Click the Cancel button in the print preview window to return to the document window. Click File on the menu bar and then point to Print.

The File menu displays (Figure 1-75).

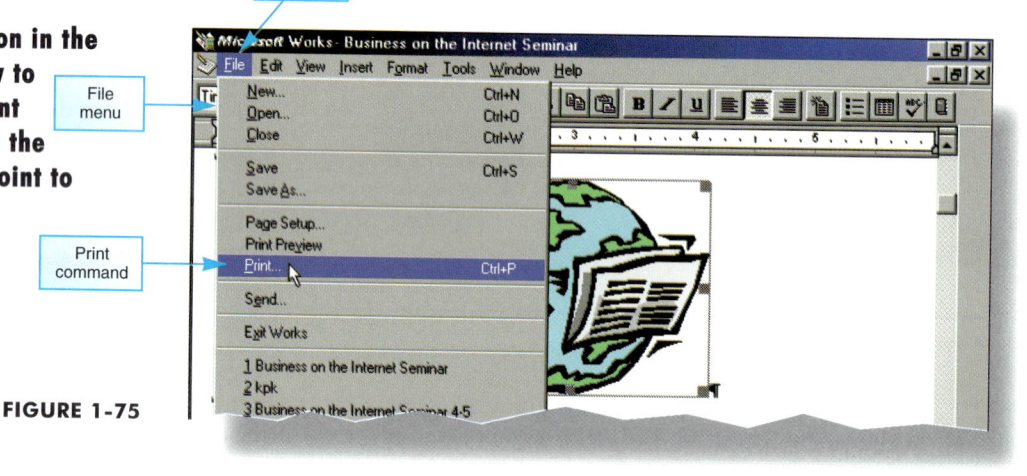

FIGURE 1-75

2 Click Print. When the First-time Help dialog box displays, point to the OK button.

*The first time you click Print in each session, Works displays the First-time Help dialog box (Figure 1-76). The **Quick tour of printing button** displays an overview of printing. The **To print your document button** displays step-by-step instructions on printing your document. The **To print a specific page or range of pages button** displays step-by-step instructions on printing a specific page or range of pages. The First-time Help dialog box will not display if you have previously clicked the Don't display this message in the future check box.*

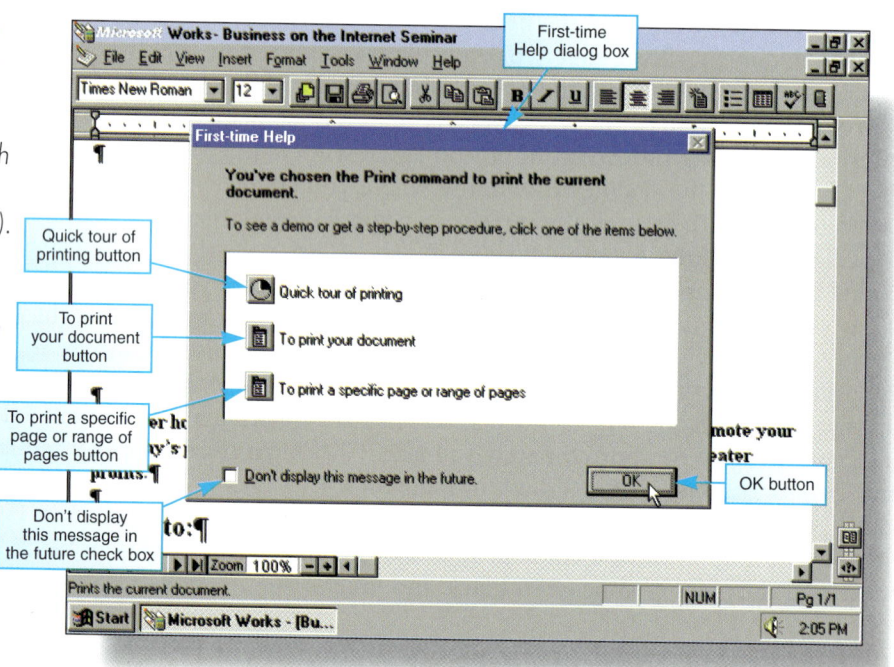

FIGURE 1-76

Printing a Document • W 1.53

3 **Click the OK button. When the Print dialog box displays, point to the OK button.**

The Print dialog box displays on the screen (Figure 1-77). Review the Print dialog box to ensure the Number of copies box contains 1 and All is selected (a small black circle appears within the All option button when it is selected). This indicates all pages will print. In the What to Print box, make sure Main Document is selected.

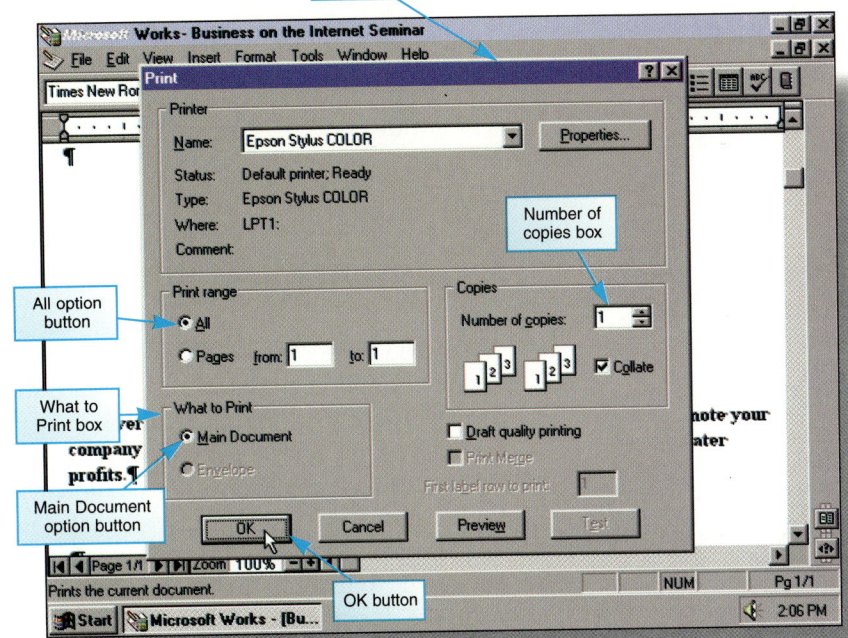

FIGURE 1-77

4 **Click the OK button.**

The Printing dialog box displays a brief message on the screen describing the status of the printing operation. The document is then printed on your printer (Figure 1-78).

OtherWays
1. Click Print button on toolbar
2. Press CTRL+P

FIGURE 1-78

After you have made entries in the Print dialog box to assure that printing will occur as you desire, you can use the Print button on the toolbar to print the document. When you click the Print button on the toolbar, the Print dialog box will not display. Printing will result based on previous entries in the Print dialog box.

Closing a Document

> **More About**
> **The Close Button**
>
> The Close button is a new innovation for Works. In previous versions of Works, the user had to click a command on a menu or a button in the Works Startup dialog box to close the window. Clicking the Close button is the fastest way to close a document or application.

When you have completed working on a document, normally you will close the document and begin work on another document or close Works. Closing a document you are working on removes the document from the screen and from random access memory. If you close a document and no other documents are open, Works displays the Works Task Launcher dialog box, which allows you to continue using Works.

You should close a document when you no longer want to work on that document, but want to continue using Works. Complete the following steps to close the document.

Steps: To Close a Document

1 Point to the Close button in the upper right corner of the document window (Figure 1-79).

FIGURE 1-79

② Click the Close button.

The text on the screen disappears and the Works Task Launcher dialog box displays, allowing you to continue to use Works (Figure 1-80).

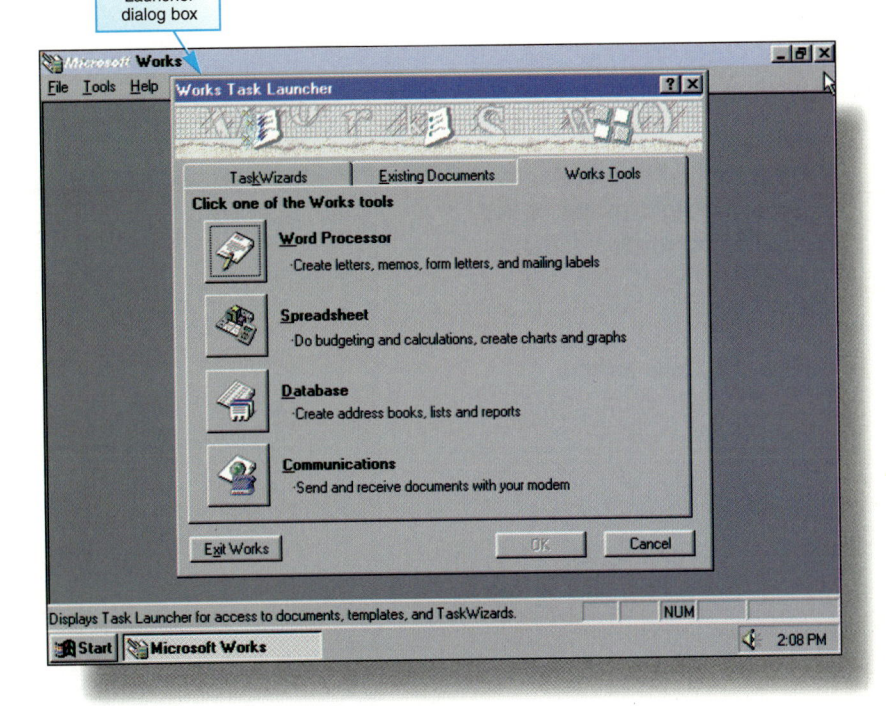

FIGURE 1-80

If you have made any changes to a document after it has been saved, a dialog box displays asking you if you want to save the changes before closing the document. Click the Yes button in the dialog box to save changes.

Closing Works

If you are finished using Works, you should **close** Works. It is important to close Works and not just turn off the machine after completing a document. The steps on the next page explain how to close Works.

> **OtherWays**
> 1. On File menu click Close
> 2. Press CTRL+W
> 3. Press CTRL+F4

W 1.56 • Project 1 • Creating a Formatted Document with Clip Art

Steps: To Close Works

1 Point to the Close button in the upper right corner of the application window (Figure 1-81).

2 Click the Close button.

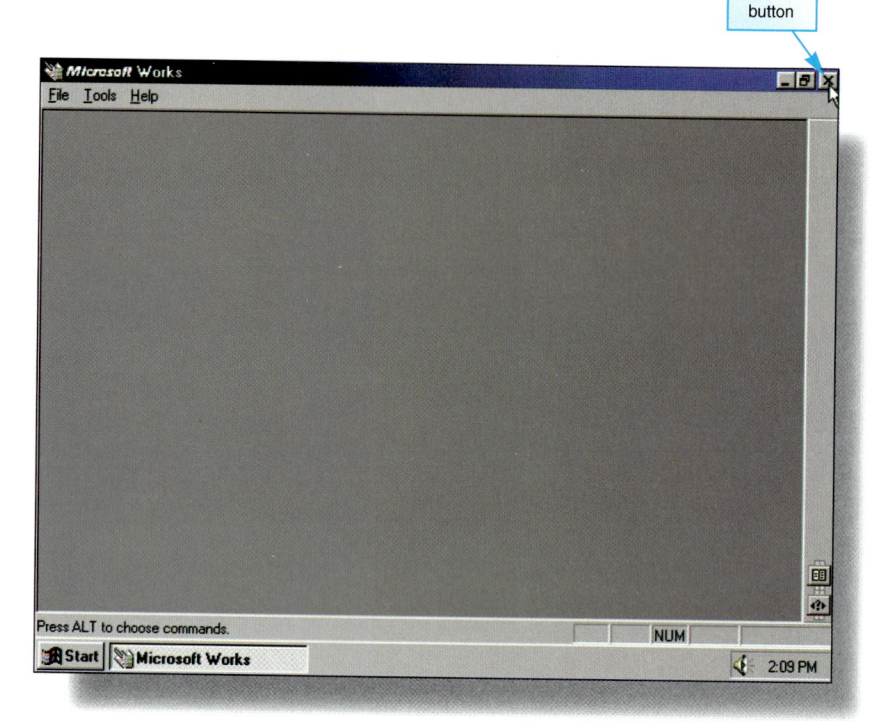

FIGURE 1-81

> **OtherWays**
> 1. On File menu click Exit Works
> 2. In Works Task Launcher dialog box, click Exit Works button
> 3. Press ALT+F4

> **More About the 3½ Floppy [A:] Window**
>
> In addition to opening a file in the 3½ Floppy [A:] window, you can accomplish other tasks. Right-click any file in the window and Works displays a context-sensitive menu with commands you can use to print, copy, delete, or rename a file.

Works is terminated, and the Microsoft Windows 95 desktop will again display. If you have made any changes to a document after it has been saved, a dialog box displays asking you if you want to save the changes before quitting. Click the Yes button in the dialog box to save changes.

Opening an Existing Document

Often after creating, saving, and printing a document and closing Works, you may want to open an existing document to make changes to that document. The easiest way to open an existing document is to use the **My Computer icon** located in the upper left corner of the desktop. My Computer allows you to access files stored on your hard disk or a floppy disk. To open the file you created in Project 1, Business on the Internet Seminar, double-click the My Computer icon, double-click the 3½ floppy [A:] icon, where the document is located, and then double-click the filename. Windows will start Microsoft Works and then open Business on the Internet Seminar. Perform the steps on the next two pages to open an existing document.

Microsoft **Works 4** Windows 95

Opening an Existing Document • W 1.57

Steps To Open an Existing Document

1 Point to the My Computer icon in the upper left corner of the desktop (Figure 1-82).

FIGURE 1-82

2 Double-click the My Computer icon. When the My Computer window opens, point to the 3½ Floppy [A:] icon.

When you double-click the My Computer icon, Windows opens the My Computer window (Figure 1-83). The My Computer window contains icons representing the hard disks, floppy disk drive, CD-ROM drive, and folder icons. The icons that display on your screen may be different.

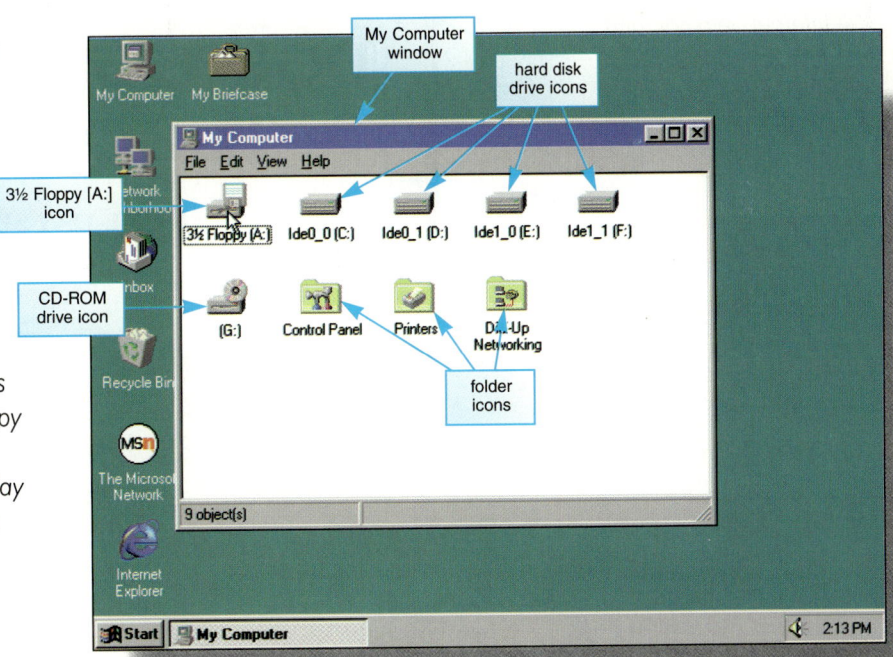

FIGURE 1-83

W 1.58 • Project 1 • Creating a Formatted Document with Clip Art

③ Double-click the 3½ Floppy [A:] icon. When the 3½ Floppy [A:] window opens, point to the Business on the Internet Seminar file icon.

When you double-click the 3½ Floppy [A:] icon, Windows opens the 3½ Floppy [A:] window (Figure 1-84) and displays the filenames on drive A.

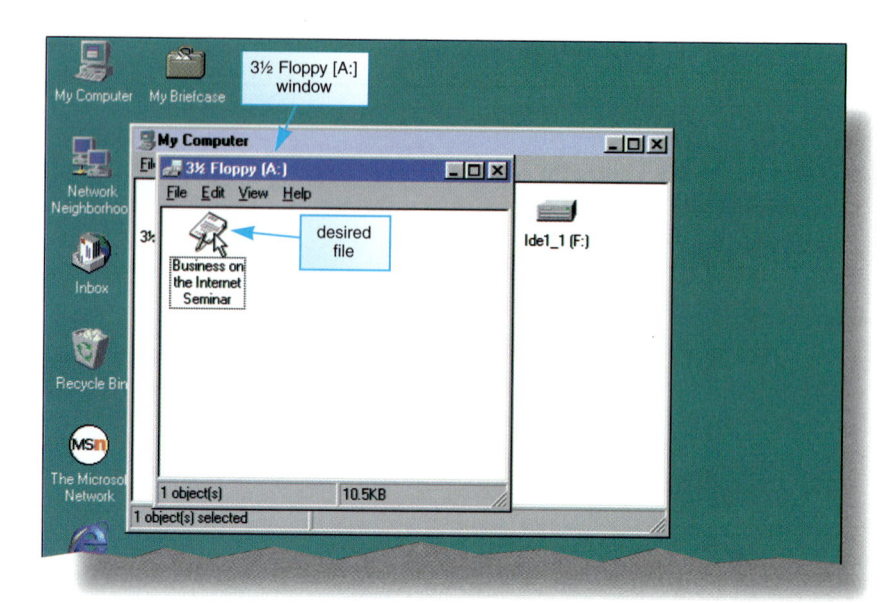

FIGURE 1-84

④ Double-click the Business on the Internet Seminar file icon.

Windows first starts Works and then opens the document, Business on the Internet Seminar, and displays it on the screen (Figure 1-85). You can revise or print the document as required.

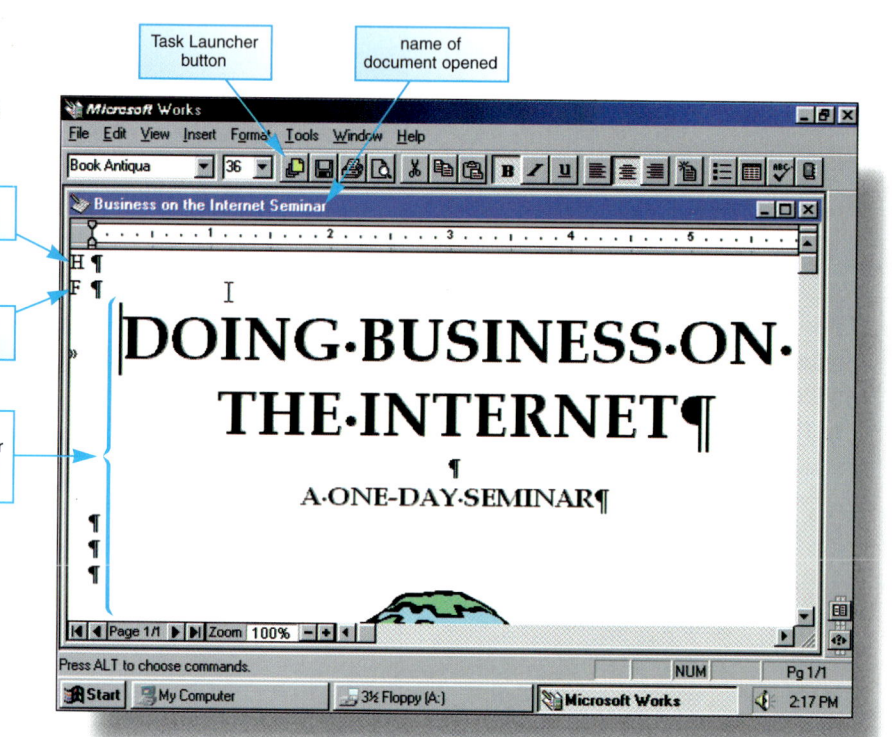

FIGURE 1-85

OtherWays

1. Click Task Launcher button on toolbar, click Existing Documents tab, click desired document, click OK button
2. On File menu click Open, click desired document, click Open button
3. Press CTRL+O

When you open an existing document in the Word Processor, Works displays a header line (H) and footer line (F) above the first line of the document (Figure 1-85). Text you type in the header line will display at the top of the first page of the document on the screen and print at the top of each page when the document is printed. Text you type in the footer line will display at the bottom of the first page on the screen of the document and print at the bottom of each page when the document is printed. The header line and footer line display at the top of the first page of a document in normal view only.

Another method of opening a file uses filenames displayed at the bottom of the File menu (Figure 1-86). Works saves the names of the last four documents on which you have worked and lists their names at the bottom of the File menu. If you want to open one of these documents, click the filename. The document will open and display on the screen.

Moving Around in a Word Processor Document

When you modify a document, you often will have to place the insertion point at different locations within the document. When using the mouse, you can place the insertion point at any location on the screen by pointing to the location and clicking. To place the insertion point at a location in the document that does not display on the screen, use the scroll bars to move the document until the desired location displays and then point and click the desired location in the document.

In some instances, you may want to use keystrokes to move larger distances in a document. Table 1-2 summarizes useful keystrokes for moving around in a document.

You can also use the UP, DOWN, LEFT, and RIGHT ARROW keys to move the insertion point through a document.

FIGURE 1-86

TABLE 1-2

TASK	KEYSTROKES
Move to the beginning of a document	CTRL+HOME
Move to the end of a document	CTRL+END
Move up one screen	PAGE UP
Move down one screen	PAGE DOWN
Move to the beginning of a line	HOME
Move to the end of a line	END

Deleting and Inserting Text in a Document

When modifying a document, you may find it necessary to delete certain characters, words, sentences, or paragraphs or to insert additional characters, words, or paragraphs. You can use a variety of methods to delete and insert text. Table 1-3 summarizes methods of deleting text.

TABLE 1-3

METHOD	RESULT
Press the DELETE key	Deletes the character to the right of the insertion point
Press the BACKSPACE key	Deletes the character to the left of the insertion point
Highlight words, sentences, or paragraphs and press the DELETE key or click Clear command on the Edit menu	Deletes highlighted information

Inserting Text

The Word Processor is initially set to allow you to insert new text between characters, words, lines, and paragraphs without deleting any of the existing text. To insert text in an existing document, place the insertion point where you want the text to appear and then type. The text to the right of the text you type will be adjusted to accommodate the insertion. For example, to insert the word, potential, before the word, customers, in the second bulleted paragraph of the announcement in Figure 1-1 on page W 1.8, place the insertion point in the space before the word, customers, by pointing and clicking and then typing the word, potential, followed by a space. Works inserts the word, potential, in the paragraph.

Overtyping Existing Text

Sometimes you may need to type over existing text. One method of doing this is to press the INSERT key on the keyboard, which causes the letters OVR to display on the status bar, and then type the new text.

When you type, the existing text will be typed over. For example, if a document contains the number 213, and it should contain the number 802, position the insertion point immediately to the left of the 2 in 213, press the INSERT key, and type 802. The number 802 will replace the number 213. To remove the overtyping status, press the INSERT key again.

You also can implement overtyping by clicking the **Options command** on the **Tools menu**. When the Options dialog box displays, click the Editing tab to display the Editing sheet. When the Editing sheet displays, click the Overtype check box and click the OK button.

Replacing Text with New Text

Another method you can use to replace existing text with new text is to highlight all the text you want to replace. When you start typing new text, the highlighted text is deleted and the new text takes its place.

Undo Command

You can use the **Undo Editing command** to reverse a typing, editing, or formatting change. For example, if you accidentally delete a paragraph, you can restore the paragraph by immediately clicking Undo. Undo Editing is effective only if you use it immediately after making a change and before taking any other action. Undo Editing is found on the Edit menu (Figure 1-87).

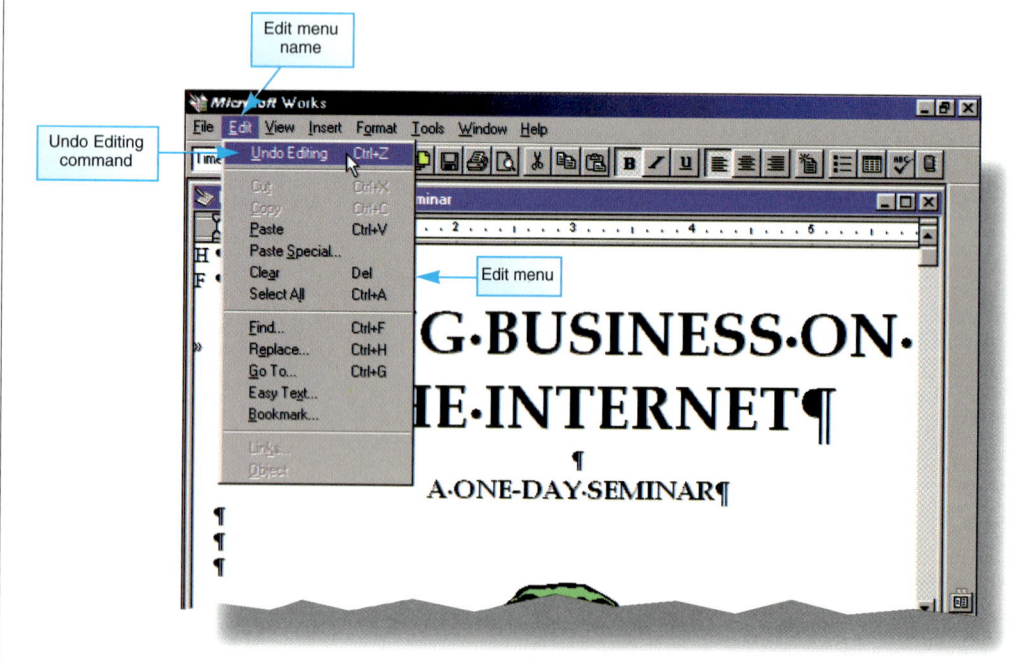

FIGURE 1-87

Undo Paragraph Formatting

To undo all paragraph formatting changes at any time and revert to the default formatting, highlight the text you want to undo, hold down the CTRL key, and press the Q key. For example, if several lines are centered and you no longer want the lines centered, highlight the lines, hold down the CTRL key, and press the Q key. You also can change and undo paragraph formatting by clicking Paragraph on the Format menu and making the appropriate entries in the Paragraph dialog box that displays.

Undo Font Styles

To undo font styles and revert to the default font and styles, highlight the text you want to undo, hold down the CTRL key, and press the SPACEBAR. For example, if a word displays in bold, italics, and underlined, and you want to remove these font styles from the word, highlight the word, hold down the CTRL key, and press the SPACEBAR. You also can click the Bold, Italic, and Underline buttons on the toolbar to undo their effect when they have been selected. Another method is to click the Font and Style command on the Format menu and make the appropriate entries in the Format Font and Style dialog box that displays.

> **More *About* Works Help**
>
> Earlier versions of Works shipped with a large manual that explained the detailed procedures of the application. With Works for Windows 95, however, you receive a thin manual less than 75 pages in length. All the instructions you need are available online as you need them.

Online Help

To assist you in learning and referencing Works, Works provides extensive **online Help**. At any time as you create or edit a document, you can display the Help window on the right side of your screen. In Figure 1-88, the Word Processor Menu displays in the Help window because a word processing document displays on the screen. The Word Processor Menu provides a list of common tasks on which you may want help when creating or editing a document.

If you need help with a task, find the topic in the Help menu and then click the topic icon. Works displays a numbered procedure on the Step-by-Step sheet (Figure 1-89 on the next page) you can follow as you complete the task in the document window. Some Step-by-Step topics contain green underlined text that when clicked provides a definition of the term. The More Info sheet displays overview information and troubleshooting information or tips.

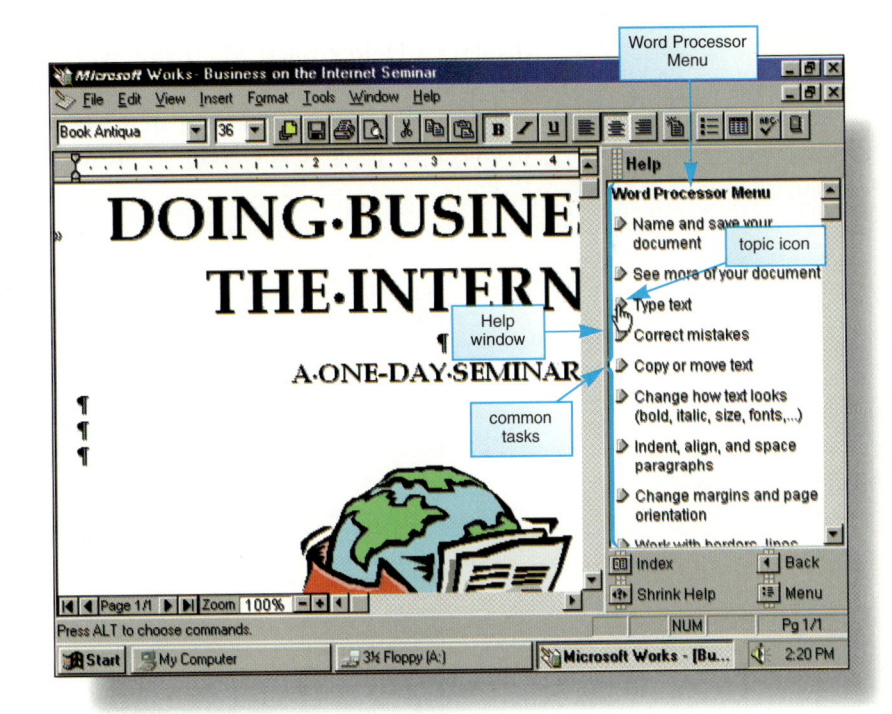

FIGURE 1-88

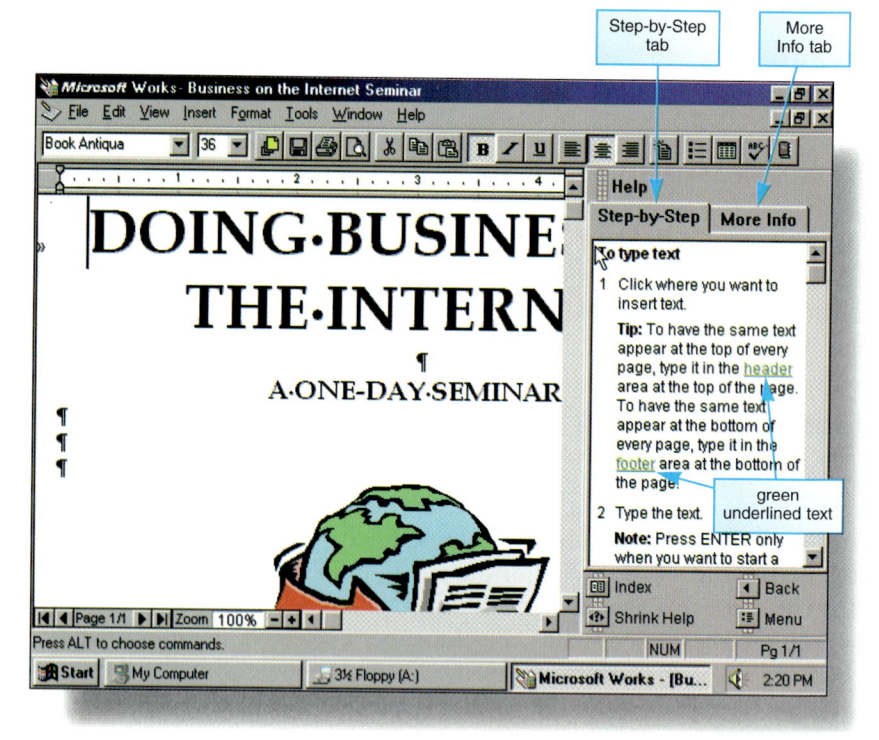

W 1.62 • **Project 1** • Creating a Formatted Document with Clip Art

FIGURE 1-89

If the topic you want is not listed in the Help menu, you can search for other Help topics by clicking the **Index button** at the bottom of the Help window. Works displays a Help Topics: Microsoft Works dialog box (Figure 1-90). The dialog box contains two tabbed sheets, Index and Contents. On the Index sheet, type a word or words for the task or item about which you desire information. Works displays the topic in the Help window. To see a listed topic, click the topic.

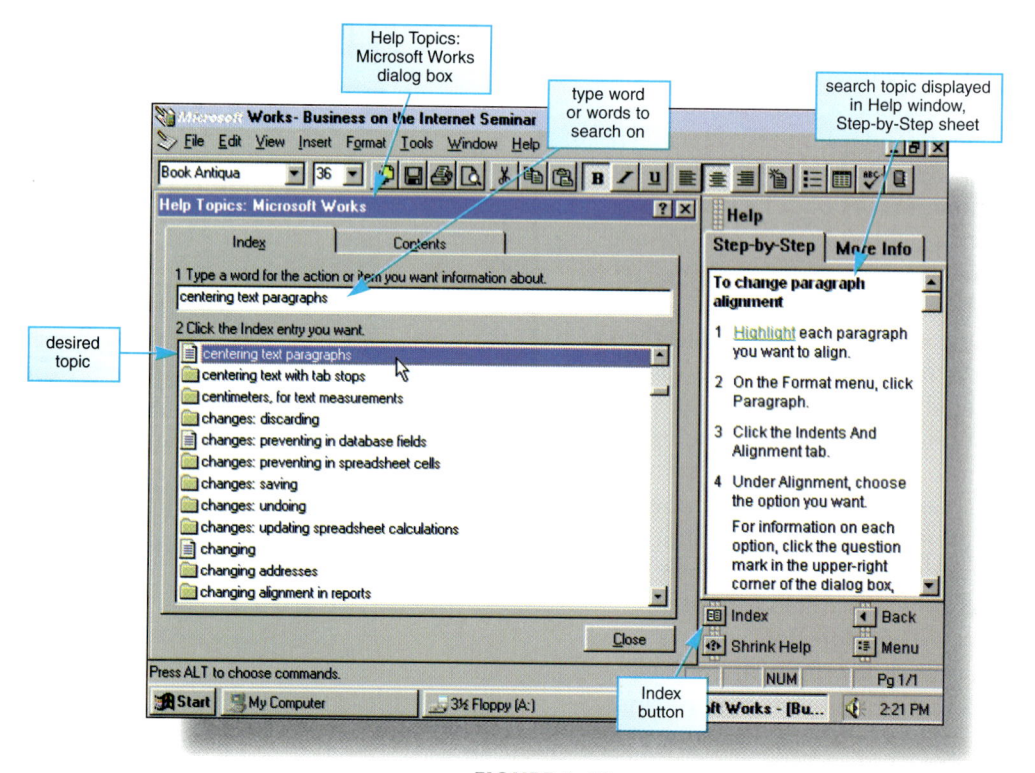

FIGURE 1-90

Microsoft **Works 4** Windows 95
Online Help • **W 1.63**

You also can get specific help for each option in a dialog box by clicking the question mark button in the upper right corner of the dialog box, and then clicking an option (Figure 1-91). Works displays information concerning the option.

> ### More *About* Help in a Dialog Box
>
> Do you want the fastest way to get additional help on any Works dialog box option? Just right-click the dialog box option you want help for and Works displays a short explanation. Right-click the explanation and Works displays a context-sensitive menu with commands that allow you to copy or print the explanation.

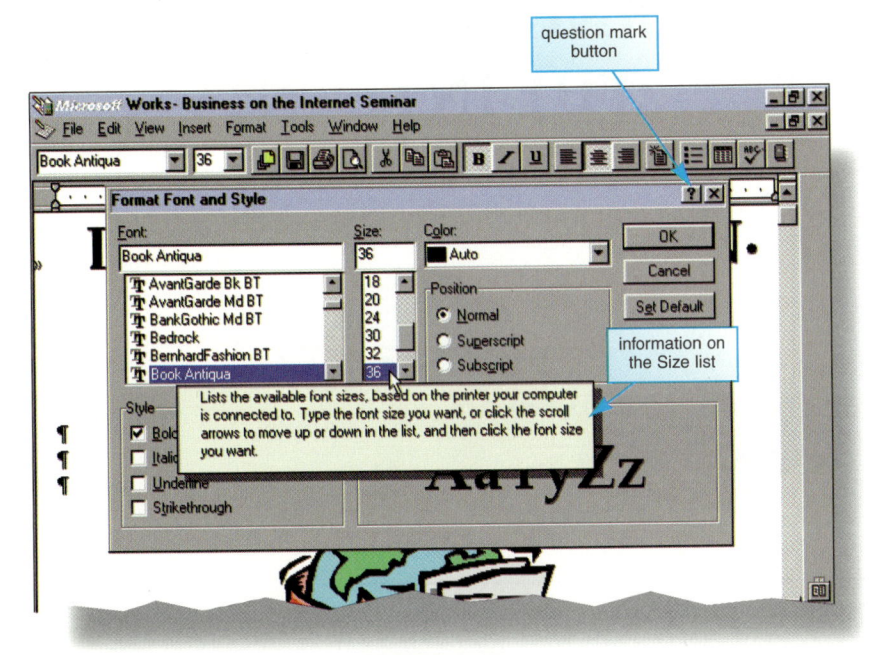

FIGURE 1-91

To learn how to use online Help, perform the following steps.

Steps To Learn Online Help

1 **Click Help on the menu bar, and then point to How to use Help.**

Works displays the Help menu (Figure 1-92).

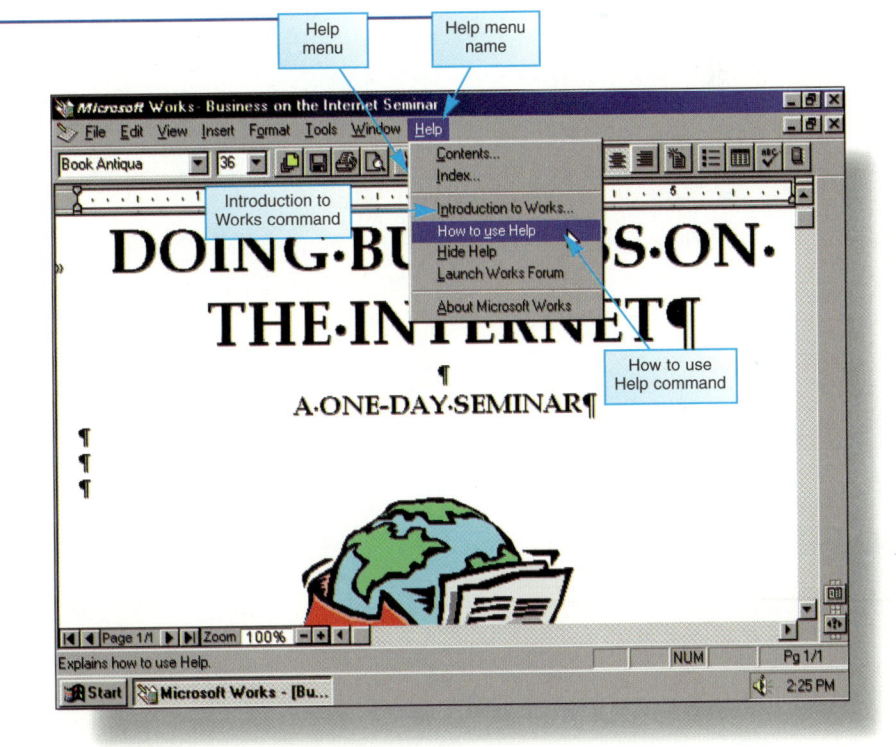

FIGURE 1-92

W 1.64 • Project 1 • Creating a Formatted Document with Clip Art

② Click How to use Help. Point to any topic.

Works displays the Help window to the right of the document window and displays the Using Help topic (Figure 1-93). When you point to a topic, the mouse pointer changes to a hand with a pointing finger.

FIGURE 1-93

Reading the topics listed in Using Help provides you with the information you need to further explore online Help.

Viewing Introduction to Works

You can view a ten-minute demonstration of the features in Works by clicking **Introduction to Works** (see Figure 1-92 on the previous page) on the Help menu. When you click Introduction to Works, the screen shown in Figure 1-94 displays. Click the forward button to go to the next screen. Click the Done button to exit the Introduction to Works demonstration.

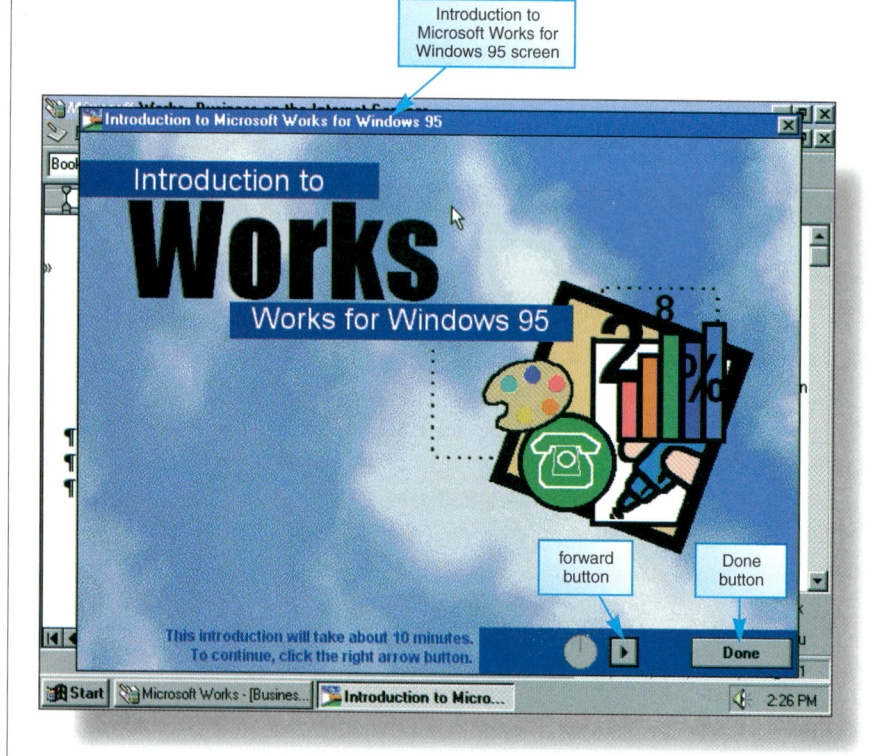

FIGURE 1-94

Project Summary

This project taught you many of the capabilities of the Works Word Processor. Important subject matter included starting Works, entering text, centering text, using fonts, increasing font size, using different font styles, previewing documents, saving a document, closing a document, closing Works, opening an existing document, inserting and deleting data, and using online Help. With a knowledge of these features of the Word Processor, you are now capable of creating a variety of documents.

What You Should Know

Having completed this project, you should now be able to perform the following tasks:

- Center Paragraphs *(W 1.29)*
- Change Fonts *(W 1.31)*
- Change Font Size *(W 1.32, W 1.34, W 1.35)*
- Change Views in the Word Processor *(W 1.17)*
- Close a Document *(W 1.54)*
- Close Works *(W 1.55)*
- Create a Bulleted List *(W 1.35)*
- Display All Characters *(W 1.21)*
- Display an Entire Document in Bold *(W 1.43)*
- Display Text in Color *(W 1.40)*
- Enter Text *(W 1.22)*
- Enter Text that Scrolls Through the Document Window *(W 1.25)*
- Insert Clip Art into a Document *(W 1.44)*

- Italicize Text *(W 1.39)*
- Maximize the Document Window *(W 1.12)*
- Open an Existing Document *(W 1.56)*
- Print a Document *(W 1.52)*
- Resize Clip Art *(W 1.47)*
- Save an Existing Document with the Same Filename *(W 1.49)*
- Save a New Document *(W 1.26)*
- Start Microsoft Works *(W 1.9)*
- Start the Word Processor *(W 1.10)*
- Use Online Help *(W 1.61)*
- Use Print Preview *(W 1.50)*
- Use Wordwrap *(W 1.23)*

Test Your Knowledge

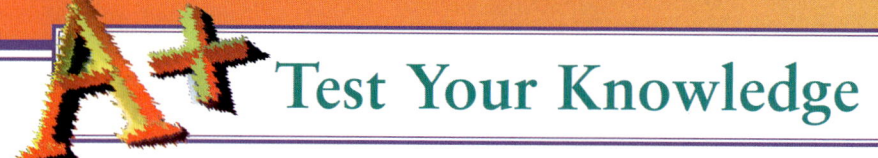

1 True/False

Instructions: Circle T if the statement is true or F if the statement is false.

T F 1. Microsoft Works is application software that provides word processing, spreadsheet, database, and communications capabilities in a single package.
T F 2. The applications within Microsoft Works are called applets.
T F 3. To start Works, click the Start button on the taskbar, point to Programs on the Start menu, point to Microsoft Works on the Programs submenu, and click Microsoft Works.
T F 4. The Microsoft Clip Gallery, which contains illustrations you can insert in documents, is an additional accessory to Works.
T F 5. The title bar in the document window contains the application name, Microsoft Works, and the name of the document you are creating.
T F 6. With Works, the default font is 12-point Arial.
T F 7. To highlight a word to be formatted, right-click the word.
T F 8. When using the Works Word Processor, the term paragraph can mean a blank line, a single character, a word, a single line, or many sentences.
T F 9. You must use print preview to make insertions or deletions in a document.
T F 10. When you close a document, click the Close button in the upper right corner of the application window.

2 Multiple Choice

Instructions: Circle the correct response.

1. When the mouse pointer is located in the document workspace area of the screen, it appears as a(n) _____.
   a. hourglass b. I-beam c. vertical bar d. block arrow
2. By default, Works uses _____-inch left and right margins and _____-inch top and bottom margins.
   a. 1, 1.25 b. 1.25, 1 c. 1.25, 1.25 d. 1.50, 1.25
3. When nonprinting characters display in the document window, spaces are indicated by _____.
   a. periods b. right-pointing arrows c. raised dots d. ¶
4. Before you change the format of a word, you must _____.
   a. highlight the first character in the word to be formatted b. right-click the word to be formatted
   c. highlight the word to be formatted d. underline the word to be formatted
5. To activate the context-sensitive menu, point to the selection and _____.
   a. double-click b. click c. right-click d. drag
6. To create a bulleted list, highlight the text, right-click the selection, and click _____.
   a. Bullets b. Style c. Font and Style d. Paragraph
7. Selected objects display _____ handles at the corners and middle points of the rectangular border.
   a. selection b. resize c. sizing d. scaling

Test Your Knowledge

8. To save an existing document using a filename different from the name under which the file is currently saved, use the _____.
    a. Save button on the toolbar
    b. Close button in the upper right corner of the document window
    c. Save As command on the File menu
    d. Save command on the File menu
9. When you close a document, _____.
    a. you close Works
    b. the document remains on the screen
    c. the document is erased from disk
    d. the Works Task Launcher dialog box displays on the screen
10. To erase a character to the right of the insertion point, press the _____.
    a. DELETE key
    b. BACKSPACE key
    c. SPACEBAR
    d. INSERT key

3 Fill In

Instructions: In Figure 1-95, a series of arrows points to the major components of the Microsoft Works Word Processor window. Identify the parts of the window in the spaces provided.

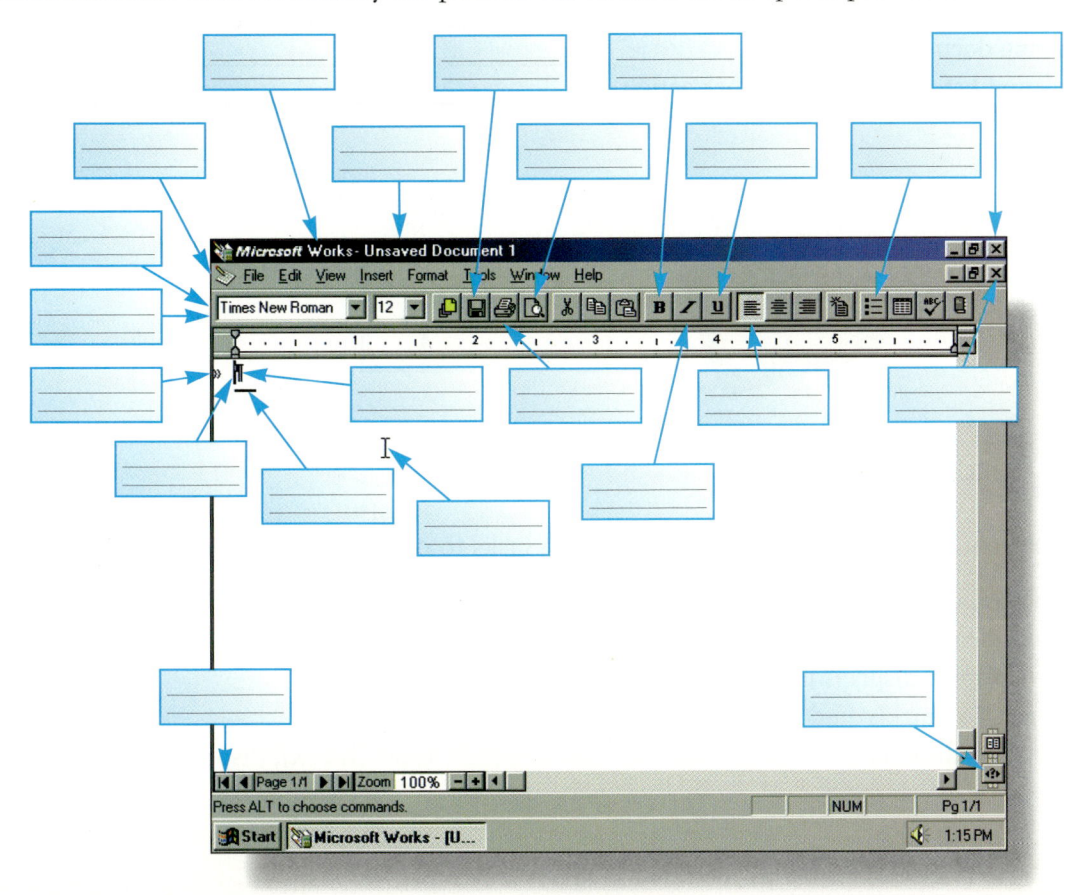

FIGURE 1-95

Test Your Knowledge

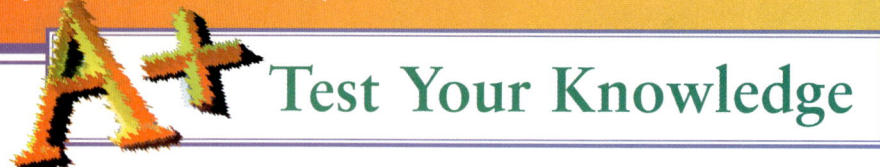

4 Fill In

Instructions: Write the appropriate command or button name to accomplish each task.

TASK	COMMAND OR BUTTON NAME
View a document in normal view	_____
Display special characters in the document window	_____
Save a new document	_____
Center a paragraph	_____
Create a bulleted list	_____
Remove bullets from a bulleted list	_____
Change text color	_____
Bold text	_____
Insert clip art	_____
Save an existing document with a different filename	_____
Print preview a document	_____
Print a document	_____
Close a document	_____
Close Works	_____
Open an existing document	_____
Reverse a deletion before taking any other action	_____

Use Help

1 Reviewing Project Activities

Instructions: Use your computer to perform the following tasks to obtain experience using online Help.

1. Start the Microsoft Works Word Processor tool.
2. Click Help on the menu bar and then click How to use Help.
3. The Using Help topic displays in the Help window.
4. Click the topic, To quickly find a specific topic (Index).
5. A numbered procedure on the topic, To quickly find a specific topic (Index), displays on the Step-by-Step sheet.

Use Help

6. Read the topic. Use the down scroll arrow to read the entire topic. In Step 4 at the bottom of the Step-by-Step sheet, several words display in green. Click the green underlined word, drag. Read the information in the pop-up definition box. Click the box to remove it from the screen. Print this topic by clicking the Print this topic icon.
7. Click the More Info tab. On the More Info sheet, click Overview. Read the Overview topic. Click Print this topic in the Overview topic. Click the Done button to close the Overview dialog box.
8. Click the Index button at the bottom of the Help window. When the Help Topics: Microsoft Works dialog box displays, type help in the 1 Type a word for the action or item you want information about text box. Below the text box, click the topic, Help: dialog box choices. Read the topic that displays on the Step-by-Step sheet. Use the down scroll arrow to view the entire screen. Click the Show an example icon. Click the Close button at the bottom of the Help Topics: Microsoft Works dialog box.
9. Click the Close button in the application window to exit Works.

2 Expanding on the Basics

Instructions: Use Works online Help to better understand the topics listed below. Print the topic or topics that substantiate your answer. If no Print this topic icon is available, then answer the question on a separate piece of paper.

1. Using the term, bullet, and the Index sheet in the Help Topics: Microsoft Works dialog box, answer the following questions.
   a. What is the definition of a bullet?
   b. How do you change the size of a bullet from 12 points to 14 points?
   c. List two ways to remove a bullet from a paragraph.
   d. How would you change the spacing between a bullet and text in a bulleted list?
2. Click Format on the menu bar and then click Font and Style. When the Format Font and Style dialog box displays, use the question mark button located in the upper right corner of the dialog box to answer the following questions.
   a. Why would you click the Set Default button in the Format Font and Style dialog box?
   b. What is the difference between the OK button and the Cancel button in the Format Font and Style dialog box?
   c. What does a check mark specify in the Strikethrough check box in the Format Font and Style dialog box?

Apply Your Knowledge

1 Creating a Bulleted List and Inserting Clip Art

Instructions: Start the Microsoft Works Word Processor tool. Open the document, Suburban Renewal, on the Student Floppy Disk that accompanies this book. The formatted document is illustrated in Figure 1-96. Create a bulleted list for the two sections of flower names and one section of vegetable names. Drag the left indent marker of each bulleted list to the 2.75-inch mark on the ruler. Change the bullet style to display an asterisk. Then, insert the clip art of vegetables from the Microsoft Clip Gallery, Plants category, in the document after the second heading line. Center the clip art. Resize the clip art until the status bar reads 60% high and 60% wide. Use Save As on the File menu to save the completed document with the filename, Fall Planting. Print the completed document.

SUBURBAN RENEWAL
Fall Planting

This month a whole new season is starting in the local gardens. The following can be planted this month:

Flowers from seed
* Alyssum
* Calendula
* Candytuft
* Carnation
* Pansy
* Viola

Flowers from bedding plants
* English daisy
* Iceland poppy
* Snapdragon
* Stock

Vegetables from seeds or starter plants
* Broccoli
* Brussels sprouts
* Celery
* Onion
* Oriental greens
* Potato
* Turnip

FIGURE 1-96

In the Lab

1 Creating and Formatting a Document Using Clip Art

Problem: As the president of the Chemistry Club, you have been asked by the club's advisor to create a flyer announcing the monthly meeting. The flyer is shown in Figure 1-97.

Instructions: Display the first heading line, CHEMISTRY CLUB, in 36-point Algerian font. Display the second heading line in 18-point Book Antiqua. The picture is clip art from the Microsoft Clip Gallery, Technology category. The next two lines display in 14-point Times New Roman font. Display the bulleted list with a three-quarter inch margin in 12-point Arial font. The first line after the bulleted list displays in 12-point Arial font. The last two lines display in dark magenta 14-point Times New Roman font. Display the entire document in bold.

After you have typed and formatted the document, save the document on a floppy disk. Use the filename Chemistry Club Meeting. Print the document, and then follow directions from your instructor for turning in the assignment.

FIGURE 1-97

In the Lab

2 Creating and Formatting a Document Using Clip Art

Problem: As an employee of the Public Relations department, you have been asked by your supervisor to create a flyer advertising the college. The flyer is shown in Figure 1-98.

Instructions: Display the first heading line, MID-WESTERN BUSINESS COLLEGE, in 30-point Arial font. Choose the illustration from the clip art in the Microsoft Clip Gallery, Business category. Display the first line below the clip art in red 20-point Times New Roman font. The next three lines display in 12-point Times New Roman font. Display the bulleted list with a one and one-half-inch margin in 14-point Arial font. The line following the bulleted list displays in 16-point Arial font. The last two lines display in 10-point Times New Roman font. Display the entire document in bold.

After you have typed and formatted the document, save the document on a floppy disk. Use the filename Mid-Western Flyer. Print the document, and then follow directions from your instructor for turning in the assignment.

MID-WESTERN BUSINESS COLLEGE

Design a New Career Path and Become a Leader

The true measure of any program is the success of its students. At MWBC, our students have real-world leadership skills and know how to succeed ethically.

Our program includes the following:

- Leadership classes
- Research on the Internet
- Academically and professionally experienced faculty
- Weekend and evening classes
- Financial aid and counseling services

Fall classes begin September 6th

For further information call
(405) 555-3835

FIGURE 1-98

3 Creating and Formatting a Document Using Clip Art

Problem: The Home Buyers Fair Committee has asked you to create a flyer announcing Home Buyers Fair. The flyer is shown in Figure 1-99.

Instructions: Create the document illustrated in Figure 1-99 using the appropriate fonts, font styles, sizes, colors, and clip art (Building category). Note the proportions of the clip art have been changed. Use Help to determine how to change the proportions of a clip art object.

After you have typed and formatted the document, save the document on a floppy disk. Use the filename Home Buyers Fair. Print the document, and then follow directions from your instructor for turning in the assignment.

FIGURE 1-99

Cases and Places

The difficulty of these case studies varies:

◗ Case studies preceded by a single half moon are the least difficult. You can complete these case studies using your own computer or a computer in the lab.

◗◗ Case studies preceded by two half moons are more difficult. You must research the topic presented using the Internet, a library, or another resource, and then prepare a brief written report.

◗◗◗ Case studies preceded by three half moons are the most difficult. You must visit a store or business to obtain the necessary information, and then use it to create a brief written report.

1 ◗ The Social Work Club on your campus is sponsoring a winter coat and blanket drive for low-income community residents. The project is one of several undertaken annually by this active club having 75 members. Most of the students are social work majors. The club president is Betsy Mans, and she can be reached at (802) 555-2829 for additional information. You have offered to help their efforts by producing a one-page flyer to hang on campus bulletin boards and a press release for the campus and local newspapers. Create the following document:

Line 1: Help warm a life. (36-point Times New Roman bold centered)
Line 2: Donate a winter coat or blanket. (24-point Times New Roman centered)
Line 3: *Insert and center an appropriate graphic from the Microsoft Clip Gallery.*
Line 4: Bring your donation to the Student Union (18-point Arial centered)
Line 5: on Monday, November 18 (18-point Arial centered)
Line 6: from 8:00 a.m. to 8:00 p.m. (18-point Arial centered)
Line 7: The Social Work Club will distribute your articles to needy families on Thanksgiving. (14-point Arial)
Line 8: Share the warmth of the holidays. (24-point Times New Roman italic centered)

Enter blank lines where appropriate to properly space the document. Use this information to write a press release to promote the winter coat and blanket drive.

Cases and Places

2 ▶ Time is in short supply for most college students, so they find waiting in line to be particularly frustrating. While you were in line at the post office this morning, you heard the clerks answering the same questions repeatedly. You think that displaying a poster with these clerks' advice might accelerate the process and shorten the lines. You discuss this idea with the Postmaster, and he recruits you to develop the poster. Design and create the following document:

Line 1: Help us deliver for you. (40-point Arial bold underlined centered)
Line 2: How you can help us: (36-point Arial bold centered)
(Lines 3 through 9 should be bulleted, 18-point Times New Roman)
Line 3: Address your letters with block capital letters.
Line 4: Do not use punctuation marks.
Line 5: Use ZIP + 4 codes.
Line 6: Print the sender's address and your return address on the same side of the envelope.
Line 7: Insure precious packages inexpensively. For example, $100 worth of insurance is just $1.60.
Line 8: Pack fragile items in sturdy boxes filled with such cushioned packing material as newspaper or popcorn.
Line 9: Buy your money orders here for only 85 cents.
Line 10: *Insert and center an appropriate graphic from the Microsoft Clip Gallery.*

Enter blank lines where appropriate to properly space the document.

3 ▶▶ Now that you are using a personal computer to complete many of your assignments, you have been suffering from a tingling sensation in your wrists, numbness in your fingers, and difficulty opening and closing your hands. During your next visit to the doctor, you mention these ailments. Your doctor informs you that you are suffering from repetitive stress, or strain, injury (RSI). This term is applied to injuries resulting from repeated movements that irritate nerves and tendons. He describes various actions you can take to alleviate or prevent RSI. They include taking short, frequent breaks of at least 10 minutes every hour, stretching the entire body, shrugging your shoulders, and rubbing your hands. You can perform some simple exercises at your desk, such as stretching your fingers, rotating your wrists, and squeezing your thumbs and fingers together. He tells you to adapt your computer workstation to fit your needs, just as you adjust the rearview mirror and seat in your car. For example, you can tilt your monitor so the top line of print on the screen is slightly below eye level and sit 14 to 24 inches away from it. Use ergonomically correct furniture that can be adjusted so the home row of keys is 29 to 31 inches above the floor and your feet are flat on the floor at a 90-degree angle. Have a good desk lamp that illuminates your work, not the screen.

You decide to summarize the doctor's advice by making a reminder list to hang on the side of your monitor. Using this information, create a one-page bulleted list of the 10 major steps you can take to help alleviate or prevent RSI. Title the document, How I can prevent RSI. Add appropriate clip art from the Microsoft Clip Gallery. Be certain to spell check your reminder list.

Cases and Places

4 ▶▶ Every year you are faced with writing thank you notes to your relatives for the birthday gifts they send you. This year you want to expedite the process by using your computer to generate the notes. You create the following form letter:

Dear [Name],
Thank you so much for the nice [gift]. I am certain I will think of you every time I use it at [place]. It was very thoughtful of you to remember my birthday. I will [action] you soon.

For each relative, use search and replace to change the words, Name, gift, place, and action to those in Figure 1-100. In addition, use the thesaurus to find a synonym for the word, nice, in each letter.

NAME	GIFT	PLACE	ACTION
Grandma	sweater	the ski resort	call
Aunt Karen	dictionary	school	see
Uncle Rich	basketball	the gym	visit
Cousin Jim	CD	my apartment	talk with you

FIGURE 1-100

5 ▶▶▶ Stress management allows you to use your awareness and mind to control your physical reactions to stress. You can learn to relieve tension and anxiety by relaxing. In turn, you can decrease your heart rate, blood pressure, and total cholesterol level. Obtain one article at least three pages long that discusses stress management. Using the concepts and techniques presented in this project, write a one-page summary of this article using the Modern Language Association's style for writing research reports. Include a footnote that cites your source and a bulleted list of the benefits of practicing stress management. Attach a cover page listing your name, your instructor's name, the course name, and current date.

6 ▶▶▶ Many students are unaware of various deadlines that occur during the semester, such as the last day for dropping a class, the first day of advanced registration, the last day of late registration, midterm week, final exam week, and holidays. You see the registrar in the cafeteria one day and propose that he create a one-half page flyer to distribute at registration. He suggests you provide him with a prototype. Design and create this document, listing important dates during the semester. Be creative in your design. If useful, add appropriate clip art from the Microsoft Clip Gallery.

7 ▶▶▶ Some campus organizations have difficulties with public relations. While the members are dedicated and talented, they simply do not know how to communicate their messages effectively to the student body and community. You have decided to use your computer expertise to help one of these groups. Locate a club on campus that seems to need assistance, whether it be in recruiting new members, promoting an event, or announcing a new program. Talk to the organization's officers and suggest how you can help. Design and create a document advertising one facet of the club. Be creative in your design. Use appropriate clip art from the Microsoft Clip Gallery.

Microsoft Works 4

Windows 95

Building a Spreadsheet and Charting Data

Objectives:

You will have mastered the material in this project when you can:

- Start the Microsoft Works Spreadsheet tool
- List the steps required to build a spreadsheet
- Describe the spreadsheet
- Highlight a cell or range of cells
- Enter text
- Enter numbers
- Use the AutoSum button to sum a range of cells in a row or column
- Copy a cell to a range of adjacent cells
- Format a spreadsheet
- Center text in a range of cells
- Add color to a spreadsheet
- Use the AutoFormat feature
- Change column widths
- Save a spreadsheet
- Print a spreadsheet
- Create a 3-D Bar chart
- Print a chart
- Close a spreadsheet
- Close Works
- Open a spreadsheet file
- Correct errors in a spreadsheet
- Clear cells and clear the entire spreadsheet

Project 2

Project 2

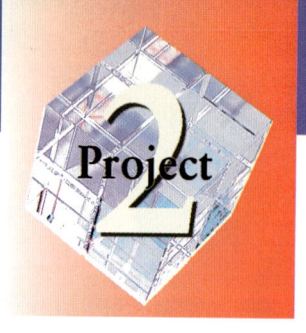

Crunching Numbers Can Be Fun

It just takes the right tool

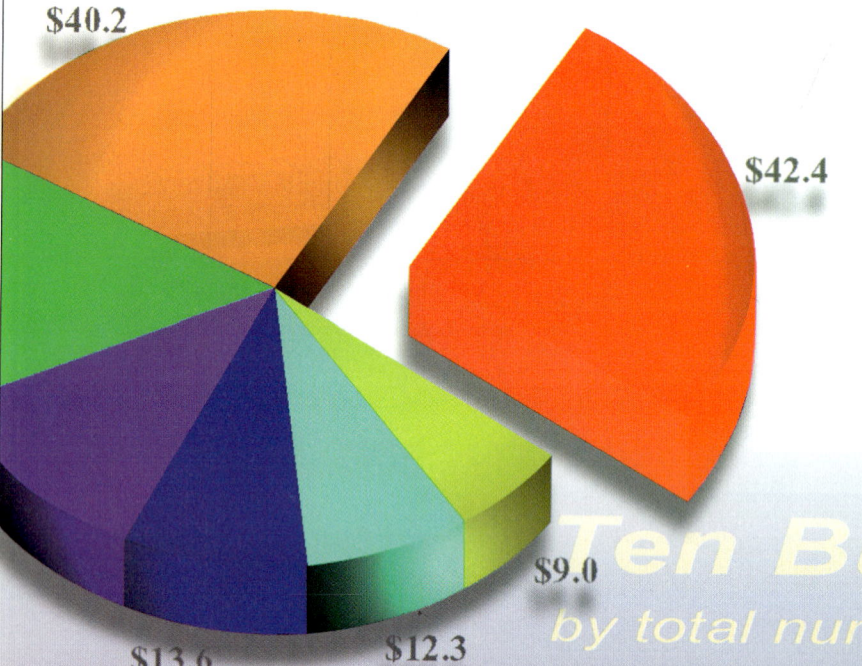

Into the crowded lecture hall strides a man in a blue suit, carrying an official-looking leather portfolio. At the podium, he calls out a name. One of the students cheers and rushes forward to receive a one million dollar check for winning the lottery! She is the same student who claimed to have created a spreadsheet for picking winning lottery numbers. If only her friends had listened... .

For now anyway, such a scene exists only in fantasy, but for lottery winners and everyone else, a spreadsheet can make many real-life situations easier to handle. Appearing on your computer monitor as a table of rows and columns, a computer spreadsheet is similar to the accountant's ledger sheet. Aided by the speed and power of the PC, a user can construct a spreadsheet to quickly and easily perform "what-if" analysis for interdependent sets of numerical data; for example, "what if the projected sales figures for July increase by 10%, how will that affect gross profit?" For the same analysis, an accountant without a computer might need hours to manually recalculate and re-enter the resulting figures on paper.

Almost everyone, especially a student on a tight budget, needs an efficient way to manage personal finances. For some, keeping track of classes and activities is a hassle that gets in the way of an education. For still others, buying a car — new or used — on a time payment plan is the beginning of major heartburn. In these three examples, the Microsoft Works Spreadsheet TaskWizards come to the rescue with ready-made templates — Accounts, Schedules, and Loan Analysis — that can be used as-is or personalized to an individual's own needs, helping to organize time and finances. Spelling checker and Easy Calc are also available to ensure spelling accuracy and to speed simple math operations.

Of course, the capabilities of spreadsheets extend beyond college into business, science, and many other fields, including managing personal affairs. Business applications are numerous and familiar, from creating business plans to calculating actuarial tables, from forecasting sales to tracking and comparing airline traffic at airports. Going beyond these traditional uses, geographic data is being merged with statistics to create color-coded maps that track such diverse factors as global warming, health care needs, criminal justice, risk of damage by flood, even maps of what is selling where. For personal use, a number of sophisticated spreadsheet programs help to manage investment portfolios, balance checkbooks, and track household inventories for insurance purposes.

Spreadsheets also have become an important tool for improving productivity in law enforcement, an area that reaches everyone. In one application, the Los Angeles Police Department uses a system based on spreadsheets to save the equivalent of 368 additional police officers by speeding the paperwork — up to 37 forms for a single incident — required of those already on the force. For certain crimes, such as car theft, spreadsheet data can be used to create maps showing crime frequency, helping police establish stakeout points.

With embedded multimedia sound and video, the expanding technology of spreadsheets opens a wide new vista of applications. For hundreds of thousands who daily use these electronic marvels, the world of "what-if?" has become the world of "what next?" Perhaps someone, someday, will even crack the lottery.

Project 2

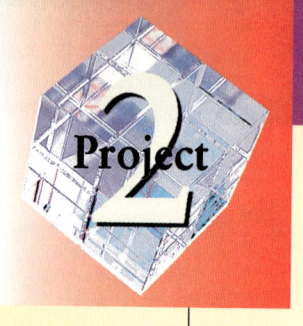

Microsoft Works 4
Windows 95

Building a Spreadsheet and Charting Data

Case Perspective

RSC Sports and Fitness Centers has experienced explosive growth since its inception three years ago. The management would like a report showing the memberships at each of their clubs. They have asked you to prepare a spreadsheet that specifies the clubs' current memberships. In particular, they want to know the total memberships for students, singles, families, and executives in the following four cities: Anaheim, Irvine, Fullerton, and Yorba Linda. They want the totals by type of memberships (Student, Single, Family, and Executive).

Your task is to develop a spreadsheet to show these memberships. In addition, the director of membership has asked to see a graphical representation of the memberships to easily illustrate this data to her sales force.

The Works Spreadsheet Tool

A **spreadsheet** is a software tool that is useful when you have a need to enter and calculate data that can be conveniently displayed in rows and columns. The Microsoft Works for Windows Spreadsheet tool allows you to enter data in a spreadsheet, perform calculations on that data, ask what-if questions regarding the data in the spreadsheet, make decisions based on the results found in the spreadsheet, chart data in the spreadsheet, and share these results with other tools within Works.

As a result of the capabilities of the Works for Windows Spreadsheet tool, you can accomplish such tasks as accounting and record keeping, financial planning and budgeting, sales forecasting and reporting, or keeping track of your basketball team's scoring averages. In addition, once you have determined the information you require, you can present it as a spreadsheet or as a chart in printed reports.

Works also allows you to change data and automatically recalculate your spreadsheet. You can place data in the spreadsheet that simulates given conditions, which then you can test and determine the results. For example, you can enter the monthly payment you want to make on a house and then determine the price of the house you can afford based on various interest rates.

Project Two

To illustrate the use of the Microsoft Works for Windows 95 Spreadsheet tool, this section of the book presents a project similar to the one you created for the Works Word Processor. Project 2 uses the Works Spreadsheet tool to produce the spreadsheet and 3-D Bar chart shown in Figure 2-1.

> **More About Spreadsheets**
>
> The first electronic spreadsheet program was VisiCalc written by Bob Frankston and Dan Bricklin in 1979. This product was originally written to run on Apple II computers. Together, VisiCalc and Apple II computers rapidly became successful. Most people consider VisiCalc to be the singlemost important reason why personal computers gained acceptance in the business world.

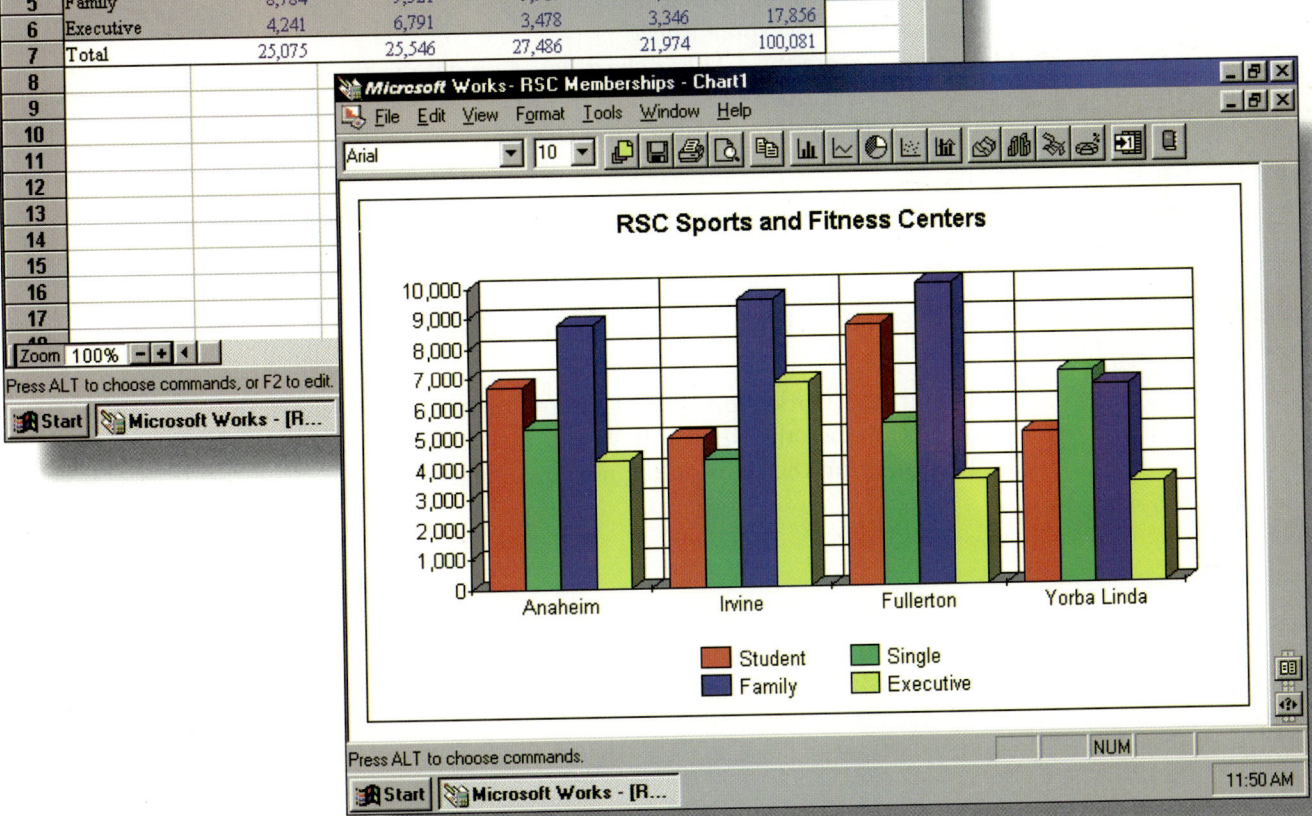

FIGURE 2-1

The spreadsheet contains RSC Sports and Fitness Centers memberships for Anaheim, Irvine, Fullerton, and Yorba Linda. Memberships fall into four categories: Student, Single, Family, and Executive. Works calculates the total memberships for each city, the total memberships for each category, and the total of all memberships in each city. The spreadsheet in this project also demonstrates the use of the various fonts, font sizes, styles, and colors in the spreadsheet. Proper spreadsheet formatting as shown in this project is an important factor in modern spreadsheet design.

The bar chart, called a 3-D Bar chart, displays the membership categories by city. Works creates the 3-D Bar chart based on the data in the spreadsheet. Each category is represented by the color indicated by the legend below the chart.

Spreadsheet Preparation Steps

The following tasks will be completed in this project.

1. Start the Works Spreadsheet.
2. Enter the report title (RSC Sports and Fitness Centers), the column titles (Anaheim, Irvine, Fullerton, Yorba Linda, and Total), and the row titles (Student, Single, Family, Executive, and Total).
3. Enter the Student, Single, Family, and Executive memberships for each of the four cities (Anaheim, Irvine, Fullerton, and Yorba Linda).
4. Enter the formulas to calculate the memberships for each city, for each category of membership, and for the total memberships.
5. Format the spreadsheet title, including adding color to the title.
6. Format the body of the spreadsheet. The membership data, city totals, and category totals are to contain commas.
7. Save the spreadsheet on disk.
8. Print the spreadsheet.
9. Create the 3-D Bar chart based on data in the spreadsheet.
10. Print the 3-D Bar chart.
11. Save the spreadsheet and chart.
12. Close Works.

The following pages contain a detailed explanation of these steps.

Starting the Works Spreadsheet

To start the Works Spreadsheet, follow the steps you used in the word processing project to open the Microsoft Works Task Launcher dialog box (Figure 2-2). Then perform the steps on the next two pages.

Starting the Works Spreadsheet • **W 2.7**

Steps To Start the Works Spreadsheet

1 Click the Works Tools tab, and then point to the Spreadsheet button in the Works Task Launcher dialog box (Figure 2-2).

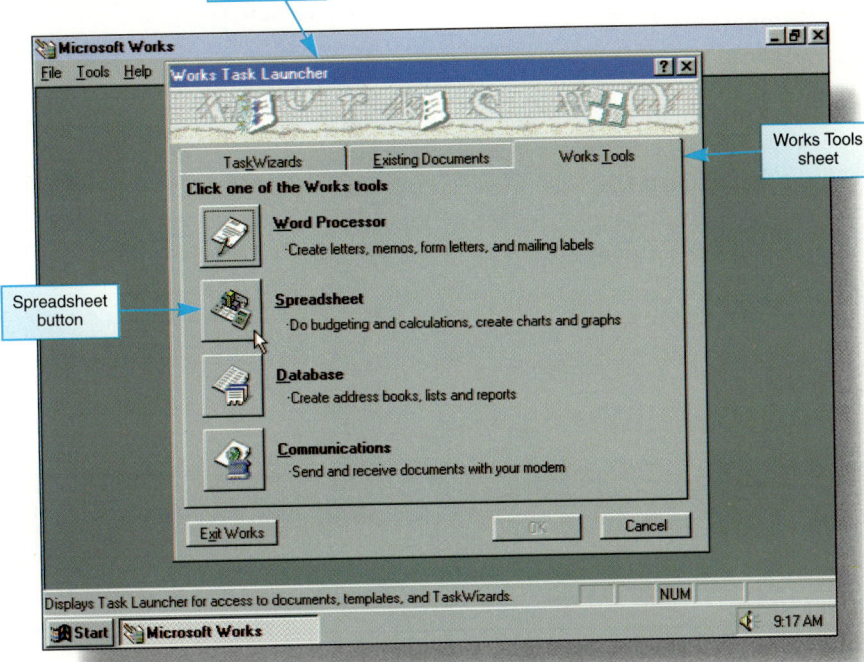

FIGURE 2-2

2 Click the Spreadsheet button. When the Microsoft Works window displays, maximize the window if necessary. If the Help window displays, click the Shrink Help button. Then point to the Unsaved Spreadsheet 1 Maximize button.

Works displays an empty spreadsheet titled Unsaved Spreadsheet 1 (Figure 2-3). The mouse pointer points to the Maximize button.

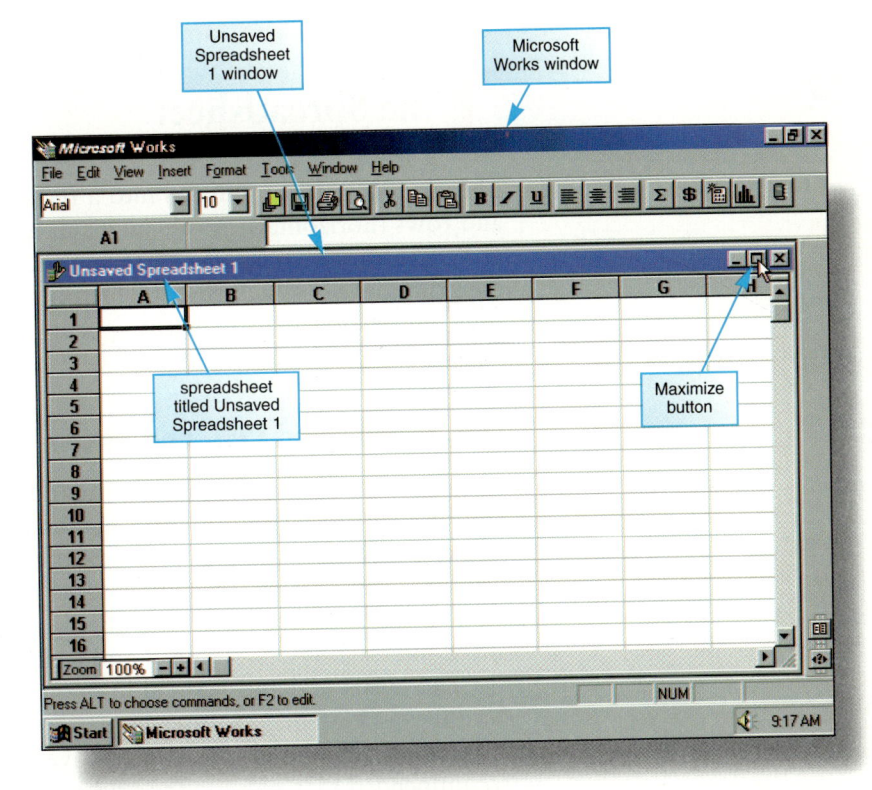

FIGURE 2-3

W 2.8 • Project 2 • Building a Spreadsheet and Charting Data

3 **Click the Maximize button in the Unsaved Spreadsheet 1 window.**

Works maximizes the spreadsheet and places the spreadsheet title, Unsaved Spreadsheet 1, in the main title bar (Figure 2-4).

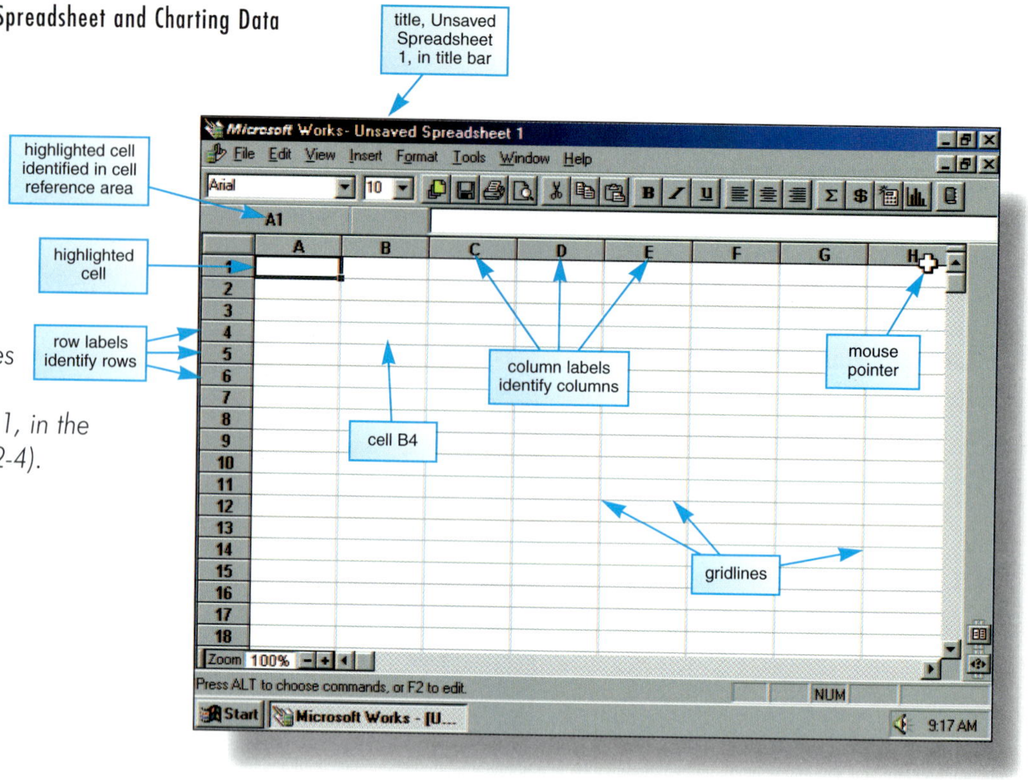

FIGURE 2-4

The following paragraphs describe the elements of the spreadsheet screen identified in Figure 2-4.

The Spreadsheet

The spreadsheet is organized into a rectangular grid containing columns (vertical) and rows (horizontal). A **column label**, which is a letter of the alphabet above the grid, identifies each **column**. A **row label**, which is a number down the left side of the grid, identifies each **row**. Eight columns (letters A through H) and eighteen rows (numbered 1 through 18) appear on the screen when the spreadsheet is maximized.

Cell, Highlighted Cell, and Mouse Pointer

The intersection of each column and each row is a **cell**. A cell is the basic unit of a spreadsheet into which you enter data. A cell is referred to by its **cell reference**, which is the coordinate of the intersection of a column and a row. To identify a cell, specify the column label (a letter of the alphabet) first, followed by the row label (a number). For example, cell reference B4 refers to the cell located at the intersection of column B and row 4 (Figure 2-4).

The horizontal and vertical lines on the spreadsheet itself are called **gridlines**. Gridlines are intended to make it easier to see and identify each cell on the spreadsheet. If desired, you can remove the gridlines from the spreadsheet but it is recommended that you use the gridlines in most circumstances.

One cell in the spreadsheet, designated the **highlighted cell**, is the one into which you can enter data. The highlighted cell in Figure 2-4 is cell A1. Works identifies the highlighted cell in two ways. First, Works places a heavy border around it. Second, the cell reference area, which is above the column labels on the left side of the screen, contains the cell reference of the highlighted cell (Figure 2-4).

The **mouse pointer** can become a number of shapes when used with the Works Spreadsheet, depending on the activity in Works and the location of the mouse pointer on the spreadsheet window. In Figure 2-4, the mouse pointer has the shape of a block plus sign. Normally, the mouse pointer displays as a block plus sign whenever it is located in a cell on the spreadsheet.

Another common mouse pointer shape is the block arrow. The mouse pointer turns into a block arrow whenever you move it outside the spreadsheet window. Other mouse pointer shapes will be described when they appear on the screen.

Spreadsheet Window

The Works Spreadsheet contains 256 columns and 16,384 rows for a total of 4,194,304 cells. The column labels begin with A and end with IV. The row labels begin with 1 and end with 16384. Only a small fraction of the spreadsheet displays on the screen at one time. You view the portion of the spreadsheet displayed on the screen through the spreadsheet window (Figure 2-5). Scroll bars, scroll arrows, and scroll boxes that you can use to move the window around the spreadsheet are located below and to the right of the spreadsheet window.

More *About* Scroll Boxes

Dragging the scroll box is the most efficient way to scroll long distances. Drag the scroll boxes in the vertical or horizontal scroll bar to move the spreadsheet view up and down, or left and right, through the document.

More *About* Scroll Bars

Clicking the scroll bar will move the spreadsheet window a full screen up or down.

More *About* Scroll Arrows

To move the spreadsheet up or down one cell at a time click the scroll arrows at the ends of the vertical scroll bars. Use the scroll arrows on the horizontal scroll bar to move the spreadsheet left or right one cell at a time.

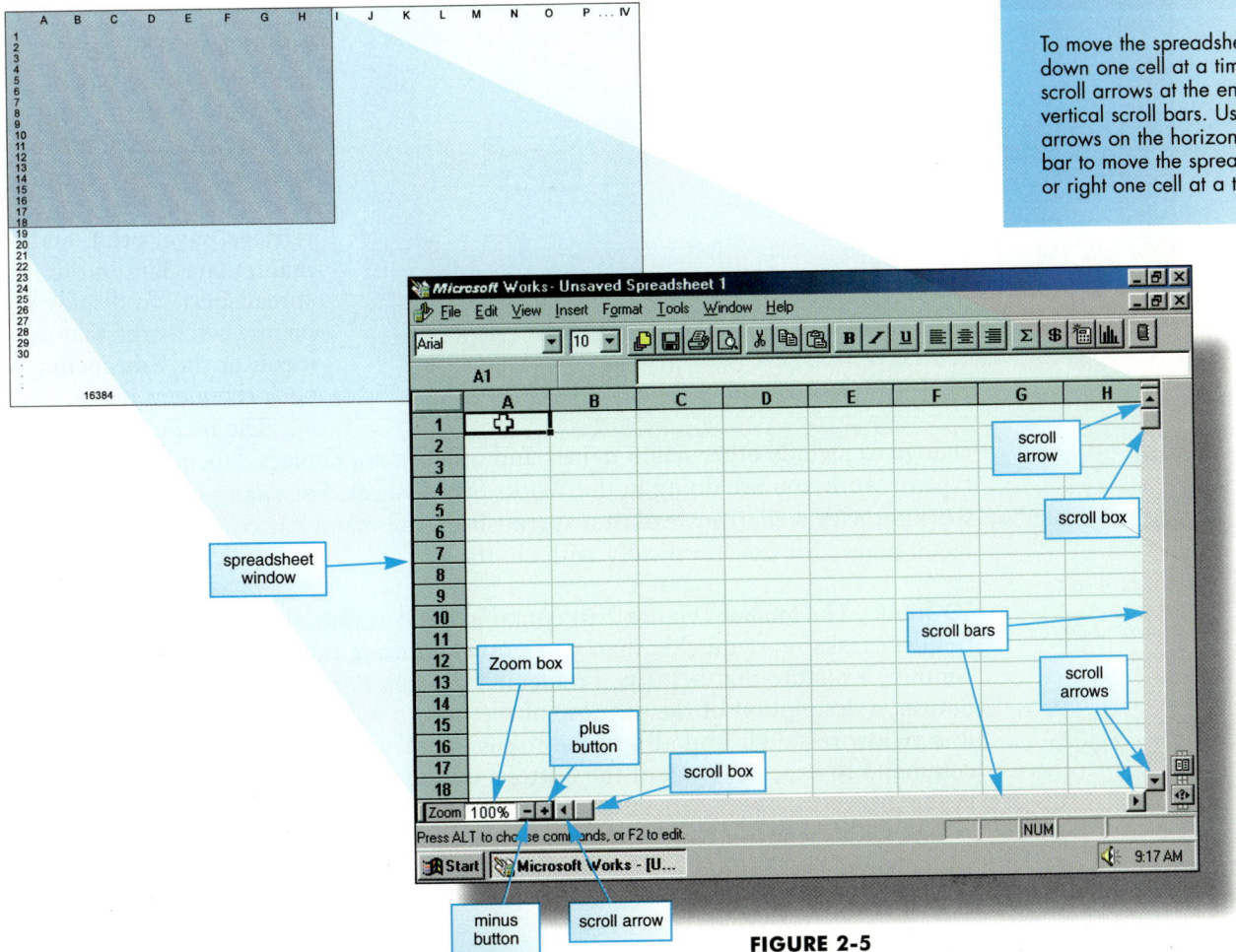

FIGURE 2-5

W 2.10 • Project 2 • Building a Spreadsheet and Charting Data

The **Zoom box** is located at the bottom left corner of the spreadsheet window. The Zoom box controls how much of a spreadsheet displays at one time in the spreadsheet window. Clicking the Zoom box displays a list of available zoom percentages to magnify or reduce your spreadsheet on the screen. You can also use the plus or minus buttons next to the Zoom box to control the display. To magnify your spreadsheet, click the plus button; to reduce your spreadsheet, click the minus button. The zoom size of the display has no effect on how the spreadsheet will look when it is printed.

Menu Bar, Toolbar, Entry Bar, and Status Bar

The menu bar, toolbar, and entry bar display at the top of the screen just below the title bar (Figure 2-6). The status bar displays at the bottom of the screen.

MENU BAR The **menu bar** displays the Works Spreadsheet menu names (Figure 2-6). Each menu name represents a menu of commands that can retrieve, save, print, and manipulate data in the spreadsheet. To display a menu such as the File menu or the Edit menu, click the menu name.

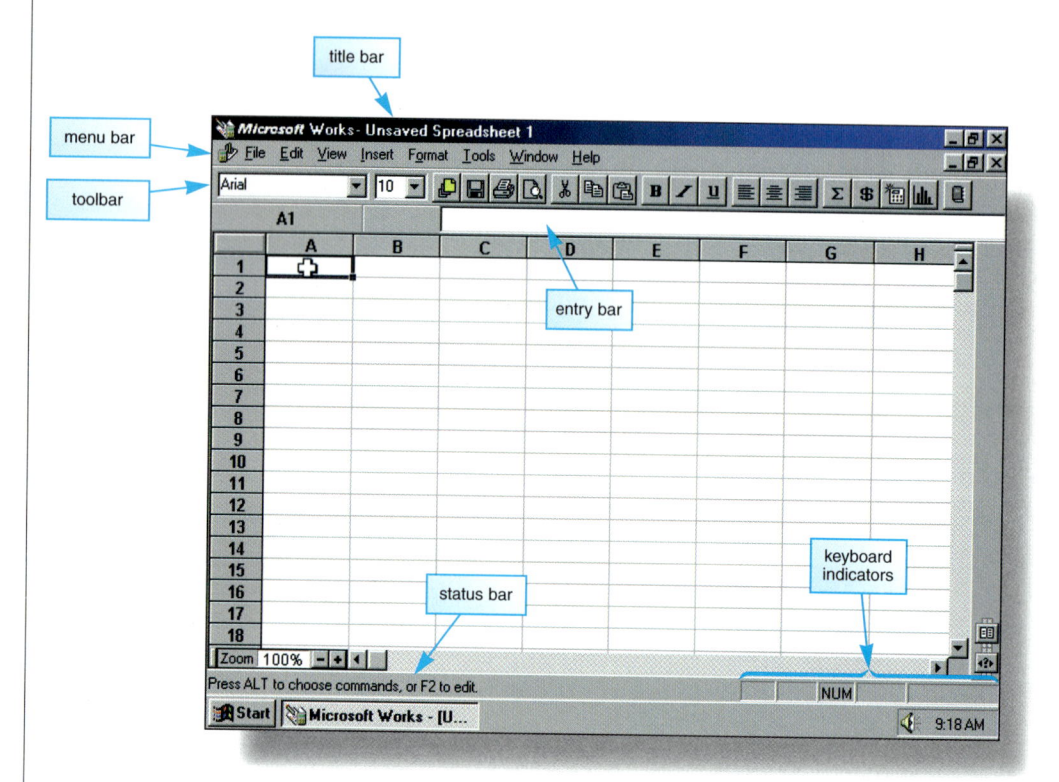

FIGURE 2-6

The menu bar can change to include other menu names and other menu choices depending on the type of work you are doing in the Works Spreadsheet. For example, if you are working with a chart instead of a spreadsheet, the menu bar consists of a list of menu names for use specifically with charts.

TOOLBAR The **toolbar** (Figure 2-6) contains buttons that allow you to perform frequent tasks more quickly than you can when using the menu bar. Each button contains a picture that helps you remember its function. If you point to the button, a description of the purpose of the button will display beneath the button in a yellow rectangle and also in the status bar. You click a button to cause a command to execute. Each of the buttons on the toolbar is explained when used in the projects.

As with the menu bar, Works displays a different toolbar when you work with charts. The buttons on the Charting toolbar are explained when charts are used.

ENTRY BAR Below the toolbar, Works displays the **entry bar** (Figure 2-6). Data that you type appears in the entry bar. Works also displays the highlighted cell reference in the cell reference area on the left side of the entry bar.

More About Scrolling Guidelines

Follow these general scrolling guidelines for viewing your spreadsheet: (1) To scroll short distances (one cell at a time), click the scroll arrows; (2) To scroll one screen at a time, click the scroll bar; (3) To scroll long distances, drag the scroll box.

More About Entry Bar

When you enter more characters in a cell than will fit in the width of the entry bar, the entry bar's text display area drops down so that you see all of the characters you are typing.

STATUS BAR The left side of the **status bar** at the bottom of the screen displays brief instructions, a brief description of the currently selected command, a brief description of the function of a toolbar button, or one or more words describing the current activity in progress.

Keyboard indicators indicating which keys are engaged, such as NUM (NUM LOCK key active) and CAPS (CAPS LOCK key active), display on the right side of the status bar within the small rectangular boxes.

Highlighting a Cell

To enter data into a cell, you must first **highlight** the cell. The easiest method to highlight a cell is to position the block plus sign mouse pointer in the desired cell and click.

An alternative method is to use the arrow keys that are located to the right of the typewriter keys on the keyboard. After you press an arrow key, the adjacent cell in the direction of the arrow on the key becomes the highlighted cell. You also can use the **TAB key** to move from one cell to another in a row.

You know a cell is highlighted when a heavy border surrounds the cell and the cell reference of the highlighted cell displays in the cell reference area in the entry bar (Figure 2-7).

Entering Text in a Spreadsheet

In the Works Spreadsheet, any set of characters containing a letter is **text**. Text is used for titles, such as spreadsheet titles, column titles, and row titles. In Project 2, the spreadsheet title, RSC Sports and Fitness Centers, identifies the spreadsheet. The column titles consist of the words Anaheim, Irvine, Fullerton, Yorba Linda, and Total. The row titles (Student, Single, Family, Executive, and Total) identify each row in the spreadsheet (Figure 2-7).

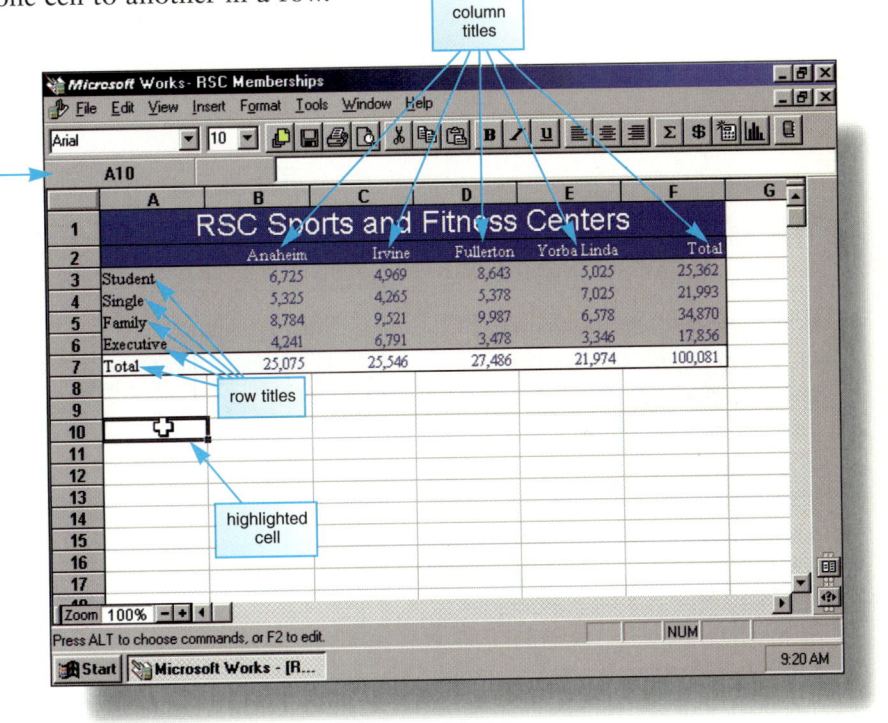

FIGURE 2-7

More *About* Labels

Whenever possible, arrange your spreadsheet so that similar items are grouped together, and label your cells as though you will not remember what they are later. Then, you won't spend as much time figuring out what you did.

Entering the Spreadsheet Title

The first task to build the spreadsheet is to complete the following steps to enter the spreadsheet title into cell A1.

Steps: To Enter the Spreadsheet Title

1 **Click cell A1 to highlight it.**

A heavy border surrounds cell A1, and cell A1 displays in the cell reference area (Figure 2-8).

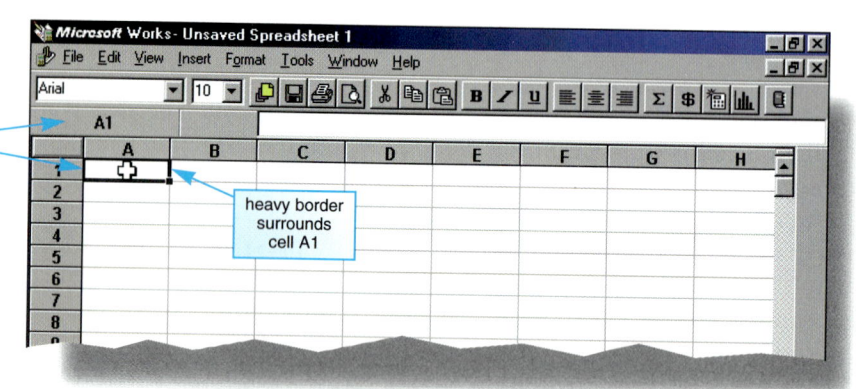

FIGURE 2-8

2 **Type** RSC Sports and Fitness Centers **in cell A1.**

When you type the first character, the heavy border surrounding the cell changes and a new message displays on the status bar (Figure 2-9). Works displays three boxes; the **Cancel box**, the **Enter box**, and the **Help box** in the entry bar. As you type characters, each character displays in the cell followed immediately by a blinking vertical bar called the **insertion point**. The insertion point indicates where the next character typed will display. Works also displays the data in the entry bar as it is typed. Notice that the mouse pointer changes from a block plus sign to an I-beam. Whenever the mouse pointer is located in the current cell when you enter data, it will change to an I-beam. If you make a typing mistake, press the BACKSPACE key until the error is erased, and then retype the text. Clicking the Help box displays the Help window to the right of the spreadsheet window.

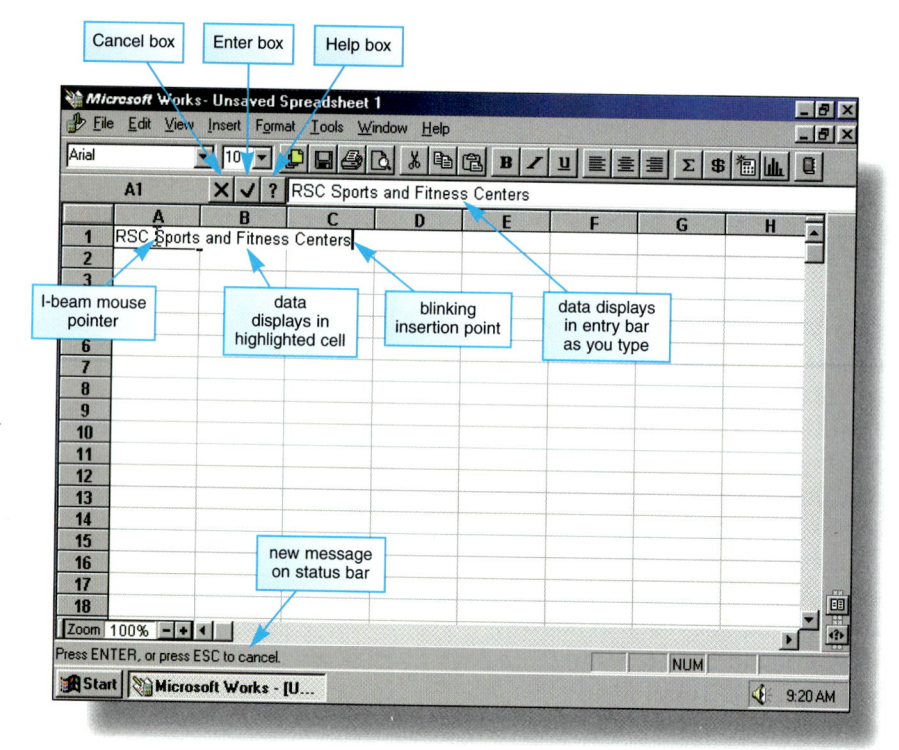

FIGURE 2-9

3 **After you type the text, point to the Enter box (Figure 2-10).**

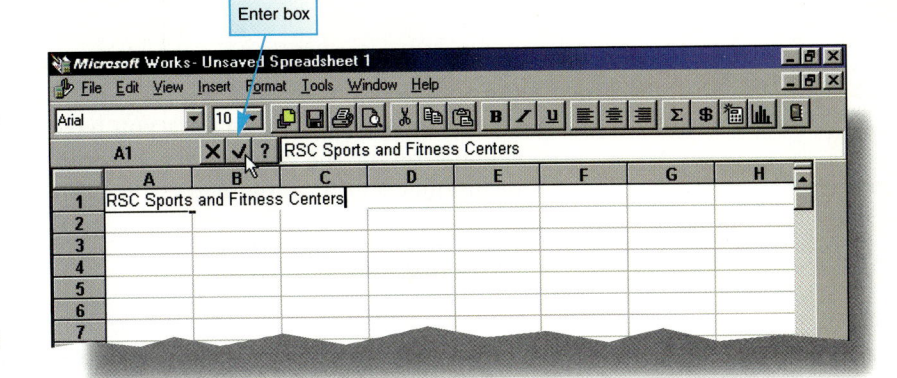

FIGURE 2-10

4 **Click the Enter box to confirm the entry.**

When you confirm the entry, Works enters the text in cell A1 (Figure 2-11).

FIGURE 2-11

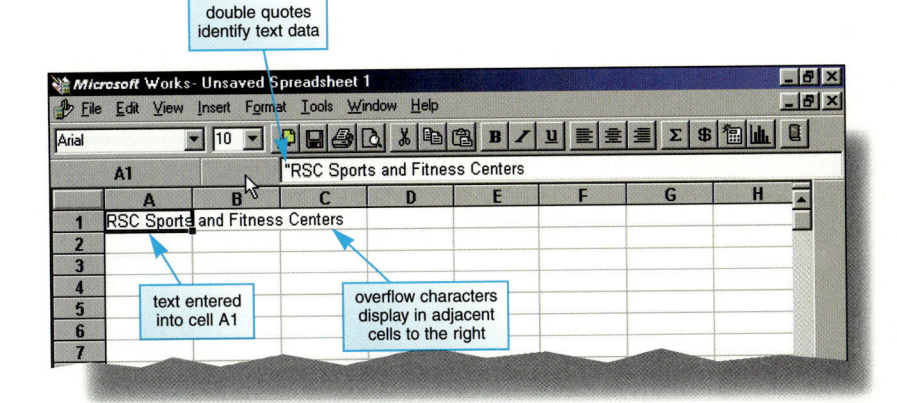

In the example in Figure 2-11, instead of using the mouse to confirm the entry, you can press the ENTER key after typing the text. Pressing the ENTER key replaces Step 3 and Step 4.

When you confirm a text entry into a cell, a series of events occurs. First, when text displays in the entry bar, it displays preceded by a double quotation mark, which indicates the entry is text and not a number or other value.

Second, Works positions the text left-aligned in the highlighted cell. Therefore, the R in the abbreviation RSC begins in the leftmost position of cell A1.

Third, when the text you enter contains more characters than can be displayed in the width of the cell, Works displays the overflow characters in adjacent cells to the right as long as these adjacent cells contain no data. In Figure 2-11, cell A1 is not wide enough to contain twenty-six characters plus four blank spaces. Thus, Works displays the overflow characters in cells B1 and C1 because the cells are empty.

Fourth, when you confirm an entry into a cell by clicking the Enter box or pressing the ENTER key, the cell into which the text is entered remains the highlighted cell.

Correcting a Mistake While Typing

If you type the wrong letter and notice the error before clicking the Enter box or pressing the ENTER key, use the BACKSPACE key to erase all the characters back to and including the ones that are wrong. The insertion point will indicate where in the text the next character you type will display. Then retype the remainder of the text entry.

W 2.14 • Project 2 • Building a Spreadsheet and Charting Data

To cancel the entire entry before confirming the entry, click the Cancel box or press the ESC key.

If you see an error in data you have already entered into a cell, highlight the cell and retype the entire entry. Later in this project, additional error-correction techniques will be explained.

Entering Column Titles

The next step is to enter the column titles consisting of the words, Anaheim, Irvine, Fullerton, Yorba Linda, and Total. To enter the column titles, select the appropriate cell and then enter the text, as illustrated in the following steps.

Steps **To Enter Column Titles**

1 **Click cell B2 to highlight it.**

A heavy border surrounds cell B2, and B2 displays in the cell reference area (Figure 2-12).

FIGURE 2-12

2 **Type** Anaheim **as the column title.**

Works displays Anaheim in the entry bar and in cell B2, which is the highlighted cell (Figure 2-13). Because the mouse pointer is located in the highlighted cell while data is entered, it changes to an I-beam.

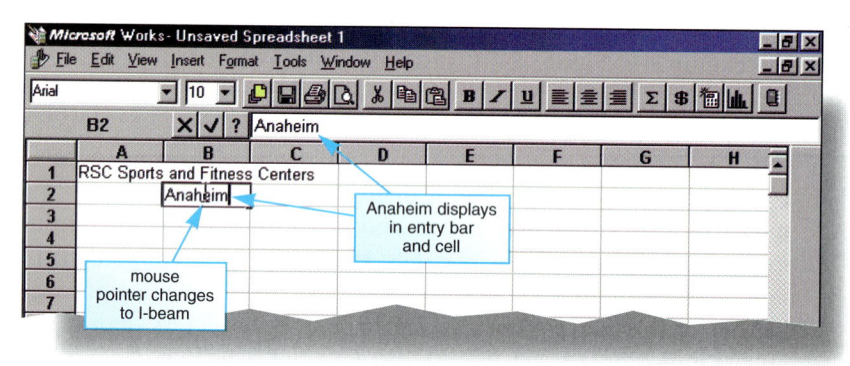

FIGURE 2-13

3 **Press the RIGHT ARROW key.**

Works highlights cell C2 (Figure 2-14). When you press an arrow key to confirm an entry, Works enters the data and then makes the adjacent cell in the direction of the arrow (up, down, left, or right) the highlighted cell.

FIGURE 2-14

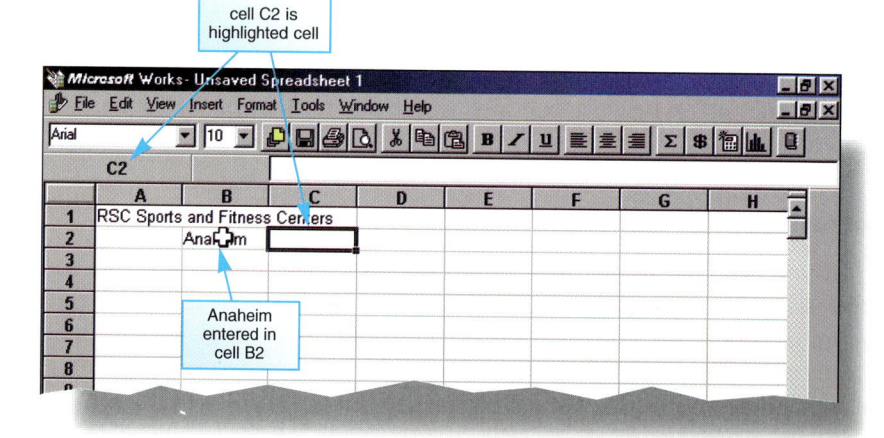

Microsoft **Works 4** Windows 95

Entering Text in a Spreadsheet • W 2.15

4 Repeat Step 2 and Step 3 for the remaining column titles. That is, enter Irvine in cell C2, Fullerton in cell D2, Yorba Linda in cell E2, and Total in cell F2. Confirm the last column title entry in cell F2 by clicking the ENTER box or pressing the ENTER key.

The column titles display as shown in Figure 2-15.

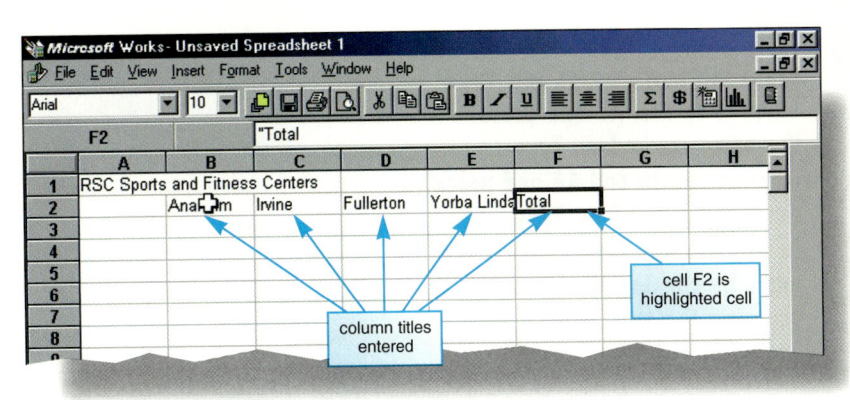

FIGURE 2-15

When confirming an entry in a cell, use the arrow keys if the next entry is in an adjacent cell. If the next entry is not in an adjacent cell, click the Enter box in the entry bar or press the ENTER key, and then use the mouse to select the appropriate cell for the next entry.

Entering Row Titles

The next step in developing the spreadsheet is to enter the row titles in column A. Complete the following steps to enter the row titles.

Steps To Enter Row Titles

1 Click cell A3 to highlight it (Figure 2-16).

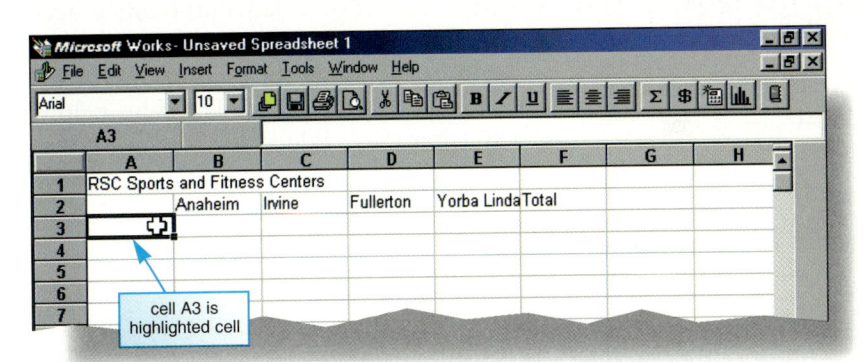

FIGURE 2-16

2 Type the row title Student and then press the DOWN ARROW key.

When you press the down arrow key, Works enters the row title, Student, in cell A3 and makes cell A4 the highlighted cell (Figure 2-17).

FIGURE 2-17

W 2.16 • Project 2 • Building a Spreadsheet and Charting Data

③ **Type** Single **in cell A4 and press the DOWN ARROW key. Type** Family **in cell A5 and press the DOWN ARROW key. Type** Executive **in cell A6 and press the DOWN ARROW key. Type** Total **in cell A7, and then confirm the entry by clicking the ENTER box or pressing the ENTER key.**

The row titles display as shown in Figure 2-18. The row titles are left-aligned in each cell. Cell A7 is the highlighted cell.

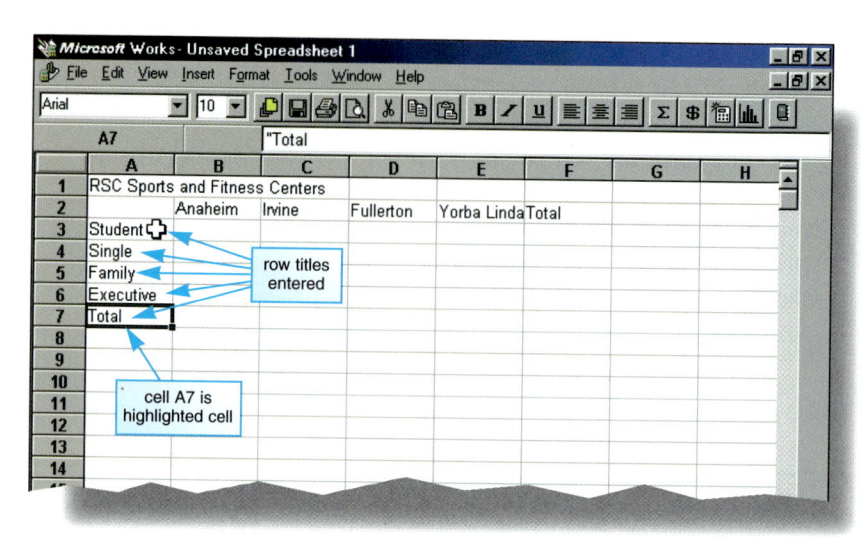

FIGURE 2-18

Entering Numbers

You can enter numbers into cells to represent amounts and other numeric values. Numbers can include the digits zero through nine and any one of the following characters:

( ) , . / $ % E e

The use of these characters is explained when they are required in a project. If a cell entry contains any other character from the keyboard, Works interprets the entry as text or a date and treats it accordingly.

In Project 2, you must enter the memberships for Anaheim, Irvine, Fullerton, and Yorba Linda for each of the categories, Student, Single, Family, and Executive in rows 3, 4, 5, and 6. The steps below and on the next two pages illustrate how to enter these values one row at a time.

More About Numbers

To enter numbers in a cell, you can use the number keys at the top of the keyboard or, when the NUM LOCK key is on, you can use the numeric key pad at the right of the keyboard. Using the key pad at the right of the keyboard is generally the fastest way to enter numbers.

Steps **To Enter Numeric Data**

① **Click cell B3 to highlight it (Figure 2-19).**

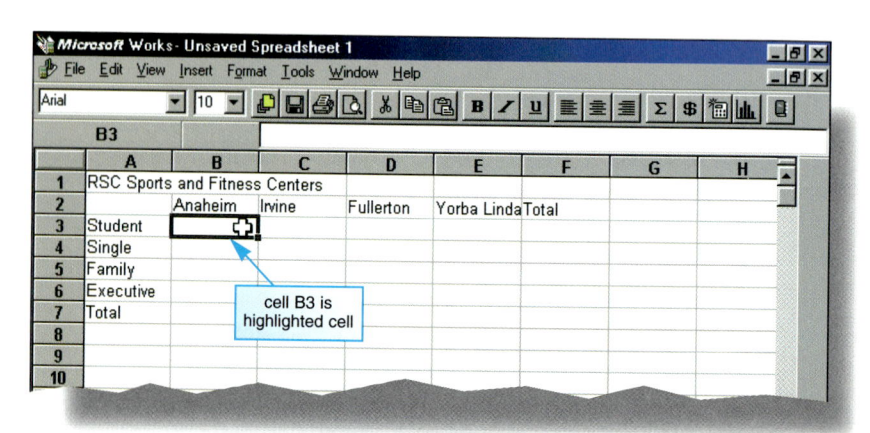

FIGURE 2-19

Microsoft **Works 4** Windows 95

ENTERING NUMBERS • W 2.17

2 **Type** 6725 **into cell B3.**

The number 6725 displays in the entry bar and in the highlighted cell (Figure 2-20). Enter the number without a comma. You will format the numbers in the spreadsheet with commas in a later step. The mouse pointer changes from a block plus sign to an I-beam.

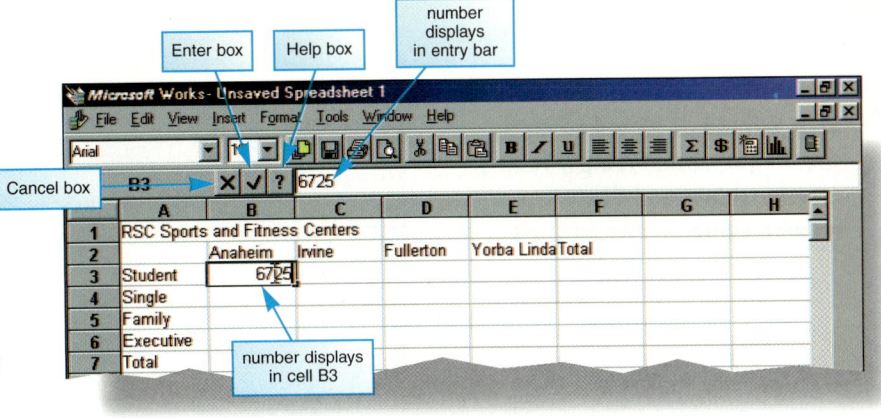

FIGURE 2-20

3 **Press the RIGHT ARROW key.**

Works enters the number 6725 into cell B3 and makes cell C3 the highlighted cell (Figure 2-21).

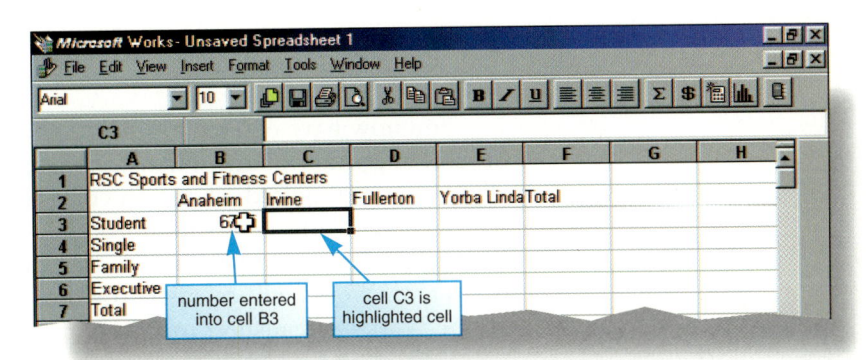

FIGURE 2-21

4 **Type** 4969 **into cell C3 and then press the RIGHT ARROW key. Type** 8643 **into cell D3 and then press the RIGHT ARROW key. Type** 5025 **into cell E3 and then press the ENTER key.**

Row 3 contains the Student memberships and cell E3 is highlighted (Figure 2-22).

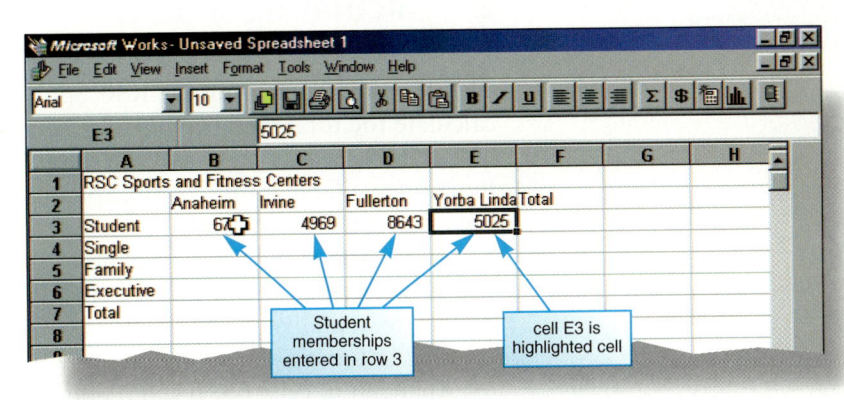

FIGURE 2-22

5 **Click cell B4 to highlight it (Figure 2-23).**

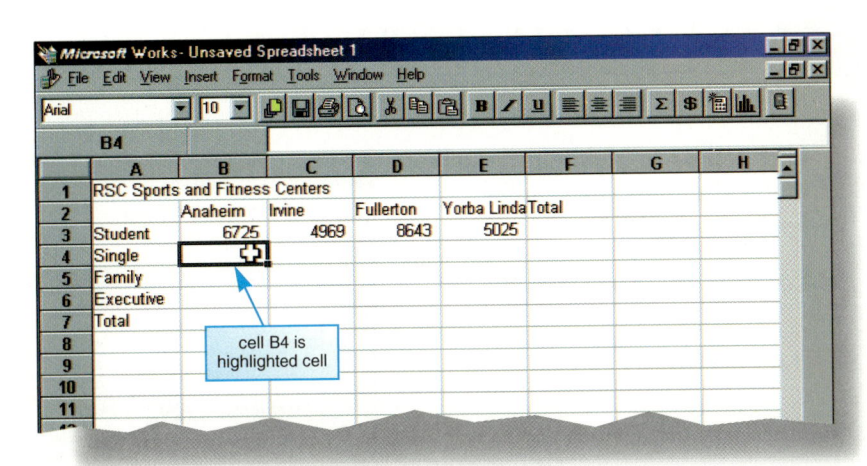

FIGURE 2-23

W 2.18 • Project 2 • Building a Spreadsheet and Charting Data

6 **Repeat the procedures used in Step 2 through Step 4 to enter the Single memberships, Family memberships, and Executive memberships.**

The Single, Family, and Executive memberships are entered in rows 4, 5, and 6, respectively (Figure 2-24).

FIGURE 2-24

You now have entered all the numbers required for this spreadsheet. Notice several important points. First, commas, which are used to separate every third digit, are not required when you enter numbers. You will add them in a later step.

Second, Works enters numbers **right-aligned** in the cells, which means they occupy the rightmost positions in the cells.

Third, Works will calculate the totals in row 7 and column F. The capability of the Works Spreadsheet tool to perform calculations is one of its major features.

Calculating a Sum

The next step in creating the RSC Sports and Fitness Centers spreadsheet is to calculate the total memberships for Anaheim. To calculate this value and enter it into cell B7, Works must add the numbers in cells B3, B4, B5, and B6. The SUM function available in the Works Spreadsheet tool provides a convenient means to accomplish this task.

To use the SUM function, you must first identify the cell into which the sum will be entered after it is calculated. Then, you can use the **AutoSum button** on the toolbar to actually sum the numbers.

The following steps illustrate how to use the AutoSum button to sum the sales for Anaheim in cells B3, B4, B5, and B6 and enter the answer in cell B7.

Steps To Sum a Column of Numbers Using the Autosum Button

1 **Click cell B7 to highlight the cell that will contain the sum for Anaheim — cell B7.**

Cell B7 is highlighted (Figure 2-25).

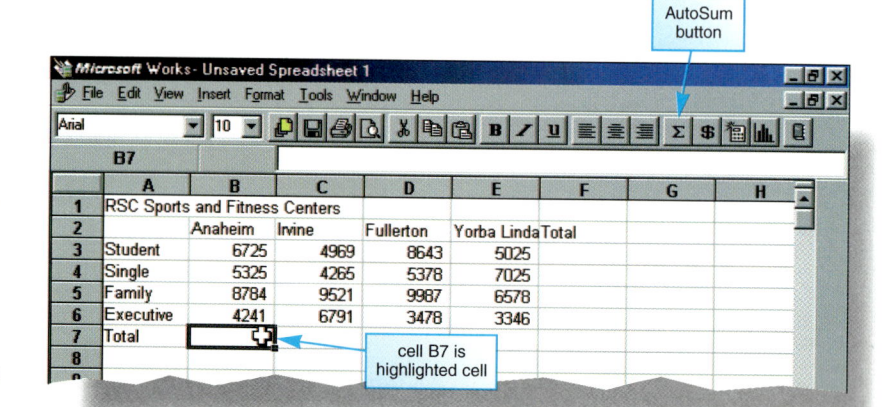

FIGURE 2-25

Microsoft **Works 4** Windows 95

Calculating a Sum • **W 2.19**

2 **Click the AutoSum button on the toolbar.**

Works responds by displaying =SUM(B3:B6) in the entry bar and in the highlighted cell (Figure 2-26). The =SUM entry identifies the SUM function. The B3:B6 entry within parentheses following the function name SUM is the way Works identifies cells B3, B4, B5, and B6 as the cells containing the values to be summed. Works also places a dark background behind the proposed cells to sum. The word POINT displays on the status bar indicating the SUM function is pointing to a range to be summed.

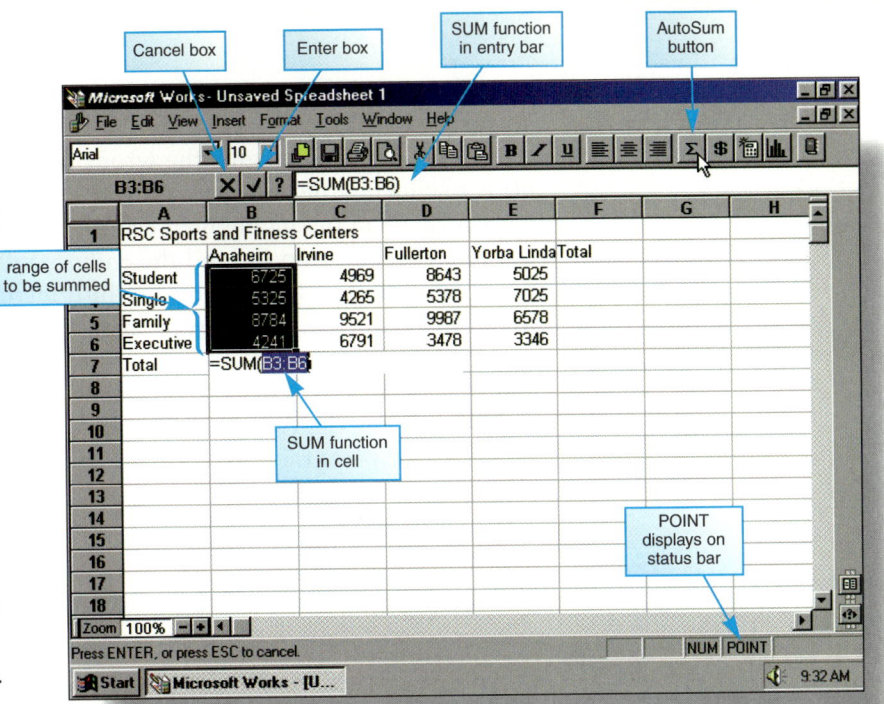

FIGURE 2-26

3 **Click the AutoSum button a second time.**

Works displays the sum of the memberships for Anaheim (6725 + 5325 + 8784 + 4241 = 25075) in cell B7 (Figure 2-27). Although the SUM function assigned to cell B7 is not displayed in the cell, it remains in the cell and displays in the entry bar when the cell is highlighted.

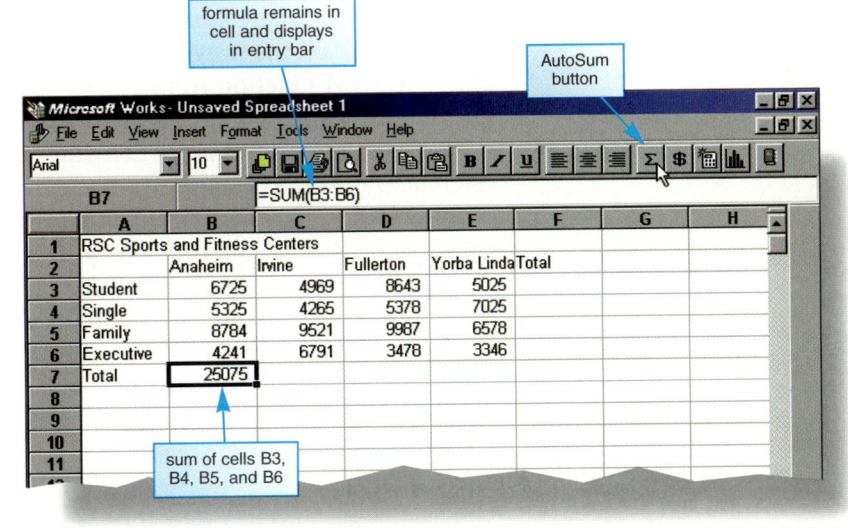

FIGURE 2-27

OtherWays

1. Press CTRL+M

To display the SUM function in a cell instead of the sum, click the cell and then click in the entry bar area.

When you enter the SUM function using the AutoSum button, Works automatically highlights what it considers to be your choice of the group of cells to sum. The group of cells, B3, B4, B5, and B6, is called a range. A **range** is a block of adjacent cells in a spreadsheet. Ranges can be as small as a single cell and as large as an entire spreadsheet. Once you define a range, you can work with all the cells in the range instead of one cell at a time. In Figure 2-26, clicking the AutoSum button defines the range, which consists of cells B3 through B6 (designated B3:B6 by Works).

More About AutoSum

Consider how fast Works completes the following sophisticated operations after clicking the AutoSum button twice: (1) Works enters the equal sign and function name; (2) scans the spreadsheet and highlights cells to be summed; (3) calculates the total; and (4) displays the result of the calculation.

W 2.20 • Project 2 • Building a Spreadsheet and Charting Data

When highlighting the range of cells to sum using the AutoSum button, Works first looks for a range with numbers above the highlighted cell, and then to the left. If Works highlights the wrong range, drag the correct range any time prior to clicking the AutoSum button a second time. You also can enter the correct range in the highlighted cell to receive the sum by typing the beginning cell reference, a colon (:), and the ending cell reference, followed by clicking the AutoSum button a second time. A third method to fix an incorrect range specified by Works is to enter the correct range in the entry bar by dragging over the range specified in the entry bar and then typing the beginning cell reference, a colon (:), and the ending cell reference, followed by clicking the AutoSum button a second time.

When using the AutoSum button, you can click it once and then click the Enter box or press the ENTER key to complete the entry. Clicking the AutoSum button a second time, however, is the quickest way to enter the SUM function.

Copying a Cell to Adjacent Cells

In the RSC Sports and Fitness Centers spreadsheet, Works also must calculate the totals for Irvine, Fullerton, and Yorba Linda. For the Irvine memberships, the total is the sum of the values in the range C3:C6. Similarly, for the Fullerton memberships, the range to sum is D3:D6 and for the Yorba Linda memberships, the range is E3:E6.

To calculate these sums, you can follow the steps shown in Figures 2-25 through 2-27 on the previous two pages. A more efficient method, however, is to copy the SUM function from cell B7 to the range C7:E7. The copy cannot be an exact duplicate, though, because different columns must be referenced for each respective total. Therefore, when you copy cell references, Works adjusts the cell references for each column. As a result, the range in the SUM function in cell C7 will be C3:C6, the range in the SUM function in cell D7 will be D3:D6, and the range in SUM function in cell E7 will be E3:E6.

The easiest way to copy the SUM function from cell B7 to cells C7, D7, and E7 is to use the fill handle. The **fill handle** is the small rectangular dot located in the lower right corner of the heavy border around the highlighted cell. To copy using the fill handle, first highlight the cell that includes the data you want to copy. Then drag the fill handle to highlight the range you want to copy to. Complete the following steps to perform this operation.

Steps To Copy One Cell to Adjacent Cells in a Row

1 Click the cell to copy – cell B7 – and position the mouse pointer on the fill handle located in the lower right hand corner of cell B7.

Cell B7 is highlighted (Figure 2-28). When you position the mouse pointer on the fill handle, the mouse pointer changes to the word FILL with a cross indicating the fill handle is selected.

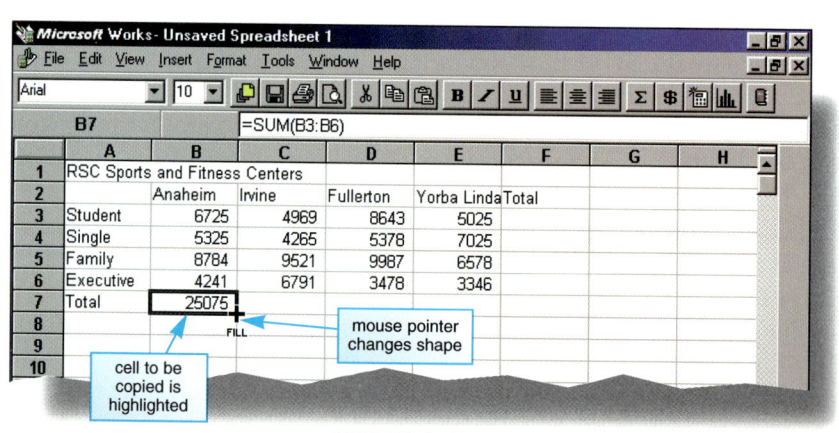

FIGURE 2-28

2 Drag the range you want to copy into (cells C7, D7, and E7).

When you drag the fill handle through the cells, Works places a border around the cell you want to copy (B7) and an outline around the range you want to copy into (C7:E7) (Figure 2-29). The contents of cell B7 display in the entry bar.

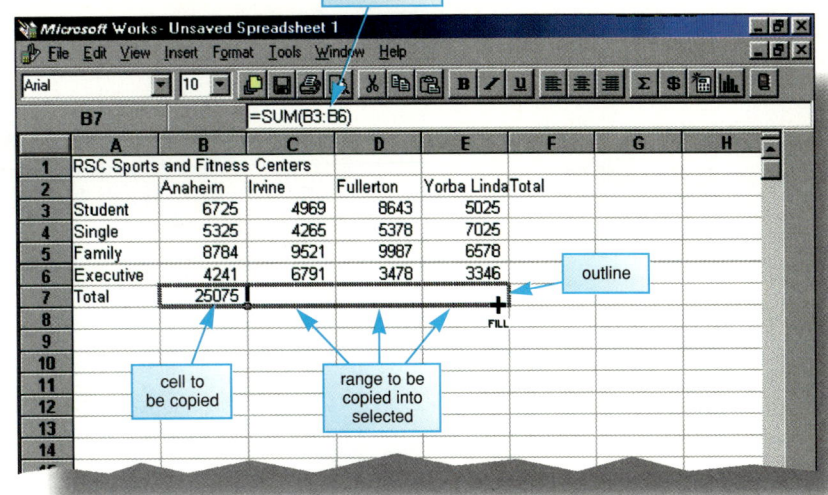

FIGURE 2-29

3 Release the mouse button.

When you release the mouse button, the mouse pointer changes to a block plus sign (Figure 2-30). Works copies the SUM function from cell B7 into the range C7:E7. In addition, Works performs calculations based on the formula in each of the cells and displays sums in cells C7, D7, and E7.

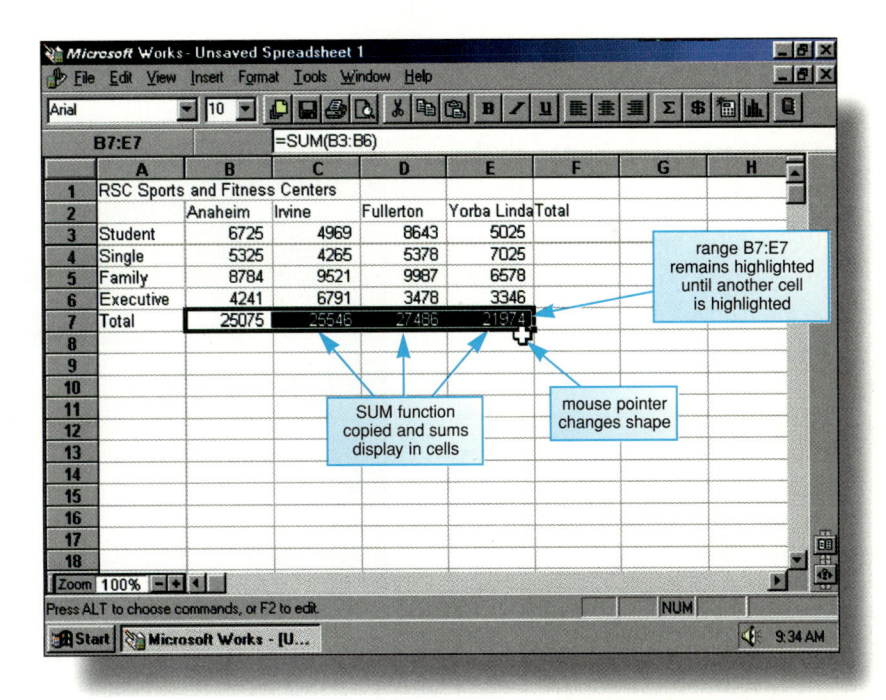

FIGURE 2-30

> **OtherWays**
> 1. On Edit menu click Fill Right
> 2. Press CTRL+R

After Works has copied the contents of a cell into a range, the range remains highlighted. To remove the range highlight, click any cell in the spreadsheet.

Summing a Row Total

The next step in building the RSC Sports and Fitness Centers spreadsheet is to total the Student memberships, the Single memberships, the Family memberships, and the Executive memberships, and then to calculate the Total memberships for the centers. These totals will be entered in column F. The SUM function is used in the same manner as totaling the memberships in row 7. Perform the steps on the next page to sum the row numbers.

Steps To Sum a Row of Numbers Using the AutoSum Button

1 Click the cell to contain the total for Student – cell F3.

Cell F3 is highlighted (Figure 2-31).

FIGURE 2-31

2 Click the AutoSum button on the toolbar.

Works responds by displaying =SUM(B3:E3) in the entry bar and in the highlighted cell (Figure 2-32). Works also places a dark background behind the proposed cells to sum. The =SUM entry identifies the SUM function. The B3:E3 entry within parentheses following the function name SUM is the way Works identifies cells B3, C3, D3, and E3 as the cells containing the values to be added.

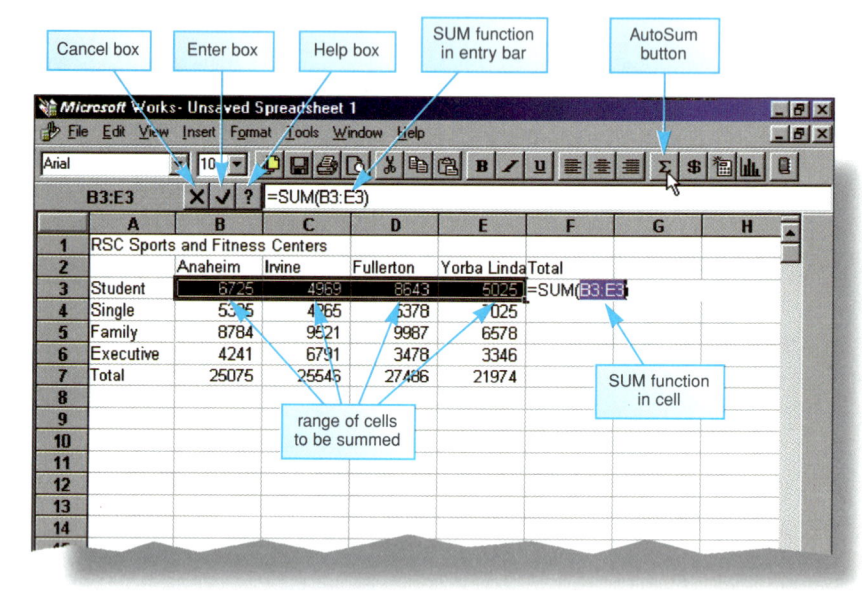

FIGURE 2-32

3 Click the AutoSum button a second time.

Works enters the formula in cell F3, displays the sum in the cell, and displays the SUM function from cell F3 in the entry bar (Figure 2-33).

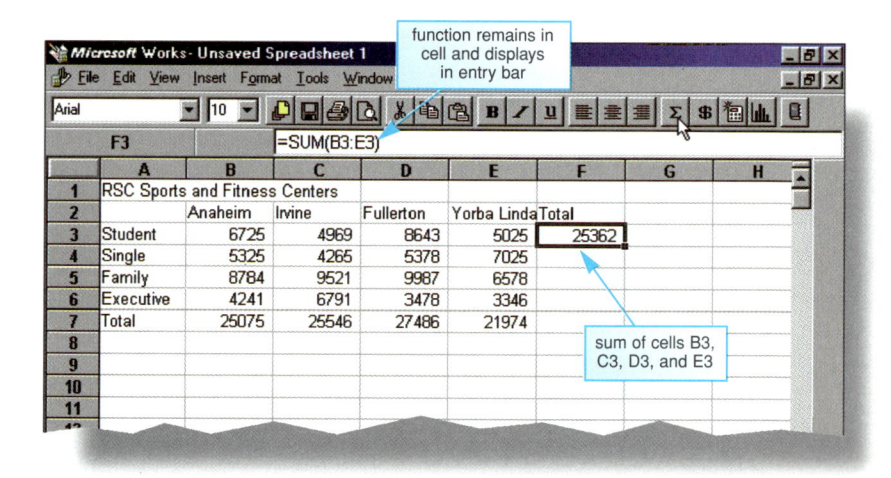

FIGURE 2-33

OtherWays

1. Press CTRL+M

Copying Adjacent Cells in a Column • **W 2.23**

As shown previously, you can accomplish Step 3 by clicking the ENTER box or pressing the ENTER key.

Copying Adjacent Cells in a Column

The next task is to copy the SUM function from cell F3 to the range F4:F7 to obtain the Total memberships for Single, Family, Executive, and the Total memberships for RSC Sports and Fitness Centers. The steps to accomplish this task follow.

Steps **To Copy One Cell to Adjacent Cells in a Column**

1 **Click cell F3. Position the mouse pointer on the fill handle located in the lower right-hand corner of cell F3. When the mouse pointer changes to the word FILL with a cross, drag the range to cell F7.**

When you drag the fill handle through the cells, Works places a border around the cell you want to copy (F3) and an outline around the range you want to copy into (F4:F7) (Figure 2-34). The contents of cell F3 display in the entry bar.

FIGURE 2-34

2 **Release the mouse button.**

When you release the mouse button, the mouse pointer changes to a block plus sign (Figure 2-35). Works fills the highlighted range with the SUM function and displays the calculated sums in each of the cells. When Works copies the function, each range reference in the function is adjusted to reflect the proper rows of numbers to sum.

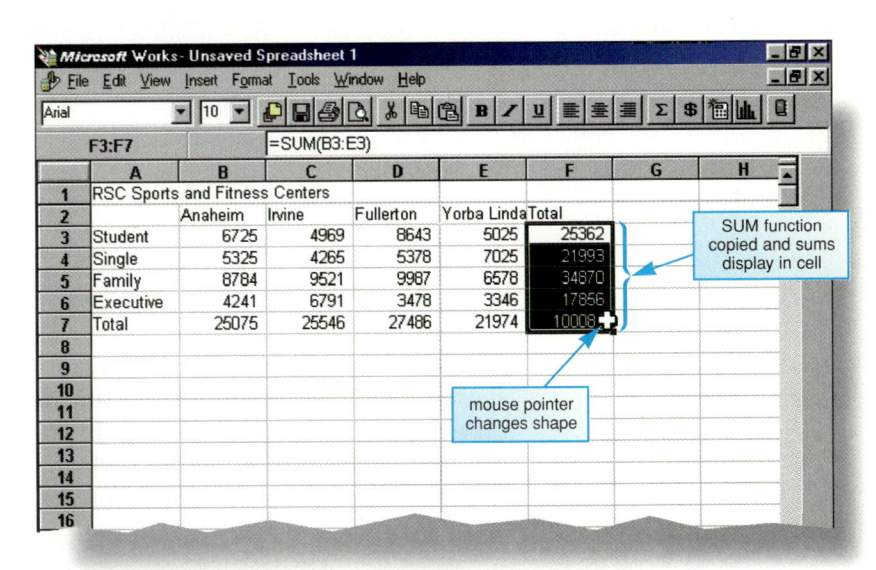

OtherWays
1. On Edit menu click Fill Down
2. Press CTRL+D

FIGURE 2-35

W 2.24 • Project 2 • Building a Spreadsheet and Charting Data

After Works copies the cell contents, the range F3:F7 remains highlighted. You can remove this highlight by clicking any cell in the spreadsheet.

Formatting the Spreadsheet

You have now entered all the text, numeric entries, and functions for the spreadsheet. The next step is to format the spreadsheet. You **format** a spreadsheet to emphasize certain entries and make the spreadsheet attractive to view and easy to read and understand.

With Works, you have the ability to change fonts, font sizes, and font styles such as bold and italic, and to color the font and cells containing the data in the spreadsheet. On the following pages you will learn how to format the spreadsheet in Project 2 as shown in Figure 2-36 and as described in the list on Page W 2.6.

1. The spreadsheet title displays in white 18-point Arial font. The cell background is dark blue. The title is centered over the columns in the spreadsheet.
2. The color of the column titles (white), row titles (black) and the remainder of the spreadsheet display as illustrated. The fonts, font sizes, styles, and colors are determined by the AutoFormat feature of Works.
3. The membership numbers, column totals, and row totals display with commas.

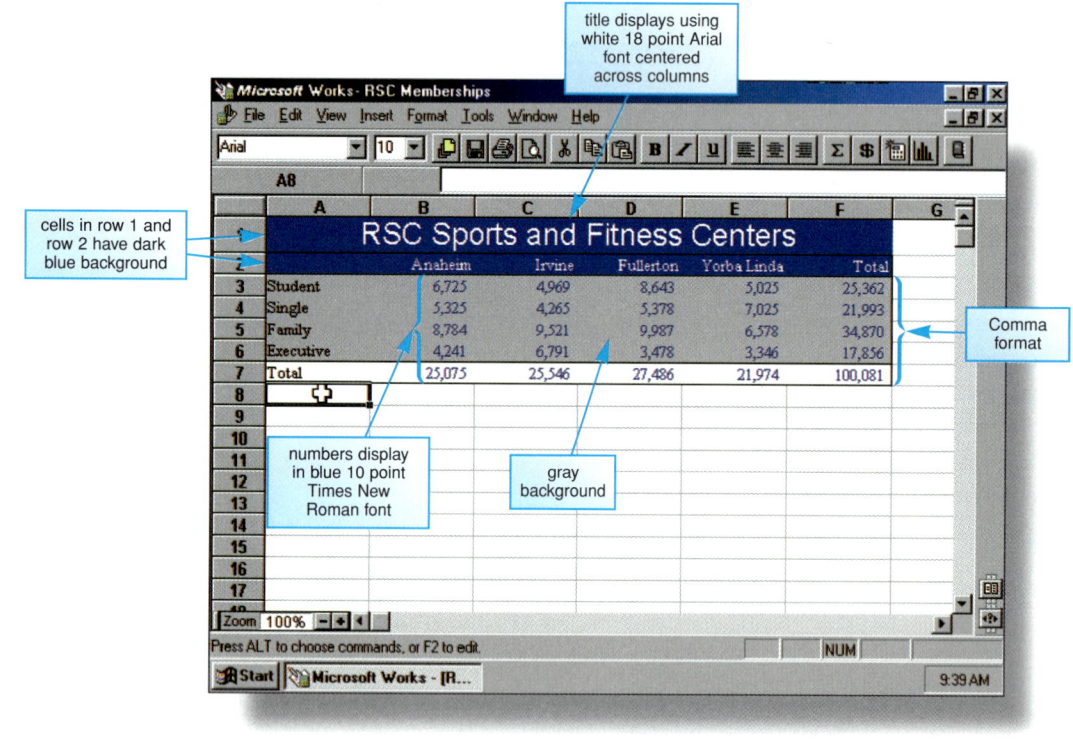

FIGURE 2-36

The following paragraphs explain how to format the spreadsheet.

Formatting Text and Changing the Color of Cells

The first step in formatting the spreadsheet is to format the title of the spreadsheet in cell A1. The spreadsheet title displays in white 18 point Arial font and is centered over columns A through F. The cell background is dark blue. Formatting can be accomplished using the Format command from the context-sensitive menu. Complete the following steps to format the title.

Microsoft **Works 4** Windows 95

Formatting Text and Changing the Color of Cells • W 2.25

Steps To Format Cells

1 **Highlight the range of cells A1:F1. Point to the highlighted cells and right-click. When the context-sensitive menu displays, point to Format.**

Cells A1 through F1 are highlighted (Figure 2-37). The context-sensitive menu displays and the mouse pointer points to the Format command.

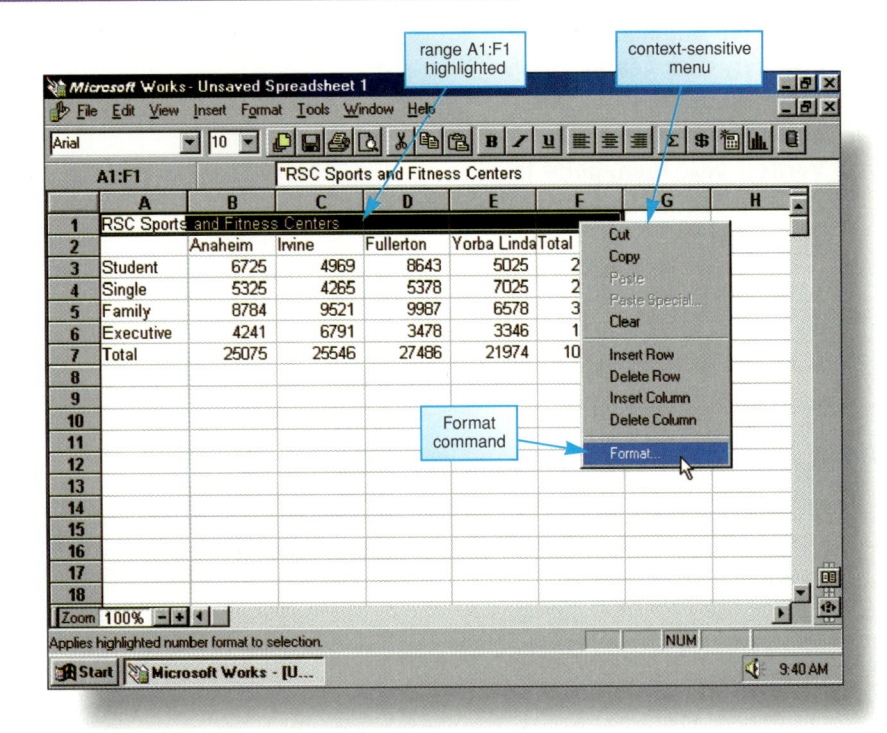

FIGURE 2-37

2 **Click Format on the context-sensitive menu. When the Format Cells dialog box displays, point to the Alignment tab.**

Works displays the Format Cells dialog box (Figure 2-38). The Format Cells dialog box contains five tabbed sheets; Number, Alignment, Font, Border, and Shading. The Number sheet displays in front of the other tabbed sheets. The mouse pointer points to the Alignment tab.

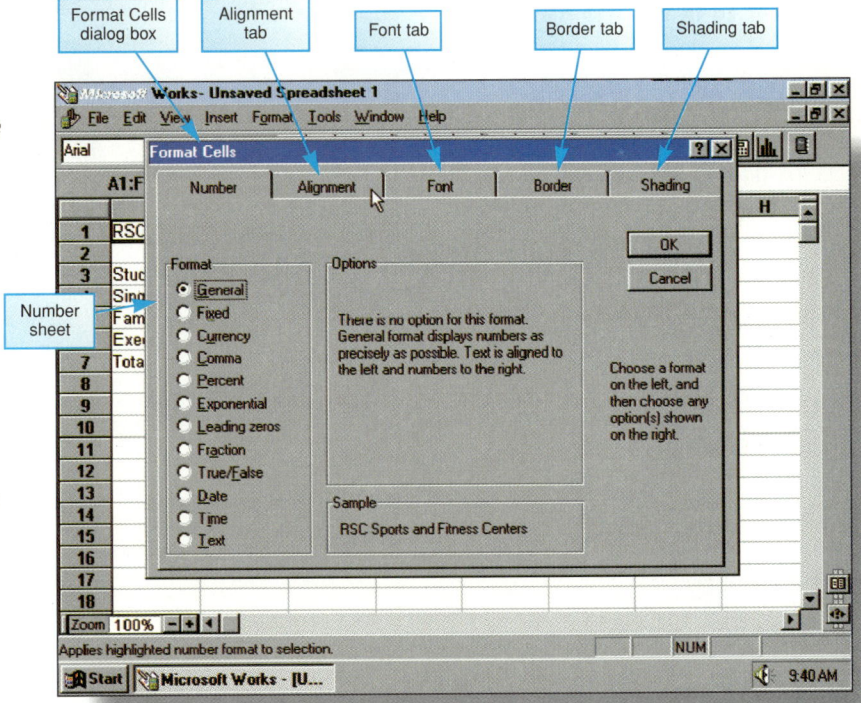

FIGURE 2-38

W 2.26 • Project 2 • Building a Spreadsheet and Charting Data

3 **Click the Alignment tab in the Format Cells dialog box. When the Alignment sheet displays, click Center across selection in the Horizontal box. Click Center in the Vertical box. Then, point to the Font tab in the Format Cells dialog box.**

When you click the Alignment tab, the Alignment sheet moves to the front (Figure 2-39). Selecting the Center across selection option button in the Horizontal box indicates the title should be centered horizontally across the selected columns. The selection of the Center option button in the Vertical box indicates that the title is to be centered vertically in the cells. The mouse pointer points to the Font tab.

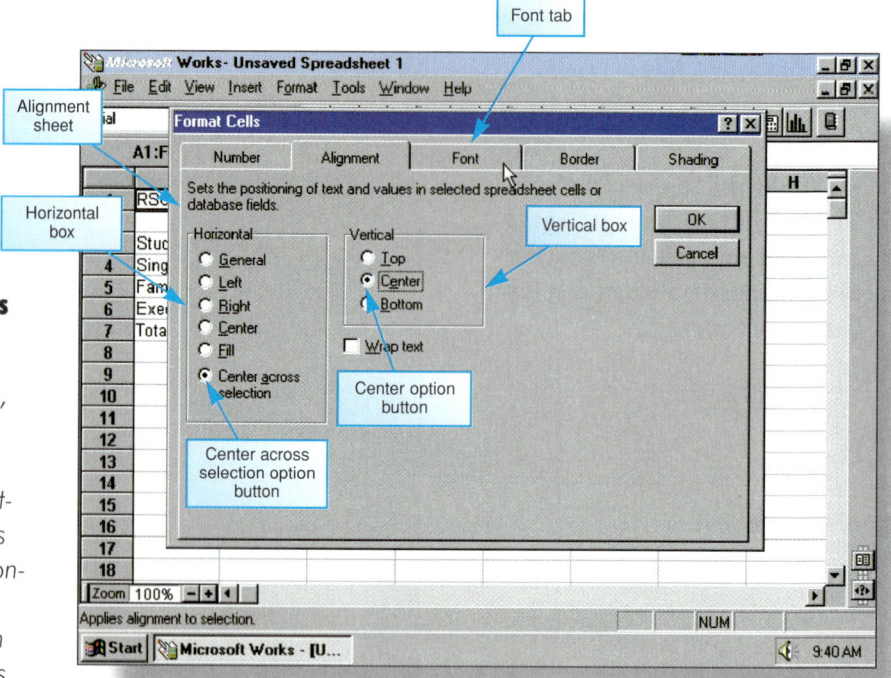

FIGURE 2-39

4 **Click the Font tab. When the Font sheet displays, point to the number 18 in the Size list box.**

Works displays the Font sheet (Figure 2-40). The default values are Arial font, 10 point size, Auto color, and no selections in the Style box. The Sample box displays an example of the text with these options in effect. Auto color displays text in black.

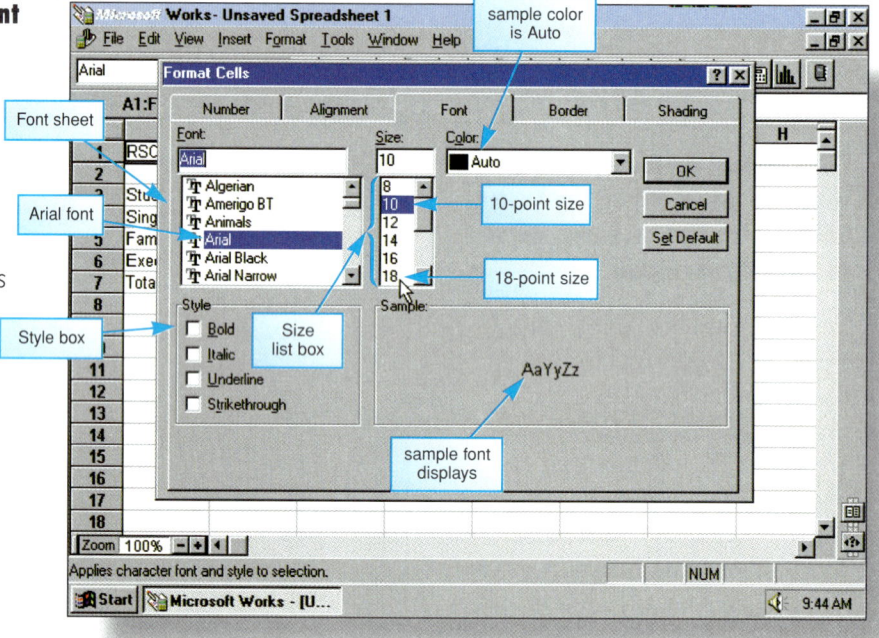

FIGURE 2-40

More About Right-Clicking

Right-clicking highlighted cells was not even available on earlier versions of Works, so you may find people familiar with Works not even considering right-clicking. Because it always produces a context-sensitive menu containing frequently used commands, however, right-clicking can be the fastest way to access commands on the menu bar.

Microsoft **Works 4** Windows 95

Formatting Text and Changing the Color of Cells • W 2.27

5 **Click 18 in the Size list box. Point to the Color drop-down list box arrow.**

Works displays a preview of 18-point Arial text in the Sample box (Figure 2-41). The mouse pointer points to the Color drop-down list box arrow.

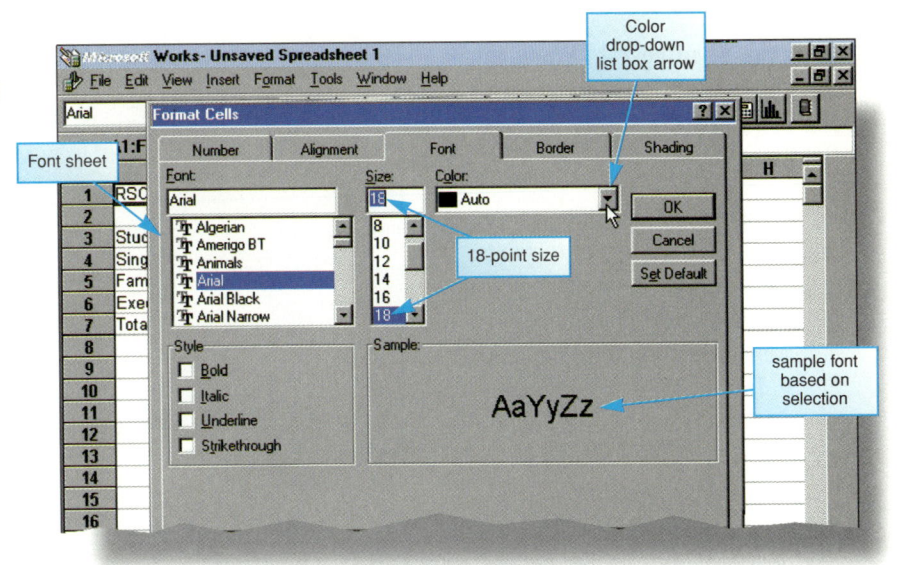

FIGURE 2-41

6 **Click the Color drop-down list box arrow. Scroll down to view the color White. Point to the color White.**

The Color drop-down list box displays and the mouse pointer points to the color White (Figure 2-42).

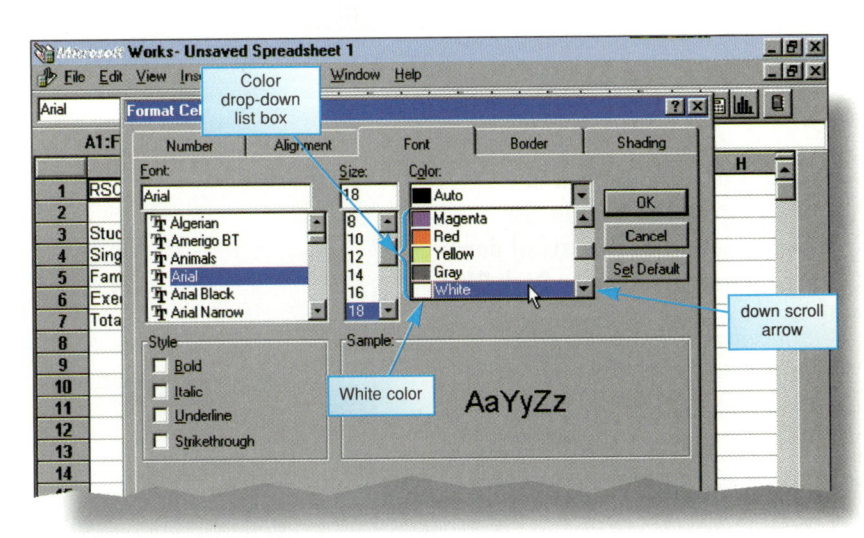

FIGURE 2-42

7 **Click White. Then, point to the Shading tab in the Format Cells dialog box.**

The color white and the word White display in the Color drop-down list box (Figure 2-43). The Sample box displays text with the current selections in effect. The mouse pointer points to the Shading tab.

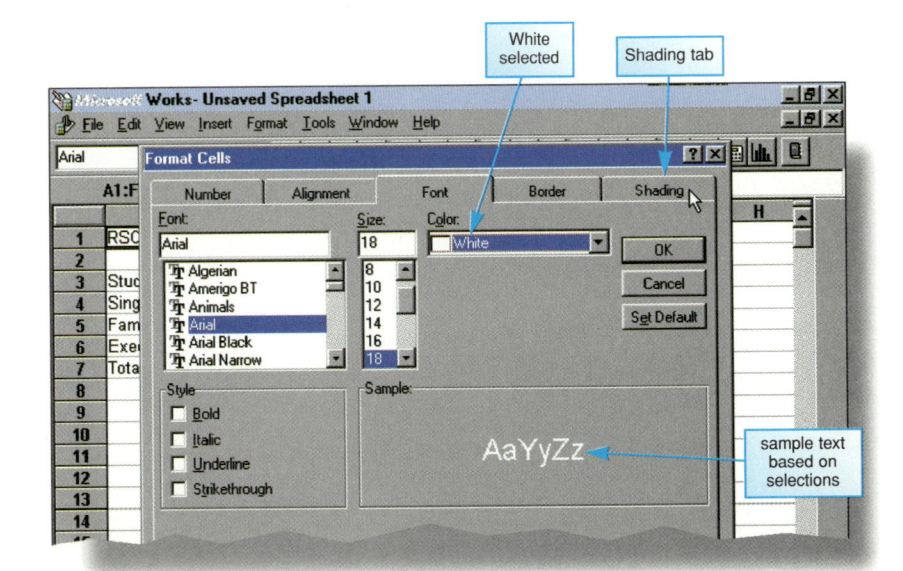

FIGURE 2-43

W 2.28 • Project 2 • Building a Spreadsheet and Charting Data

8 **Click the Shading tab. When the Shading sheet displays, point to the solid pattern in the Pattern list box.**

Works displays the Shading sheet (Figure 2-44). A series of rectangular boxes displays in the Pattern list box. The first rectangular box is highlighted and contains the word None. This box is followed by a series of boxes with various patterns you can select. The first pattern below None is the solid pattern. Below the Pattern list box the description of the selected pattern displays None, indicating no pattern is selected. The mouse pointer points to the solid pattern.

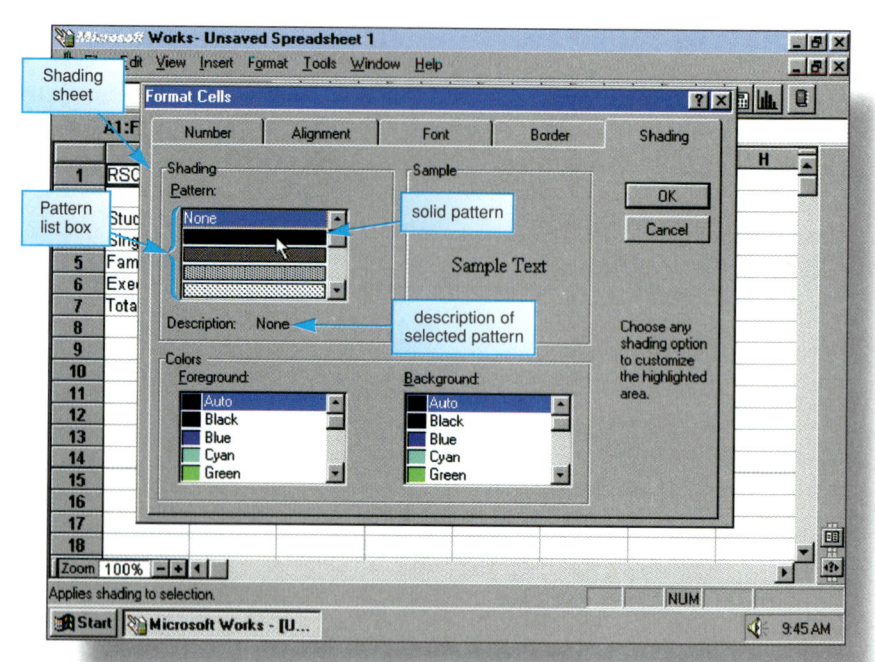

FIGURE 2-44

9 **Click the solid pattern in the Pattern list box. In the Foreground list box, scroll down and point to the color Dark Blue.**

The solid pattern in the Pattern list box is selected (Figure 2-45). The description of the selected pattern displays Solid (100%) below the Pattern list box. The foreground color is the color that will display in the highlighted cells. The mouse pointer points to the color Dark Blue.

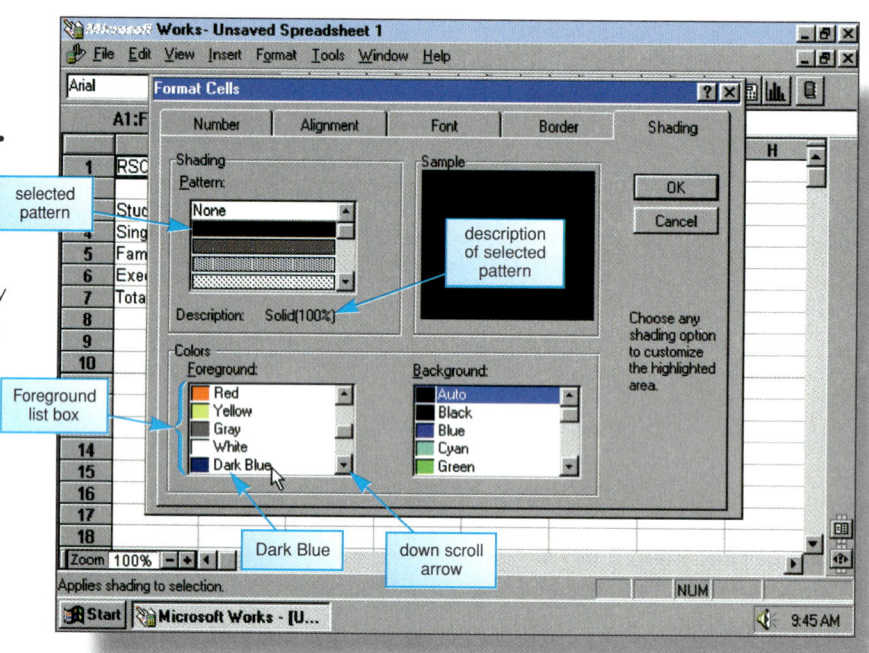

FIGURE 2-45

Microsoft **Works 4** Windows 95

Formatting Text and Changing the Color of Cells • W 2.29

10 **Click Dark Blue. Point to the OK button in the Shading sheet.**

Dark Blue is highlighted in the Foreground list box (Figure 2-46). The solid pattern selected in the Pattern list box changes to dark blue. A preview of the solid pattern, Dark Blue, displays in the Sample box of the Shading sheet. The mouse pointer points to the OK button.

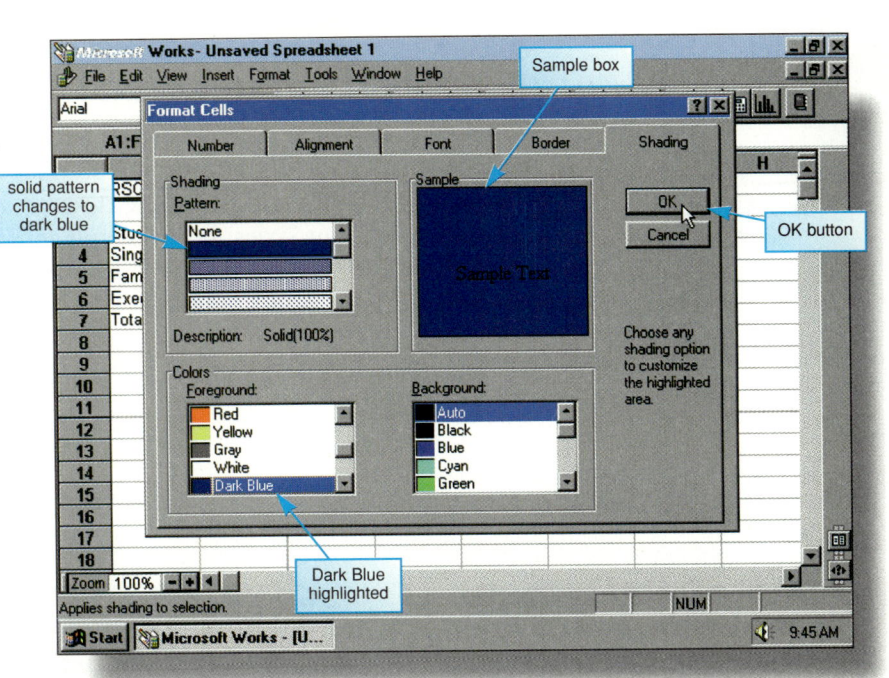

FIGURE 2-46

11 **Click the OK button in the Format Cells dialog box. Click any cell to remove the highlight.**

Works displays the foreground color in cells A1 through F1 in dark blue (Figure 2-47). The title displays in white 18-point Arial font and is centered across columns A through F. Notice that when the font size is increased to 18 point, Works automatically increases the height of row 1 so the enlarged text displays properly.

FIGURE 2-47

> **OtherWays**
> 1. On Format menu click Alignment, Font and Style, Border, or Shading, click OK button

The background color in the Colors box of the Shading sheet (see Figure 2-45) can be used when a pattern other than solid is selected. Patterns other than solid may use both a foreground and background color.

W 2.30 • Project 2 • Building a Spreadsheet and Charting Data

More About AutoFormat

After you apply a format to a highlighted range with the AutoFormat command, you can apply additional formatting. For example, you can increase the thickness of a border or change the foreground shading color of the cells.

Using the AutoFormat Command

Works provides an AutoFormat feature that enables you to format a spreadsheet in a variety of styles without going through a series of individual steps to select color, font and font styles, borders, and so forth. AutoFormat allows you to select one of fifteen different, predefined formats to apply to a spreadsheet. AutoFormat sets the alignment, fonts, patterns, column width, cell height, and borders automatically to match the style option you select.

The following steps explain how to use the Works AutoFormat feature.

Steps   To Use AutoFormat

1 **Highlight cells A2:F7 by dragging the mouse pointer from cell A2 through cell F7. Click Format on the menu bar and then point to AutoFormat.**

Cells A2 through F7 are highlighted (Figure 2-48). The Format menu displays. The mouse pointer points to the AutoFormat command.

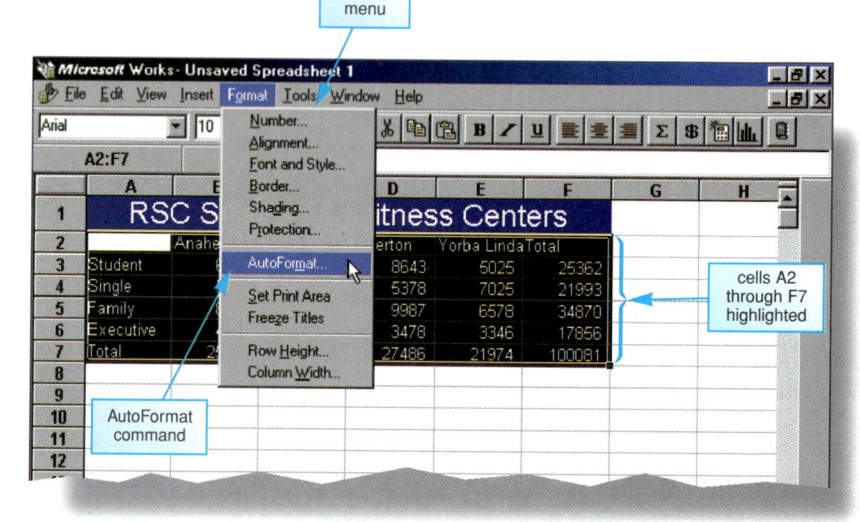

FIGURE 2-48

2 **Click AutoFormat.**

Works displays the AutoFormat dialog box (Figure 2-49). The Select a format list box displays a list of preformatted styles. You can click the down scroll arrow to display additional styles. The Plain style is the default format. A sample of this style displays in the Example box. The Example box shows how the highlighted cells in the spreadsheet will display based on the selection in the Select a format list.

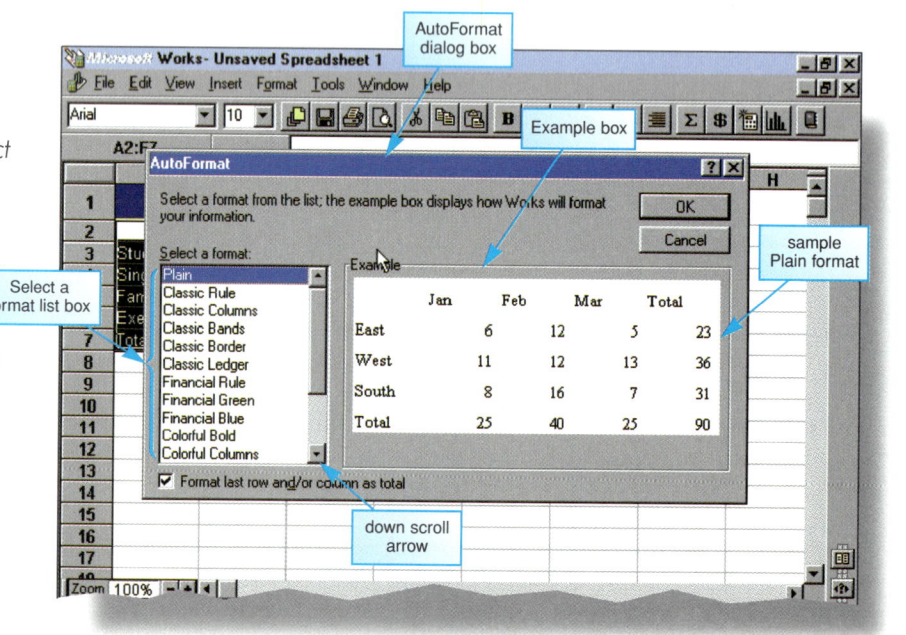

FIGURE 2-49

3 **In the Select a format list box, click Classic Bands. Ensure the Format last row and/or column as total check box displays a check mark. Point to the OK button.**

Works displays a sample of Classic Bands in the Sample box (Figure 2-50). A check mark in the Format last row and/or column as total check box specifies that you want Works to format the last row of the selected range as a total row for easy identification.

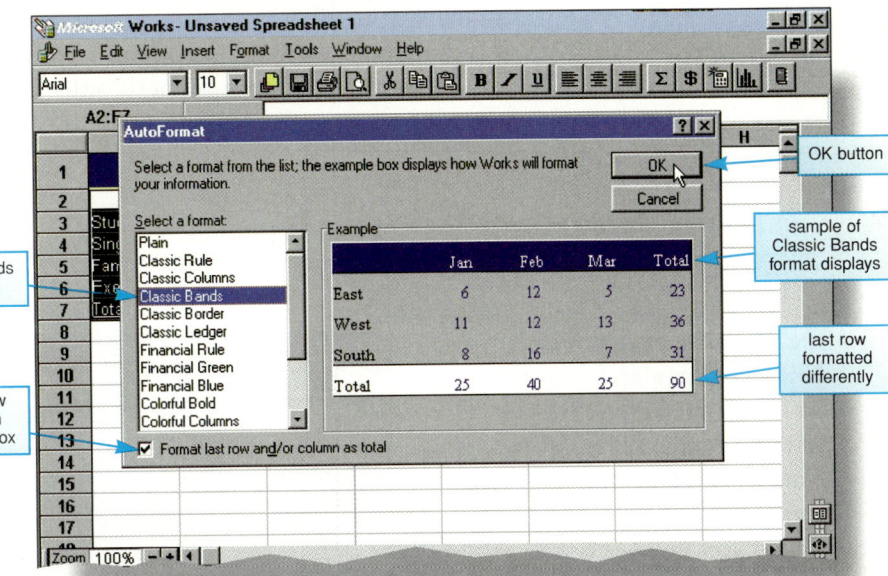

FIGURE 2-50

4 **Choose the OK button in the AutoFormat dialog box. Click any cell to remove the highlight.**

Works applies the predefined format style Classic Bands to the highlighted spreadsheet (Figure 2-51). The spreadsheet displays with the fonts, font styles, colors, and borders as illustrated. Works formats row 7 with a white background color for easy identification.

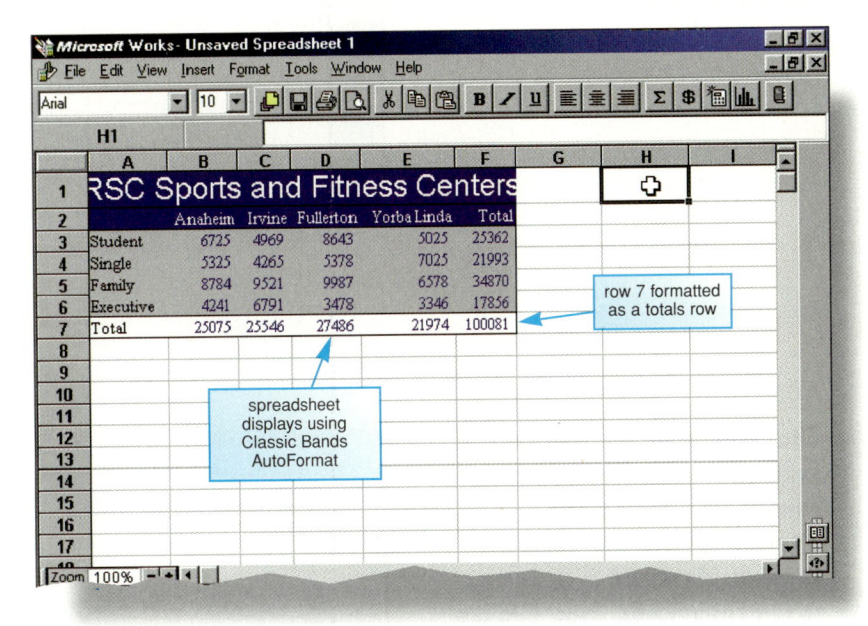

FIGURE 2-51

You can apply additional formatting to the spreadsheet. In Project 2, the numbers in cells B3 through F7 are to contain commas if necessary. This requires additional formatting.

Comma Format

The numeric values in rows 3, 4, 5, 6, and 7 are to be formatted with commas. In Works this requires the use of the Comma format. When you use the **Comma format**, by default, Works places two digits to the right of the decimal point (including zeroes), and a comma separates every three digits to the left of the decimal point. Because the numeric values in rows 3 through 7 are whole

W 2.32 • Project 2 • Building a Spreadsheet and Charting Data

numbers, you will apply the Comma format and specify zero digits to the right of the decimal point and a comma separating every three digits to the left of the decimal point. To format numeric values in the Comma format, complete the following steps.

Steps To Display Numbers with the Comma Format

1 **Highlight the range of cells B3:F7 by dragging from cell B3 to cell F7. Right-click the selected range and point to Format on the context-sensitive menu.**

Cells B3 through F7 are highlighted (Figure 2-52). The context-sensitive menu displays and the mouse pointer points to the Format command.

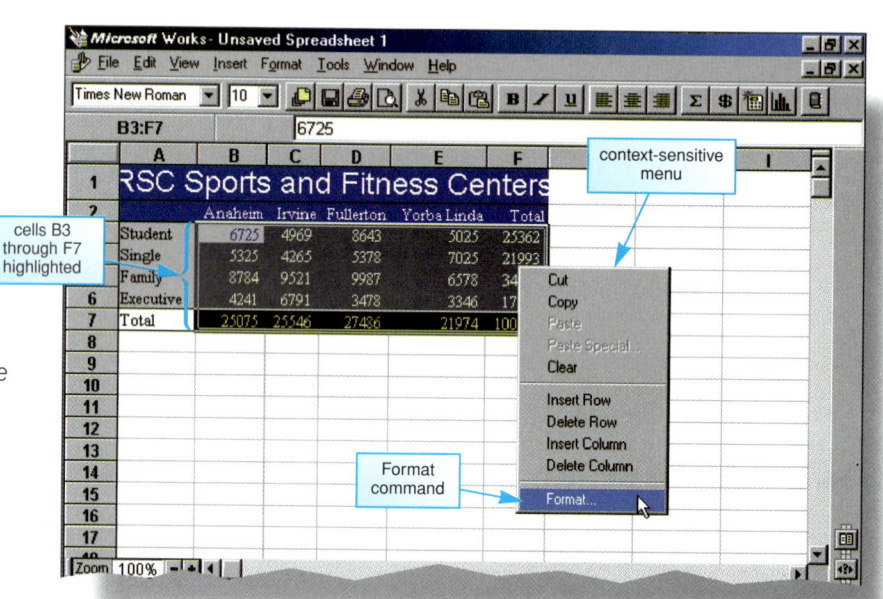

FIGURE 2-52

2 **Click Format on the context-sensitive menu. When the Format Cells dialog box displays, ensure the Number sheet displays and click Comma in the Format box. Type 0 in the Decimal places text box in the Comma box of the Options box. Then, point to the OK button.**

The Comma option button is selected and the mouse pointer points to the OK button (Figure 2-53). The value 0 displays in the Decimal places text box. The Sample box shows how the numbers will display in the cells formatted with the Comma format. The mouse pointer points to the OK button.

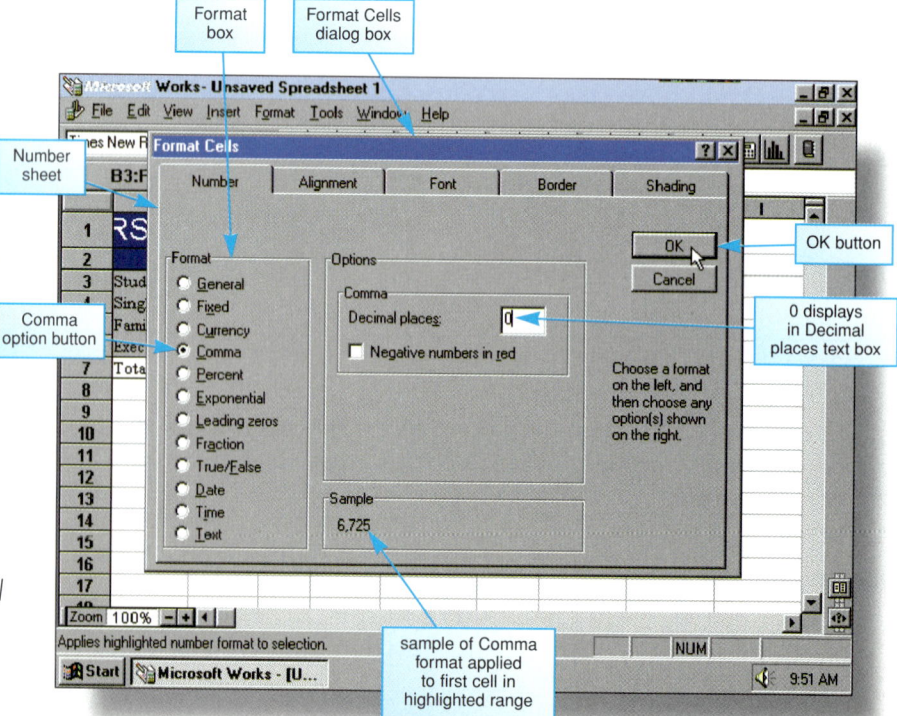

FIGURE 2-53

3 **Click the OK button in the Format Cells dialog box. Click any cell to remove the highlight.**

Works formats the range of cells B3:F7 using the Comma format with commas every three digits to the left (Figure 2-54).

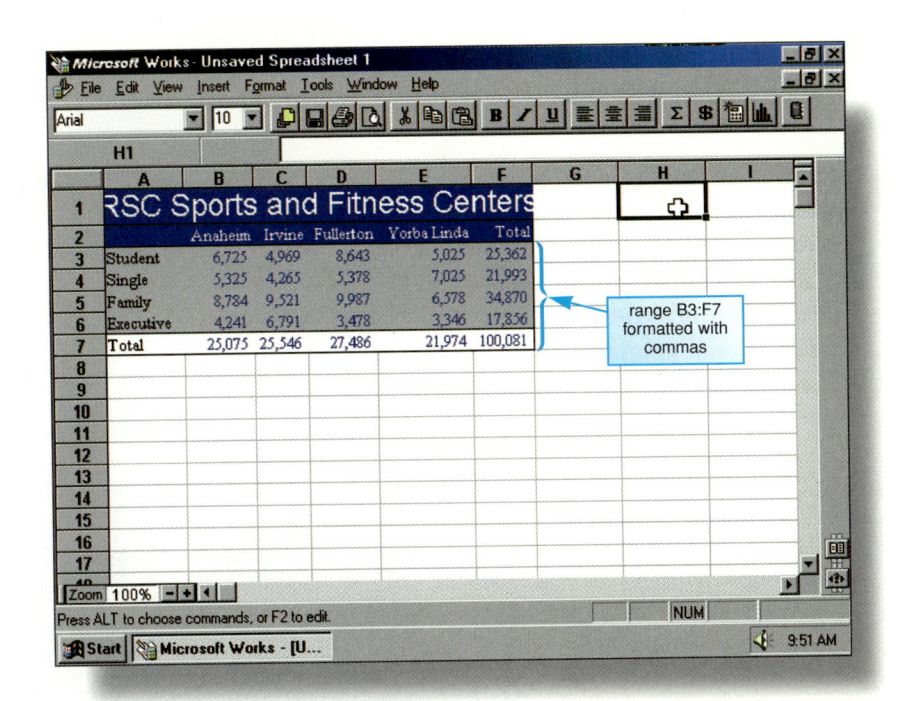

FIGURE 2-54

> **OtherWays**
> 1. On Format menu click Number, click Comma, click OK button
> 2. Press CTRL+, (comma)

Changing Column Widths

The next step in formatting the spreadsheet is to change the column widths. The default column width is ten characters. You change column widths for several reasons. First, changing the column width increases the space between each column and often makes the spreadsheet easier to read. Also, in some instances the values you enter into a cell or the values Works calculates in a cell will not fit in a ten-character wide cell. When this occurs, you must change the width of the column to a size that can accommodate the entry in the cell.

The AutoFormat feature changes column width to a best fit to accommodate the numbers in each of the columns. Adding formatting such as the Comma format may require increasing the column width. In this project when the formatting was changed by adding commas, the columns became too narrow for good readability. Therefore, the column width of columns A through F should be changed to twelve to improve the readability of the spreadsheet.

Works provides the capability to change each column individually or you can change the width of a group of columns. In the following example, the columns will be changed as a group, which requires highlighting all columns to be changed and then choosing the Column Width command from the context-sensitive menu. To complete the task, perform the steps on the next two page.

W 2.34 • Project 2 • Building a Spreadsheet and Charting Data

Steps   To Change Column Widths

1 **Position the mouse pointer on column heading A and drag across column headings B, C, D, E, and F to highlight columns A through F. Right-click the selection and point to Column Width on the context-sensitive menu.**

Columns A through F are highlighted (Figure 2-55). The context-sensitive menu displays and the mouse pointer points to the Column Width command.

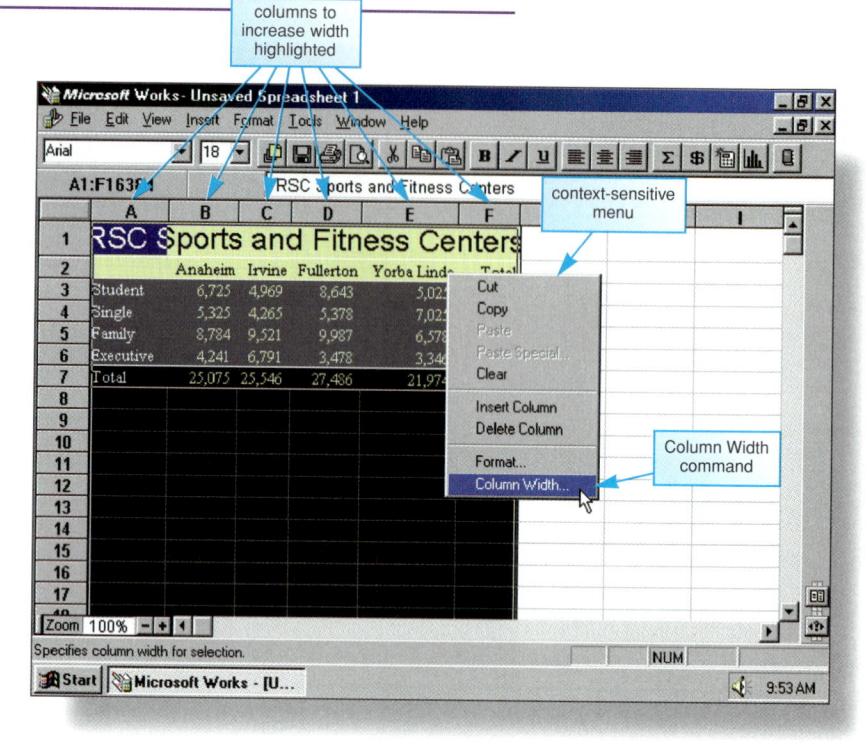

FIGURE 2-55

2 **Click Column Width. When the Column Width dialog box displays, type 12 in the Column width text box. Point to the OK button.**

Works displays the Column Width dialog box (Figure 2-56). The number 12 has been typed in the Column width text box. The mouse pointer points to the OK button.

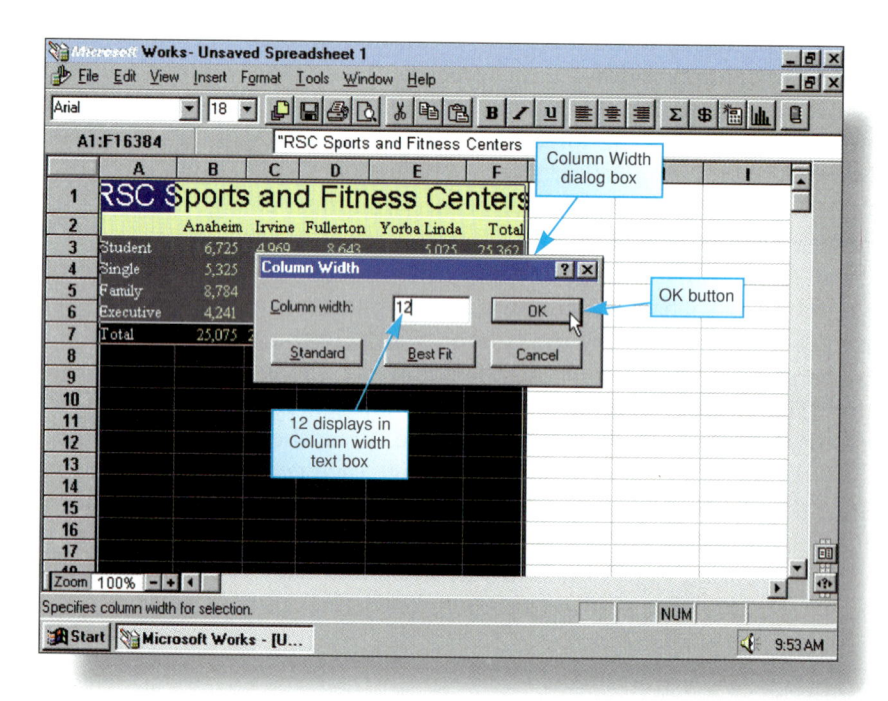

FIGURE 2-56

Saving a Spreadsheet • W 2.35

3 **Click the OK button in the Column Width dialog box. Click any cell to remove the highlight.**

Works makes columns A through F twelve characters wide (Figure 2-57). Notice most of column G and all of columns H and I have moved off the screen.

FIGURE 2-57

> **OtherWays**
> 1. On Format menu click Column Width, type desired width in Column width text box, click OK button

Works provides a number of methods that can be used to change the column width. To quickly change the width of a single column, place the mouse pointer over the column border (the right or left vertical line in the column label area) and drag. When the column is as large or small as you want, release the mouse button.

To quickly adjust the column width for best fit, double-click the column letter. This will adjust the column width to fit the longest entry in the column. To obtain best fit, you also can click the Best Fit button in the Column Width dialog box. If more than one column is highlighted, Works applies an appropriate width to each column.

If, at a later time, you want to change these columns back to the default value, highlight the desired columns, right-click the selected columns, click Column-Width command, and then click the Standard button in the Column Width dialog box.

Checking the Spelling on the Spreadsheet

The spreadsheet is now complete. All the data is entered and the formatting is complete. You should now check the spelling on the spreadsheet using the **Spelling command** on the Tools menu. To check the spelling, complete the following steps.

TO CHECK SPELLING

Step 1: Click Tools on the menu bar.
Step 2: Click Spelling.
Step 3: If any errors are found, perform the steps to correct the errors.

Saving a Spreadsheet

If you accidentally turn off your computer or if electrical power fails, you will lose all your work on the spreadsheet unless you have saved it on disk. Therefore, after you have worked on a spreadsheet for a period of time, or when you complete the spreadsheet, you should save it on hard disk or a floppy disk. When saving the spreadsheet for the first time, use the **Save button** on the toolbar.

> **More About The Undo Feature**
>
> Remember the Undo feature from the Word Processor tool? It is available with the Spreadsheet tool as well. Click Undo on the Edit menu immediately after performing the operation you want to undo.

W 2.36 • Project 2 • Building a Spreadsheet and Charting Data

You can save a spreadsheet on hard disk or on a floppy disk. In Project 2, you are to save the spreadsheet on a floppy disk located in drive A. You can use the procedure explained below and on the next page, however, for either hard disk or floppy disk.

Steps To Save a Spreadsheet

1 Point to the Save button on the toolbar (Figure 2-58).

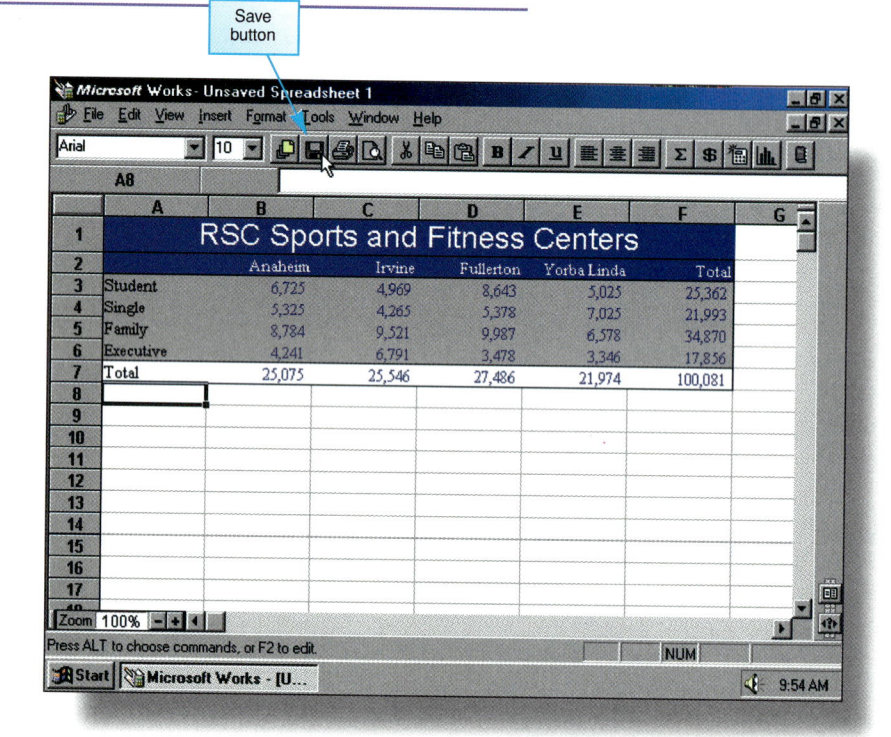

FIGURE 2-58

2 Click the Save button on the toolbar. When the Save As dialog box displays, type RSC Memberships in the File name text box. Click the Save in box arrow. Click the 3½ floppy [A:] icon in the Save in list and then point to the Save button.

Works displays the Save As dialog box (Figure 2-59). The filename you type displays in the File name text box. This is the name Works will use to store the file. Drive A (3½ Floppy [A:]) is selected in the Save In box. The mouse pointer points to the Save button.

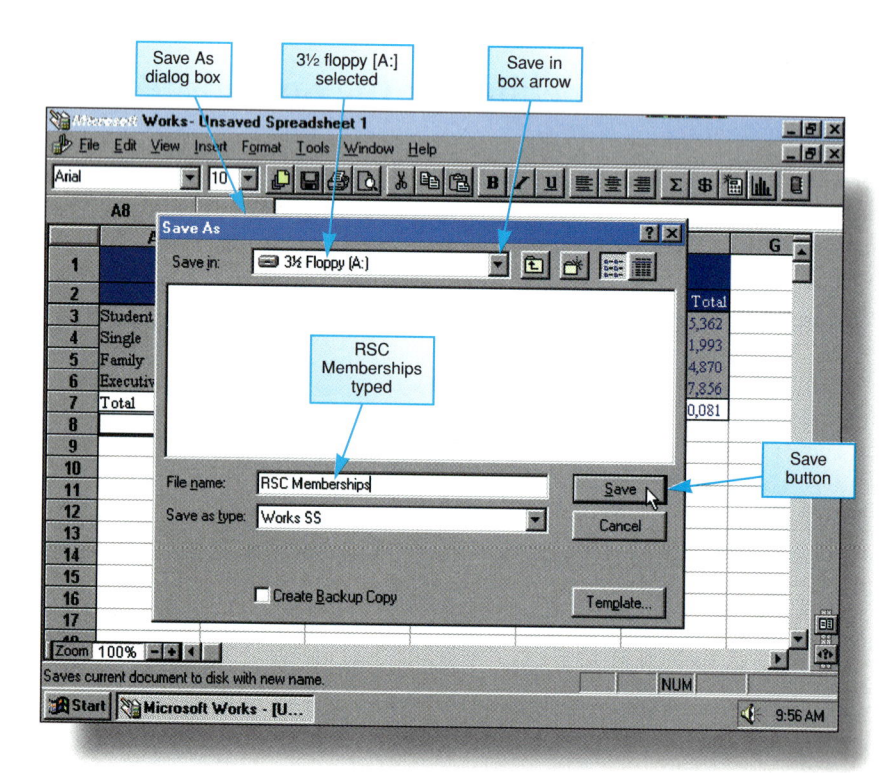

FIGURE 2-59

3 **Click the Save button in the Save As dialog box.**

Works saves the file on the designated disk drive, drive A, and places the filename in the title bar (Figure 2-60).

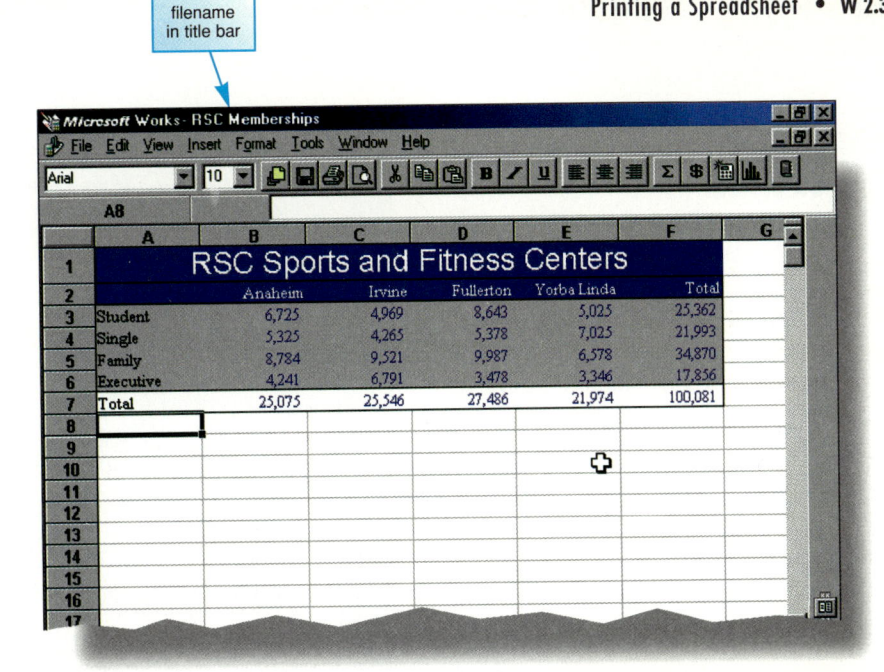

FIGURE 2-60

> **OtherWays**
> 1. On File menu click Save As, enter filename, click OK button
> 2. Press CTRL+S

Printing a Spreadsheet

After you save the spreadsheet, the next step is to print the spreadsheet. To print a spreadsheet, click Print on the File menu, as explained in the steps below and on the next page.

Steps   To Print a Spreadsheet

1 **Click File on the menu bar and then point to Print.**

Works displays the File menu and the mouse pointer points to the Print command (Figure 2-61).

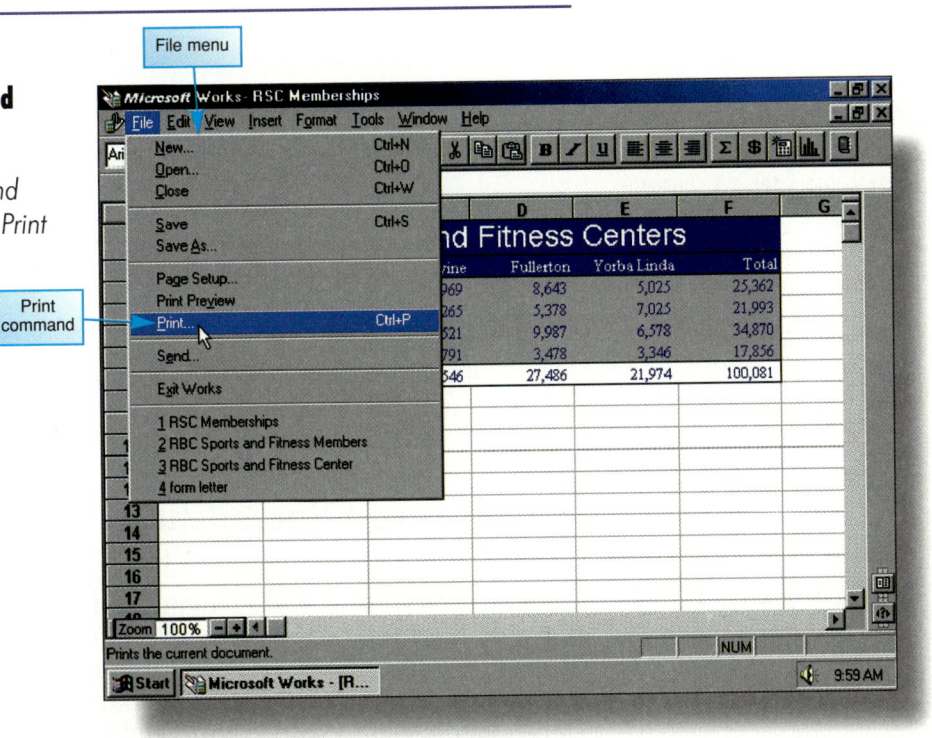

FIGURE 2-61

W 2.38 • Project 2 • Building a Spreadsheet and Charting Data

② Click Print. When the Print dialog box displays, point to the OK button.

Works displays the Print dialog box (Figure 2-62). The default for the dialog box is that one copy of the spreadsheet is to print and all pages in the document are to print.

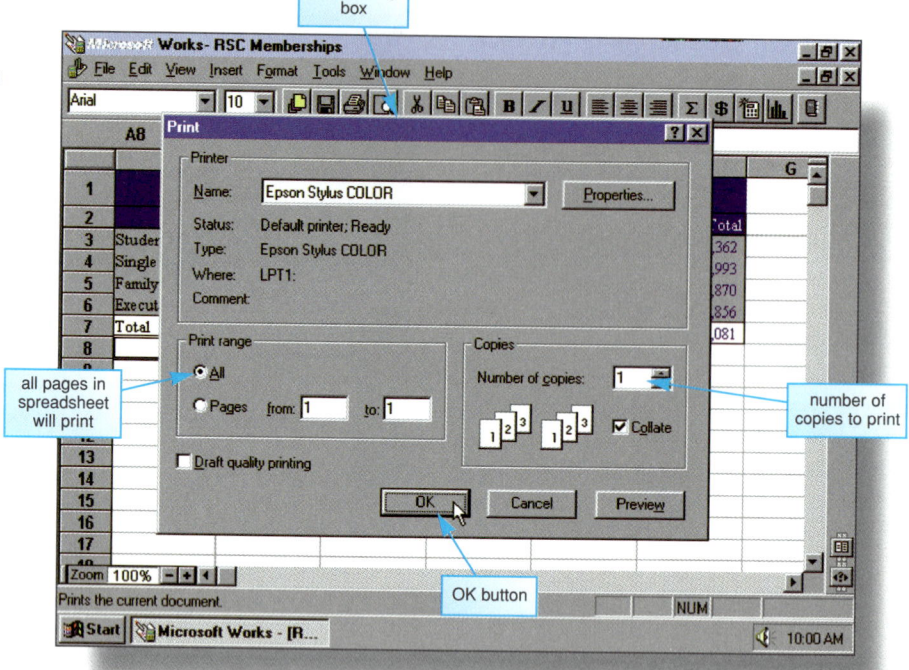

FIGURE 2-62

③ Click the OK button in the Print dialog box.

Works momentarily displays a Printing dialog box. Then, the document is printed on the printer (Figure 2-63).

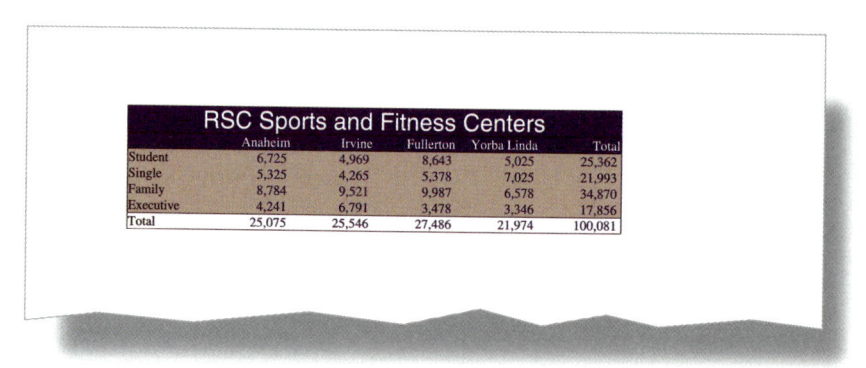

FIGURE 2-63

OtherWays
1. On toolbar, click Print button
2. Press CTRL+P

If a color printer is used, the output will appear as illustrated. If a black and white printer is used, the spreadsheet will print in shades of black, gray, and white.

If you have used the Print command previously and know that proper entries are contained in the Print dialog box, you can click the Print button on the toolbar to cause the spreadsheet to print.

Charting a Spreadsheet

In addition to creating and printing the spreadsheet, Project 2 requires a portion of the data in the spreadsheet to be charted. A **chart** is a graphical representation of the data in the spreadsheet. You are to create a 3-D Bar chart of the memberships for Anaheim, Irvine, Fullerton, and Yorba Linda for each of the four categories (Student, Single, Family, and Executive). With a 3-D Bar chart, memberships are represented by a series of vertical bars that are shaded to give a three-dimensional effect.

Microsoft **Works 4** Windows 95
Charting a Spreadsheet • **W 2.39**

To create the 3-D Bar chart, perform the steps below and on the next page.

Steps: To Create a 3-D Bar Chart

1 **Highlight the cells to be charted (A2:E6) and then point to the New Chart button on the toolbar.**

The highlighted cells include the column titles, row titles, and memberships for Anaheim, Irvine, Fullerton, and Yorba Linda (Figure 2-64). The totals are not included because they do not present meaningful comparisons on a Bar chart. The mouse pointer points to the New Chart button.

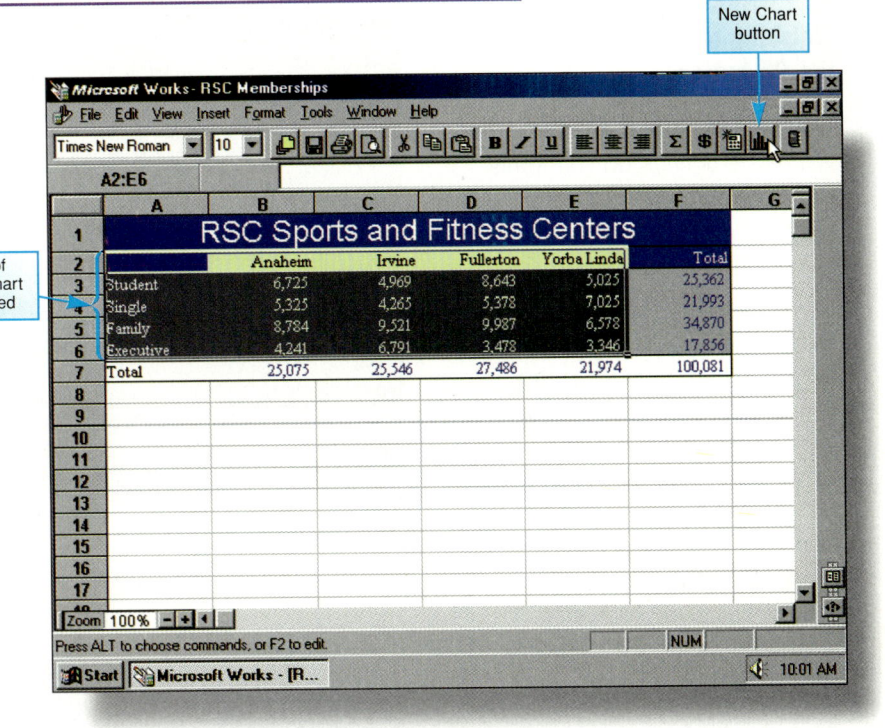

FIGURE 2-64

2 **Click the New Chart button on the toolbar. When the New Chart dialog box displays, point to the 3-D Bar chart in the What type of chart do you want? box located on the Basic Options sheet.**

Works displays the New Chart dialog box (Figure 2-65). Twelve types of charts display in the What type of chart do you want? box on the Basic Options sheet. The Works default chart (Bar chart) is selected. The chart name that is selected (Bar) displays above the chart types. A sample of the chart that will display is shown in the Your Chart box. The mouse pointer points to the 3-D Bar chart.

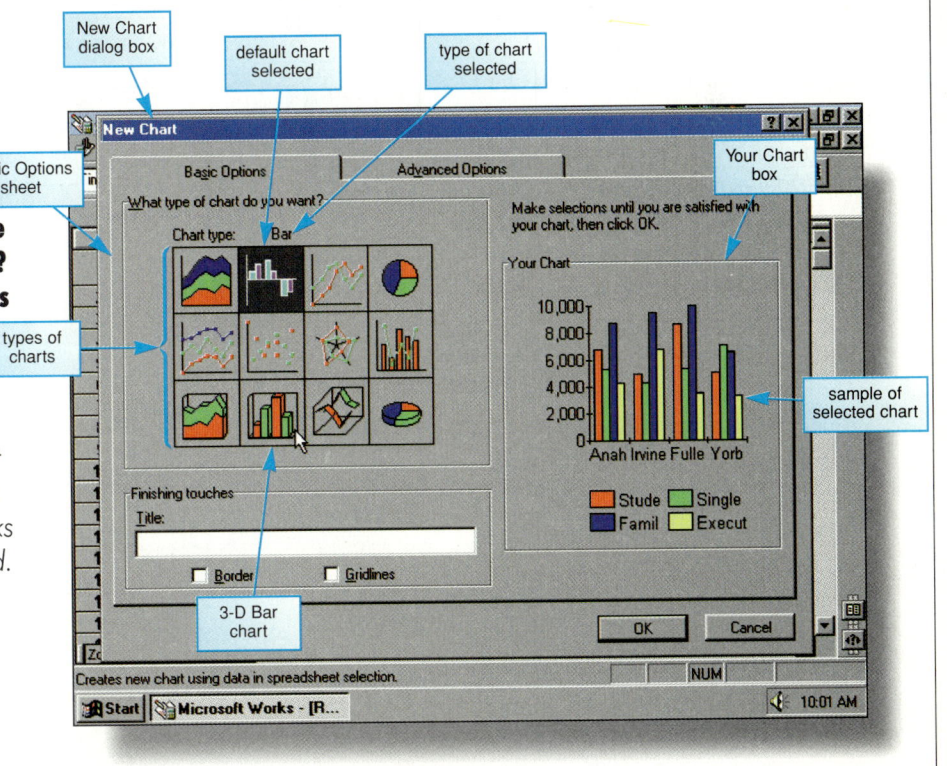

FIGURE 2-65

W 2.40 • Project 2 • Building a Spreadsheet and Charting Data

3 ▶ Click 3-D Bar chart. Press the TAB key and type RSC Sports and Fitness Centers in the Title text box. Click Border, and then click Gridlines located in the Finishing touches box. Point to the OK button.

The 3-D Bar chart is selected in the What type of chart do you want? box (Figure 2-66). The title for the chart displays in the Title box. The check mark in the Border check box instructs Works to place a border around the chart. The check mark in the Gridlines check box informs Works to include gridlines on the chart. The Your Chart box contains a sample of the chart that will display. You can enter a maximum of 39 characters including spaces in the Title box.

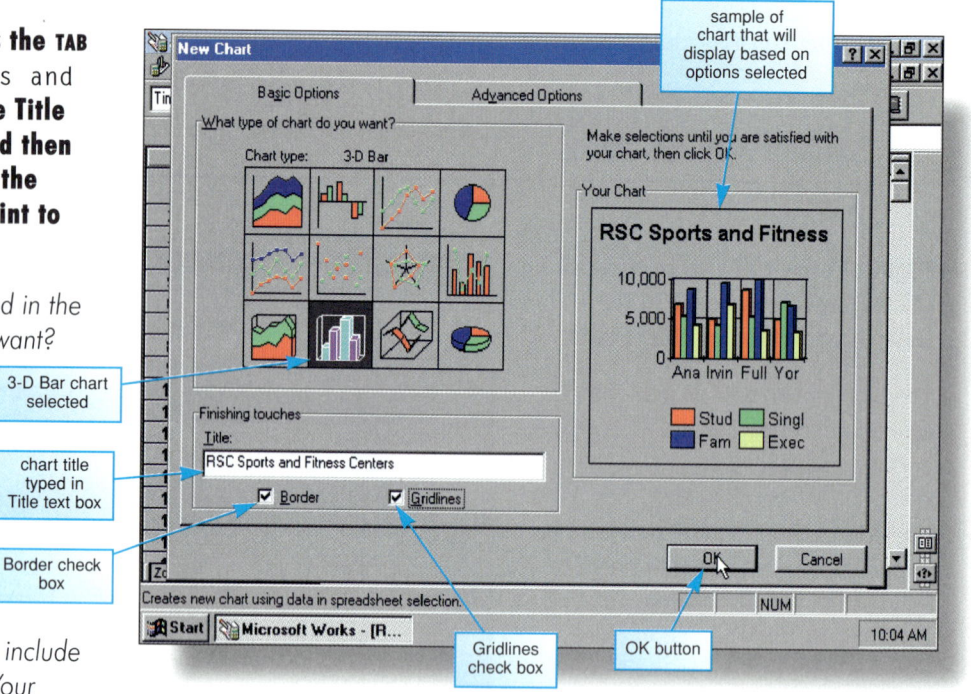

FIGURE 2-66

4 ▶ Click the OK button in the New Chart dialog box.

Works displays the chart with the title RSC Memberships - Chart1 in the title bar (Figure 2-67). The chart title displays centered above the chart. The cluster of bars for each city (Anaheim, Irvine, Fullerton, and Yorba Linda) is called a **category**. All the category labels together are called the **category (X) series**. Each bar (red for Student, green for Single, blue for Family, and yellow for Executive) represents the memberships for each item in the spreadsheet and is called the **Y-series**, or the **value series**. The chart legend indicates the item each color represents. The Charting toolbar displays below the menu bar. The horizontal gridlines originate from each number on the y-axis. The vertical gridlines separate each category on the x-axis. A border displays around the chart.

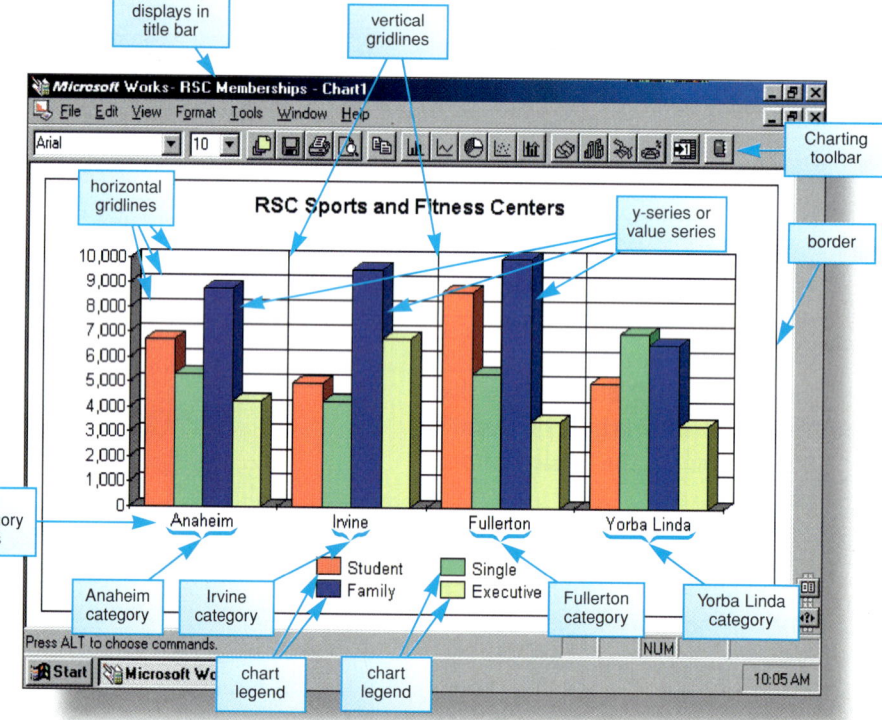

FIGURE 2-67

> ### OtherWays
> 1. On Tools menu click Create New Chart, click 3-D Bar button, click desired options, click OK button

Microsoft **Works 4** Windows 95
Printing the Chart • **W 2.41**

A spreadsheet file can contain a total of eight charts.

To remove the vertical gridlines from the chart, click the Vertical (Y) axis command on the Format menu in the chart window. In the Format Vertical Axis dialog box, remove the check mark from the Show gridlines check box. To remove the horizontal gridlines from the chart, click the Horizontal (X) axis command on the Format menu in the chart window. In the Format Horizontal Axis dialog box, remove the check mark from the Show gridlines check box.

To remove the border around the chart, click the Border command on the Format menu.

Printing the Chart

You can print the chart by clicking the Print button on the Charting toolbar. By default, Works attempts to fill the entire page with the chart when printing. Therefore, if you want to print a chart with proper proportions, you should first click the **Page Setup command** on the File menu and click Screen Size. Works reduces the chart to the size of your computer screen, which is approximately one-quarter page. Then click the Print button on the toolbar. Perform the steps below and on the next two pages to print the chart with the proper proportions.

> **More** *About*
> **Printing a Chart**
>
> If you work with a color monitor but print in black and white, the colors you see on screen are replaced with patterns in black and white. To view the chart as it will appear when printed, click Display as Printed on the View menu. Works displays the chart as it will appear when printed in black and white.

Steps To Print a Chart

1 **Click File on the menu bar and then point to Page Setup.**

Works displays the File menu and the mouse pointer points to the Page Setup command (Figure 2-68).

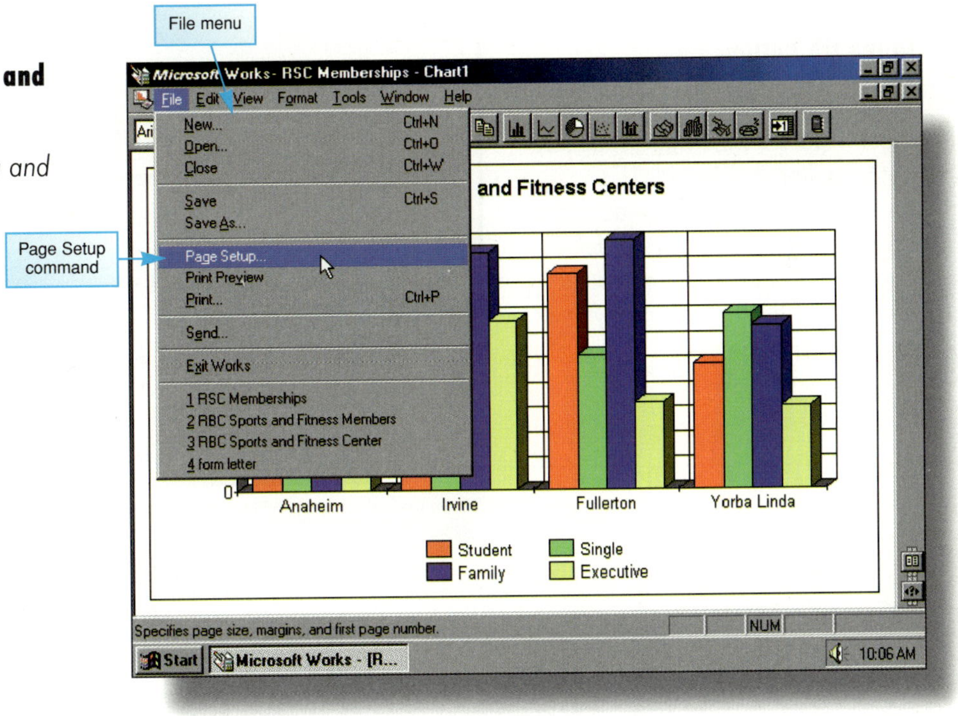

FIGURE 2-68

W 2.42 • Project 2 • Building a Spreadsheet and Charting Data

2 **Click Page Setup. When the Page Setup dialog box displays, point to the Other Options tab.**

The Page Setup dialog box displays and the mouse pointer points to the Other Options tab (Figure 2-69).

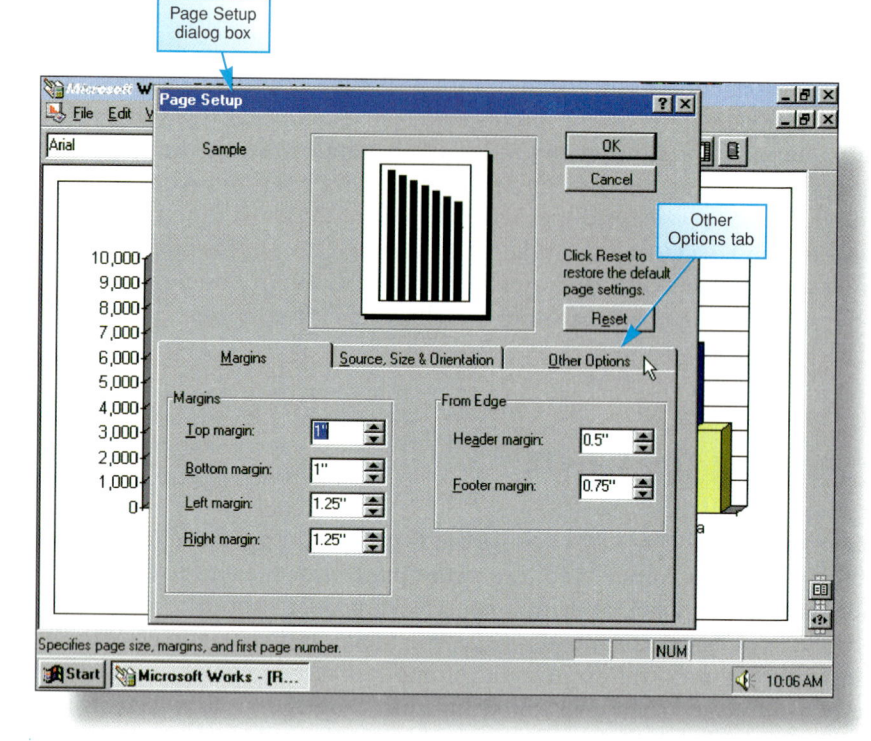

FIGURE 2-69

3 **Click the Other Options tab in the Page Setup dialog box. Click Screen size in the Size box. Point to the OK button.**

Works displays the Other Options sheet (Figure 2-70). The Screen size option button is selected. This option instructs Works to reduce the chart from the default size of full page to the size of your computer screen, which is approximately one-quarter of a page.

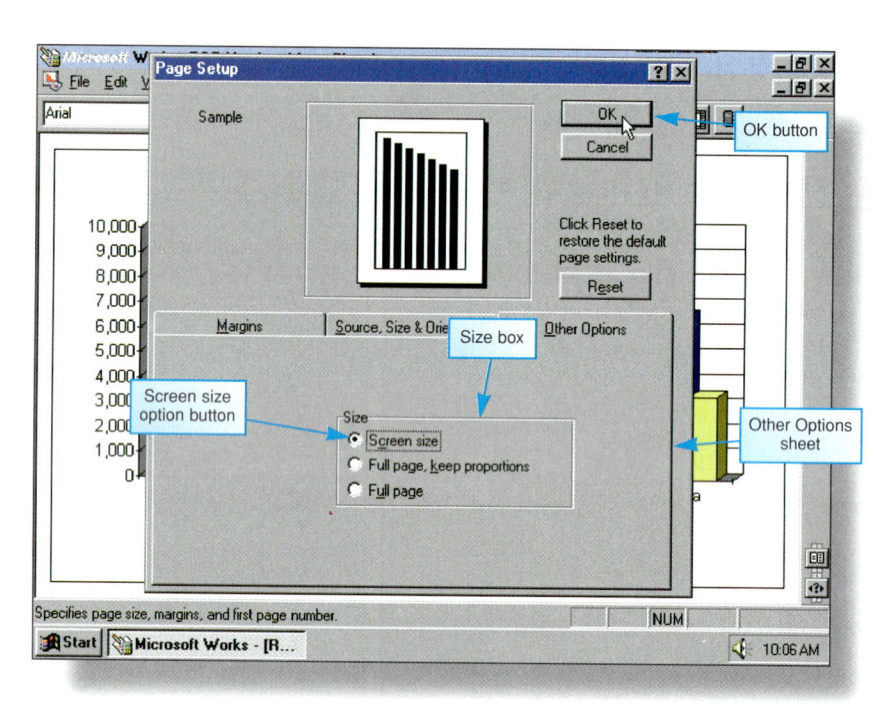

FIGURE 2-70

Microsoft Works 4 Windows 95

Printing the Chart • W 2.43

4 **Click the OK button in the Page Setup dialog box. Point to the Print button on the toolbar.**

Works removes the Page Setup dialog box (Figure 2-71). The mouse pointer points to the Print button on the toolbar.

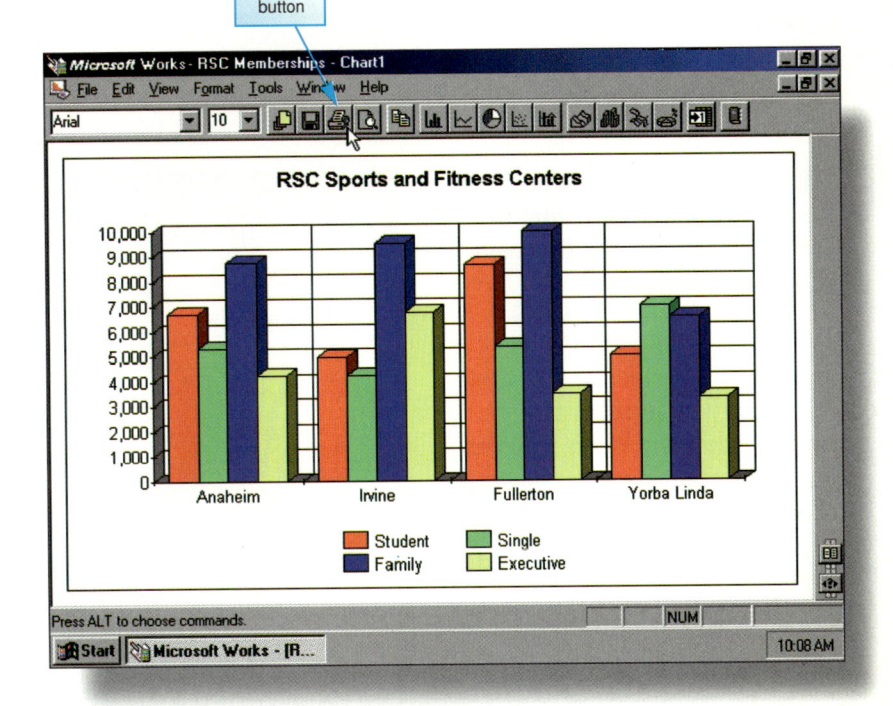

FIGURE 2-71

5 **Click the Print button on the toolbar.**

Works prints the chart on the top one-quarter of the page (Figure 2-72).

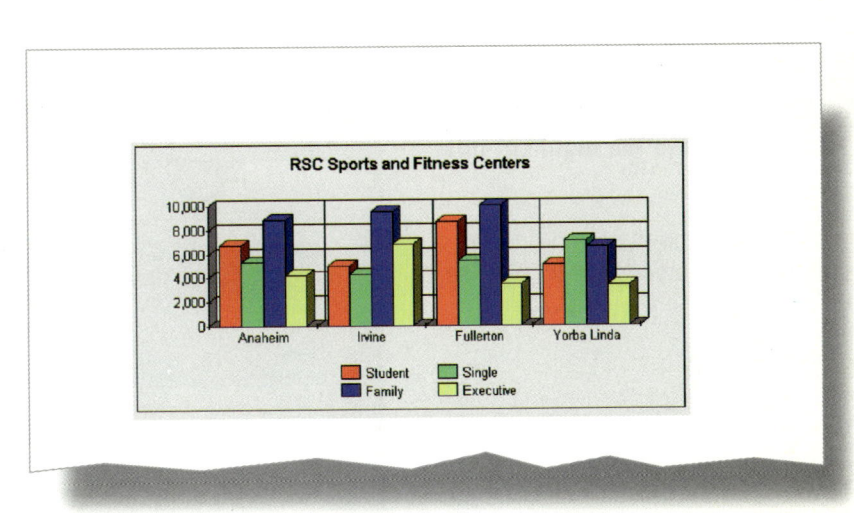

FIGURE 2-72

> **OtherWays**
> 1. On File menu in the chart window, click Print
> 2. Press CTRL+P

Viewing the Spreadsheet

When you create a chart, Works displays the chart window on top of the spreadsheet. To view the spreadsheet, click the filename of the spreadsheet on the Window menu in the chart window as illustrated in the steps on the next page.

W 2.44 • Project 2 • Building a Spreadsheet and Charting Data

Steps: To View the Spreadsheet

1 **Click Window on the menu bar in the chart window and point to RSC Memberships, the filename of the spreadsheet.**

The Window menu displays and lists the open windows in the application (Figure 2-73). The chart is the active window and Works indicates this by the check mark next to the chart name RSC Memberships - Chart1.

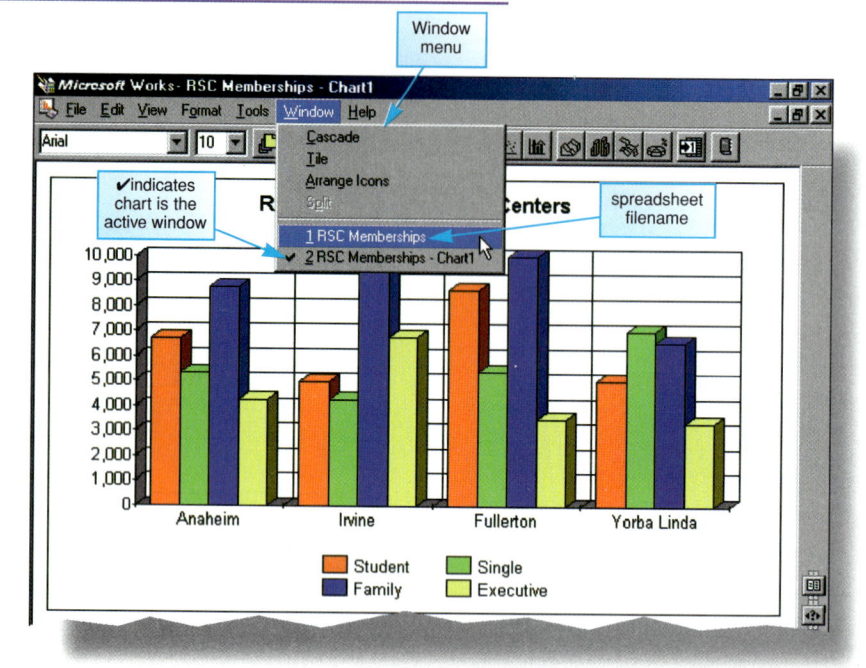

FIGURE 2-73

2 **Click RSC Memberships. Click any cell to remove the highlight from the cells.**

Works displays the spreadsheet and makes the spreadsheet window the active window (Figure 2-74).

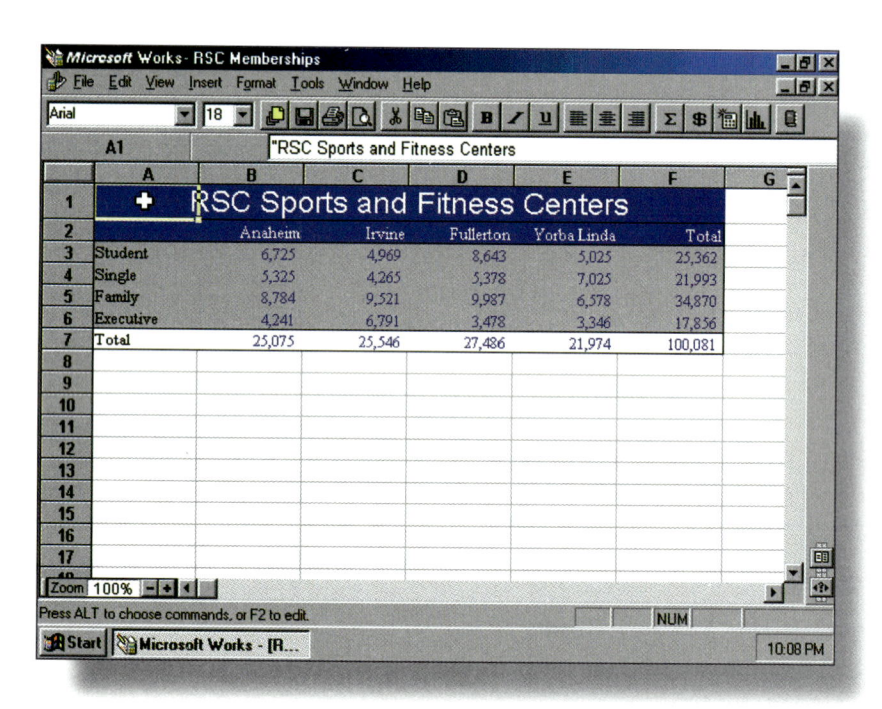

FIGURE 2-74

OtherWays
1. On View menu, click spreadsheet filename

To move back to the chart window, click the chart name on the Window menu.

Saving the Spreadsheet and Chart

If you want to save the chart with the spreadsheet, save the spreadsheet again using techniques previously explained. The chart will be saved with the spreadsheet. To view the chart at a later time (for example, after you have closed the spreadsheet file), open the spreadsheet file and then choose the Chart command from the View menu.

Closing a Spreadsheet

Once you complete the spreadsheet and chart, you can close the spreadsheet and work on another spreadsheet or another Works project. To close the spreadsheet, perform the following steps.

Steps: To Close the Spreadsheet

1 **Point to the Close button in the upper right-hand corner of the spreadsheet window.**

The mouse pointer points to the Close button in the upper right-hand corner of the spreadsheet window (Figure 2-75).

2 **Click the Close button.**

The spreadsheet closes and the Works Task Launcher dialog box displays, allowing you to continue to use Works.

FIGURE 2-75

> **OtherWays**
> 1. On File menu, click Close
> 2. Press CTRL+W
> 3. Press CTRL+F4

You can close a chart without closing the entire spreadsheet file by clicking the Close command from the File menu in the chart window.

If you have made any changes to a spreadsheet after it has been saved, a dialog box appears asking you if you want to save the changes before closing the spreadsheet. Click the Yes button in the dialog box to save changes.

Closing Works

After you have completed all your tasks, normally you will want to close Works and return to the Windows 95 desktop. To close Works, perform the steps on the next page.

Steps **To Close Works**

1 Point to the Close button in the upper right-hand corner of the application window.

The mouse pointer points to the Close button in the upper right-hand corner of the application window (Figure 2-76).

2 Click the Close button.

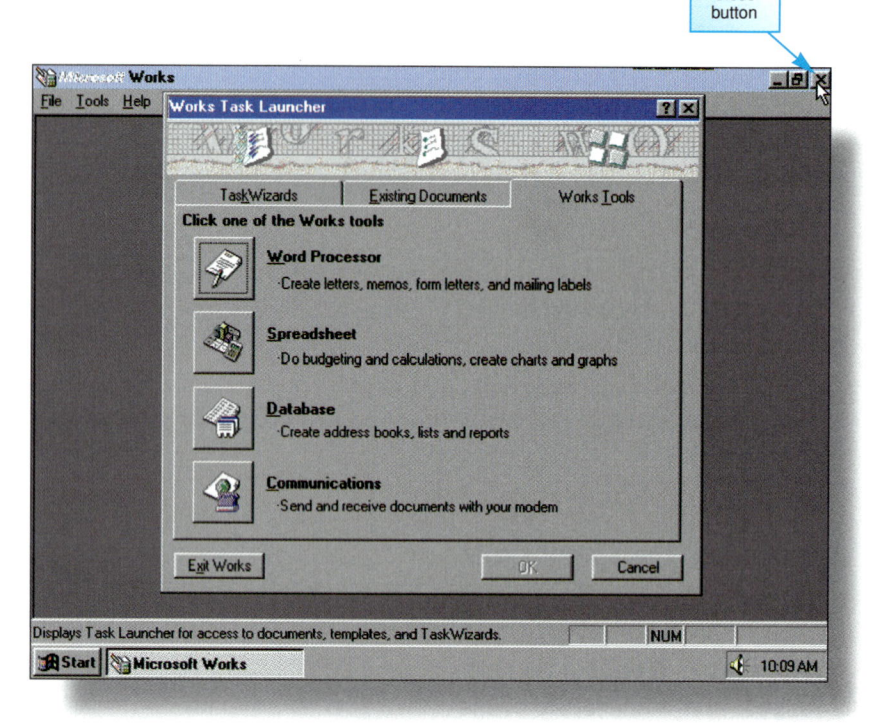

FIGURE 2-76

OtherWays
1. On File menu, click Exit Works
2. In Works Task Launcher dialog box, click Exit Works button
3. Press ALT+F4

Works is terminated, and the Microsoft Windows 95 desktop will again display. If you have made any changes to a spreadsheet after it has been saved, a dialog box appears asking you if you want to save the changes before exiting. Click the Yes button in the dialog box to save changes.

Opening an Existing Spreadsheet File

Once you have saved a spreadsheet on disk, you may need to retrieve the spreadsheet to make changes to it or otherwise process it. To retrieve the spreadsheet, you must open the spreadsheet. Opening a spreadsheet means the spreadsheet is retrieved from the disk into main memory. The easiest way to open an existing document is to use the **My Computer icon** located in the upper left corner of the desktop. Perform the following steps to open an existing spreadsheet.

Microsoft **Works 4** Windows 95

Opening an Existing Spreadsheet File • **W 2.47**

Steps To Open An Existing Spreadsheet File

1 Point to the My Computer icon in the upper left corner of the desktop.

The mouse pointer points to the My Computer icon on the desktop (Figure 2-77).

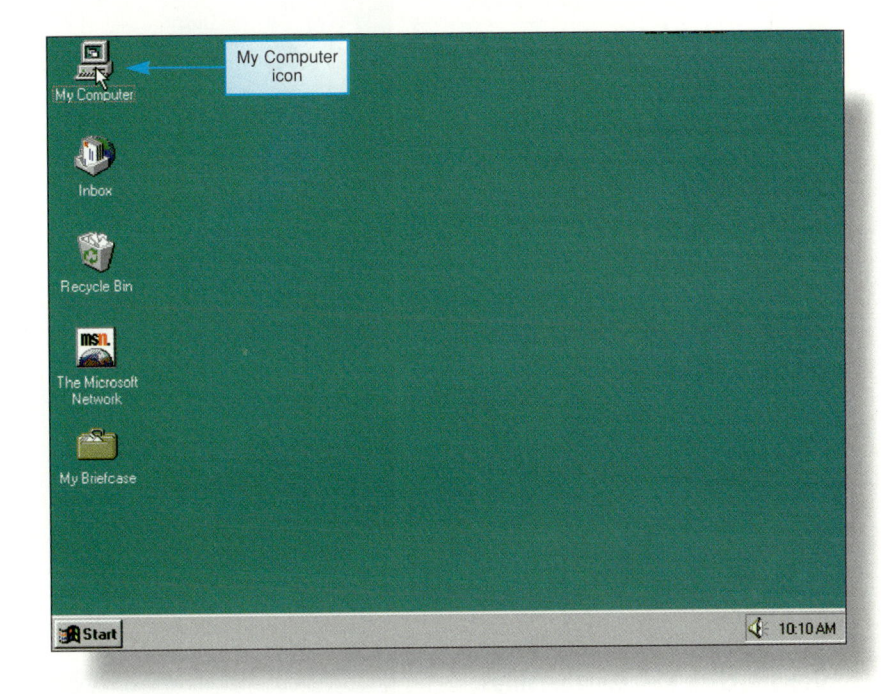

FIGURE 2-77

2 Double-click the My Computer icon. When the My Computer window opens, point to the 3½ Floppy [A:] icon.

When you double-click the My Computer icon, Windows 95 opens the My Computer window (Figure 2-78). The My Computer window contains icons representing the hard disk, floppy disk drive, CD-ROM drive, and two folder icons. Drive A in Figure 2-78 is a 3½ floppy disk drive. The icons that display on your screen may be different. The mouse pointer points to the 3½ Floppy [A:] icon.

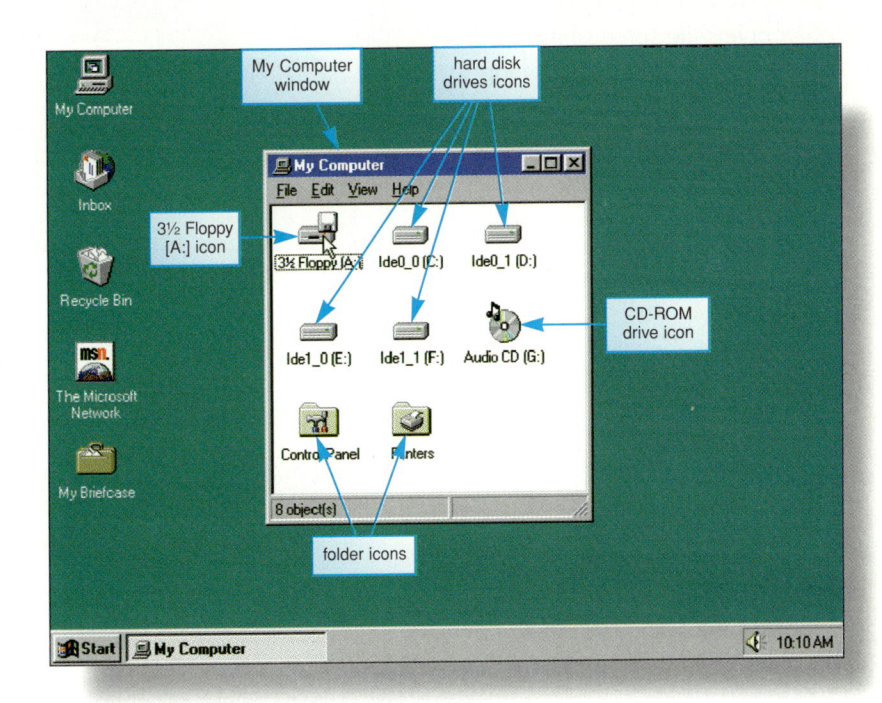

FIGURE 2-78

W 2.48 • Project 2 • Building a Spreadsheet and Charting Data

3 **Double-click the 3½ Floppy [A:] icon. When the 3½ Floppy [A:] window opens, point to the RSC Memberships icon.**

When you double-click the 3½ Floppy [A:] icon, Windows 95 opens the 3½ Floppy [A:] window (Figure 2-79) and displays the filenames on drive A. The mouse pointer points to the RSC Memberships icon. The charting icon identified with the file indicates the file is a spreadsheet.

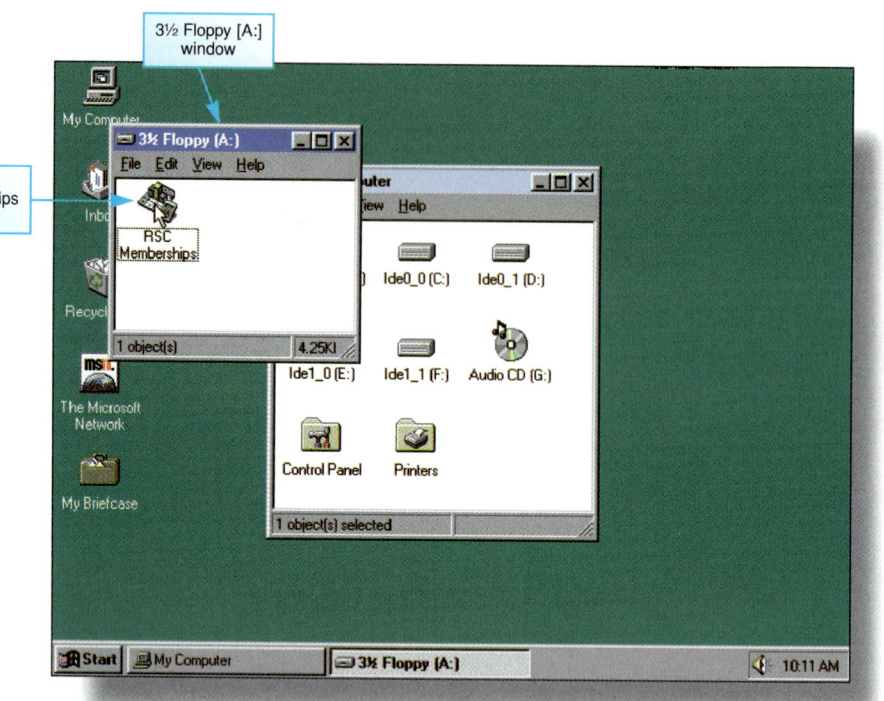

FIGURE 2-79

4 **Double-click RSC Memberships.**

Windows 95 first starts Works and then opens the spreadsheet, RSC Memberships, and displays it on the screen (Figure 2-80). You can revise or print the spreadsheet as required.

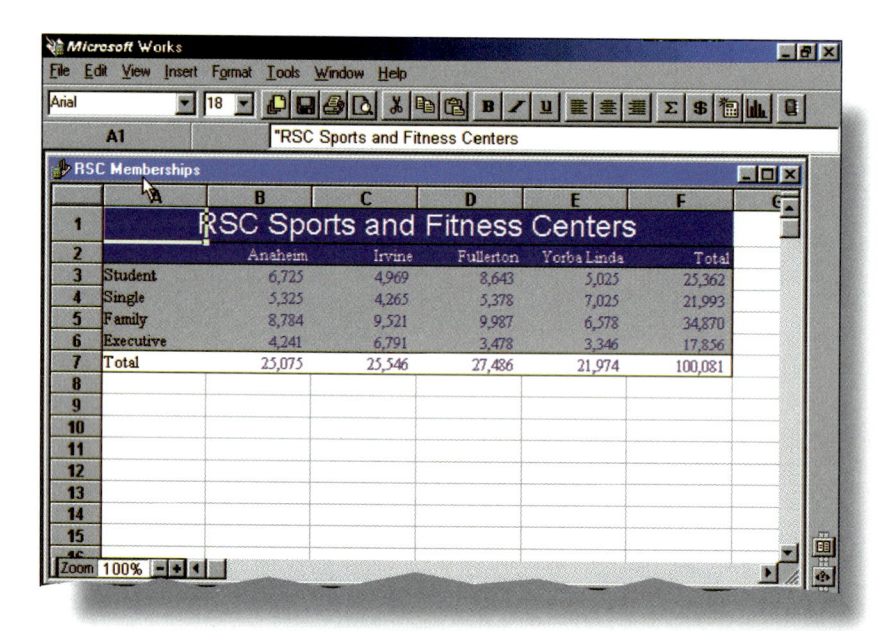

FIGURE 2-80

OtherWays
1. On toolbar click Task Launcher button, click Existing Documents tab, click desired document, click OK button
2. On File menu click Open, click desired document, click Open button
3. Press CTRL+O

You also can click one of the filenames at the bottom of the File menu to open that file.

Correcting Errors

When you create a spreadsheet, the possibility exists that you may make an error by entering the wrong text or data in a cell. In addition, it is possible that you must change a value in a cell even though it was correct when you entered it.

Works provides several methods for changing data in a spreadsheet and correcting errors. These methods are explained below.

Correcting Errors Prior to Entering Data into a Cell

If you notice an error in the entry bar prior to confirming the entry and entering the data into a cell, do one of the following:

1. Use the BACKSPACE key to erase back to the error and then type the correct characters. If the error is too severe, click the Cancel box in the entry bar or press the ESC key to erase the entire entry in the entry bar and reenter the data from the beginning.

Editing Data in a Cell

If you notice an error in the spreadsheet after confirming the entry and entering the data, highlight the cell with the error and use one of the following methods to correct the error.

1. If the entry is short, retype it and click the ENTER box or press the ENTER key. The new entry will replace the old entry. Remember that you must highlight the cell containing the error before you begin typing.
2. If the entry in the cell is long and the errors are minor, you may want to edit the entry rather than retype it. To edit an entry in a cell:
   a. Highlight the cell containing the error.
   b. Click the first character in error in the entry bar. Works places the insertion point at the location you clicked in the entry bar.
   c. Make your changes.

When you type characters in the entry bar, Works inserts the character and moves all characters one position to the right.

To delete a character in the entry bar, place the insertion point to the left of the character you want to delete and then press the DELETE key, or place the insertion point to the right of the character you want to delete and then press the BACKSPACE key.

While the insertion point is located in the entry bar, you may have occasion to move it to various points in the bar. Table 2-1 illustrates the means for moving the insertion point in the entry bar.

> **More** *About*
> **Saving a Works Spreadsheet**
>
> When saving a Works spreadsheet for the first time, check to make sure that Works SS is displayed in the Save as type box. If it is not displayed, click the Save as type down arrow and click Works SS.

TABLE-2-1

TASK	MOUSE	KEYBOARD
Move the Insertion Point to the Beginning of Text	Click to left of first character	Press HOME
Move the Insertion Point to the End of Text	Click to right of last character	Press END
Move the Insertion Point One Character to the Left	Click one character to left	Press LEFT ARROW
Move the Insertion Point One Character to the Right	Click one character to right	Press RIGHT ARROW
Move the Insertion Point Anywhere in the Entry Bar	Click entry bar at appropriate position	Press LEFT ARROW or RIGHT ARROW
Highlight One or More Characters	Drag mouse pointer over the characters	Press SHIFT+LEFT ARROW or SHIFT+RIGHT ARROW
Delete Highlighted Characters	None	Press DELETE

When you have finished editing an entry, click the Enter box or press the ENTER key.

Understanding how to correct errors or change entries in a spreadsheet is an important skill.

Clearing a Cell or Range of Cells

It is not unusual to enter data into the wrong cell or range of cells. In such a case, to correct the error you may want to delete, or clear, the data. Never highlight a cell and press the SPACEBAR to enter a blank character and assume you have cleared the cell. A blank character is text and is different from an empty cell even though the cell may appear empty.

Works provides a variety of methods to clear the contents of a cell or a range of cells. The various methods are explained in the following paragraphs.

TO CLEAR CELL CONTENTS — DELETE KEY

Step 1: Highlight the cell or range of cells.
Step 2: Press the DELETE key.

TO CLEAR CELL CONTENTS — EDIT MENU AND CLEAR COMMAND

Step 1: Highlight the cell or range of cells.
Step 2: Click Edit on the menu bar and click Clear.

TO CLEAR CELL CONTENTS — EDIT MENU AND CUT COMMAND OR CUT BUTTON

Step 1: Highlight the cell or range of cells.
Step 2: Click Edit on the menu bar and click Cut; or click the Cut button on the toolbar.

Each of these methods has differences you should understand. In the first method, when you press the DELETE key, the data in the cell or cells is cleared but the formatting remains. Thus, even after you clear the cells using the DELETE key, formatting such as dollar formats, bold, italic, underlining, and so on remain. To clear the formatting, you must individually turn off each of the formatting features or use the Cut command for clearing the cells.

When you use the Edit menu and Clear command, the data in the cell or range of cells is cleared, but the formatting remains. This method has the same effect as using the DELETE key.

When you use the Cut command from the Edit menu or click the Cut button on the toolbar, Works clears both the data and the formatting from the cell or range of cells. Actually, the data and the associated formatting are placed on the Windows Clipboard for potential pasting elsewhere, but if you never paste the data into the same or another Works document, in effect, the data and formatting have been entirely cleared from the spreadsheet.

Clearing the Entire Spreadsheet

Sometimes so many major errors are made with a spreadsheet that it is easier to start over. To clear an entire spreadsheet, follow these steps.

TO CLEAR THE ENTIRE SPREADSHEET

Step 1: Highlight the entire spreadsheet by clicking the box located just above row 1 and immediately to the left of column A, or click Select All on the Edit menu.

Step 2: Follow any of the three methods specified previously to clear the cell contents. The method used should be based on whether you want the formatting to remain.

An alternative to the previous steps is to click Close on the File menu and not save the spreadsheet. Works closes the spreadsheet. You can then click the Spreadsheet button in the Works Task Launcher dialog box to begin working on your new spreadsheet.

Project Summary

In this project, you have learned to start the Microsoft Works Spreadsheet tool, enter both text and numeric data into the spreadsheet, calculate the sum of numeric values in both rows and columns, and copy formulas to adjacent cells in both rows and columns. In addition, you have seen how to display the title centered across columns, display the title with color, and you learned how to use the AutoFormat feature to format a spreadsheet. Using the steps and techniques presented, you changed column widths and formatted numeric data in the Comma format.

Next, you learned to save a spreadsheet, print a spreadsheet, create a chart from spreadsheet data, print the chart, and open a spreadsheet. Finally, after completing the project, you know how to correct errors on the spreadsheet.

What You Should Know

Having completed this project, you should now be able to perform the following tasks:

- Change Column Widths *(W 2.33)*
- Clear Cell Contents *(W 2.50)*
- Clear the Entire Spreadsheet *(W 2.51)*
- Close the Spreadsheet *(W 2.45)*
- Close Works *(W 2.45)*
- Copy One Cell to Adjacent Cells in a Column *(W 2.23)*
- Copy One Cell to Adjacent Cells in a Row *(W 2.20)*
- Create a 3-D Bar Chart *(W 2.39)*
- Display Numbers with the Comma Format *(W 2.32)*
- Enter Column Titles *(W 2.14)*
- Enter Numeric Data *(W 2.16)*
- Enter Row Titles *(W 2.15)*
- Enter the Spreadsheet Title *(W 2.12)*
- Format Text and Change the Color of Cells *(W 2.24)*
- Open an Existing Spreadsheet File *(W 2.46)*
- Print a Chart *(W 2.41)*
- Print a Spreadsheet *(W 2.37)*
- Save a Spreadsheet *(W 2.35)*
- Start the Works Spreadsheet *(W 2.6)*
- Sum a Column of Numbers Using the AutoSum Button *(W 2.18)*
- Sum a Row of Numbers Using the AutoSum button *(W 2.22)*
- Use the AutoFormat command *(W 2.30)*
- View the Spreadsheet *(W 2.43)*

Test Your Knowledge

1 True/False

Instructions: Circle T if the statement is true or F if the statement is false.

T F 1. You can start the Works Spreadsheet by clicking the Spreadsheet button in the Works Task Launcher dialog box.
T F 2. The intersection of each column and each row is a cell.
T F 3. A Works spreadsheet contains a total of 256 columns and 8,192 rows.
T F 4. If text you enter in a cell contains more characters than can be displayed in the width of the cell, the overflow characters will always display in adjacent cells to the right.
T F 5. Works enters numbers right-aligned in cells.
T F 6. When using the AutoSum button to sum a column or row of values, Works always highlights the correct range to sum.
T F 7. You can use the fill handle to copy the contents of one cell to adjacent cells in a column or row.
T F 8. To quickly adjust the column width for best fit, double-click the cell displaying the largest entry in the column.
T F 9. To print a spreadsheet, click the Print button on the Charting toolbar.
T F 10. Clicking Close on the File menu in the chart window closes the spreadsheet file and displays the Works Task Launcher.

2 Multiple Choice

Instructions: Circle the correct response.

1. A _____ is a block of adjacent cells in a spreadsheet.
   a. group b. highlight c. chart d. range
2. To enter numbers into a cell, the cell must be _____.
   a. empty
   b highlighted
   c. defined as a number
   d. formatted with the Comma format
3. To change a cell's background color, click _____.
   a. Format on the context-sensitive menu
   b. Color on the Format menu
   c. Format cells on the Format menu
   d. the Format button on the toolbar
4. Works enters numbers _____-aligned in a cell.
   a. left b. center c. right d. decimal
5. After highlighting a range to chart, clicking the New Chart button on the toolbar will display _____.
   a. a 2-D Bar chart
   b. a 3-D Bar chart
   c. the New Chart dialog box
   d. a blank chart window with a Charting toolbar

Test Your Knowledge

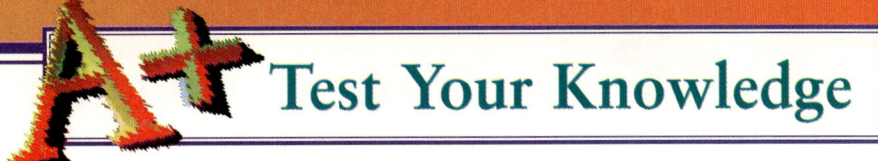

6. A chart title may contain up to _____ characters including spaces.
   a. 20   b. 30   c. 39   d. 40
7. You can save up to _____ charts for each spreadsheet.
   a. two   b. six   c. eight   d. ten
8. To print a chart, _____.
   a. click Print on the File menu in the charting window
   b. click the Print button in the spreadsheet window
   c. click Print on the File menu in the spreadsheet window
   d. press CTRL+P in the spreadsheet window
9. To delete a character in the entry bar, _____.
   a. place the insertion point at the right of the character to delete and then click the Cancel button
   b. place the insertion point to the left of the character to delete and then press the BACKSPACE key
   c. place the insertion point to the left of the character to delete and then press the SPACEBAR
   d. place the insertion point to the right of the character to delete and then press the BACKSPACE key
10. To clear both the data and the formatting from a cell, click _____.
    a. the DELETE key
    b. the Cut button on the toolbar
    c. Clear on the Edit menu
    d. the BACKSPACE key

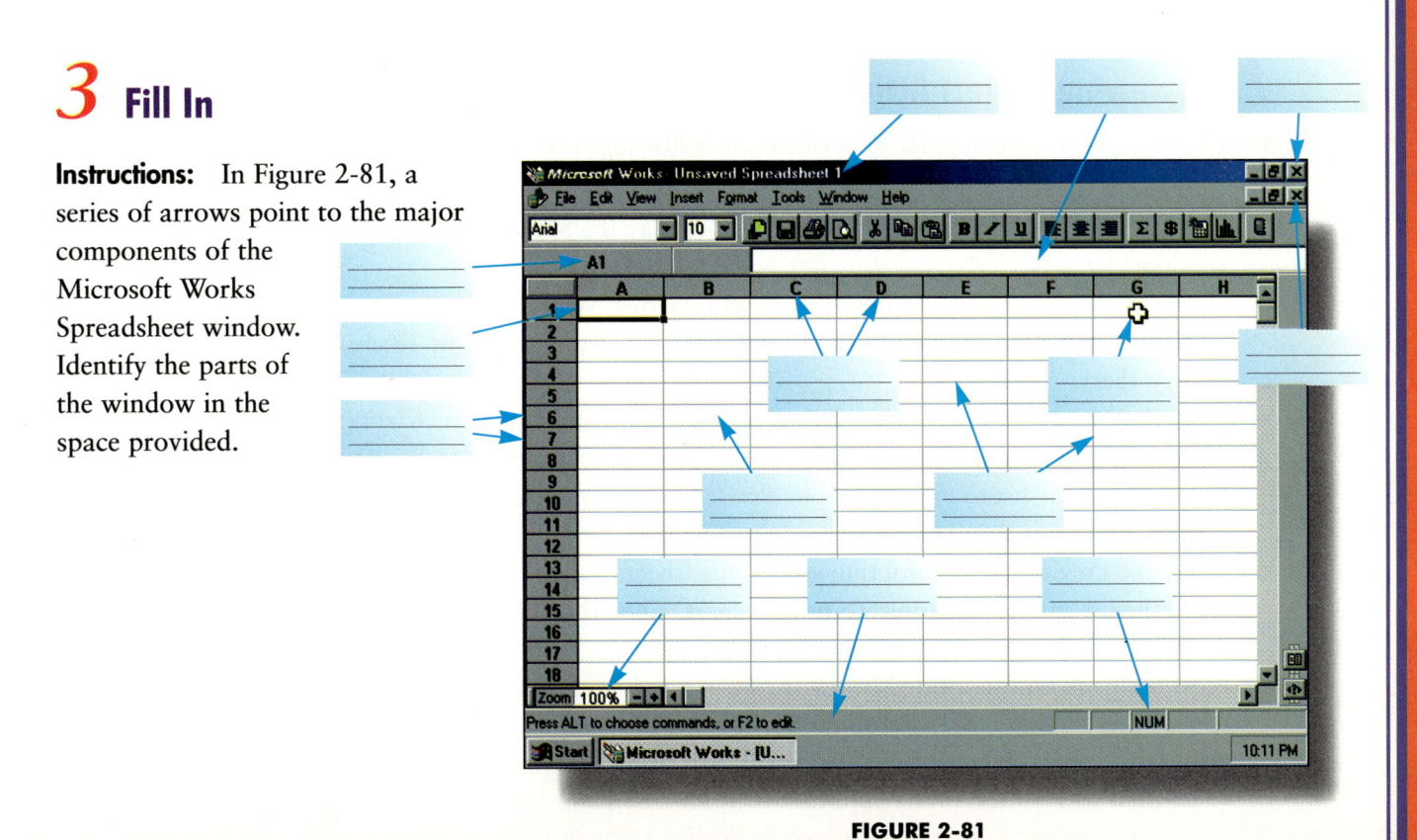

3 Fill In

Instructions: In Figure 2-81, a series of arrows point to the major components of the Microsoft Works Spreadsheet window. Identify the parts of the window in the space provided.

FIGURE 2-81

Test Your Knowledge

4 Fill In

Instructions: Write the appropriate command or button name to accomplish each task.

TASK	COMMAND OR BUTTON NAME
Display a chart	_____
Change a cell's background color	_____
Save a new spreadsheet	_____
Create a chart	_____
Add a column of numbers	_____
Apply the Comma format to a cell	_____
Change text color	_____
Center text across columns	_____
Print a spreadsheet	_____
Print a chart	_____
Close a spreadsheet	_____

Use Help

1 Reviewing Project Activities

Instructions: Use your computer to perform the following tasks to obtain experience using online Help.

1. Start the Microsoft Works Spreadsheet tool.
2. Click the Shrink Help button if necessary to display the Spreadsheet and Charting Menu in the Help window.
3. Click Create a chart in the Spreadsheet and Charting Menu. When the Creating a chart topic displays in the Help window, click To create a chart. Read and print To create a chart on the Step-by-step sheet.
4. Click the More Info tab. Click Quick tour. View the Quick tour on charting. Click the Done button.
5. Click the Menu button located below the Help window to return to the Spreadsheet and Charting Menu. Scroll the list to view the topic, Preview and print your spreadsheet or chart. Click the Preview and print your spreadsheet or chart icon.
6. When the Previewing and printing your spreadsheet or chart topic displays in the Help window, scroll the list to view the topic To print a chart. Click the To print a chart icon. Read and print the To print a chart topic.
7. Press the Back button located below the Help window to view the Previewing and printing your spreadsheet or chart topic. Scroll the list to view the topic To print your spreadsheet. Click the To print your spreadsheet icon. Read and print To print your spreadsheet.
8. Click the Close button in the application window to close Works.

Microsoft **Works 4** Windows 95
Use Help • W 2.55

? Use Help

2 Expanding on the Basics

Instructions: Use Works online Help to better understand the topics listed below. Print the topic or topics that substantiate your answer. If no Print this topic icon is available, then answer the question on a separate piece of paper.

1. Using the key term, shortcut keys: spreadsheet highlighting, and the Index sheet in the Help topics: Microsoft Works dialog box, display and print the shortcut keys to highlight spreadsheet entries. Then answer the following questions.
    a. Which key or combination of keys highlights an entire column?
    b. Which key or combination of keys highlights an entire row?
    c. Which key or combination of keys highlights an entire spreadsheet?
2. Using the key term, changing number formats on spreadsheets, and the Index sheet in the Help topics: Microsoft Works dialog box, display the topic, To change the number format on spreadsheets. Read the Step-by-Step sheet and More Info sheet and then answer the following questions.
    a. How do you quickly format numbers as currency?
    b. What is General format?
    c. When will Works automatically format a cell as currency or percentage?
    d. How do you enter the fraction 1/16 into a spreadsheet cell?
    e. What should be done if you see #### instead of your entry in a cell?

Apply Your Knowledge

1 Charting Spreadsheet Data

Instructions: Start the Microsoft Works Spreadsheet Tool. Open the spreadsheet, Underwater Aquarium Sales, on the Student Floppy Disk that accompanies this book (Figure 2-82). Chart the range A2:E5 as a 3-D chart. Add the title, Underwater Aquarium Sales - Projections. Add a border and gridlines to the 3-D Bar chart. Print the 3-D chart.

FIGURE 2-82

In the Lab

1 Building a Regional Guitars Sold Spreadsheet

Problem: As the regional sales manager for Goodtime Music Company, you have been asked to analyze the yearly guitar sales for the region. The regional guitar sales are shown in Table 2-2. The spreadsheet and chart are shown in Figure 2-83.

TABLE 2-2

	WEST	NORTH	SOUTH	EAST
Classical	5456	6782	5460	6000
Steel String	8457	7321	10540	9303
Electric	10250	9561	9652	11275
Bass	6541	4556	7485	7126

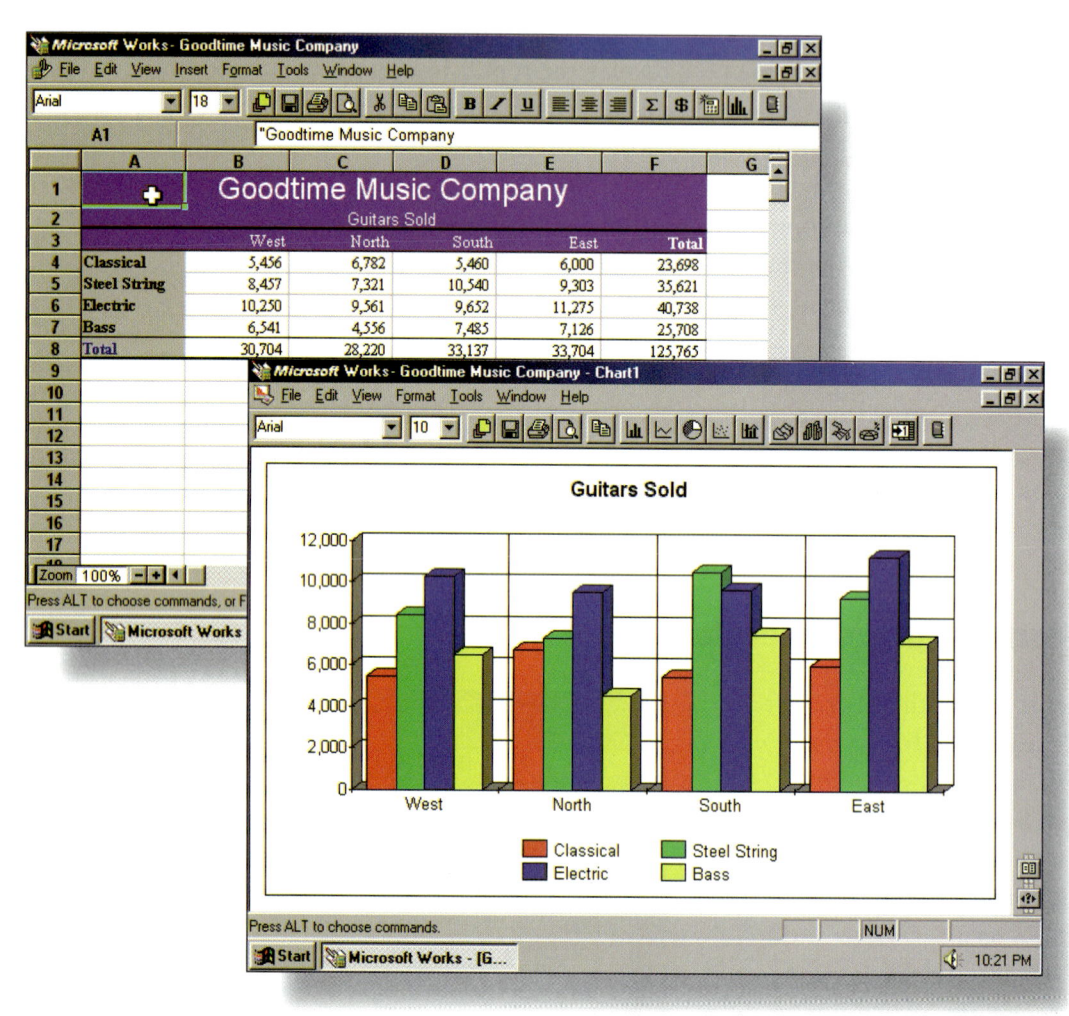

FIGURE 2-83

In the Lab

Instructions: Perform the following tasks:

1. Create the spreadsheet shown in Figure 2-83 using the numbers in Table 2-2.
2. Calculate the totals for the four regions, the guitar categories, and the company.
3. Format the spreadsheet title, Goodtime Music Company, as white 18-point Arial font and centered over columns A through F. Format the spreadsheet subtitle, Guitars Sold, as white 10-point Arial font and centered over columns A through F. Add a dark magenta solid pattern to the foreground of cells A1:F2.
4. Use AutoFormat and the Classic Columns table format for the remaining portion of the spreadsheet. The numbers display using the Comma format.
5. The column width should be 12 for columns A through F.
6. Print the spreadsheet you create.
7. Create the 3-D Bar chart from the spreadsheet data.
8. Print the 3-D Bar chart.
9. Save the spreadsheet with the chart using the filename, Goodtime Music Company.
10. Follow directions from your instructor for turning in this assignment.

2 Building a Current Employees Spreadsheet

Problem: As the director of human resources for the West Coast Fire Department, you have been asked to prepare a report of all employees by department. The current employees are shown in Table 2-3. The spreadsheet and chart are shown in Figure 2-84.

TABLE 2-3

	NORTH DIVISION	HILLS DIVISION	PARK DIVISION	OCEAN DIVISION
Firefighters	725	969	643	525
Engineers	325	265	378	425
Inspectors	784	521	687	578
Mechanics	241	791	478	346

In the Lab

Building a Current Employees Spreadsheet (continued)

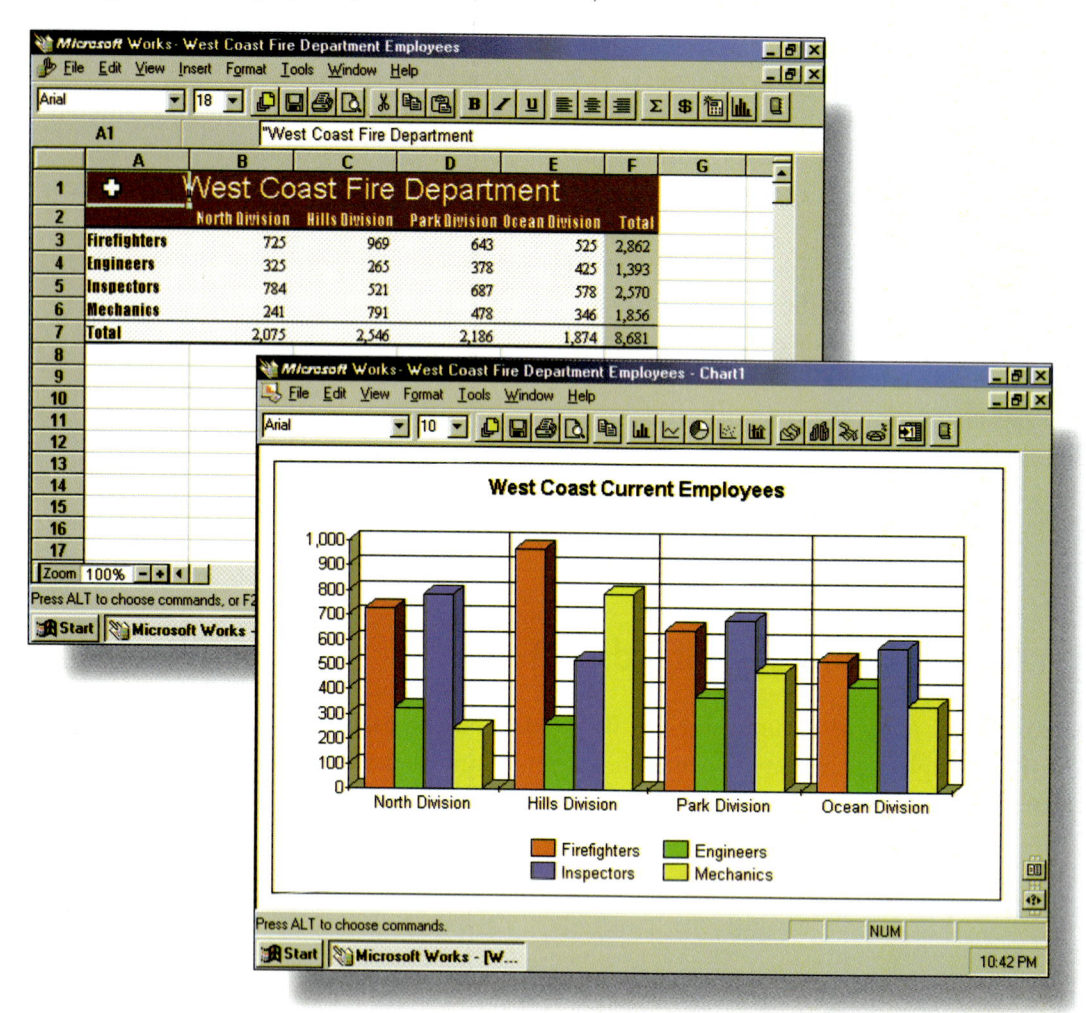

FIGURE 2-84

Instructions: Perform the following tasks:

1. Create the spreadsheet shown in Figure 2-84 using the numbers in Table 2-3.
2. Calculate the totals for the four divisions, the employee categories, and the department.
3. Format the spreadsheet title, West Coast Fire Department, as white 18-point Arial font and centered over columns A through F. Add a dark magenta solid pattern to the foreground of cells A1:F1.
4. Use AutoFormat and the Colorful Columns table format for the remaining portion of the spreadsheet. The numbers display using the Comma format.
5. The column width should be 12 for columns A through E. Column F width should be 6.
6. Print the spreadsheet you create.
7. Create the 3-D Bar chart from the spreadsheet data. Add the title, West Coast Current Employees, to the chart. Also include a border and gridlines for the chart. Print the 3-D Bar chart.

In the Lab

8. Save the spreadsheet with the chart using the filename, West Coast Fire Department Employees.
9. Follow directions from your instructor for turning in this assignment.

3 Building a Computer Software Sales Spreadsheet

Problem: As the director of marketing for Computer Software, Inc., you have been asked to prepare a report of software sales for the past four quarters. The sales are shown in Table 2-4. The spreadsheet and chart are shown in Figure 2-85 on the next page.

TABLE 2-4

	QTR1	QTR2	QTR3	QTR4
Business	22990	33250	11987	22789
Database	42230	22564	11257	22461
Education	11196	21495	31856	11797
Graphics	21950	31023	21256	31789
Games	22520	33154	33937	44330

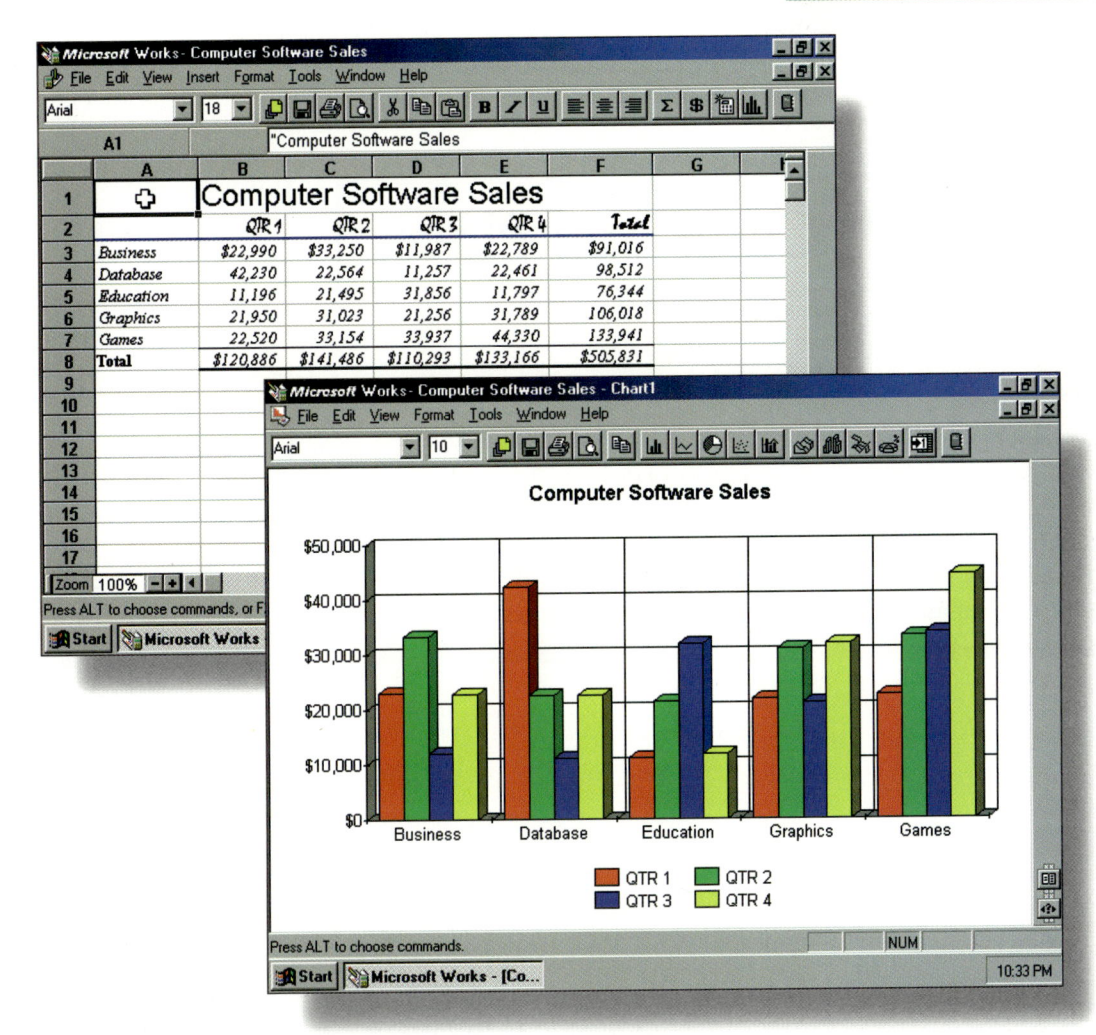

FIGURE 2-85

In the Lab

Building a Computer Software Sales Spreadsheet *(continued)*

Instructions: Perform the following tasks:

1. Create the spreadsheet shown in Figure 2-85 using the numbers in Table 2-4 on the previous page.
2. Calculate the totals for the four quarters, the software categories, and the company.
3. Format the spreadsheet title, Computer Software Sales, as 18-point Arial font and centered over columns A through F.
4. Use AutoFormat and the Financial Blue table format for the remaining portion of the spreadsheet.
5. The column width should be 12 for columns A and F.
6. Print the spreadsheet you create.
7. Create the 3-D Bar chart from the spreadsheet data. Add the title, Computer Software Sales, to the chart. Also include gridlines for the chart.
8. Print the 3-D Bar chart.
9. Save the spreadsheet with the chart using the filename, Computer Software Sales.
10. Follow directions from your instructor for turning in this assignment.

Cases and Places

The difficulty of these case studies varies:

▶ Case studies preceded by a single half moon are the least difficult. You can complete these case studies using your own computer or a computer in the lab.
▶▶ Case studies preceded by two half moons are more difficult. You must research the topic presented using the Internet, a library, or another resource, and then prepare a brief written report.
▶▶▶ Case studies preceded by three half moons are the most difficult. You must visit a store or business to obtain the necessary information, and then use it to create a brief written report.

Cases and Places

1 ▸ To save money, you are considering changing your car's oil, oil filter, and air filter yourself instead of going to the dealer or a local garage. You examine newspaper ads and make a few telephone calls to determine the prices of these items (Figure 2-86) to decide where to shop for these supplies.

TYPE OF RETAILER	QUARTS OIL	OIL FILTER	AIR FILTER	TOTAL COST
Discount	$5.95	$2.50	$4.25	
Auto parts	$4.95	$2.88	$3.55	
Auto dealer	$7.50	$5.50	$6.95	
Mini-mart	$9.00	$7.00	$9.10	

FIGURE 2-86

With this data, you want to produce a spreadsheet to analyze the total costs for five quarts of oil, an oil filter, and an air filter. Use the concepts and techniques presented in the project to create the spreadsheet.

2 ▸ You frequently fly to various cities to visit family and for business. In an attempt to earn a free ticket based on your mileage, you keep a record of the distance flown on four airlines during the past four years (Figure 2-87). Use the concepts and techniques presented in this project to prepare a spreadsheet to accumulate your distance flown on each airline and during each year.

AIRLINE	1992	1993	1994	1995
American	156	532	248	832
United	432	1043	341	963
Northwest	1865	621	832	2779
Continental	439	311	1521	379

FIGURE 2-87

3 ▸ The number of new cars and trucks sold has increased each year from 1991 to 1995, as indicated in Figure 2-88.

MODEL YEAR	DOMESTIC CARS (THOUSANDS)	IMPORT CARS SOLD (THOUSANDS)	DOMESTIC TRUCKS SOLD (THOUSANDS)	IMPORT TRUCKS SOLD (THOUSANDS)
1991	6,276	2,313	3,582	333
1992	6,195	2,140	4,026	247
1993	6,595	2,011	4,789	199
1994	7,173	1,977	5,499	155
1995	7,167	1,803	5,666	170

FIGURE 2-88

With this data, you want to create a spreadsheet to examine these increases. Use the concepts and techniques presented in this project to create the spreadsheet. Calculate the total domestic cars, import cars, domestic trucks, and import trucks sold each year and the total vehicles sold in each of the four categories for the past five years. Also, include bar graphs showing the number of domestic and import cars and the domestic and import trucks sold each year.

Cases and Places

4 ▶▶ Medical and fitness experts recommend aerobic exercise for at least 30 minutes three times weekly. You have decided to visit your campus' fitness center between classes and on weekend mornings in an attempt to improve your health. You speak with a fitness trainer who develops an aerobic training schedule for you. In addition, she recommends 30 minutes of spot toning on alternate days. You decide to exercise by using the treadmill for 24 minutes on Monday, Wednesday, and Friday, the stepper for 18 minutes on Tuesday, Thursday, and Saturday, and the rower for 18 minutes on Sunday, Wednesday, and Saturday. Also, you plan to use free weights for 30 minutes every other day beginning on Monday. Use the concepts and techniques presented in this project to prepare a spreadsheet to record the total minutes spent exercising on each piece of equipment and with the free weights each week. Chart your progress for four weeks. Then create a bar graph illustrating your exercise efforts.

5 ▶▶ The director of your school's fitness center has asked you to help her arrange more efficient scheduling of the facilities. She has asked you to determine which activities appeal to various age groups during the day. You administer a survey to all students and staff using the fitness center during the week and collect data on their ages and preferred activities. You discover that among students ages 17 – 21, 1143 participate in aerobics, 643 in swimming, 2,534 in toning, 423 in volleyball, 943 in running or walking, and 210 in tennis. Among students ages 22 – 29, 2338 participate in aerobics, 893 in swimming, 3021 in toning, 354 in volleyball, 1,932 in running or walking, and 521 in tennis. Among students ages 30 – 39, 964 participate in aerobics, 421 in swimming, 1950 in toning, 301 in volleyball, 1021 in running or walking, and 402 in tennis. Among students ages 40 – 49, 643 participate in aerobics, 398 in swimming, 978 in toning, 97 in volleyball, 793 in running or walking, and 389 in tennis. Among students ages 50 and older, 297 participate in aerobics, 318 in swimming, 419 in toning, 76 in volleyball, 521 in running or walking, and 320 in tennis. Using this information, create a spreadsheet showing the age groups that participate in each of these activities. Include a bar graph to illustrate your data.

6 ▶▶▶ The United States Post Office has started new services and has introduced new products in recent years. Visit your local post office, and ask the postmaster how the facility derives some of its revenues. In particular, find out how many first class commemorative and regular postage stamps (self-adhesive and regular), post cards (single and double), certificates of mailing, certified mail, money orders, and return receipts are sold each week for a two-month period. Using this information, together with the techniques presented in this project, create a spreadsheet showing the total for each category. Include a bar graph to illustrate your data.

7 ▶▶▶ Health experts recommend individuals obtain 10-20 percent of their total daily calories from fat, which for most people would be approximately 20 – 40 grams per day. Keep track of the total fat grams you consume daily during breakfast, lunch, dinner, and snacks for one week. You can determine the number of fat grams by examining the labels on the products, tables in nutrition books, or pamphlets at local fast food restaurants. Use the concepts and techniques presented in this project to prepare a spreadsheet. Include totals for each day of the week and each meal of the week to determine which days and meals are the healthiest for you. Include a bar graph to illustrate your data.

Microsoft *Works 4*

Windows 95

Using Form Design to Create a Database

Objectives:

You will have mastered the material in this project when you can:

- Define the elements of a database
- Start the Works Database tool
- Identify all elements on the Works Database screen
- Change a field size in form design view
- Correct errors when entering field names
- Save a database file
- Position fields in form design view
- Insert clip art into a form
- Enter a title in form design view using WordArt
- Format a title in form design view using WordArt
- Insert a rectangle into a form
- Add color to an object
- Format the field names in form design view
- Enter a text label in form design view
- Display the database in form view
- Enter text and numeric data into a database in form view
- Display the next record, previous record, first record, and last record in form view
- Display the database in list view
- Format the database in list view
- Change font size in list view
- Set field widths in list view
- Print the database in list view and form view

Project 3

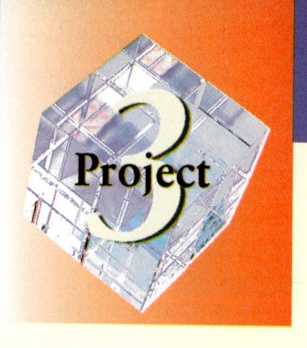

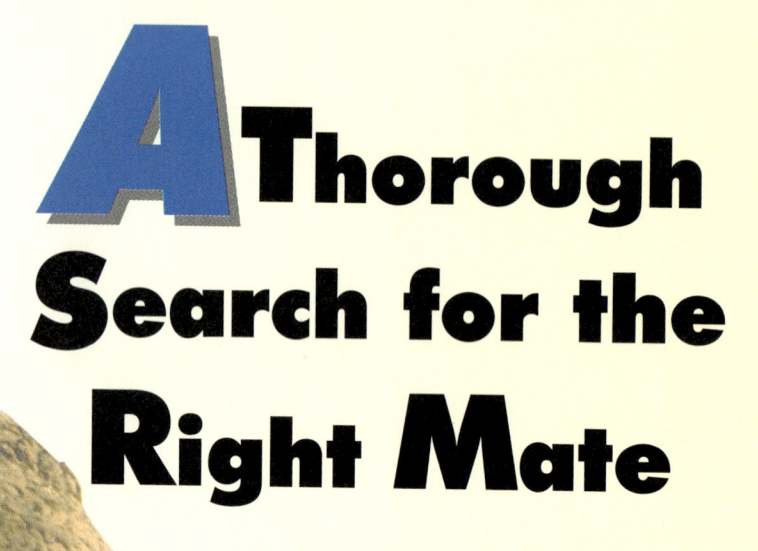

A Thorough Search for the Right Mate

Thoroughbred Database Worth Millions to Matchmaker

What is the world coming to when Thoroughbred horses depend on computers for a date? Barry Weisbord of Lexington, Kentucky — known as the Matchmaker to the Horsey Set — parlayed an enthusiasm for the race track into a business that did $61 million in trading the first year. He pioneered the use of computer databases and sophisticated statistical software to virtually control the breeding of Thoroughbreds. At his company's black-tie auctions, bidders compete for the right to breed mares to top Thoroughbred studs. At stake are the rights to gene pools that go back twenty-four generations, to the mid-1600s.

This is just one example of the numerous business, scientific, and personal databases that help people organize and process the mountains of information modern society collects. A computer database, such as one developed using the Microsoft Works Database tool, is a catalog of information about a particular subject: people, space programs, sales, books, movies, and so on. Using the computer's speed, data on a subject can be rapidly sorted according to different characteristics to find common denominators; say, all the movies directed by John Huston in which he also had an acting role. The more information about a given subject, the more useful a database becomes.

From keeping track of names, addresses, and phone numbers to creating a personal inventory of books, CDs, and videos, managing information is as important for students as for businesses. To make it easier to get started, Microsoft Works Database TaskWizards provide preprogrammed layouts, called templates. Among the many TaskWizards available are Address Book, Phone List, Loan Analysis, Schedule (classes and activities), and Student & Membership Information (club and team rosters). All you must do is simply add data.

Besides the many home and personal applications, databases are used for a multitude of business and scientific functions. Some databases keep track of genetic factors that aid in developing new disease-fighting drugs. Others organize satellite data for use in oil exploration or receive information from point-of-sale transactions that help refine retail merchandising. Still others track demographics and buying patterns to enhance consumer marketing.

As the world expands into the era of connectivity via the Internet and private networks, information sharing is now more flexible than ever. With the concept of distributed databases, individuals or groups can physically hold the storage medium where the information is kept, but anyone, anywhere, can access and use — even update — the data. Numerous data storage locations, often separated by thousands of miles, also can be linked electronically to form a single virtual database.

Behind the scenes, computer databases assume greater importance every day in the management of government, business, science, and personal activities. For those who know how to use them, databases can be the Thoroughbreds they ride to success on the information superhighway.

Project 3

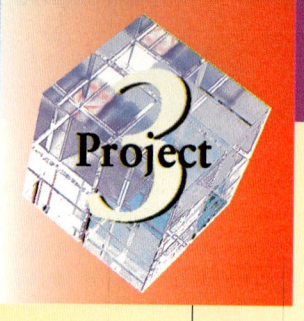

Microsoft Works 4
Windows 95

Using Form Design to Create a Database

Case Perspective

The RSC Sports and Fitness Centers has grown rapidly as an expert in the field of exercise and health fitness providing state-of-the-art workout and health fitness facilities. The management has asked you to design and create a database of current members belonging to the facilities.

The information for the database can be found in the Membership department of the RSC Sports and Fitness Centers. Leanne Barchucci, assistant director of membership, maintains current information on all members. You have been asked to design and then create a database to hold information on each member of the centers. Leanne has requested an attractively designed database form that can be used to enter member information.

You are to analyze the data available on each member and create a database of all current members at the RSC Sports and Fitness Centers. Once the database is designed, you are to enter the information for each member in the database.

Introduction

In Projects 1 and 2, you have used the Microsoft Works Word Processor and Spreadsheet tools. In this project, you will be learning about and using the Database tool.

The **Works Database tool** allows you to create, store, sort, and retrieve data. Many people record data such as the names, addresses, and telephone numbers of friends and business associates, records of investments, and records of expenses for income tax purposes. These records must be arranged so the data can be accessed easily when required.

The term **database** describes a collection of data organized in a manner that allows access, retrieval, and use of that data. The Works Database tool allows you to create a database; add, delete, and change data in the database; sort the data in the database; retrieve the data in the database; and create reports using the data in the database.

Project Three

Project 3 shows you how to create a database using Microsoft Works. The database created in this project is shown in Figure 3-1. This database contains information about members belonging to the RSC Sports and Fitness Centers. The information for each member is stored in a record. A **record** contains all the information for a given person, product, or event. For example, the first record in the database contains information about Mr. Nimiira A. Sanji.

fields

DATE JOINED	TITLE	FIRST NAME	M.I.	LAST NAME	ADDRESS	CITY	STATE	ZIP	OCCUPATION	TYPE	CHARGE	DUES	KIDS CENTER
5/12/96	Mr.	Nimiira	A.	Sanji	79 Fuller	Orange	CA	92667	Teacher	Executive	Y	$120.00	$12.50
5/12/96	Dr.	Albert	G.	Sandler	26 Irning	Yuma	AZ	85364	Doctor	Family	Y	$89.00	$12.50
5/15/96	Ms.	Midge	W.	Maclone	94 Bourne	Placentia	CA	92670	Attorney	Single	N	$45.00	$12.50
5/15/96	Dr.	Edward	R.	Guen	170 Tremont	Irvine	CA	92715	Doctor	Family	N	$89.00	
5/17/96	Mr.	Rubin	E.	Gordon	1539 Centre	Yorba Linda	CA	92686	Teacher	Family	Y	$89.00	$12.50
5/25/96	Mr.	Ivan	I.	Fenton	228 Seaver	Irvine	CA	92715	Accountant	Single	Y	$45.00	$12.50
5/26/96	Mr.	David	L.	Dirsa	47 Concord	Orange	CA	92667	Salesrep	Student	Y	$35.00	
5/31/96	Mr.	Julian	P.	Coulon	216 Summer	Tustin	CA	92680	Teacher	Family	Y	$89.00	
6/1/96	Mr.	Jacob	W.	Chase	35 Chilton	Fullerton	CA	92635	Salesrep	Student	Y	$35.00	$12.50
6/1/96	Mrs.	Michele	Q.	Bovie	14 St. Lukes	Irvine	CA	92715	Accountant	Family	Y	$89.00	
6/3/96	Mr.	Stefano	U.	Branchi	58 Sullivan	Orange	CA	92667	Accountant	Family	Y	$89.00	
6/6/96	Mr.	Antonio	V.	Alonso	2468 Allston	Tustin	CA	92680	Teacher	Single	N	$45.00	$12.50
6/10/96	Mr.	Gabriel	A.	Vidal	40 Concord	Reno	NV	89503	Nurse	Executive	Y	$120.00	
6/12/96	Ms.	Olivia	D.	Brown	4 Hyde Park	Orange	CA	92667	Teacher	Student	Y	$35.00	
6/12/96	Ms.	Cathy	E.	Wain	520 Beacon	Santa Ana	CA	92705	Nurse	Single	Y	$45.00	$12.50
6/13/96	Dr.	Bei	F.	Wu	205 Kent	Santa Ana	CA	92705	Teacher	Executive	Y	$120.00	$12.50

records

FIGURE 3-1

A record consists of a series of fields. A **field** contains a specific piece of information within a record. For example, in the database shown in Figure 3-1, the first field is the Date Joined field, which contains the date on which the person joined. The Title field identifies the person as Mr., Mrs., Ms., or Dr. The First Name, M.I., and Last Name fields contain the first name, middle initital, and last name of each of the members.

The remaining fields in each of the records are:

1. Address: Street address of the member.
2. City: City in which the member lives.
3. State: State in which the member lives.
4. Zip: Zip code of the member's city.
5. Occupation: The occupation of the member.
6. Type: The type of membership held by the member. Four memberships are available – Student, Single, Family, and Executive.
7. Charge: Specifies whether the member has been approved to charge food and merchandise in the center on his account. If a member has charge privileges, this field will contain a Y, otherwise the field contains an N.
8. Dues: The monthly amount paid by each member for the use of the exercise and health facility.
9. Kids Center: The additional monthly amount paid by each member for the use of the Kids Center while at the center.

Each of these fields contains information for each member record. Thus, for record one, the member's first name is Nimiira, the middle initial is A., the last name is Sanji, he lives at 79 Fuller, Orange, CA. In record two, the First Name field contains Albert, the middle initial contains G., and the Last Name field contains Sandler. Dr. Sandler lives in Yuma, AZ, has a family membership on which he has charge privileges. He pays $89 a month for the use of the facility and $12.50 a month for the use of the Kids Center.

It is important you understand that a record consists of one or more fields. When you define the database, you will define each field within a record. After you define the fields, you can enter data for as many records as are required in your database.

Creating the Database

The following tasks will be completed in this project to create the database shown in Figure 3-1 on the previous page.

1. Start Microsoft Works and choose the Database tool.
2. Enter the field names and field formats required for the database. This step results in the database structure.
3. Change the size of fields in form design view, in which a single record displays on the screen.
4. Position the fields in form design view.
5. Save the database structure.
6. Insert clip art in the title area of the form. Enter the title, RSC Sports and Fitness Centers, and format the title with special effects. Place a thin rectangular bar below the clip art and title in the form.
7. Color the title and the thin rectangle below the title. Place a color border around the field entries.
8. Enter the text labels, MEMBER INFORMATION and ACCOUNT INFORMATION, as identifying labels to the sections of each member's record. Format the text labels.
9. Enter the data for the records in the database in form view.
10. Save the database with the data you have entered.
11. Switch to list view where the entire database displays on the screen.
12. Format the database in list view.
13. Print the database in form view.
14. Print the database in list view.

The following pages contain a detailed explanation of these tasks and terms.

Starting Microsoft Works

To start Microsoft Works, follow the steps you have used in previous projects to open the Microsoft Works Task Launcher dialog box (Figure 3-2). The following step summarizes the procedure.

More *About* Creating a Database

To create a database quickly, the TaskWizards listed on the Works Task Launcher can be used. For example, the Address Book, Phone List, Employee Profile, and Business Inventory are wizard-generated databases that step the user through the creation of predesigned forms based on the Database tool. Database wizards are identified in the TaskWizards window by the Cards icon that displays to the left of the wizard name.

Microsoft Works 4 Windows 95
Creating a Database • W 3.7

TO START MICROSOFT WORKS

Step 1: Click the Start button on the taskbar, point to Programs, point to the Microsoft Works folder on the Programs submenu, point to Microsoft Works on the Microsoft Works submenu, and then click Microsoft Works. When the Works Task Launcher dialog box displays, click the Works Tools tab and point to the Database button.

The Microsoft Works application program opens and the Works Task Launcher dialog box displays (Figure 3-2).

You have now started Works and are ready to use the Database tool.

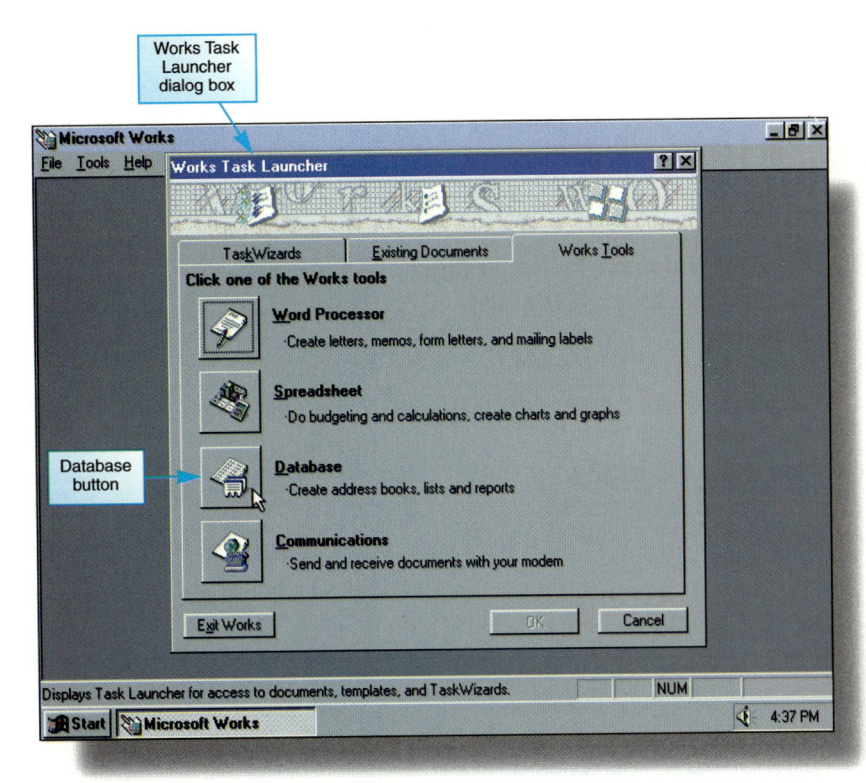

FIGURE 3-2

Creating a Database

The next step is to start the Microsoft Works Database tool. When you start the Microsoft Works Database tool, Works opens the Create Database dialog box where you add fields to create your database. Each field has a format that indicates the type of data that can be stored in the field. The formats you will use in this project are:

1. **Text** – The field can contain any characters.

2. **Number** – The field can contain only numbers. Fields are assigned this type so they can be used in arithmetic operations. Fields that contain numbers but will not be used for arithmetic operations are usually assigned a format of Text. The Dues field and Kids Center field contain numbers and are assigned the Number format. The values in these fields display with dollar signs and decimal points.

3. **Date** – The field can contain text or numbers in a recognizable date format, such as 05/12/99 or May 12, 1999. The Date Joined field is assigned the Date format.

The field names and field formats are shown in Table 3-1.

> **More About**
> **Database Formats**
>
> When assigning formats to fields that contain numbers but will not be used for arithmetic operations, use the Text format. For example, a Zip code field should be assigned the Text format because Zip codes will not be involved in any arithmetic. Also, Zip codes that begin with zero must be assigned the Text format. Otherwise, the Zip code 01075 will turn into 1075. Zip codes and phone numbers that include hyphens cannot use the Number format either.

TABLE 3-1

FIELD NAME	FIELD FORMAT	FIELD NAME	FIELD FORMAT
Date Joined	Date	State	Text
Title	Text	Zip	Text
First Name	Text	Occupation	Text
M.I.	Text	Type	Text
Last Name	Text	Dues	Number
Address	Text	Charge	Text
City	Text	Kids Center	Number

W 3.8 • Project 3 • Using Form Design to Create a Database

To create the database, perform the following steps.

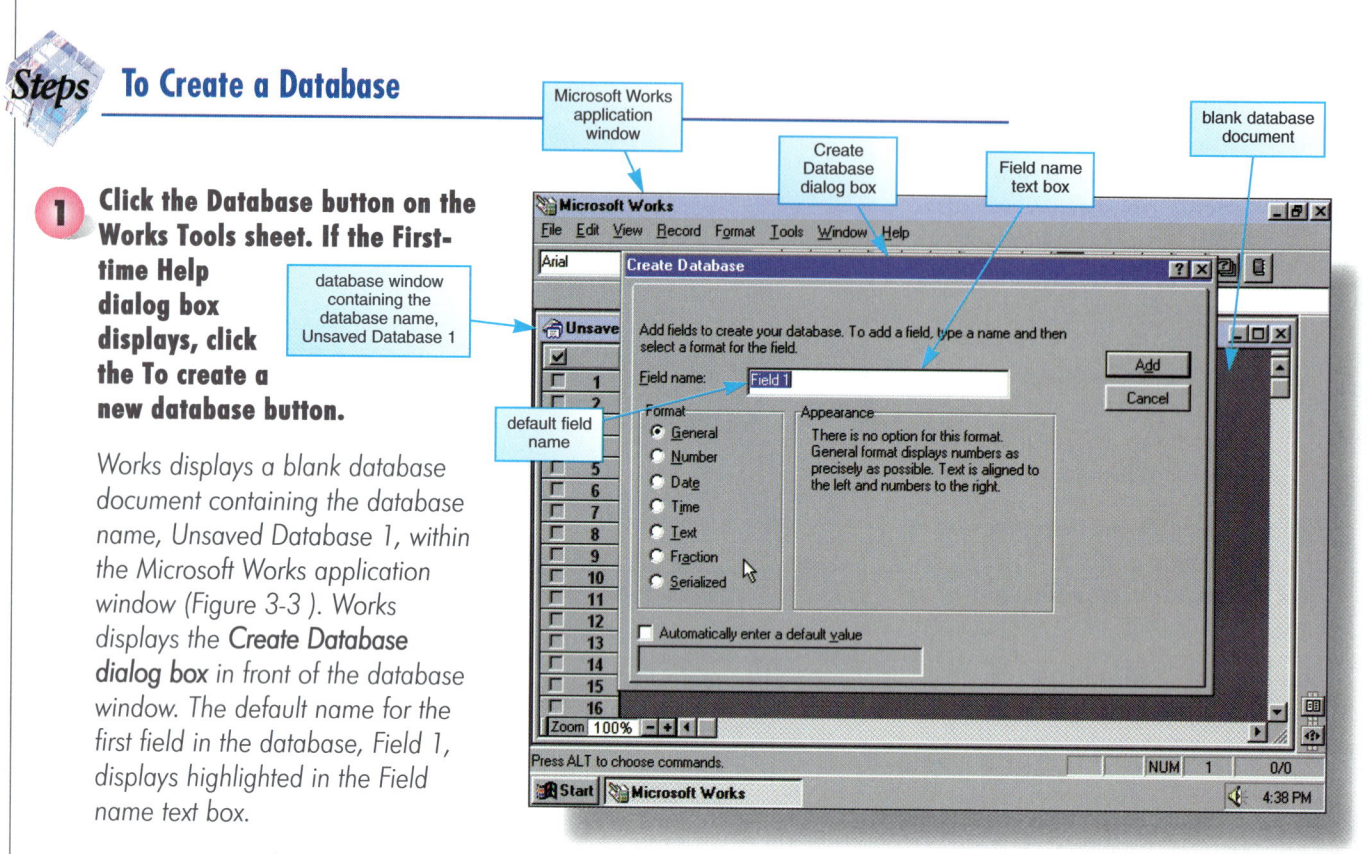

Steps To Create a Database

1 Click the Database button on the Works Tools sheet. If the First-time Help dialog box displays, click the To create a new database button.

Works displays a blank database document containing the database name, Unsaved Database 1, within the Microsoft Works application window (Figure 3-3). Works displays the **Create Database dialog box** in front of the database window. The default name for the first field in the database, Field 1, displays highlighted in the Field name text box.

FIGURE 3-3

2 Type Date Joined in the Field name text box. Click Date in the Format box. Verify the first date format is highlighted in the Appearance list. Then point to the Add button.

Works displays the field name you typed in the Field name text box (Figure 3-4). When you click Date in the Format box, Works displays the Appearance box with a list of available formats for a date. The current date in the MM/DD/YY format is highlighted in the Appearance list.

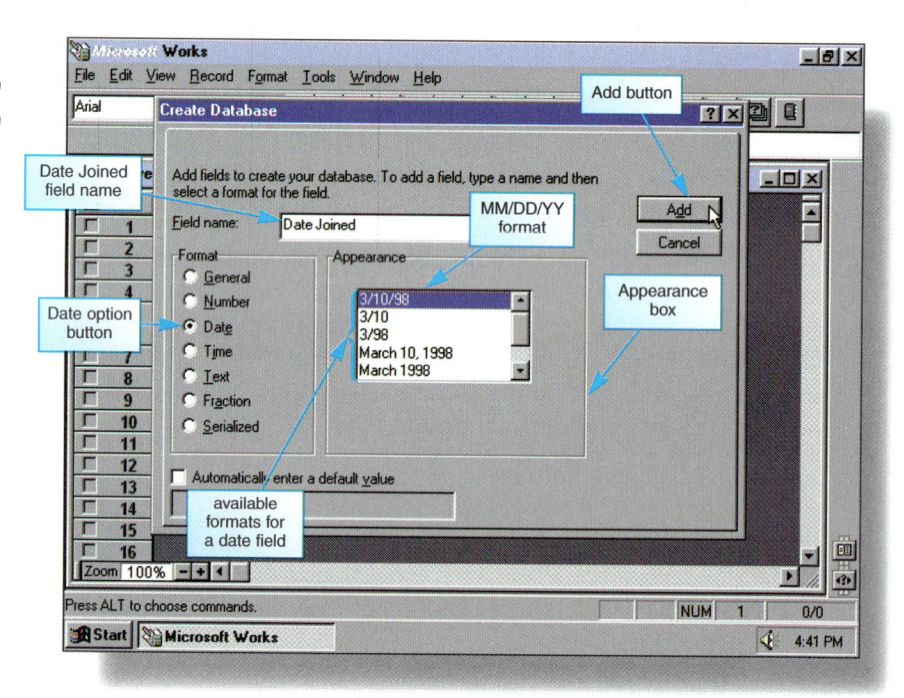

FIGURE 3-4

Microsoft **Works 4** Windows 95

Creating a Database • **W 3.9**

3 **Click the Add button. Type** `Title` **in the Field name text box, click Text in the Format box, and point to the Add button.**

Works adds the Date Joined field to the database document located behind the Create Database dialog box (Figure 3-5). The dialog box remains open, ready to accept another field definition. The field name, Title, displays in the Field name text box. The Text option button is selected indicating any characters, symbols, or numbers can be entered in the field. Works displays information on the Text format in the Appearance box.

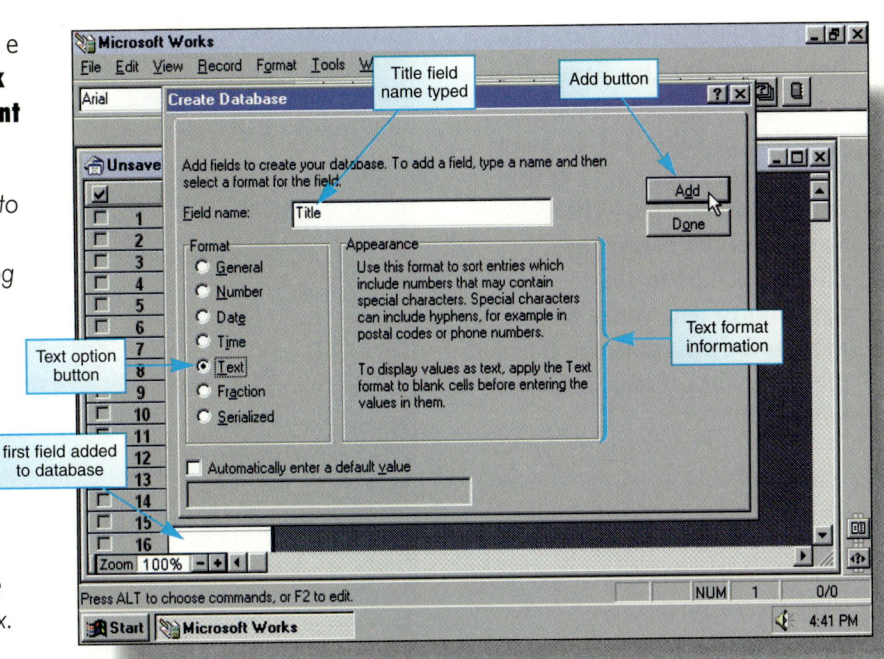

FIGURE 3-5

4 **Click the Add button to enter the Title field. Repeat Step 3 above to enter the field names for First Name, M.I., Last Name, Address, and City using the format specified in Table 3-1 on page W 3.7. Type** `State` **in the Field name text box. Click Text in the Format box. Click Automatically enter a default value. Type** `CA` **in the Automatically enter a default value text box. Then, point to the Add button.**

Works adds the fields for Title, First Name, M.I., Last Name, Address, and City to the database document (Figure 3-6). In the Create Database dialog box, the field name, State, displays in the Field name text box. The Text option button is selected. A check mark displaying in the Automatically enter a default value check box instructs Works to enter the value you type automatically for every record.

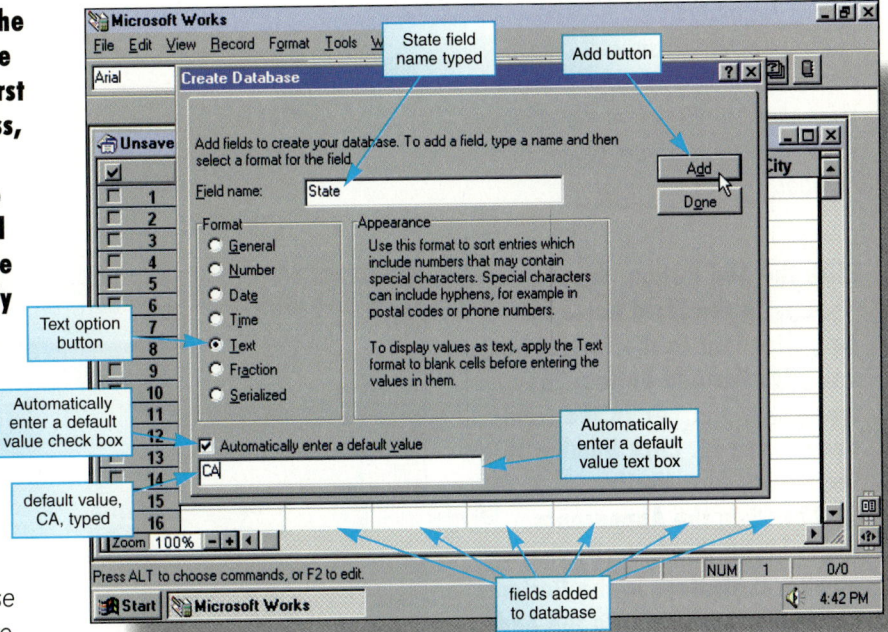

FIGURE 3-6

5 Click the Add button. Enter the field names for Zip, Occupation, and Type using the format specified in Table 3-1 on page W 3.7. Then, type Dues in the Field name text box. Click Number in the Format box. Click $1,234.56 in the Appearance list. Verify the number 2 displays in the Decimal places list box. Point to the Add button.

Works adds the State, Zip, Occupation, and Type fields to the database. The field name, Dues, displays in the Field name text box (Figure 3-7). When you click the Number option button, Works displays a list of available formats for a number. The $1,234.56 format is highlighted and the value 2 displays in the Decimal places list box. These selections instruct Works to add a dollar sign, a comma every three digits to the left of the decimal point, and two decimal places to a number.

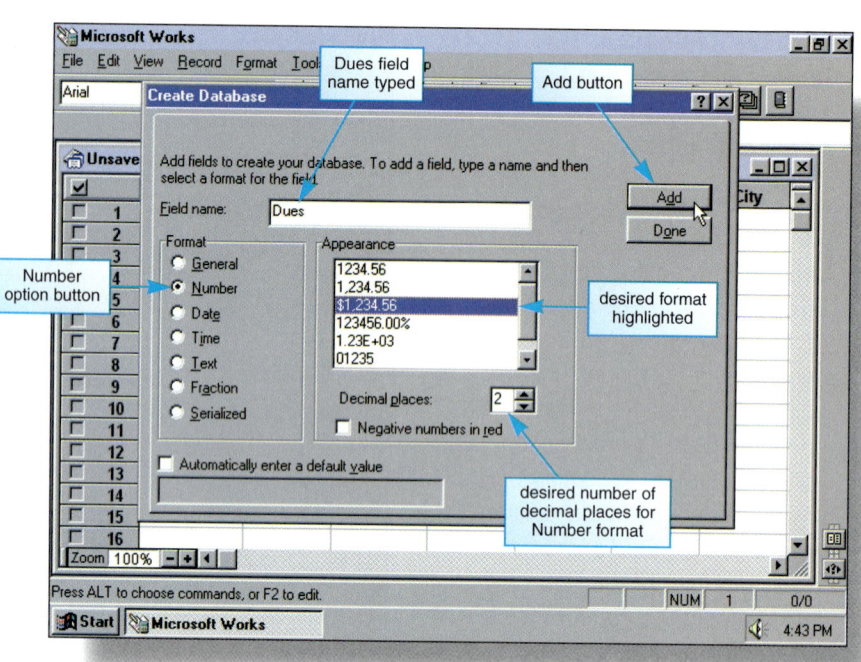

FIGURE 3-7

6 Click the Add button. Type Charge in the Field name text box, click Text in the Format box, and click the Add button. Then, type Kids Center in the Field name text box. Click Number in the Format box. Verify $1,234.56 in the Appearance list is highlighted. Verify the number 2 displays in the Decimal places list box. Point to the Add button.

Works adds the Charge field to the database. The field name, Kids Center, displays in the Field name text box (Figure 3-8). The $1,234.56 format is highlighted.

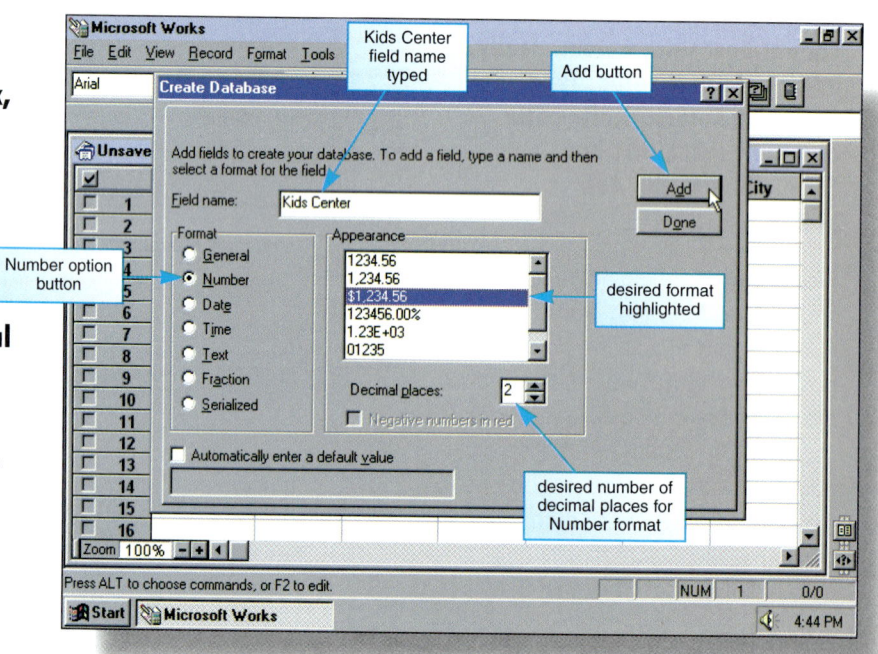

FIGURE 3-8

Microsoft **Works 4** Windows 95
Creating a Database • **W 3.11**

7 **Click the Add button. When Works displays Field 15 in the Field name text box, point to the Done button.**

Works adds the Kids Center field to the database. The default field name, Field 15, displays in the Field name text box (Figure 3-9).

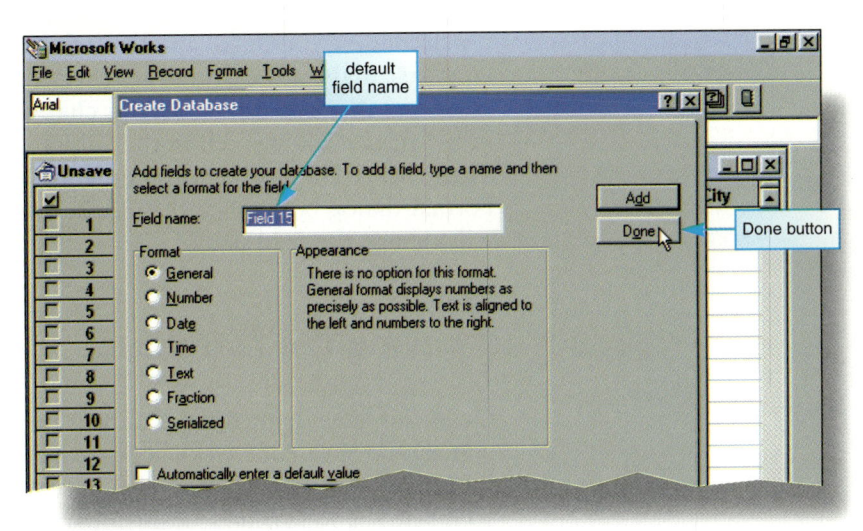

FIGURE 3-9

8 **Click the Done button in the Create Database dialog box. If the Help window displays, click the Shrink Help button to minimize the window.**

Works displays the records in the database in a grid that resembles a spreadsheet (Figure 3-10). The screen in Figure 3-10 is presented in **list view**, *which allows you to view multiple records at the same time. The field names identify each column and the record numbers identify each row. The Date Joined field for record 1 is highlighted by a dark border around the field. Only the first seven fields display on the screen. Use the scroll arrows, scroll boxes, or scroll bars to view the additional fields. The right side of the toolbar contains six new buttons. These buttons are explained as they are used. The List View button is light gray and is recessed, indicating the screen is showing the database in list view.*

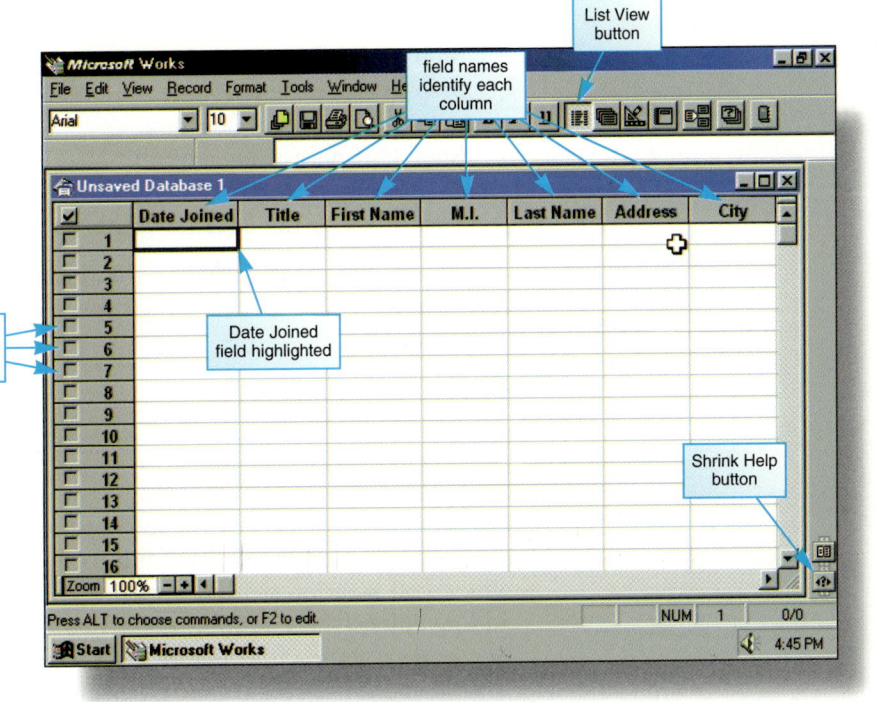

FIGURE 3-10

You should note several points when entering the fields for a database. First, choose the field names with care so they reflect the contents of the field. In all subsequent uses of the database, you will refer to the data in the fields by these names, so it is important to be able to easily identify the contents of the fields. The maximum number of characters in a field name is fifteen characters, including spaces and punctuation. A field name can contain any character except a single quotation mark. You can enter up to 256 fields into your database.

**More *About*
Entering Default Values**

Using a default value in any field in a database that contains identical information saves time entering the data. The default value will not appear, however, until you enter data in at least one other field in the record.

Second, if you make an error while typing a field name in the Create Database dialog box, you can correct the error by backspacing to remove the error and then typing the correct characters. If you notice an error in a field name in list view, click any cell in the column that contains the incorrect field name. Then click Field on the Format menu and enter the correct field name in the Format dialog box. Click the OK button in the Format dialog box and Works will change the field name.

Saving the Database

Once you have defined the database by specifying all the field names, normally you should save your work so an accidental loss of power does not destroy it. To save your work on a floppy disk in drive A using the filename RSC Members, complete the following steps.

TO SAVE THE DATABASE

Step 1: Click the Save button on the toolbar.
Step 2: Type the filename, RSC Members, in the File name text box in the Save As dialog box.
Step 3: If necessary, click the 3½ Floppy [A:] icon in the Save in drop-down list box.
Step 4: Click the Save button in the Save As dialog box.

Works will save the file on the floppy disk in drive A and will place the name, RSC Members, in the title bar of the Works window.

Form Design View

After you have entered the field names into the database, the next step is to position the fields on a form so they are easy to read and use. You use the form design view to arrange fields on a form. **Form design view** is a database view in which you position fields on a form, insert graphics, or customize the form by adding color, labels, and borders. The final form design view of the database in this project is shown in Figure 3-11. Notice that each of the fields in the database is arranged on the page for ease of reading.

Four different elements are displayed in the form shown in Figure 3-11. The first is a clip art display in the upper left corner of the form. The second element contains the words, RSC Sports and Fitness Centers. RSC Sports and Fitness Centers is the name of the sports and fitness club. The words, RSC Sports and Fitness Centers, were created using a Works accessory called WordArt. **WordArt** allows you to display words on a database form in a variety of shapes and styles. You also may display a title on a database form using the standard fonts available as part of Works. In database terminology, when using standard font styles, the title would be called a **text label**. MEMBER INFORMATION and ACCOUNT INFORMATION shown in Figure 3-11 are text labels. A dark blue rectangle displays below the clip art and WordArt.

The third element on the form is the field name. A **field name** distinguishes a field from all other fields in the database. For example, in Figure 3-11, you can see that the field containing the date joined is called Date Joined, the field name for title is Title, the field for the first name is First Name, and so on. A field name always ends with a colon (:). In form design view, you can format each of the field

Microsoft **Works 4** Windows 95

Formatting the Database Form in Form Design View • W 3.13

names in a style that makes the form easy to read. In the database for Project 7, each of the field names displays in bold and italics.

The fourth element on the form is the field entry. A **field entry** is the actual data in the field. In Figure 3-11, the field entry for the Date Joined field is 5/12/96. The field entry for the Title field is Mr., the field entry for the First Name field is Nimiira, and so on. Field entries can contain any characters you wish and can be a maximum of 256 characters. By default, Works assigns a field width of 20 to each field. The default font is Times New Roman and the default point size is 12.

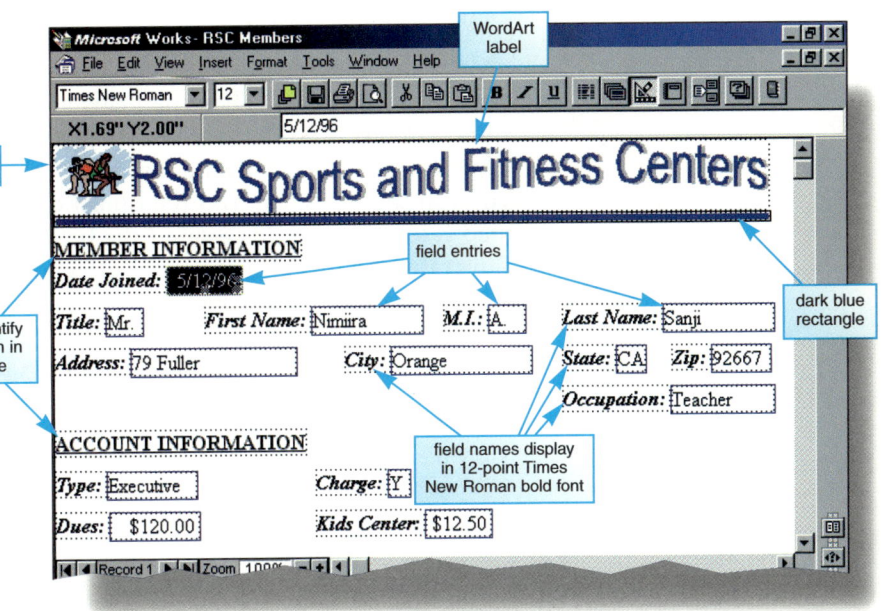

FIGURE 3-11

Notice that dotted lines display around all elements in form design view. This indicates you can select the elements for editing or change their locations on the form. In Figure 3-11, the field entry for Date Joined is highlighted, indicating it is selected. Three square handles display on the corners of the selected area. You can select the field name and the field entry area separately in form design view.

An important design decision is to determine the width of the field. You want the field to be large enough to contain the largest field entry but no larger. In most cases, you will be able to determine the proper width based on the maximum number of characters in the field entry, but the field width you specify when defining the field will not always correspond to the number of characters actually in the field because many fonts, such as Times New Roman, use variable-width characters. For example, when using 12-point Times New Roman, to place twenty letter i's in a field requires a width of 10, while placing twenty letter m's in a field requires a width of 37. If you use a font with a fixed width for each character, such as Courier New, then the width you choose will correspond exactly to the number of characters in the field. When you choose the width, estimate as closely as you can while remembering you can easily change the width of a field at a later time.

The field widths for the form design view of the database in Project 3 are shown in Table 3-2.

TABLE 3-2

FIELD NAME	FIELD WIDTH	FIELD NAME	FIELD WIDTH
Date Joined	10	State	4
Title	5	Zip	8
First Name	15	Occupation	14
M.I.	5	Type	12
Last Name	15	Dues	12
Address	22	Charge	3
City	19	Kids Center	9

Formatting the Database Form in Form Design View

After you have entered the field names, the next step is to format the form so it is easy to read and use. You use the form design view of the database to format the form. Because someone may have to enter thousands of records into the database, the form should be easy to read and use.

W 3.14 • Project 3 • Using Form Design to Create a Database

Formatting the form consists of a number of separate tasks. The first is to change the margins of the form in form design view. The next task is to change the size of the fields. Then the fields are positioned on the form. Next you are to insert clip art in the title area; type, position, and format the title, RSC Sports and Fitness Centers, on the database form; place a border below the title; and add color in the title area. You then must change the style of the field names. The final step is to add a border around the field entries. Figure 3-11 on the previous page illustrates the form for Project 3 after formatting. The technique for formatting is explained on the following pages.

Displaying the Database in Form Design View

The first step in formatting the form is to display the database in form design view. Perform the following steps to display the database in form design view.

Steps To Display the Database in Form Design View

1 Point to the Form Design button on the toolbar (Figure 3-12).

FIGURE 3-12

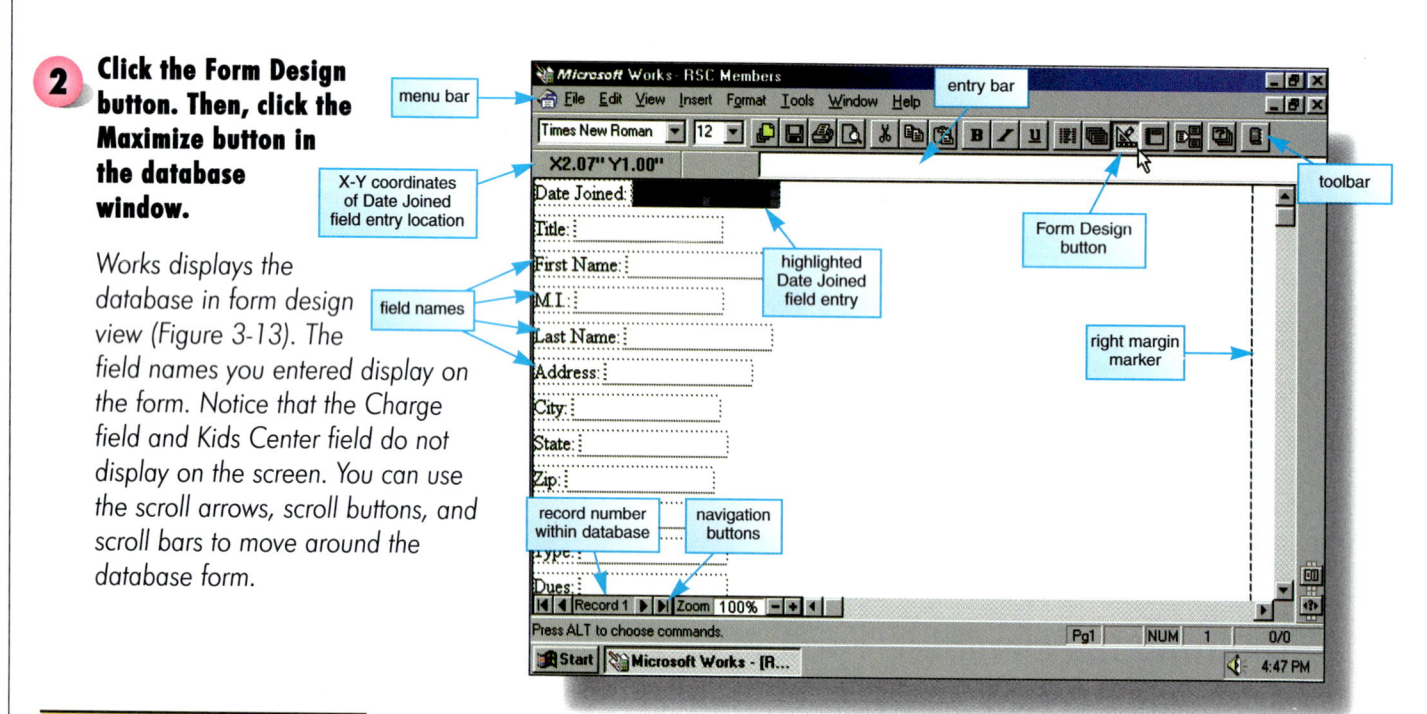

2 Click the Form Design button. Then, click the Maximize button in the database window.

Works displays the database in form design view (Figure 3-13). The field names you entered display on the form. Notice that the Charge field and Kids Center field do not display on the screen. You can use the scroll arrows, scroll buttons, and scroll bars to move around the database form.

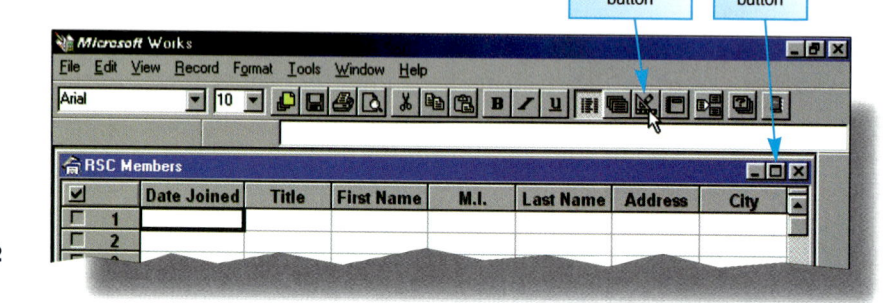

FIGURE 3-13

OtherWays
1. On View menu click Form Design
2. Press CTRL+F9

Although you can see in Figure 3-13 that the database window appears much the same as the word processing window and the spreadsheet window, some important differences are present. These differences are noted below.

MENU BAR The **menu bar** in the Works Database is the same as the menu bar in the Spreadsheet. The menu names are File, Edit, View, Insert, Format, Tools, Window, and Help. Most of the Database menus, however, contain additional or different commands from the corresponding Works Spreadsheet menu. These commands are explained as they are used.

TOOLBAR The **toolbar** contains many of the same buttons as the Word Processor and Spreadsheet toolbars; however, the Database toolbar also contains a number of unique buttons on the right side of the toolbar. These buttons are explained as they are used. In Figure 3-13, the Form Design button is light gray and is recessed, indicating the screen is showing the database in form design view.

ENTRY BAR The Database **entry bar** functions in much the same manner as the Spreadsheet entry bar. When you type an entry into the database, the entry will display in the entry bar. The X and Y values shown in Figure 3-13 indicate the **X-Y coordinates** of the highlighted field on the screen. The X value specifies the number of inches from the left edge of the form. The Y value specifies the number of inches from the top of the form. In Figure 3-13, the X coordinate is 2.07" and the Y coordinate is 1.00". This means the field entry for Date Joined is located 2.07 inches from the left edge of the form and 1.00 inch from the top of the form.

RIGHT MARGIN MARKER The **right margin marker** is the dashed vertical line down the right side of the screen in Figure 3-13. It marks the right margin on the form. The default margin setting is 1.25 inches on the right of the form.

SCROLL BAR The **scroll bar**, in addition to the normal scroll arrows, scroll box, and scroll bar, contains navigation buttons and a Zoom box. You use **navigation buttons** to move from record to record. The function of each of the buttons is described in Figure 3-14. The use of these buttons with a loaded database will be illustrated later.

The Zoom box is located to the right of the navigation buttons. The **Zoom box** controls how much of the record displays at one time in the database window. Clicking the Zoom box displays a list of available zoom percentages to magnify or reduce your database on the screen. You also can use the plus or minus buttons next to the Zoom box to control the display. To magnify your display, click the **plus button**. To reduce your display, click the **minus button**.

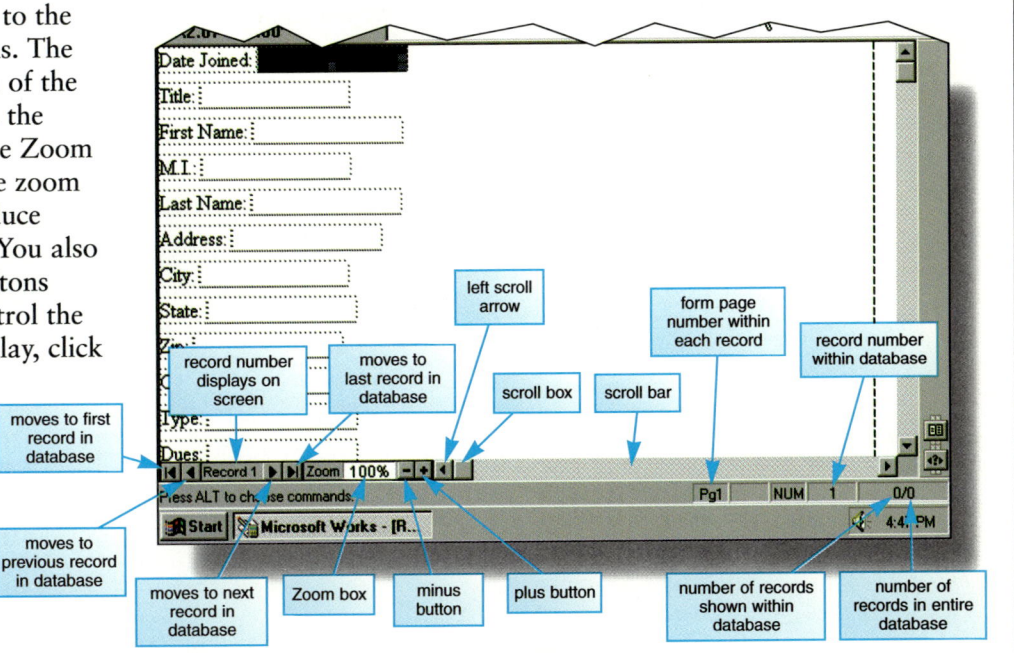

FIGURE 3-14

STATUS BAR The **status bar** contains information regarding the database and the record currently displayed on the screen (see Figure 3-14 on the previous page). The entry Pg1 indicates that the screen shows page 1 of the record on the screen. In some instances, a record may consist of more than one form page. Works allows a maximum of eight pages to a record. The entry 1 following the NUM indicator indicates that record number 1 in the database is displayed on the screen. The next value, a number 0 (zero) separated from another number 0 (zero) by a slash (0/0), specifies the record number currently displaying in the database and the total number of records stored in the database. Works allows a maximum of 32,000 records in a database.

Changing Form Margins

In this project, you must increase the area into which you will enter data to create the form shown in Figure 3-11 on page W 3.13. This requires setting the left and right margin to .75 inch each. To change the margins on the database form, perform the following steps.

Steps   To Change the Margins on the Database Form

1. **Click File on the menu bar and then point to Page Setup (Figure 3-15).**

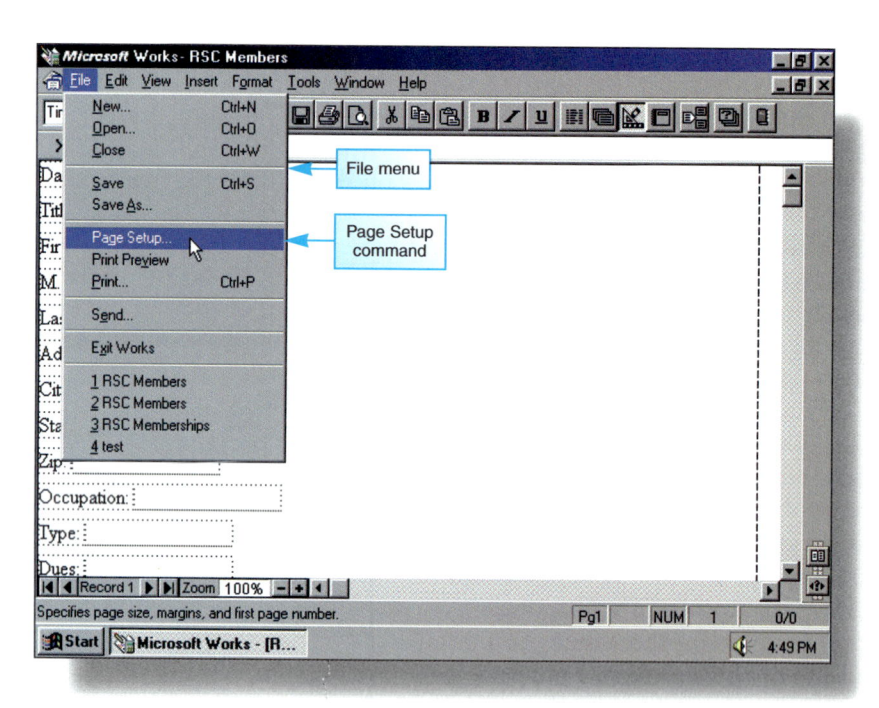

FIGURE 3-15

Microsoft **Works 4** Windows 95

Formatting the Database Form in Form Design View • **W 3.17**

2 **Click Page Setup. When the Page Setup dialog box displays, ensure the Margins sheet displays. Change the Left margin to .75 and the Right margin to .75. Point to the OK button.**

Works displays the Page Setup dialog box (Figure 3-16). The left and right margins have been changed to .75.

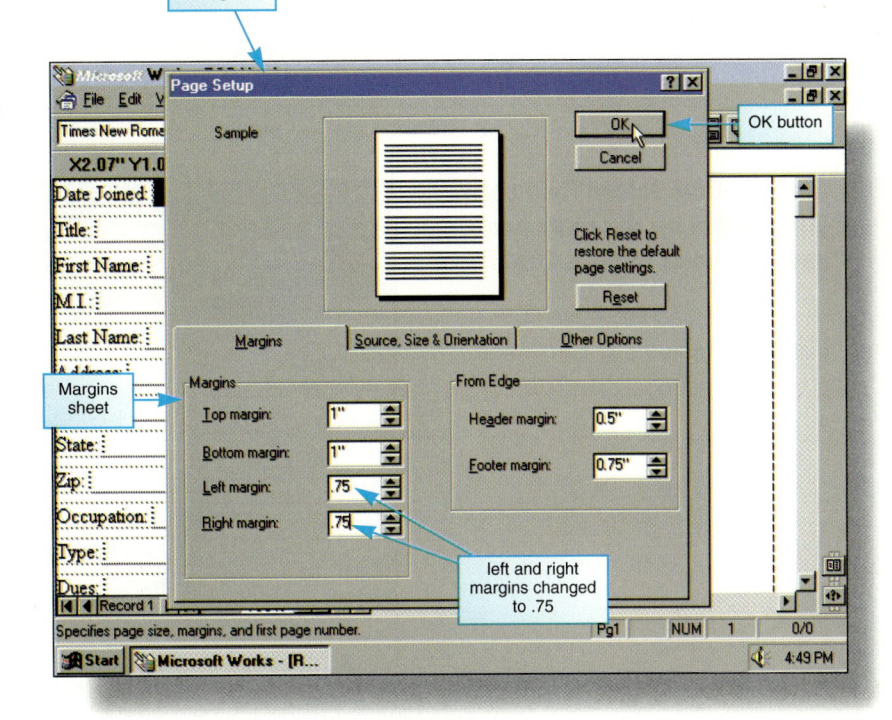

FIGURE 3-16

3 **Click the OK button.**

The Works database form design view document screen displays (Figure 3-17). The dotted right margin line is not visible because of the change in margins. Works also has moved the default X–Y coordinates of the Date Joined field entry to the new location of X1.57" Y1.00".

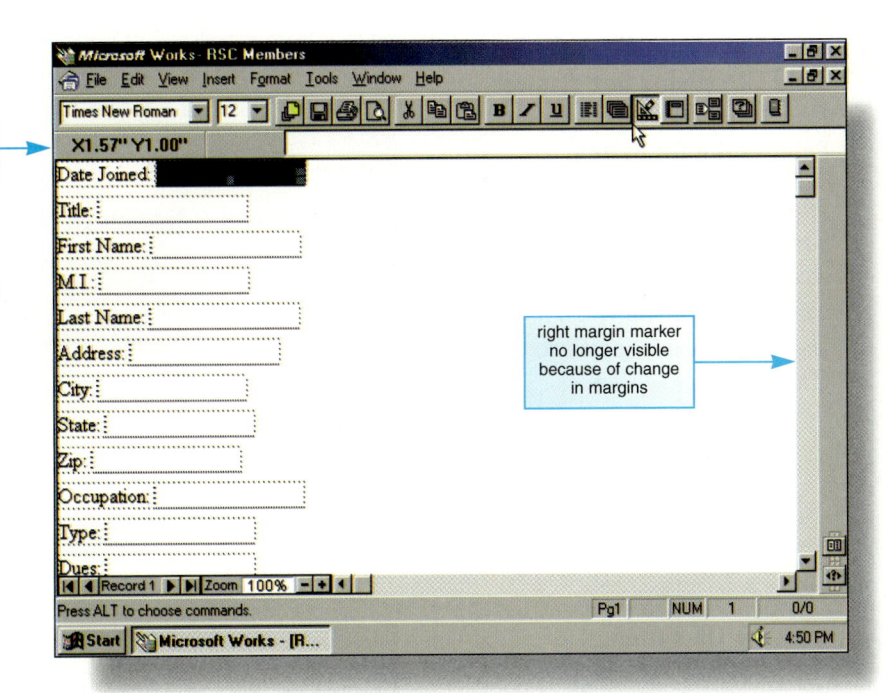

FIGURE 3-17

Setting Field Widths

The next step in formatting the form is to set the field widths for each of the fields in form design view. Table 3-2 on page W 3.13 shows the field widths for the form design view of the database. Perform the steps on the next two pages to set the field widths.

More *About*
Field Widths and Heights

In form view, the field width can be between 1 and 325 characters and the field height can be between 1 and 325 lines. When a field's height is more than one line, Works wraps the text to the next line when the text is longer than the field's width.

W 3.18 • Project 3 • Using Form Design to Create a Database

Steps: To Set Field Widths in Form Design View

1) Click the Date Joined field entry. Click Format on the menu bar and then point to Field Size.

The Date Joined field entry is highlighted and the Format menu displays (Figure 3-18).

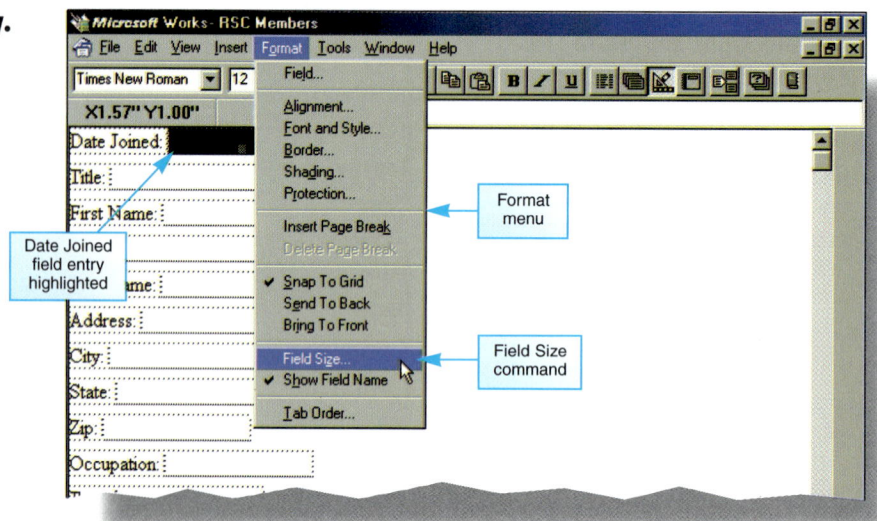

FIGURE 3-18

2) Click Field Size. When the Format Field Size dialog box displays, type 10 in the Width text box. Point to the OK button.

Works displays the Format Field Size dialog box (Figure 3-19). The value 10, which is the new field size, displays in the Width text box. The mouse pointer points to the OK button.

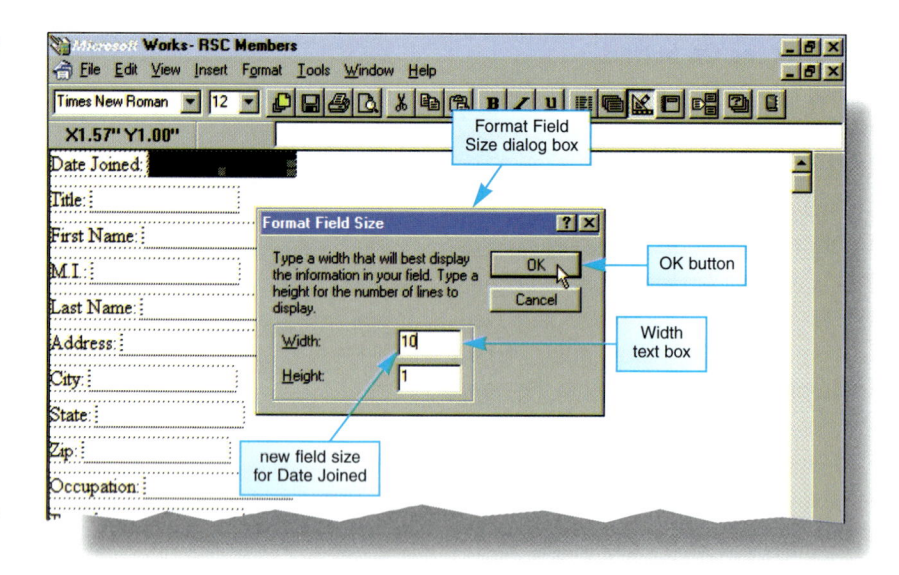

FIGURE 3-19

3) Click the OK button.

Works changes the width of the Date Joined field entry to 10 (Figure 3-20).

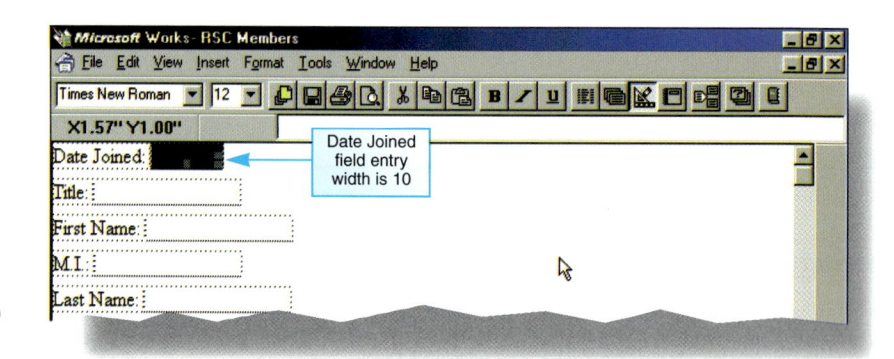

FIGURE 3-20

4 **Use Steps 1 through 3 to set the remainder of the field entries to their proper widths as specified in Table 3-2 on page W 3.13.**

The field entry widths are set to their new sizes (Figure 3-21). Notice that the Date Joined, Title, and First Name fields have scrolled off the screen.

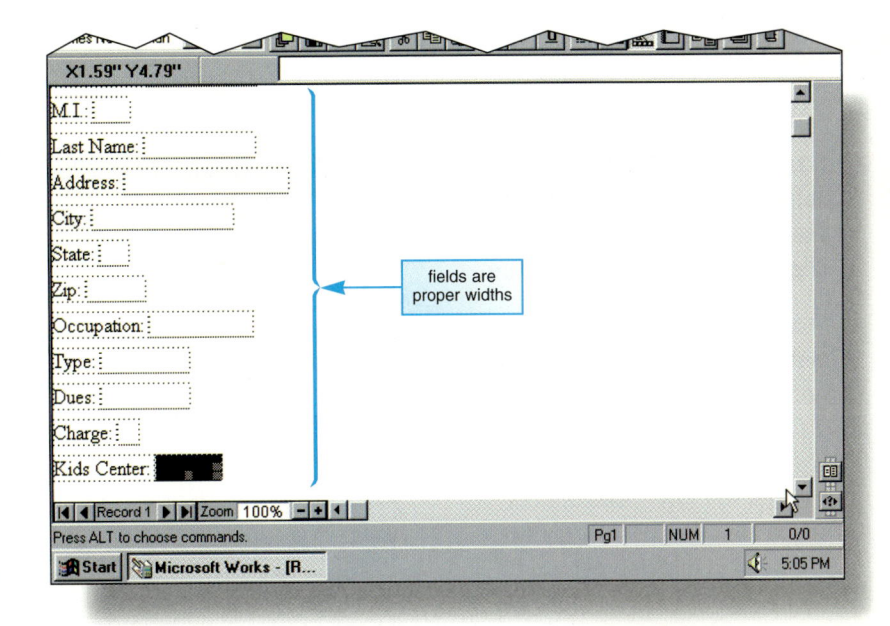

FIGURE 3-21

> **OtherWays**
> 1. Click field entry, click top right handle and drag to desired width

Positioning Fields on the Form

The first task of positioning the fields in the proper location requires that you determine **X-Y coordinates** for each of the fields. You can do this by dragging the field names and field entries to various locations until you are satisfied with their placement on the form. The coordinates in Table 3-3 are specified to assist in illustrating the technique of dragging fields in form design view. They were determined after moving the fields into various locations and then finally deciding on the best form layout. These locations can be modified at a later time, as will be seen when the clip art and form title are entered and formatted.

Perform the steps beginning on the next page to position the fields on the form.

TABLE 3-3

FIELD NAME	X COORDINATE	Y COORDINATE
Date Joined	X0.75"	Y1.00"
Title	X0.75"	Y1.33"
First Name	X2.00"	Y1.33"
M.I.	X4.00"	Y1.33"
Last Name	X5.00"	Y1.33"
Address	X0.75"	Y1.67"
City	X3.17"	Y1.67"
State	X5.00"	Y1.67"
Zip	X5.92"	Y1.67"
Occupation	X5.00"	Y2.00"
Type	X0.75"	Y2.67"
Dues	X0.75"	Y3.00"
Charge	X2.92"	Y2.67"
Kids Center	X2.92"	Y3.00"

> **More *About***
> **Positioning Fields on a Form**
>
> When positioning fields on a form consider which fields are always filled and which fields are seldom filled. Entering data is faster and more efficient if the user does not need to press the TAB key to skip over seldom-used fields. Group the most often-used fields together at the top of the form.

W 3.20 • Project 3 • Using Form Design to Create a Database

Steps: To Position Fields on the Form

1 **Scroll the screen up so the Date Joined field is visible. Highlight the Last Name field name by clicking the words, Last Name.**

Works highlights the Last Name field name with a dark background and the block arrow mouse pointer displays with the word DRAG below it (Figure 3-22). You often will find it easier to move fields out of sequence. The Last Name field is moved in this step because it occupies the rightmost position on the second line of the form.

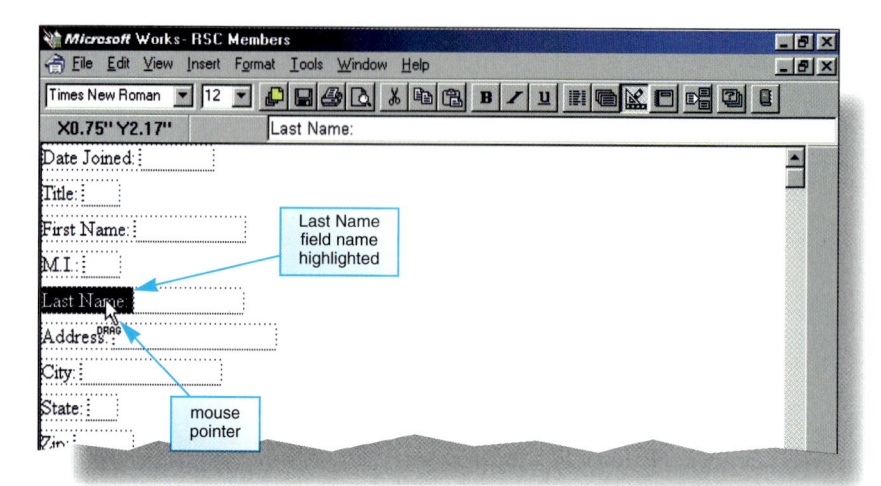

FIGURE 3-22

2 **Drag the Last Name field toward its location.**

As you drag the field, Works displays a dotted outline of both the field name and the field itself (Figure 3-23). The word MOVE displays below the mouse pointer. The coordinates of the outline are changed as you drag the outline. The field you drag remains highlighted and does not move while you drag.

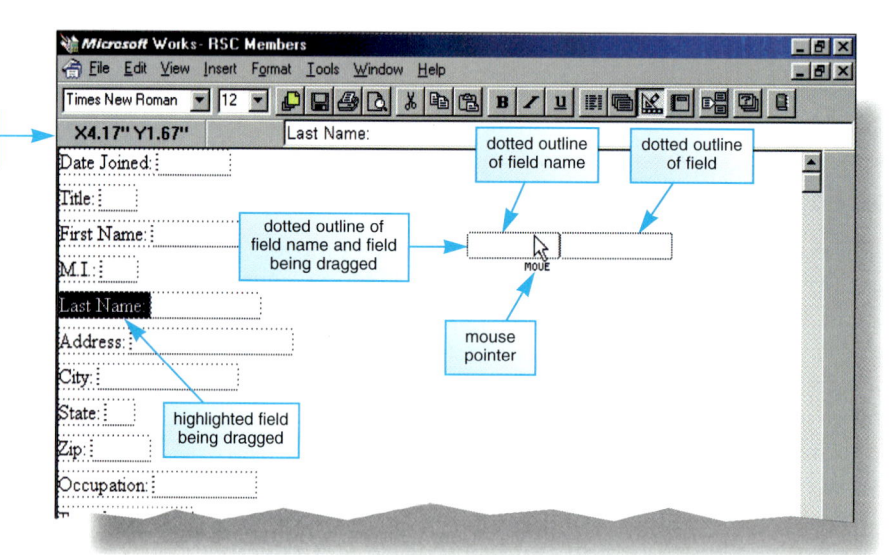

FIGURE 3-23

3 **When the dotted outline is at the desired location (X5.00" Y1.33"), release the left mouse button.**

Works moves the highlighted field to the location of the dotted outline (Figure 3-24). After being moved, the field name remains highlighted.

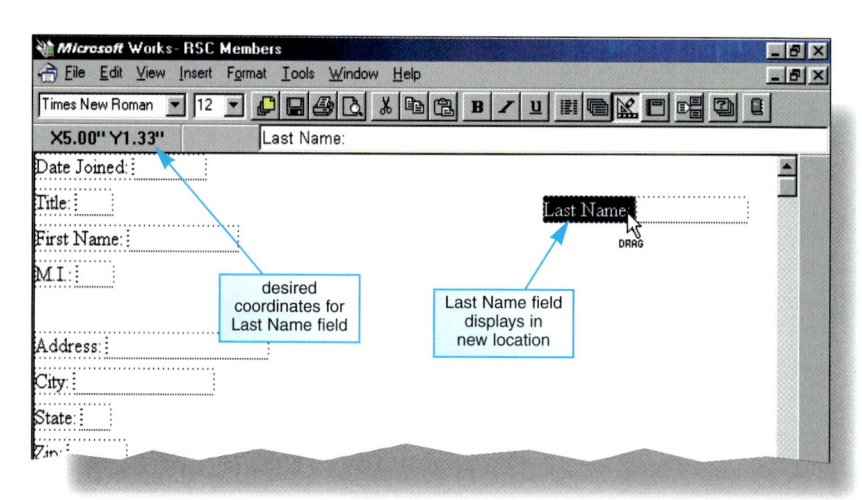

FIGURE 3-24

Formatting the Database Form in Form Design View • **W 3.21**

4 Using the same technique, move the M.I. field to coordinates X4.00" Y1.33", the First Name field to coordinates X2.00" Y1.33", and the Title field to coordinates X0.75" Y1.33".

The fields are moved to the prescribed locations (Figure 3-25). Each of the fields is on the same line (Y coordinate 1.33").

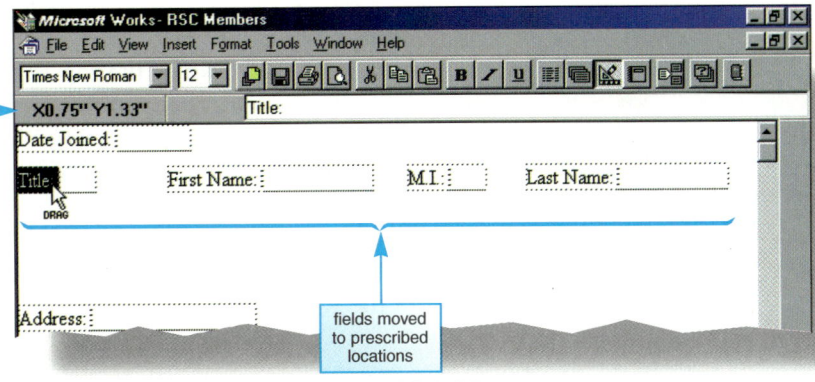

FIGURE 3-25

5 Drag the Zip, State, City, Address, and Occupation fields to their proper locations, as specified in Table 3-3 on page W 3.19.

Each of the fields is positioned in its proper location (Figure 3-26).

FIGURE 3-26

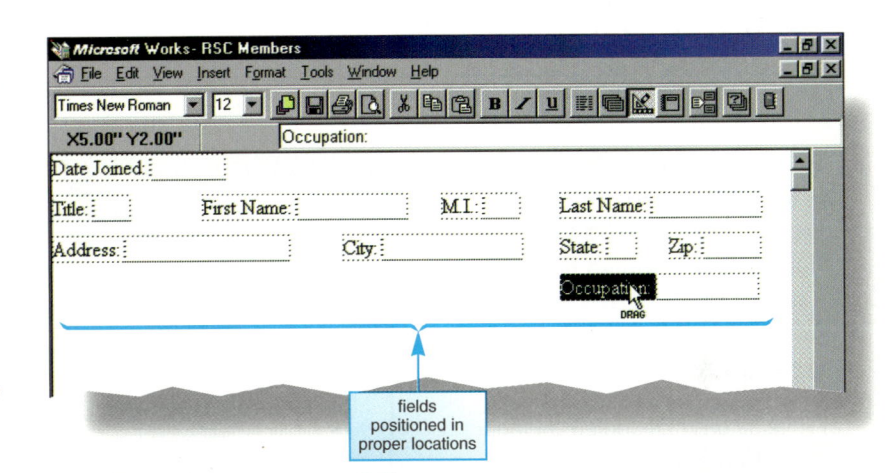

6 Use the down scroll arrow to view the remaining fields. Drag the remaining fields to their proper locations as specified in Table 3-3. Scroll up to view all fields in their proper locations.

All the fields are positioned in their proper locations (Figure 3-27).

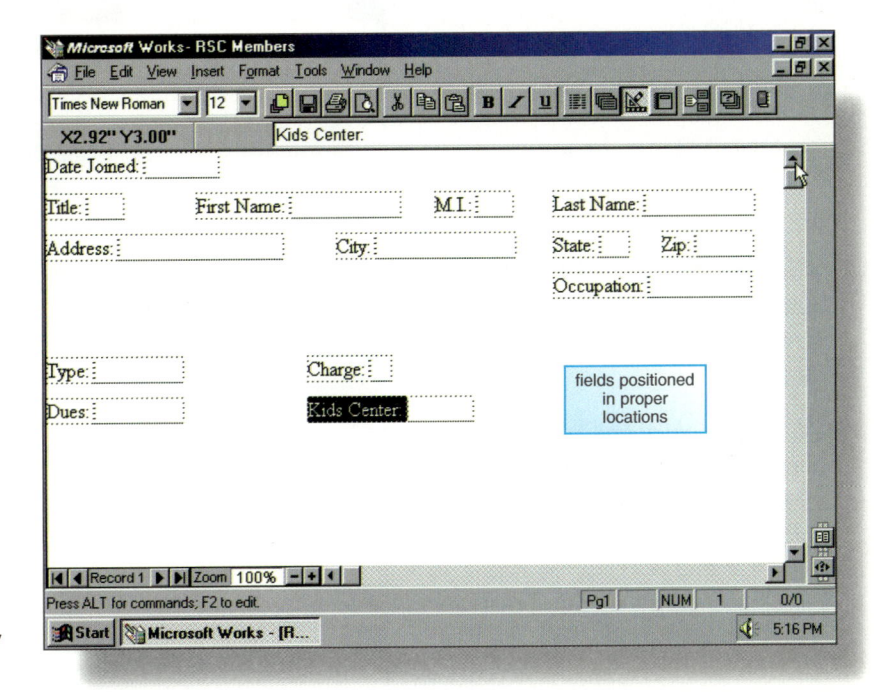

FIGURE 3-27

OtherWays

1. On Edit menu click Position Selection

You should note that even after arranging the fields in the form, at any time you can move the fields to make the form more attractive and easier to read.

W 3.22 • Project 3 • Using Form Design to Create a Database

More About
Selecting Field Names

To select many fields at one time in form view, you can save time by drawing a lasso around the fields. Click at one corner of the block, and then drag to the opposite corner to lasso the block.

Moving the Field Names as a Unit

You must make room at the top of the form because the clip art will be inserted in the top left corner of the form and the title will be entered and increased in size and formatted using WordArt. The title will occupy an area approximately one inch at the top of the form. Below the title, you also will insert a bar and a text label to identify the information located after the label. To provide for this area at the top of the form, move the field names down approximately one inch. To move the field names down as a unit on the form, perform the following steps.

Steps   To Move Field Names as a Unit

1 **Scroll up and click the Date Joined field name. Hold down the CTRL key and click the Title field name. Continue this process until all fields on the database form are highlighted. Release the CTRL key.**

All fields are highlighted on the form (Figure 3-28).

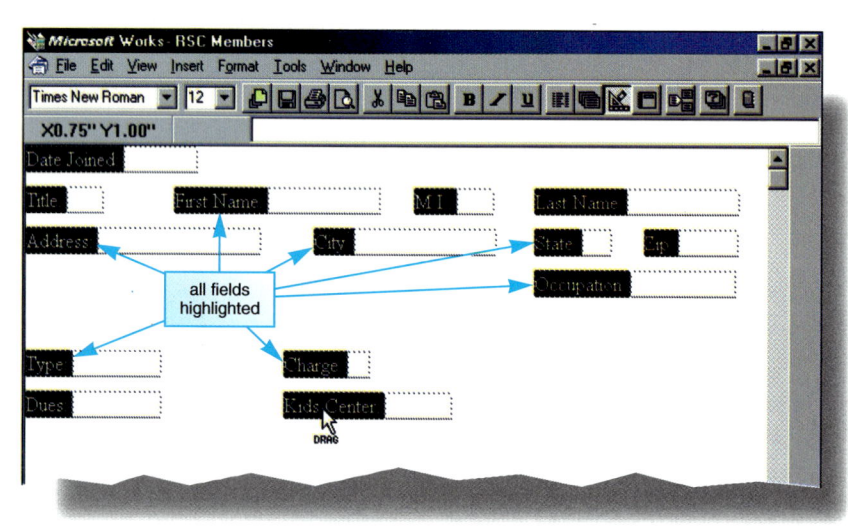

FIGURE 3-28

2 **Click the Date Joined field name and drag all fields down by dragging the Date Joined field down.**

After you highlight all field names, dragging a single field name will drag all field names as a unit (Figure 3-29).

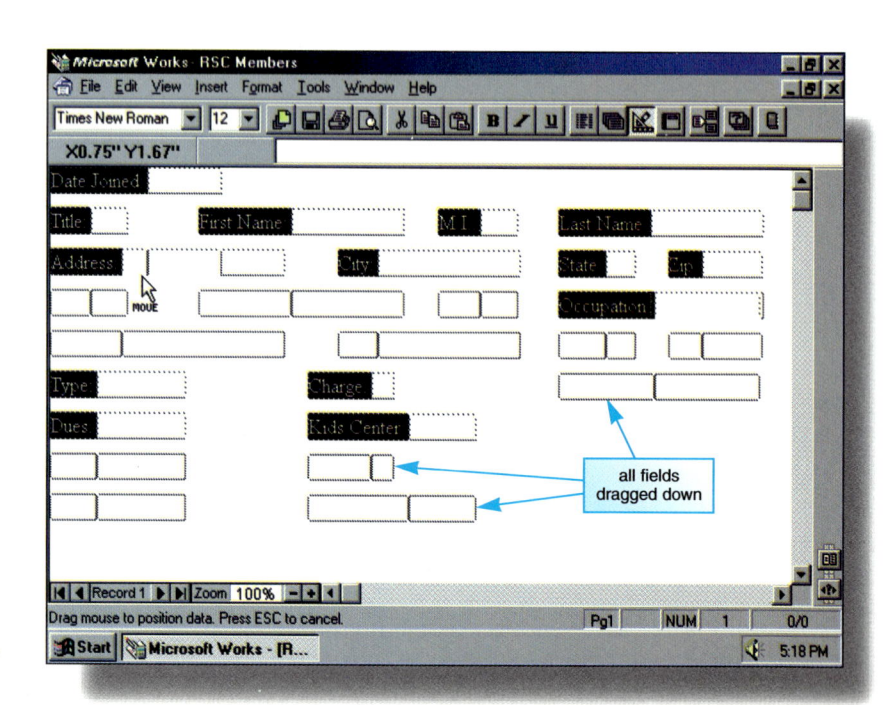

FIGURE 3-29

Formatting the Database Form in Form Design View • W 3.23

3 **When the coordinates are X0.75" Y2.00", release the left mouse button.**

The fields are repositioned on the database form (Figure 3-30). The Date Joined field is positioned at coordinates X0.75" Y2.00". The other fields retain their relative positions.

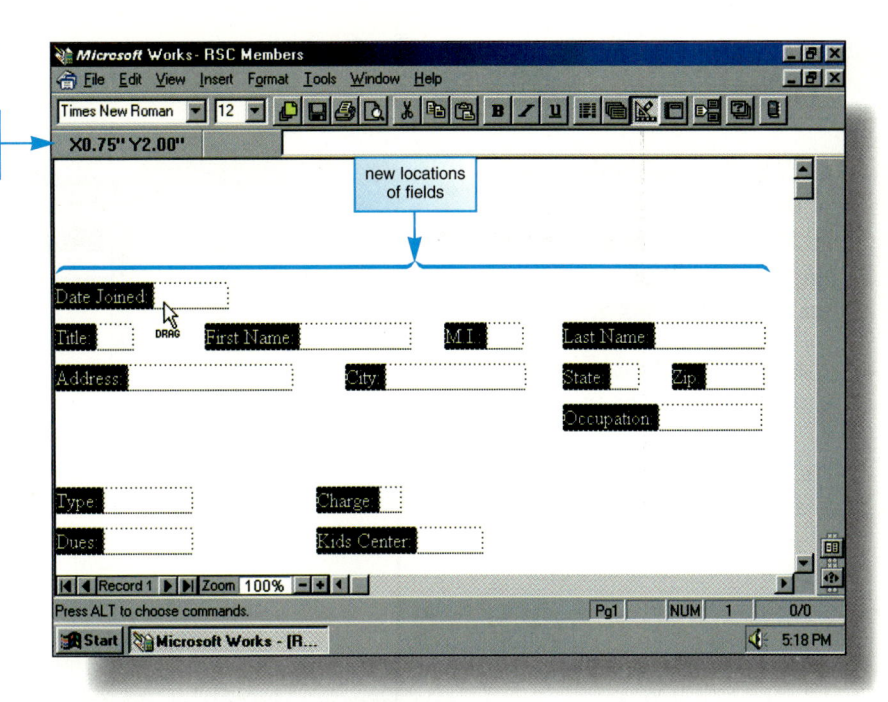

FIGURE 3-30

Importing Clip Art from Microsoft Clip Gallery Live on the World Wide Web

Recall from Project 1 that you used Microsoft Clip Gallery to insert a clip art image into a document. Because the number of clip art images in the Microsoft Clip Gallery is limited, sometimes you may not find one that enhances your document. Microsoft maintains a **Web site** on the **World Wide Web** called **Microsoft Clip Gallery Live** that contains files for clip art, pictures, sounds, and motion.

You can find clip art images (clips) in Microsoft Clip Gallery Live by searching for clips using keywords or you can browse for clips by selecting a category that best describes the topic the clip will represent.

To access the Microsoft Clip Gallery Live Web site, you must have access to the World Wide Web and Web browser software. You access the World Wide Web through an **Internet service provider**, called an **ISP**. This project, for example, uses **The Microsoft Network (MSN)** to access the Web and uses the **Microsoft Internet Explorer** Web browser. If you do not have an ISP, your instructor will provide the clip art file used in this project.

The Microsoft Clip Gallery 3.0 dialog box contains a **Connect to Web for additional clips button** that connects to the Microsoft Clip Gallery Live Web site. Perform the steps on the following pages to insert clip art from Microsoft Clip Gallery Live.

W 3.24 • Project 3 • Using Form Design to Create a Database

Steps: To Insert Clip Art from Microsoft Clip Gallery Live

1 **Click in the upper left corner of the form at the coordinates X0.75" Y1.00". Click Insert on the menu bar and then point to ClipArt.**

The insertion point is positioned in the upper left corner on the form at the coordinates X0.75" Y1.00" and the Insert menu displays (Figure 3-31).

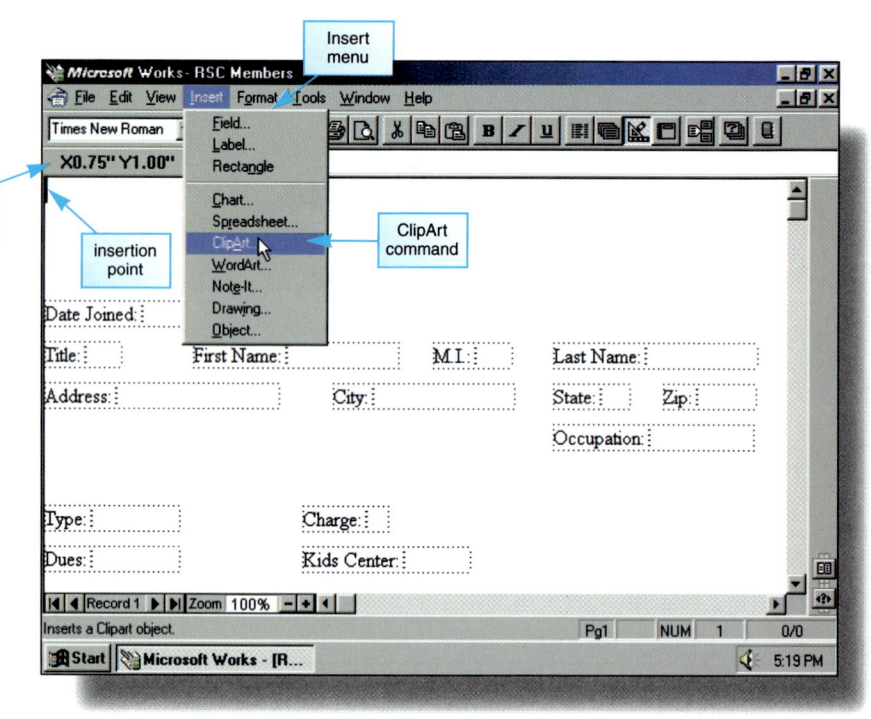

FIGURE 3-31

2 **Click ClipArt. When the Microsoft Clip Gallery 3.0 dialog box displays, point to the Connect to Web for additional clips button.**

The Microsoft Clip Gallery 3.0 dialog box opens and displays the Clip Art sheet (Figure 3-32).

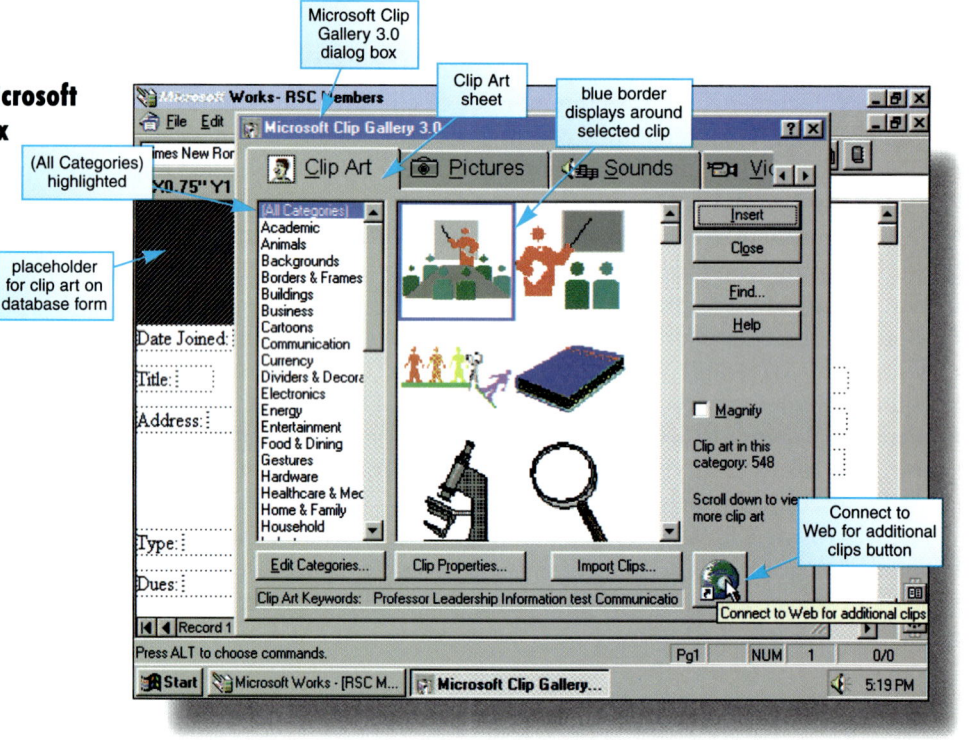

FIGURE 3-32

Microsoft **Works 4** Windows 95

Formatting the Database Form in Form Design View • **W 3.25**

3 **Click the Connect to Web for additional clips button. Connect to the World Wide Web as required by your browser software and ISP. When the Microsoft Clip Gallery Live start page displays, read the End-User License Agreement for Microsoft Software. Click the Accept button.**

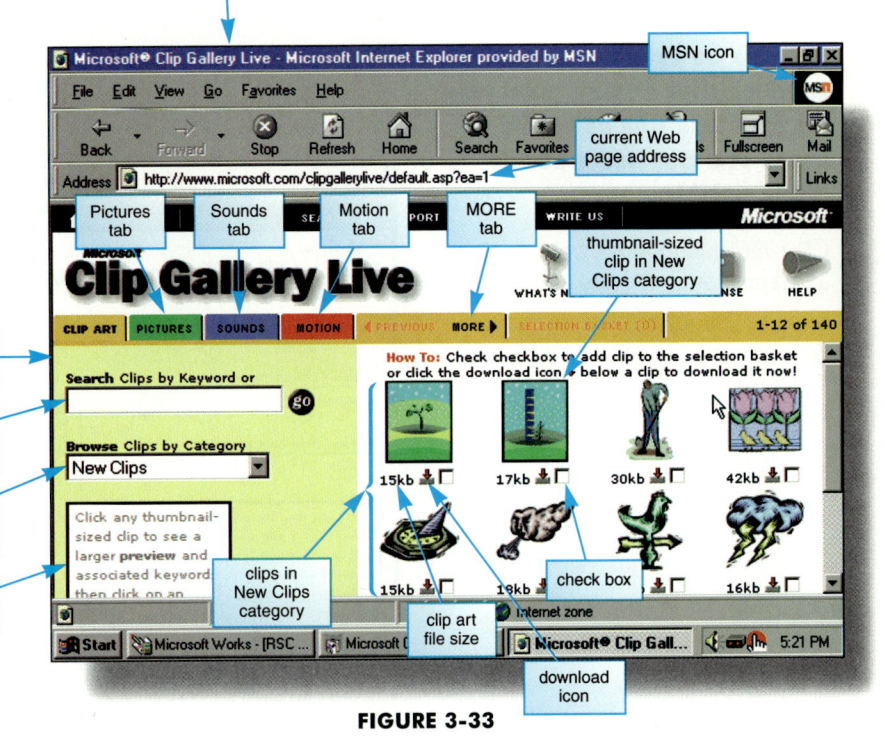

If you are using a modem, Microsoft Clip Gallery displays a dialog box that connects you to the World Wide Web via your ISP. If you are directly connected to the World Wide Web through a computer network, the dialog box does not display. The Microsoft Clip Gallery Live Web page loads and displays four tabbed sheets labeled Clip Art, Pictures, Sounds, and Motion (Figure 7-33). The Clip Art sheet displays the Search Clips by Keyword text box and the Browse Clips by Category text box. The text, New Clips, displays in the Browse Clips by Category text box indicating the clips that display are from the New Clips category. Each clip displays as a thumbnail-sized sketch. Under each clip is the file size, the download icon, and a check box. The preview box displays below the Browse Clips by Category text box.

FIGURE 3-33

4 **Click the Search Clips by Keyword text box. Type** weights **and then point to the Go button.**

The keyword, weights, displays in the Search Clips by Keyword text box (Figure 3-34).

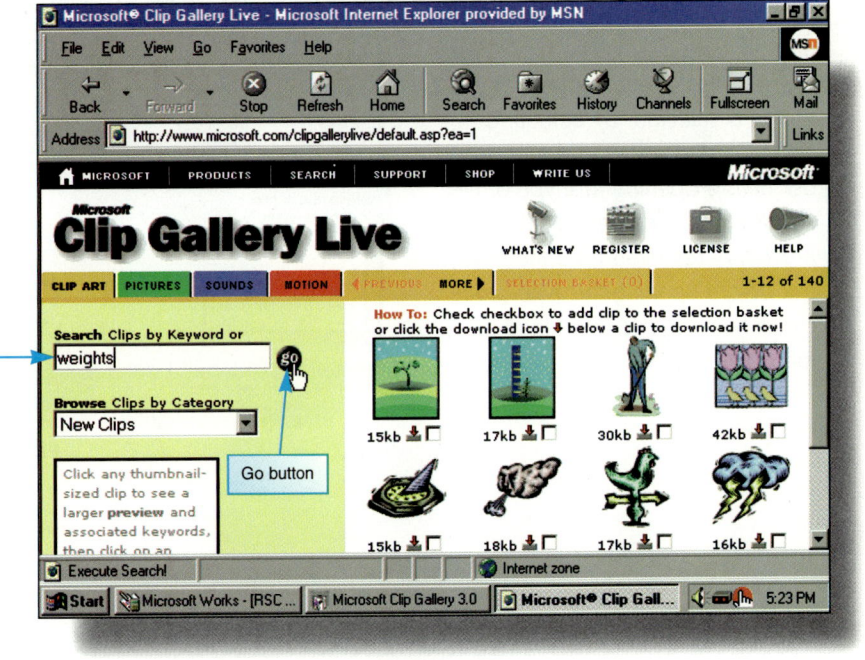

FIGURE 3-34

W 3.26 • Project 3 • Using Form Design to Create a Database

5) **Click the Go button. When all matching clips display, point to the download icon below the image of a man and a woman lifting weights.**

Clips matching the keyword, weights, display (Figure 3-35). New Clips no longer displays in the Browse Clips Category text box. The results of the search, 1-12 of 14, display above the clips indicating a total of 14 clips match the keyword and the first 12 clips display on this page.

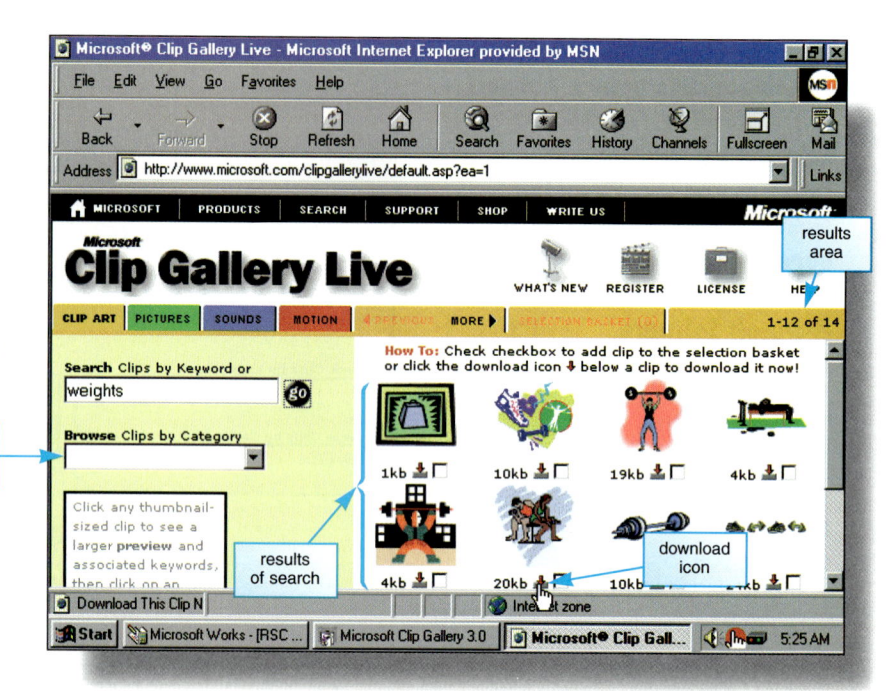

FIGURE 3-35

6) **Click the download icon below the desired clip. When the File Download dialog box displays, click Open this file from its current location. Point to the OK button.**

The File Download dialog box displays (Figure 3-36). The Open this file from its current location option button is selected. By default, a check mark displays in the Always ask before opening this type of file check box. If the check mark was previously removed from the Always ask before opening this type of file check box, the File Download dialog box will not display.

FIGURE 3-36

Formatting the Database Form in Form Design View • **W 3.27**

7 **Click the OK button. When the Microsoft Clip Gallery 3.0 dialog box displays, ensure the desired clip art is selected. Point to the Insert button.**

The desired clip art is added to the Microsoft Clip Gallery in the Downloaded Clips category (Figure 3-37). Keywords for this clip art display at the bottom of the Clip Art sheet.

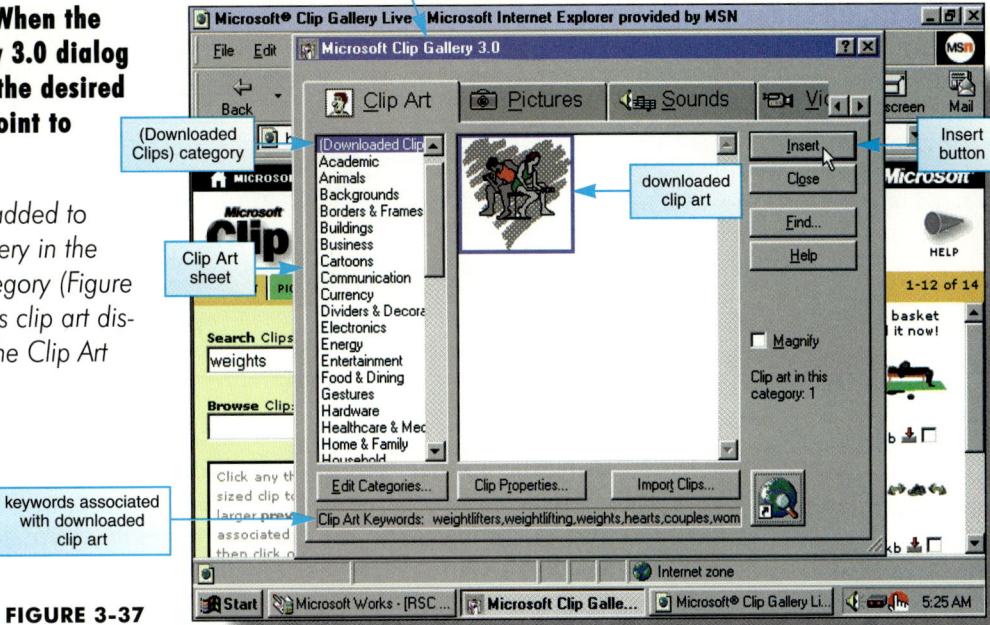

FIGURE 3-37

8 **Click the Insert button. Right-click the clip art and then point to Format Picture.**

The clip art is inserted at the location of the insertion point and the context-sensitive menu displays (Figure 3-38). A rectangular box containing dotted lines and resize handles surrounds the clip art indicating the clip art is an object and may be moved or resized.

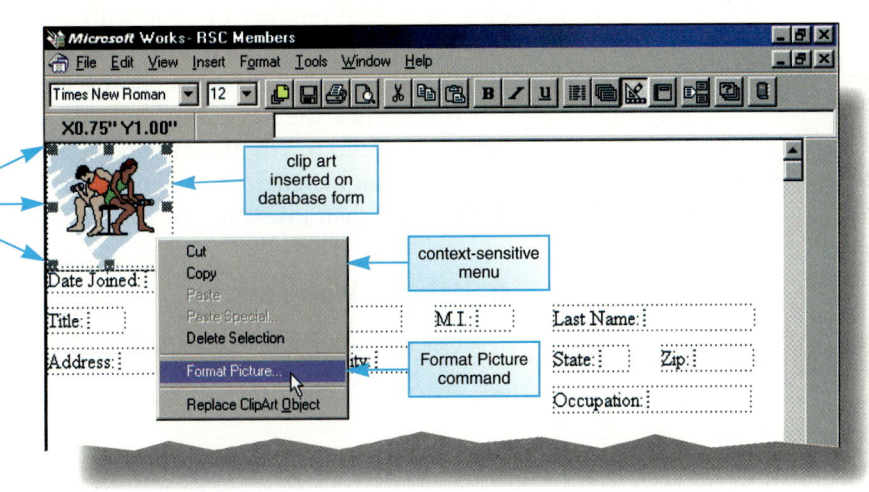

FIGURE 3-38

9 **Click Format Picture. When the Format Picture dialog box displays, in the Size box, type .67 in the Width text box and type .58 in the Height text box. Point to the OK button.**

The Format Picture dialog box displays with the values you entered, indicating you want the width to be .67 inch and the height to be .58 inch. (Figure 3-39). The Format Picture dialog box allows you to control the size of an object precisely.

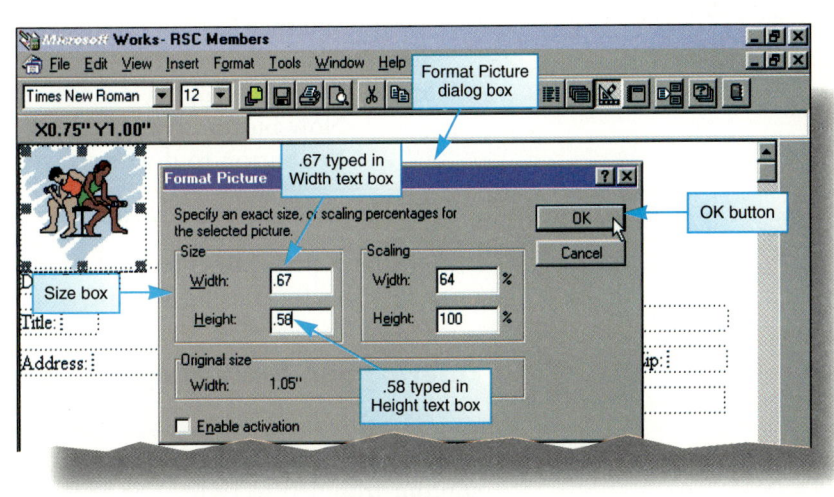

FIGURE 3-39

10 **Click the OK button.**

The resized clip art displays on the database form (Figure 3-40).

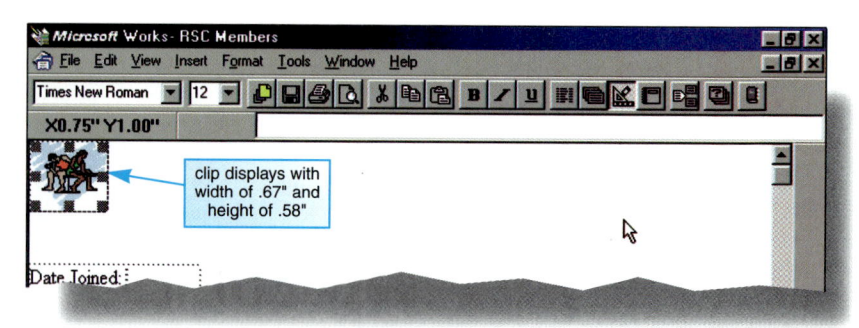

clip displays with width of .67" and height of .58"

FIGURE 3-40

Using the Format Picture command allows more precise control over the sizing in applications where the exact size is important.

Steps 1 through 7 on the previous pages illustrate downloading a single clip to the Microsoft Clip Gallery. To download more than one clip at a time, click the check box under each clip you want to download. The clips will be stored in the Selection Basket. The **Selection Basket** is a temporary location where multiple clips are stored and then downloaded all at once. The Selection Basket stores up to 120 clips or a total number of clips with a cumulative file size of 2 MB, whichever you reach first. Individual clips may be removed from the Selection Basket by clearing the check box under the selected clip.

If you click the Save this file to disk option button in the File Download dialog box in Step 6, you download the file to a disk. If you save clip art on a disk, you must double-click the file name in Exploring – My Computer to decompress the file and then insert it into the Microsoft Clip Gallery.

Quitting a Web Session

Once you have downloaded your clip art, quit your Web session by performing the following steps.

TO QUIT A WEB SESSION

Step 1: Right-click the Microsoft Clip Gallery Live – Microsoft Internet Explorer button on the taskbar. If you are not using Microsoft Internet Explorer, right-click the button for your browser.
Step 2: Click Close on the shortcut menu.
Step 3: When the MSN – Connected dialog box displays, click the Hang-Up Now button to disconnect. If you are using a different ISP, click the Yes button to disconnect.

The browser software closes and the ISP connection is terminated.

The next step is to enter and format the title, RSC Sports and Fitness Centers, on a database form using WordArt.

Entering and Formatting a Title on a Database Form Using WordArt

The title on the database form, RSC Sports and Fitness Centers, displays using special effects; that is, the characters in the title display in a wave-like contour from left to right. The characters in the title also display in navy with a

Formatting the Database Form in Form Design View • W 3.29

silver shadow. To create a title with special effects, Works provides an accessory called **WordArt**. Complete the steps beginning on the next page to enter and format a title using WordArt.

Steps To Enter and Format a Title Using WordArt

1 **Position the insertion point at the coordinates X1.50" Y1.00". Click Insert on the menu bar and then point to WordArt.**

The Insert menu displays (Figure 3-41). The insertion point is located at the coordinates X1.50" Y1.00". This is the position where Works will insert the title on the database form.

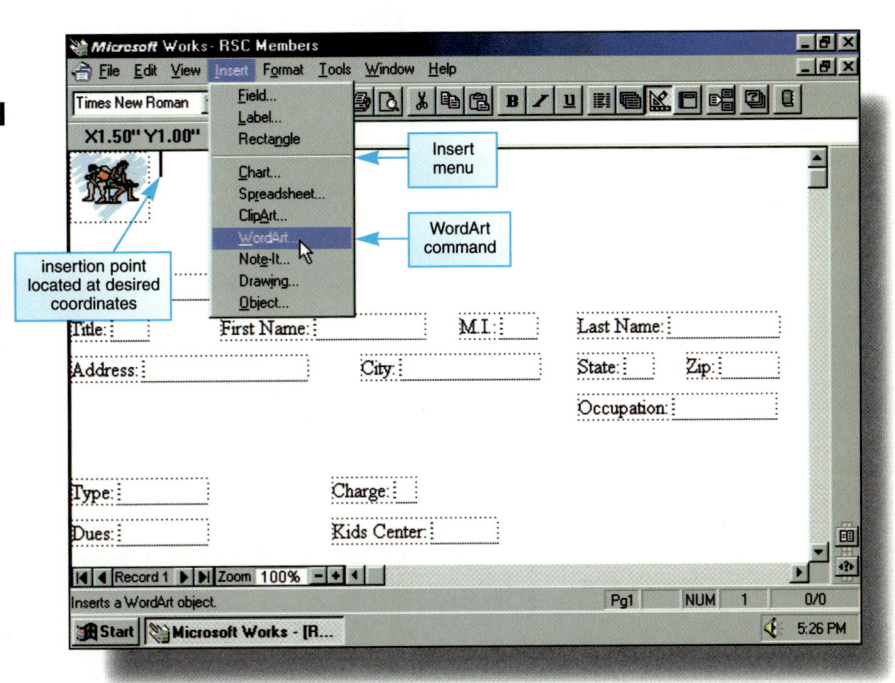

FIGURE 3-41

2 **Click WordArt.**

The Enter Your Text Here box displays (Figure 3-42). The default text, Your Text Here, is highlighted in the box. A shaded outline area containing the words, Your Text Here, displays above the window. After you type and display text, the text will display in the shaded outline area on the database form. A new menu bar and new toolbar also display. The toolbar contains a number of buttons unique to WordArt that assist in using WordArt. The buttons used in this project will be explained as needed. When you use WordArt, you are using the OLE 2.0 facilities of Works for Windows 95.

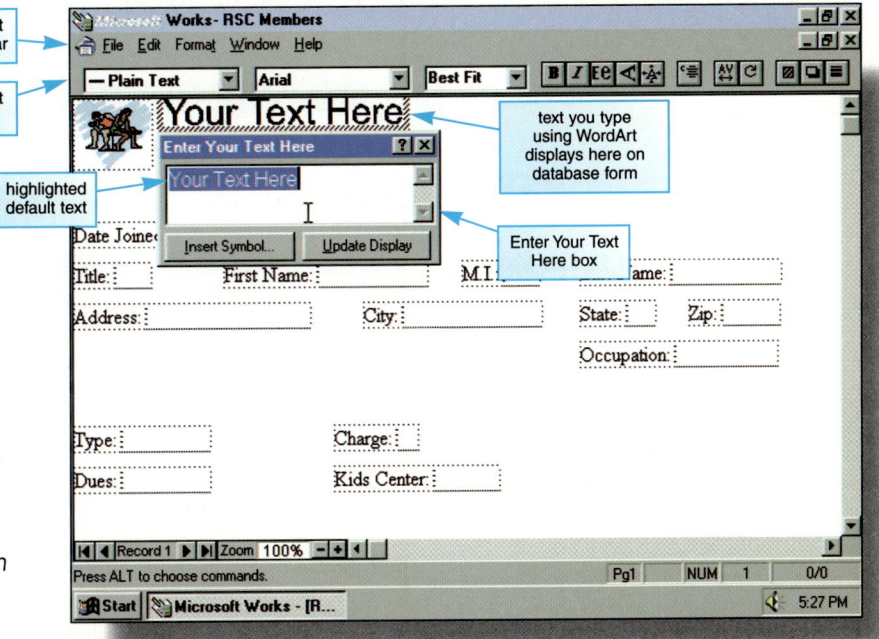

FIGURE 3-42

W 3.30 • Project 3 • Using Form Design to Create a Database

3 **Type** RSC Sports and Fitness Centers **in the Enter Your Text Here box and then click the Update Display button in the box.**

Works displays the words, RSC Sports and Fitness Centers, in the box as you type (Figure 3-43). When you click the Update Display button, the words, RSC Sports and Fitness Centers, display in the shaded outline area on the database form.

FIGURE 3-43

4 **Click the Shape box arrow on the toolbar. When the Shape drop-down list box displays, point to the first box on the right in the fourth row.**

The Shape drop-down list box displays and the **Wave 2** *shape is highlighted (Figure 3-44).*

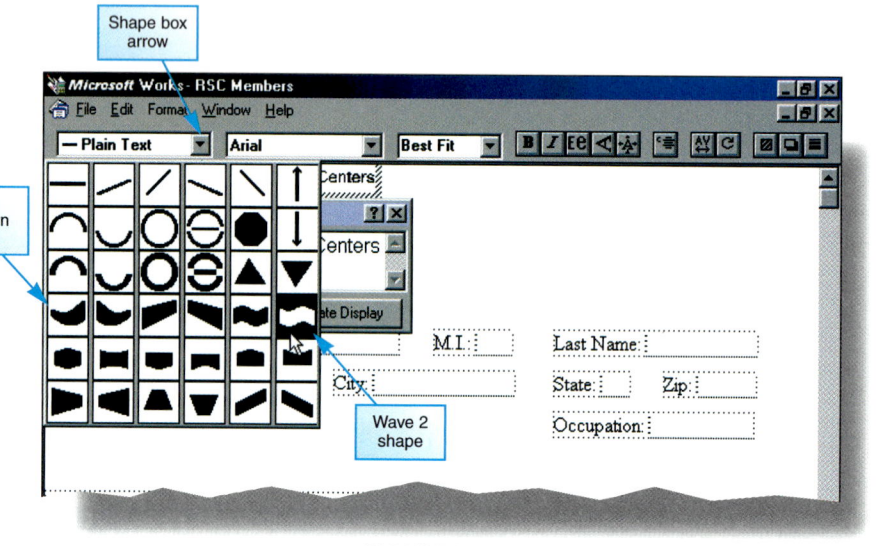

FIGURE 3-44

5 **Click Wave 2. Point to the Stretch button on the toolbar.**

The words, RSC Sports and Fitness Centers, display in the object area on the form in compressed text (Figure 3-45). The shape you clicked, Wave 2, displays in the Shape box.

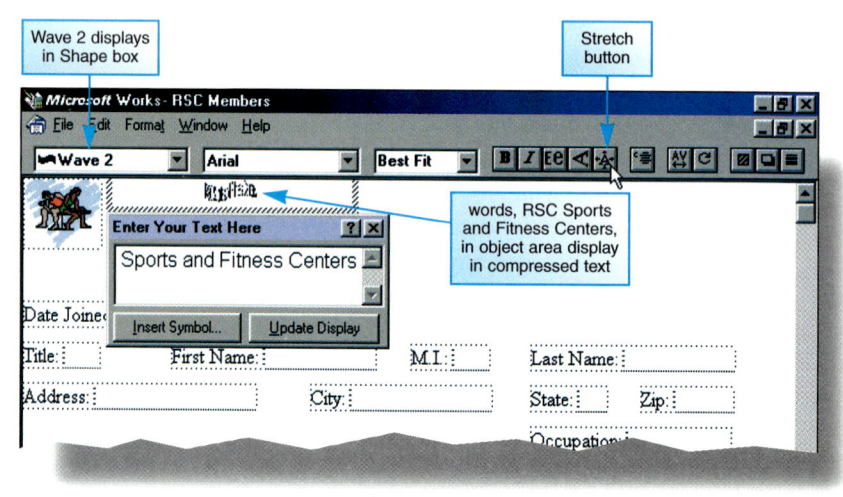

FIGURE 3-45

Formatting the Database Form in Form Design View • W 3.31

6 **Click the Stretch button. Then, click the Shadow button on the toolbar.**

WordArt displays the words, RSC Sports and Fitness Centers, with a Wave 2 effect in the object area on the database form (Figure 3-46). The Shadow dialog box displays. The Choose a Shadow box displays eight special effects for shadows. The Shadow Color box displays Silver as the default color of the shadow.

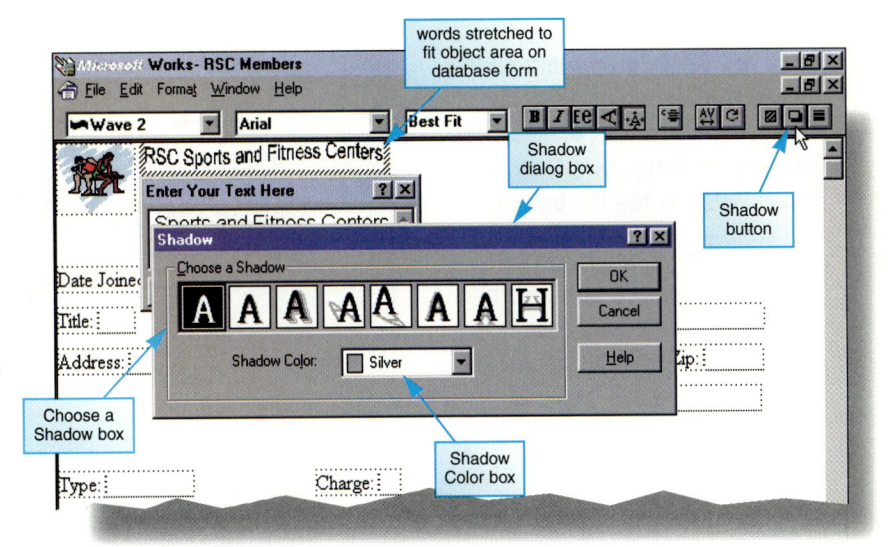

FIGURE 3-46

7 **Click the second box on the left in the Choose a Shadow box. Then, point to the OK button.**

WordArt displays the words, RSC Sports and Fitness Centers, with a silver shadow within the object area on the database form (Figure 3-47).

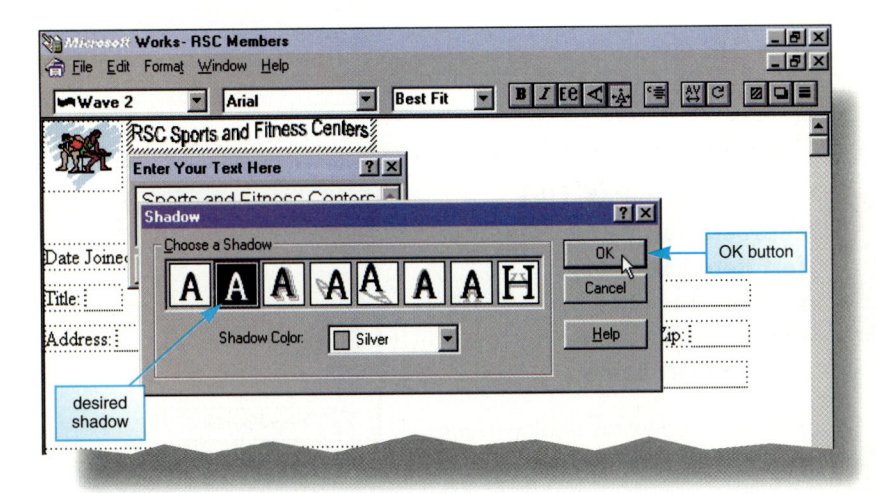

FIGURE 3-47

8 **Click the OK button. Click the Shading button on the toolbar.**

The words, RSC Sports and Fitness Centers, contain a shadow effect, and the Shading dialog box displays (Figure 3-48). In the Style box, twenty-four fill patterns are provided for the characters in the WordArt object. The Color box contains the foreground and background fill colors.

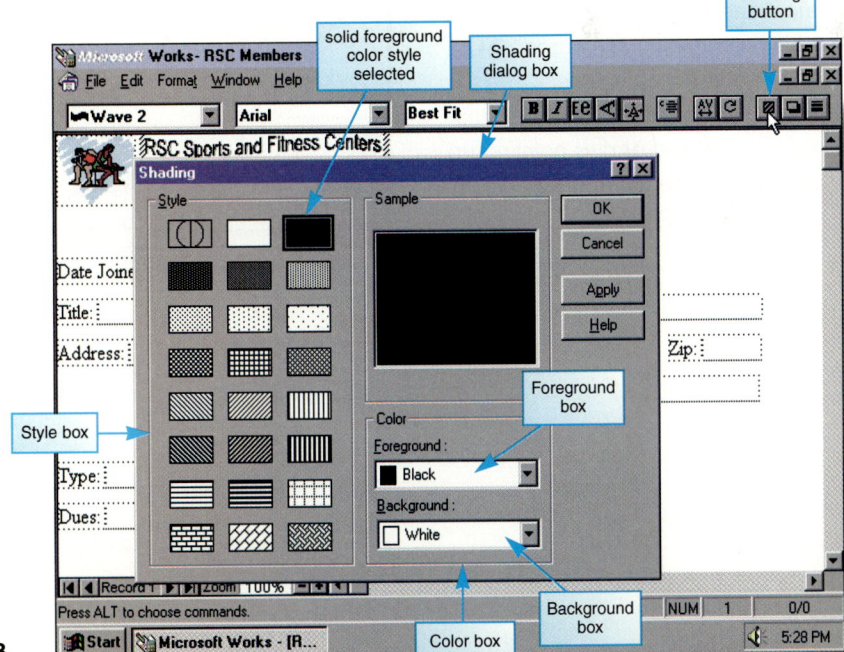

FIGURE 3-48

W 3.32 • Project 3 • Using Form Design to Create a Database

9) **Click the solid foreground style box in the Style box. Click the Foreground box arrow, scroll the list to view Navy, and then click Navy. Point to the OK button.**

The solid foreground style box is selected in the Style box (Figure 3-49). The Foreground drop-down list box displays Navy. The Sample box displays the solid navy fill pattern to be applied to the text on the database form.

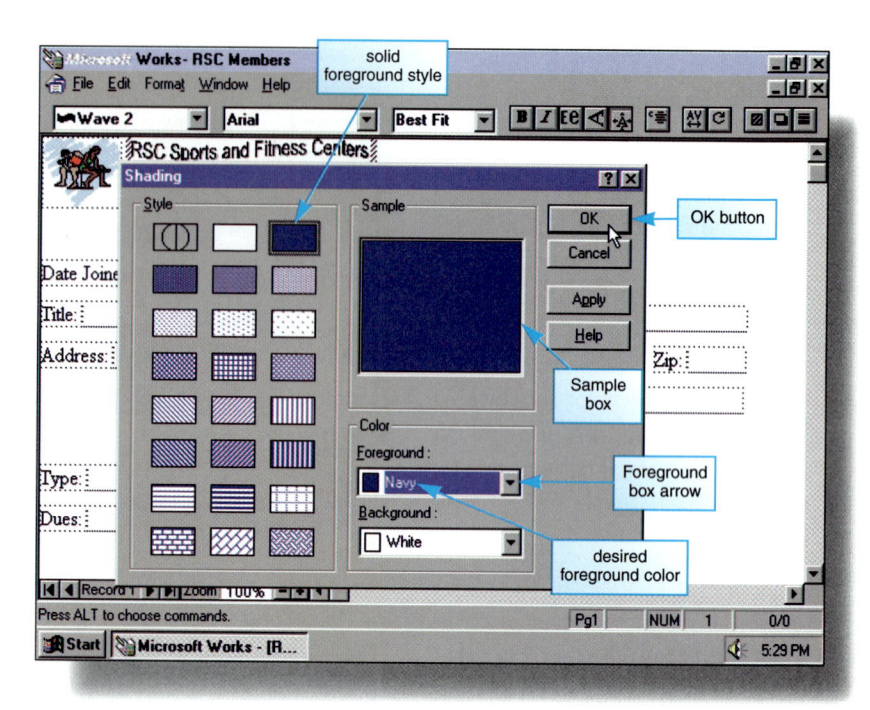

FIGURE 3-49

10) **Click the OK button. Click anywhere outside the Enter Your Text Here box. Then, point to the bottom center resize handle on the object border.**

The formatted words display (Figure 3-50). The X coordinate is 1.50" and the Y coordinate is 1.00". These coordinates refer to the leftmost and topmost position of the object containing the words, RSC Sports and Fitness Centers. The mouse pointer displays with a small square box and arrows pointing up and down. The word RESIZE displays below the arrows.

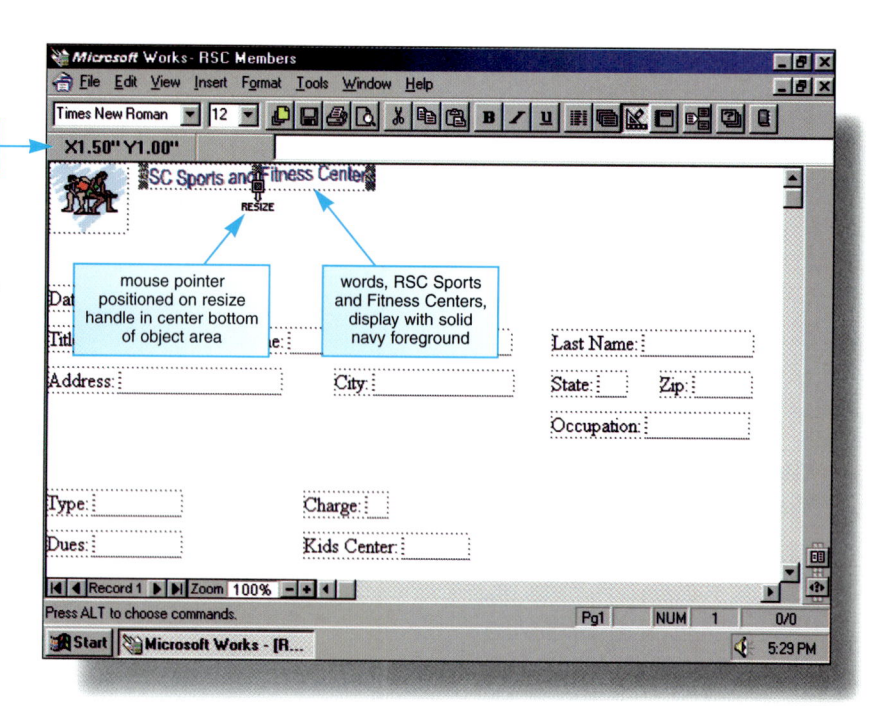

FIGURE 3-50

Microsoft **Works 4** Windows 95

Formatting the Database Form in Form Design View • **W 3.33**

11 **Drag the resize handle down to approximately the bottom of the fitness clip art. With the mouse pointer inside the WordArt object, drag the WordArt object to the left until the object is adjacent to the right border of the clip art object. Place the mouse pointer on the right center resize handle.**

As you drag the resize handle down, the object expands vertically (Figure 3-51). The object area moves to the left. Dragging the resize handle in the lower right corner expands the rectangular box both vertically and horizontally at one time. For some individuals, a two-step approach makes it easier to control the vertical and horizontal expansion.

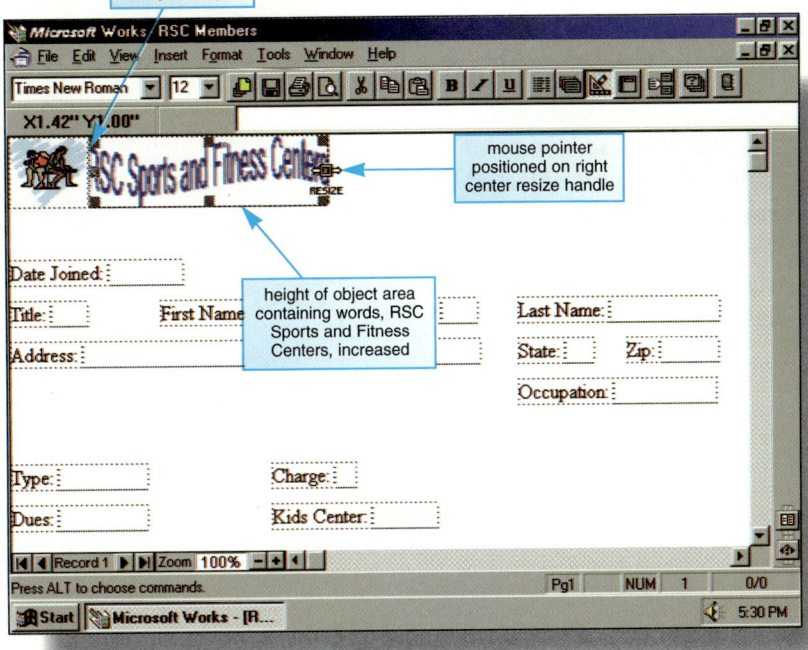

FIGURE 3-51

12 **Drag the right center resize handle to the right approximately one-quarter of an inch from the edge of the screen.**

The words, RSC Sports and Fitness Centers, expand horizontally to fill the object area (Figure 3-52).

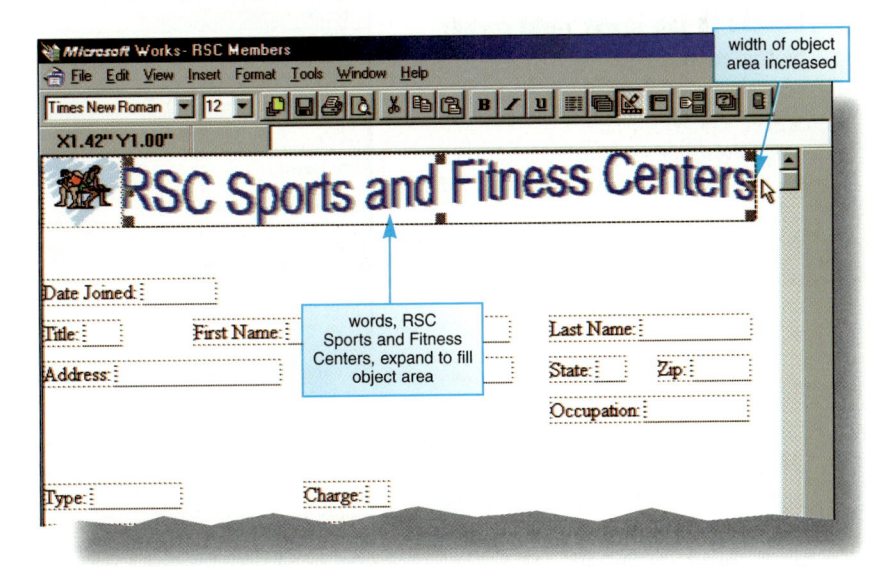

FIGURE 3-52

The words, RSC Sports and Fitness Centers, have now been formatted as required. WordArt provides many special effects for text when using Microsoft Works. To edit the object, double-click the embedded object to open WordArt and make the desired changes to the object.

Inserting a Rectangular Bar Below the Title

To further enhance the title area, the area is to contain a rectangular bar below the clip art and the words, RSC Sports and Fitness Centers (see Figure 3-11 on page W 3.13). Complete the steps on the next page to insert the bar.

W 3.34 • Project 3 • Using Form Design to Create a Database

Steps To Insert a Rectangular Bar in the Title Area

1 **Position the insertion point below the clip art object at the coordinates X0.75" Y1.58" and then right-click. Point to Insert Rectangle.**

The context-sensitive menu displays (Figure 3-53).

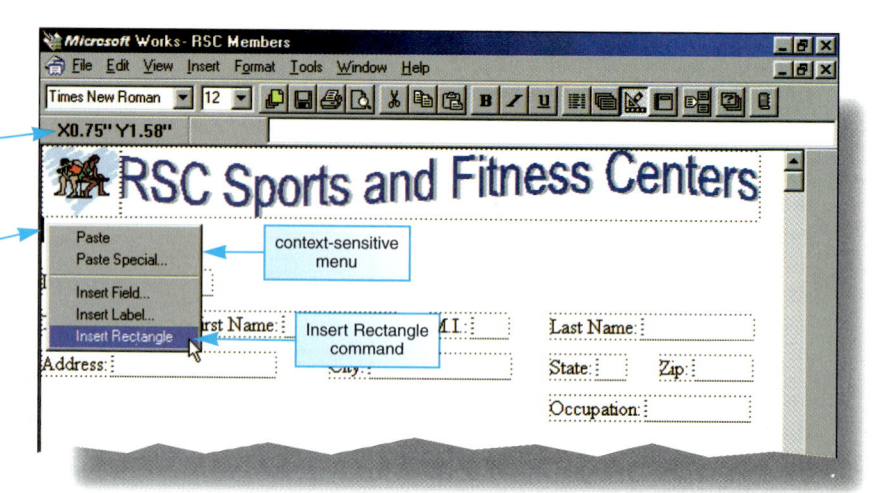

FIGURE 3-53

2 **Click Insert Rectangle. When the rectangle displays, position the mouse pointer on the resize handle in the lower right corner of the rectangle.**

Works displays a rectangle containing dotted lines and resize handles on the database form (Figure 3-54).

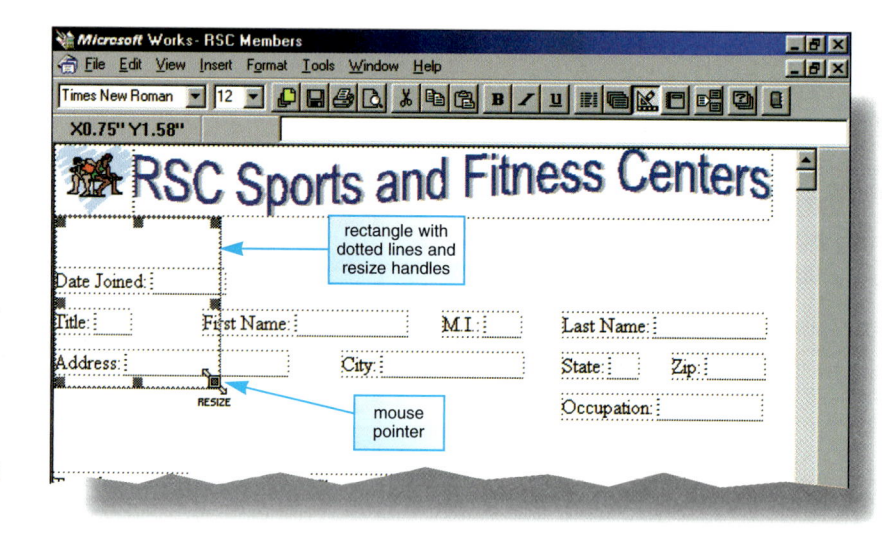

FIGURE 3-54

3 **Drag the resize handle up to the bottom of the clip art and to the right until the rectangle is the same width as the WordArt.**

Works displays the resized rectangle below the clip art and the words, RSC Sports and Fitness Centers (Figure 3-55).

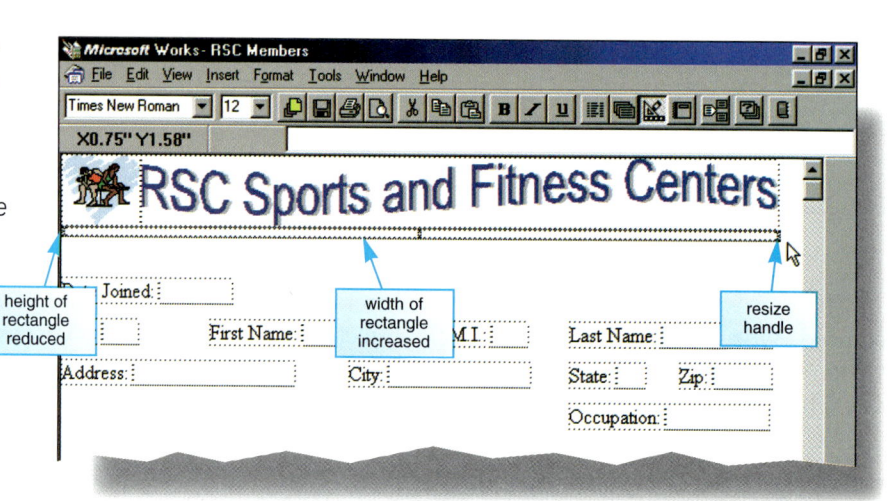

FIGURE 3-55

OtherWays

1. On Insert menu in form design view click Rectangle

Adding Color to the Rectangle

The next step is to add color to the rectangle. Dark blue displays in the rectangular bar below the clip art and the words, RSC Sports and Fitness Centers. To add color, perform the following steps.

Steps: To Add Color to the Rectangular Bar

1 **Right-click the rectangle and then point to Shading.**

The rectangle contains resize handles indicating it is selected, and the context-sensitive menu displays (Figure 3-56).

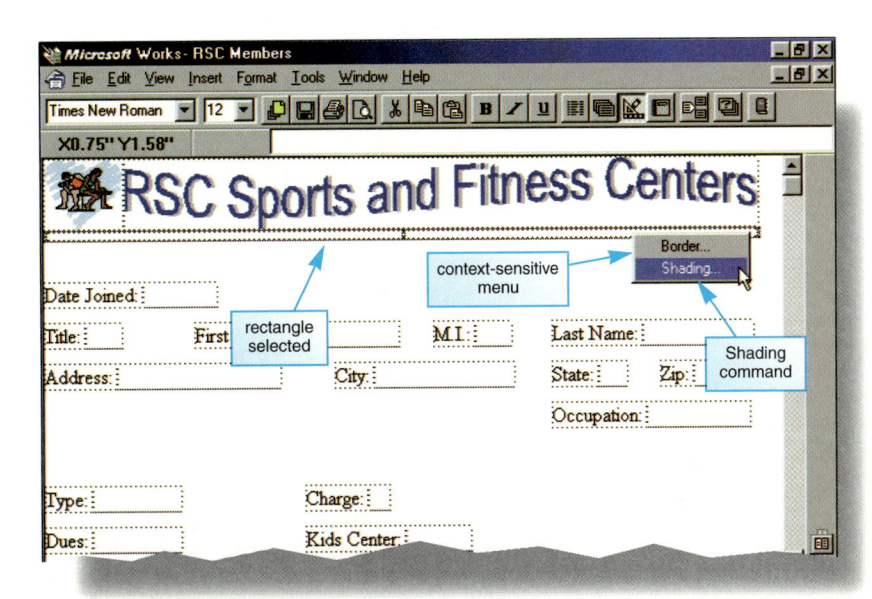

FIGURE 3-56

2 **Click Shading. When the Format dialog box displays, click the solid pattern in the Pattern list box on the Shading sheet. Scroll down the Foreground list box in the Colors box to display Dark Blue. Then, click Dark Blue. Point to the OK button.**

Works displays the Format dialog box (Figure 3-57). The solid pattern is selected in the Pattern list box and Dark Blue is highlighted in the Foreground list box. The Sample box displays a sample of the pattern and color.

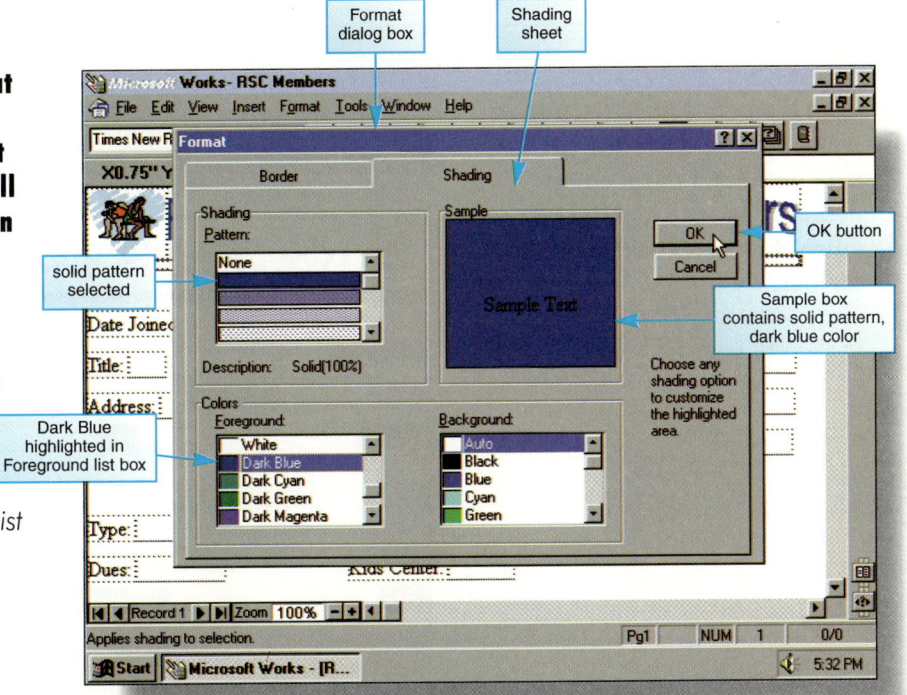

FIGURE 3-57

W 3.36 • Project 3 • Using Form Design to Create a Database

3 **Click the OK button. Click anywhere on the form to remove the selection.**

Works displays the rectangle with a solid pattern that is a dark blue color (Figure 3-58).

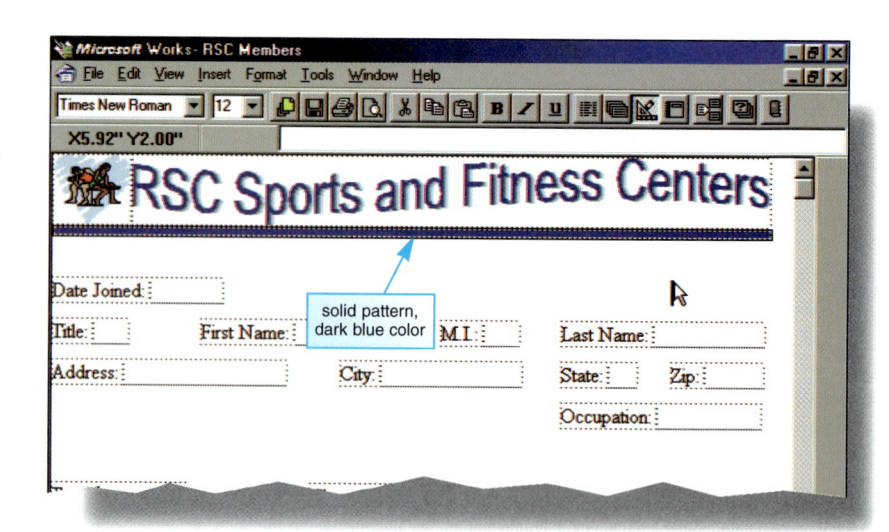

FIGURE 3-58

Most database forms in a modern computing environment use color to enhance the appearance of the form.

Formatting Field Names

To give further emphasis to the field names on the database form, each field name is to display in bold and italics. The steps on the next page explain how to display the field names in bold and italics.

Steps **To Format the Field Names**

1 **Click the Date Joined field name. While holding down the CTRL key, click each field name on the database form to highlight it. Point to the Bold button on the toolbar.**

Each field name on the database form is highlighted (Figure 3-59).

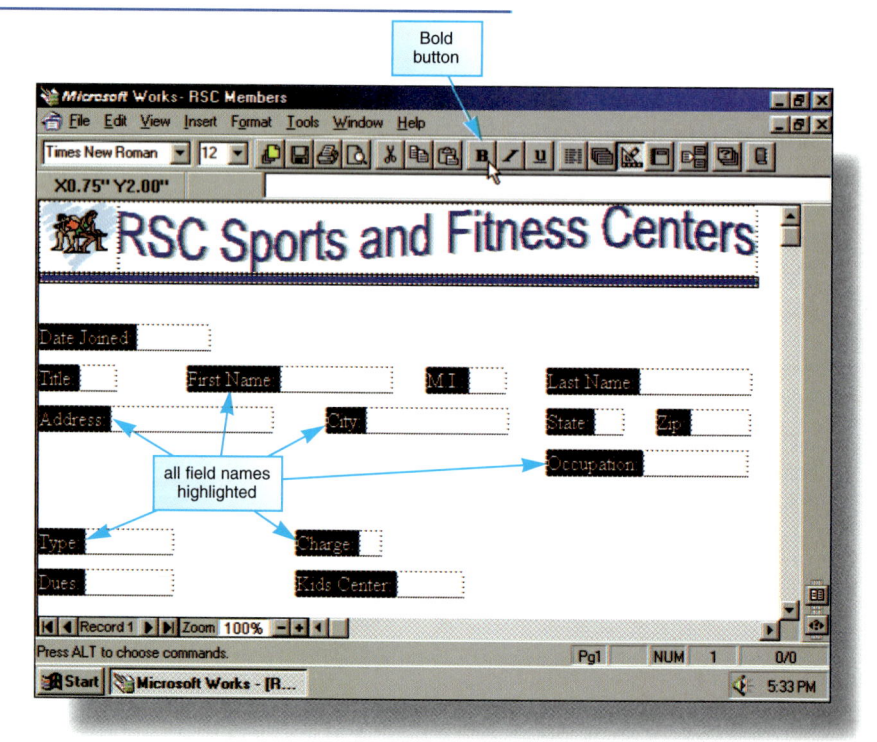

FIGURE 3-59

Microsoft **Works 4** Windows 95

Formatting the Database Form in Form Design View • **W 3.37**

2 Click the Bold button. Click the Italic button on the toolbar. Click anywhere on the database form to remove the highlighting.

Each field name on the database form displays in bold and italics (Figure 3-60).

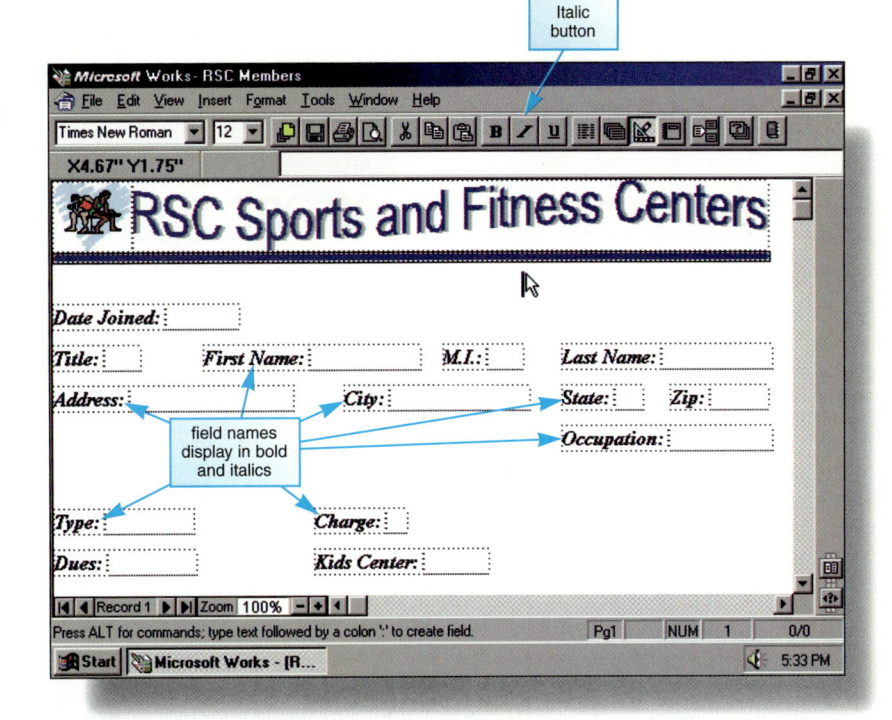

FIGURE 3-60

Adding a Border on Fields

The next step in developing the format of the database form is to add a color border to the fields. This technique precisely defines for the user where data is to appear. To accomplish this task, it is recommended that you first remove the field lines and then add the color borders. Perform the following steps to accomplish this task.

Steps To Remove Field Lines and Add a Border on Fields

1 Click the Date Joined field. While holding down the CTRL key, click each field to highlight it. Click View on the menu bar and then point to Field Lines.

All fields are highlighted, and the View menu displays (Figure 3-61).

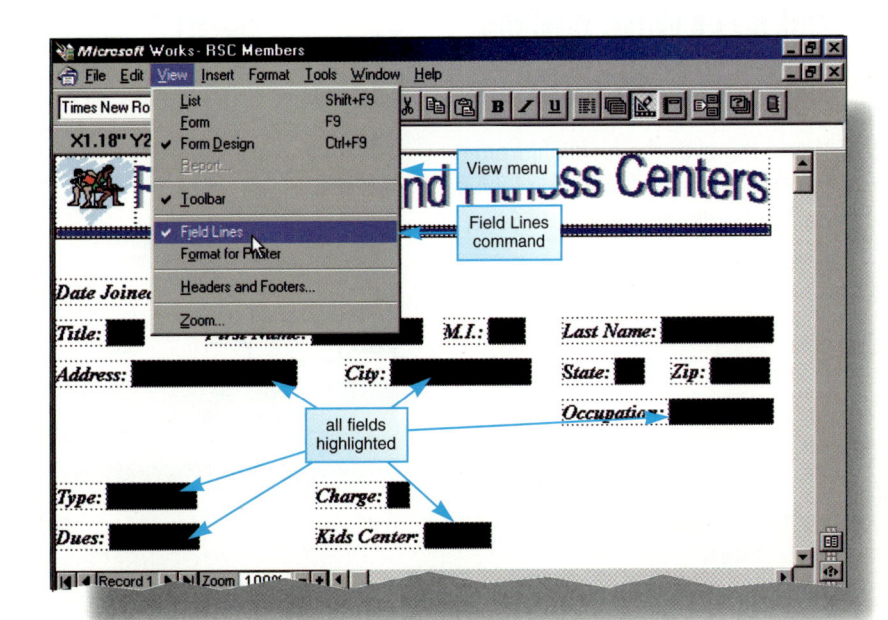

FIGURE 3-61

W 3.38 • Project 3 • Using Form Design to Create a Database

2 **Click Field Lines. Right-click the Date Joined field and then point to Border.**

The field lines no longer show and the context-sensitive menu displays (Figure 3-62).

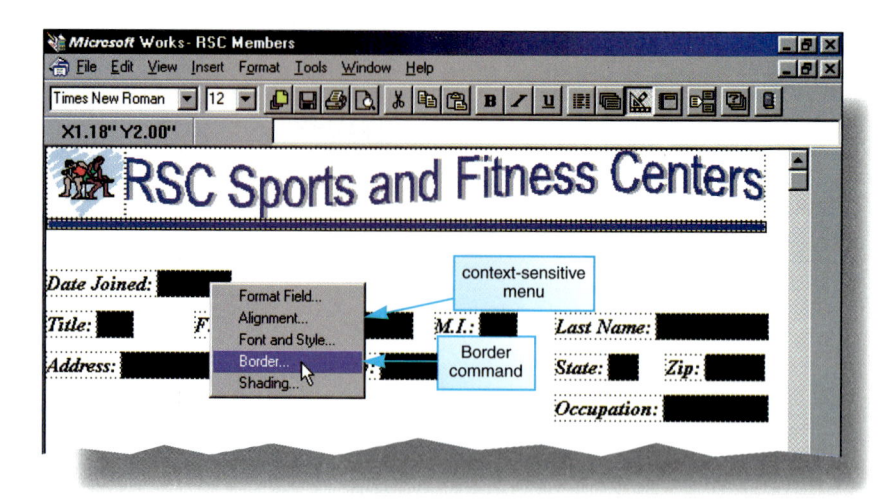

FIGURE 3-62

3 **Click Border on the context-sensitive menu. When the Format dialog box displays, click the Outline box in the Border box and scroll down the Color drop-down list to view Dark Blue. Click Dark Blue. Then, point to the OK button.**

The Format dialog box displays the selected entries (Figure 3-63).

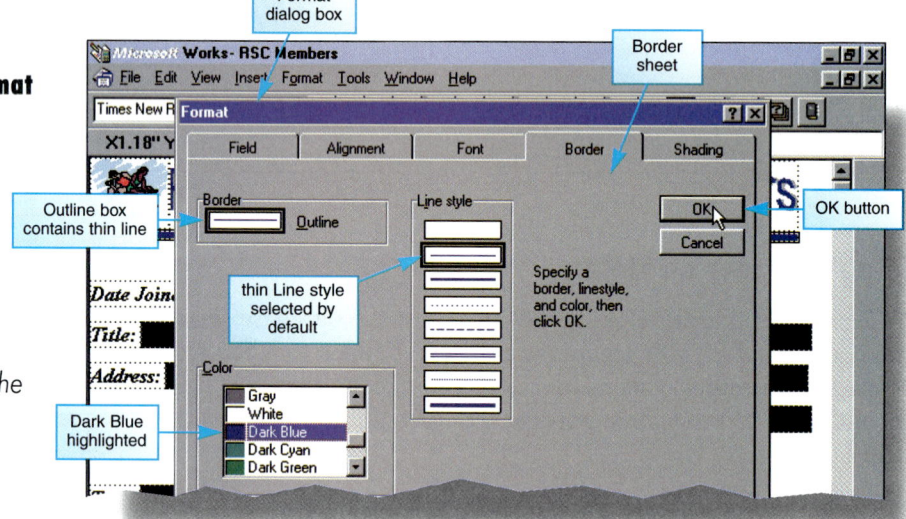

FIGURE 3-63

4 **Click the OK button. Then, click the form to remove the highlights from the fields.**

Works removes the highlight from the fields and applies the dark blue outline border to all fields (Figure 3-64).

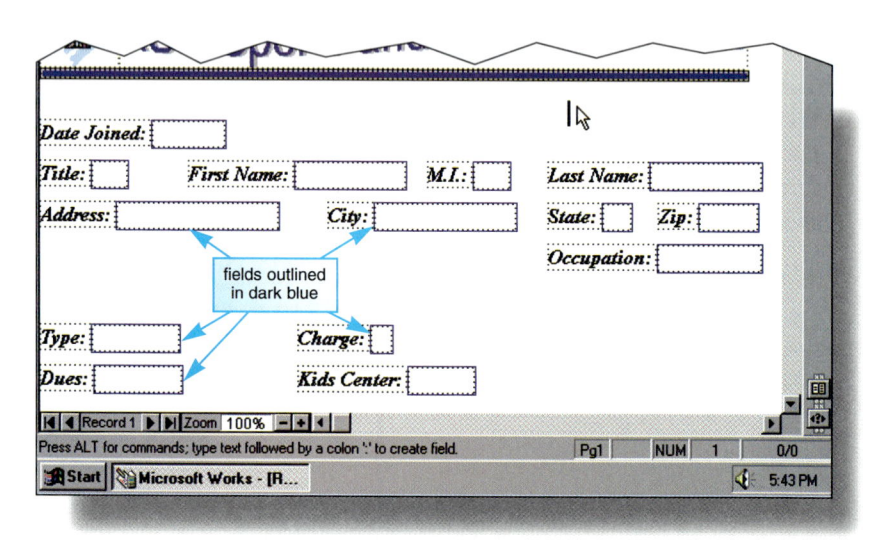

FIGURE 3-64

OtherWays

1. On Format menu in form design view, click Border

Microsoft Works 4 Windows 95

Formatting the Database Form in Form Design View • **W 3.39**

Adding Text Labels to the Database Form

The next step in formatting the form is to add two text labels to the database form. A **text label** is identifying information placed on a database form. Text labels can be any length and can contain any words or numbers that provide the description or instructions you need. The two text labels that display on the form are MEMBER INFORMATION and ACCOUNT INFORMATION as illustrated in Figure 3-13 on page W 3.14. To add the text labels, perform the following steps.

Steps To Add Text Labels to the Database Form

1 **Click at the coordinates X0.75" Y1.75".**

Works displays the insertion point at the coordinates X0.75" Y1.75" (Figure 3-65).

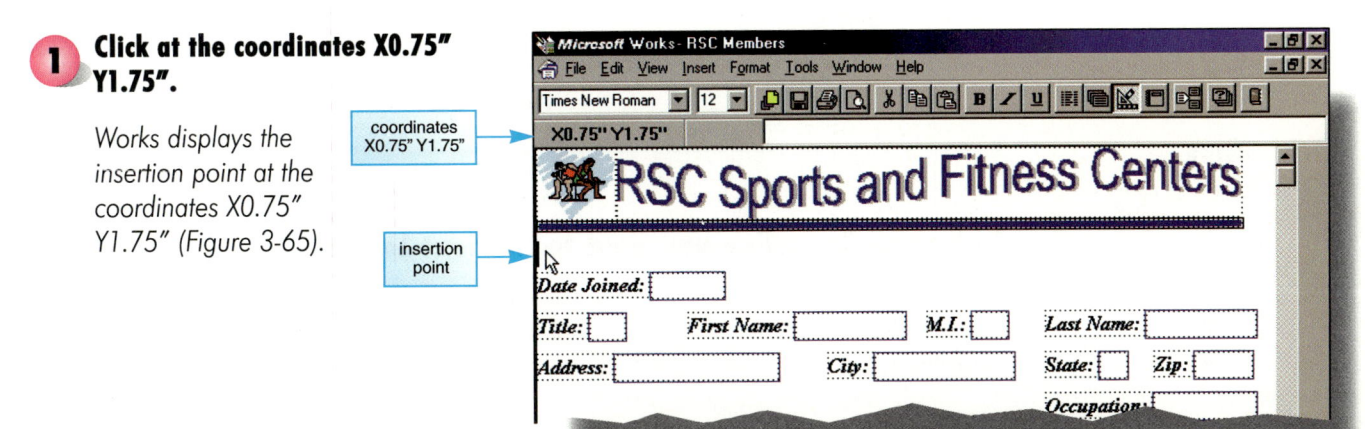

FIGURE 3-65

2 **Press the CAPS LOCK key and then type MEMBER INFORMATION as the text label.**

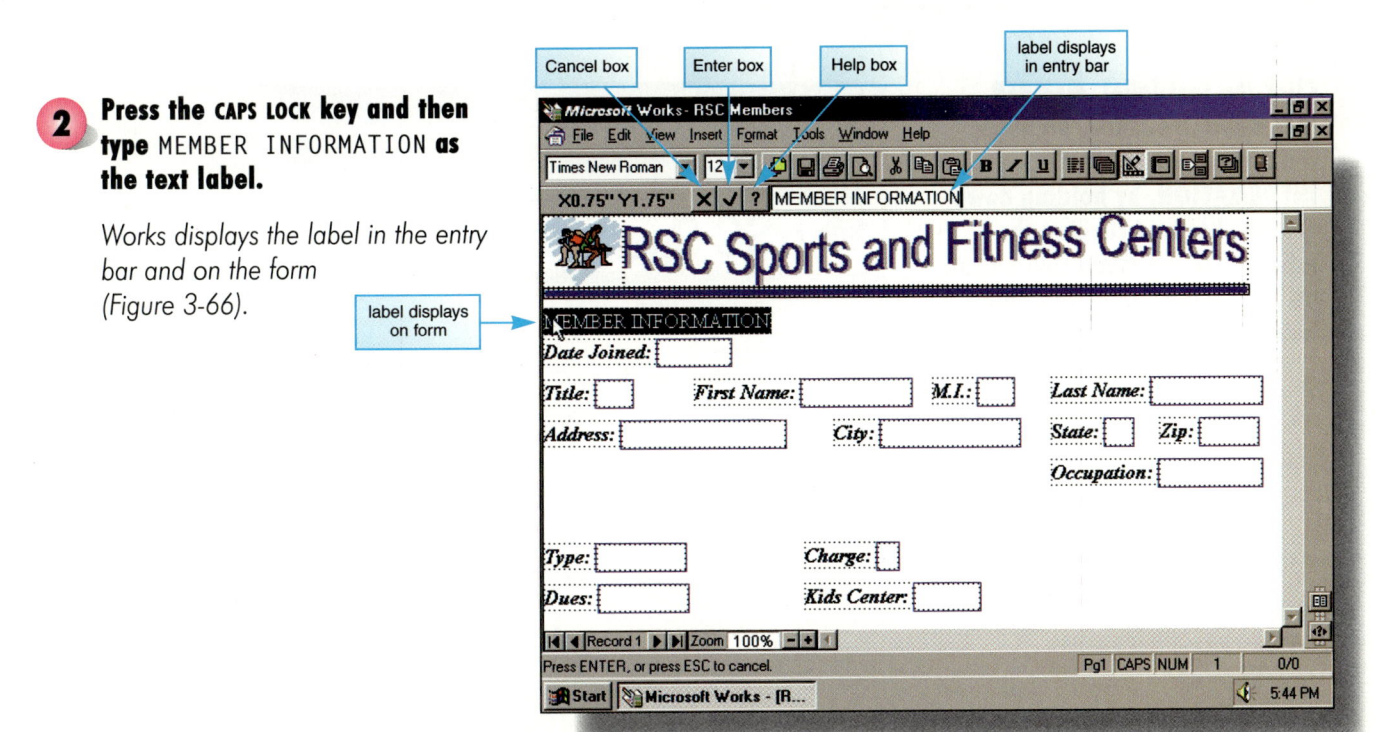

Works displays the label in the entry bar and on the form (Figure 3-66).

FIGURE 3-66

W 3.40 • Project 3 • Using Form Design to Create a Database

3 Click the Enter box or press the ENTER key. Click at the coordinates X0.75" Y3.33". Type ACCOUNT INFORMATION and then click the Enter box or press the ENTER key. Then, press the CAPS LOCK key.

Works enters the text labels on the database form at the coordinates X0.75" Y1.75" and X0.75" Y3.33" (Figure 3-67).

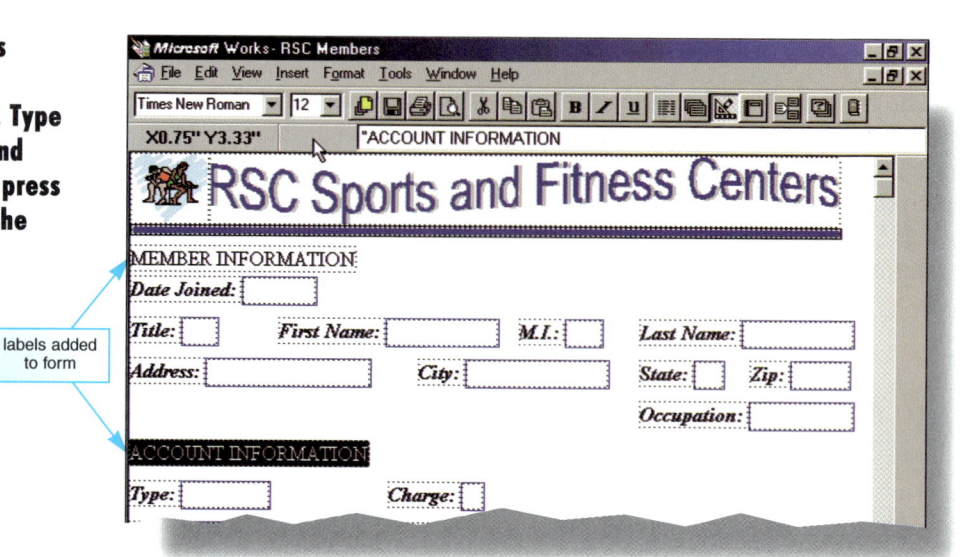

FIGURE 3-67

OtherWays
1. On Insert menu in form design view click Label, type desired text label, click OK button

Adding an Underline and Bold to the Text Labels

The final task in developing the format of the database form is to add a single underline below the text labels and display the labels in bold. Perform the following step to accomplish this task.

Steps To Underline and Apply Bold to Text Labels

1 Click the text label, MEMBER INFORMATION. Then, highlight the text label, ACCOUNT INFORMATION, by holding down the CTRL key and clicking the label. Click the Underline button on the toolbar. Click the Bold button on the toolbar.

The text labels display with a single underline and bold (Figure 3-68).

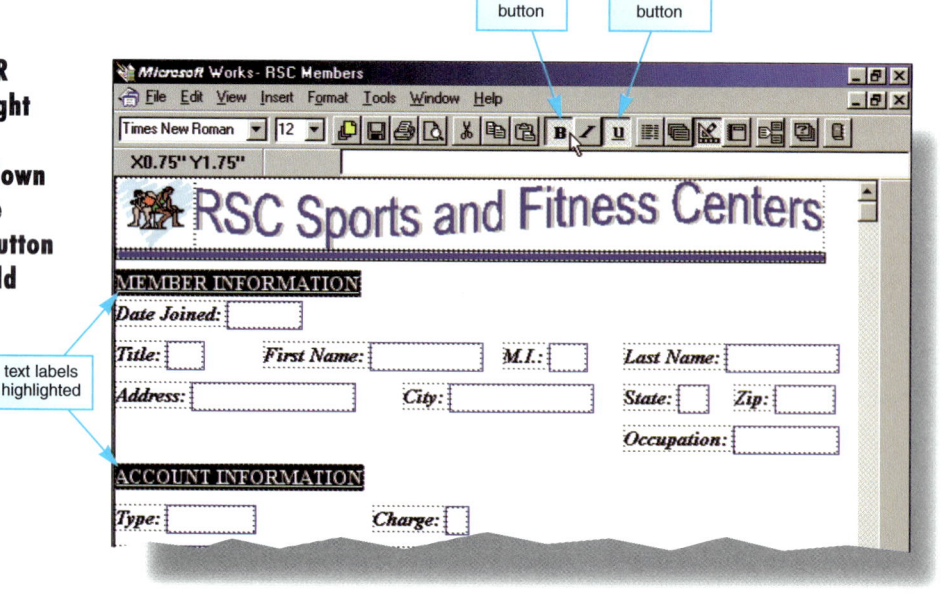

FIGURE 3-68

OtherWays
1. On Format menu in form design view click Font and Style, click Underline, click Bold, click OK button

The format of the database form is now complete. In most cases, you should save the completed form on disk. To save the database, click the Save button on the toolbar.

Entering Data into the Database in Form View

The fields contained within each record of the database constitute the structure of the database. The **structure** defines the fields within the database. The whole purpose of a database is to enter data so the data is available for printing, sorting, querying, and other uses. Therefore, the next step is to enter data into the database. The data can consist of text, numbers, formulas, and even functions.

Changing to Form View

Thus far, you have viewed the database in form design view. To type information into fields on a form, you use form view. **Form view** allows you to enter information into the database one record at a time. To change to form view perform the following steps.

> **More About Form View**
>
> Displaying one record at a time in form view is the easiest way to work with a database. Form view is similar to having a stack of paper forms inside your computer. You can also see titles, graphics, and other enhancements on the form.

Steps To Change to Form View

1 Point to the Form View button on the toolbar (Figure 3-69).

FIGURE 3-69

2 Click the Form View button.

The database displays in form view (Figure 3-70). Form view resembles form design view except no dotted lines surround the field names, field entries, or the objects on the database form. Works places a black background in the Date Joined field. The coordinates of the fields do not display in form view. The Record menu name replaces the Insert and Format menu names on the toolbar.

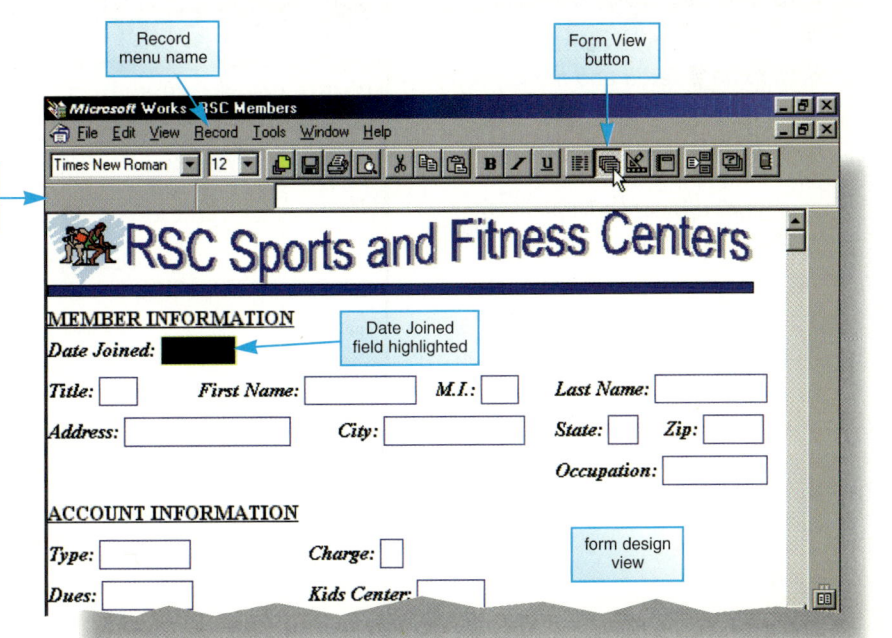

FIGURE 3-70

> **OtherWays**
>
> 1. On View menu click Form
> 2. Press F9

Entering Data into the Database

To enter data, highlight the field where you want to enter the data and then type the data. To enter the data for the first record in the database, complete the following steps.

Steps: To Enter Data into the Database

1 **Ensure the Date Joined field is highlighted. Type** 5/12/96 **into the field.**

The date joined displays in the entry bar and in the field (Figure 3-71).

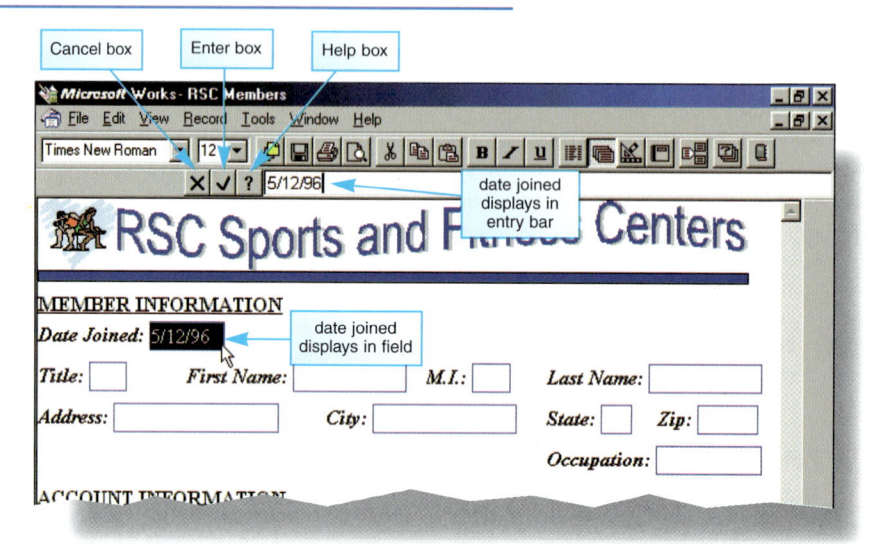

FIGURE 3-71

2 **Press the TAB key.**

Works enters the date into the Date Joined field and highlights the next field, Title, (Figure 3-72). When you press the TAB key, it causes both the data to be entered and the highlight to be moved from the previous field. If you press the ENTER key or click the Enter box, the data is entered but the highlight is not moved. Pressing the TAB key is the most efficient technique to enter data into a database. Notice when you enter information in the first field in the database, Works automaticallly enters CA in the State field because this field was formated with the default value of CA.

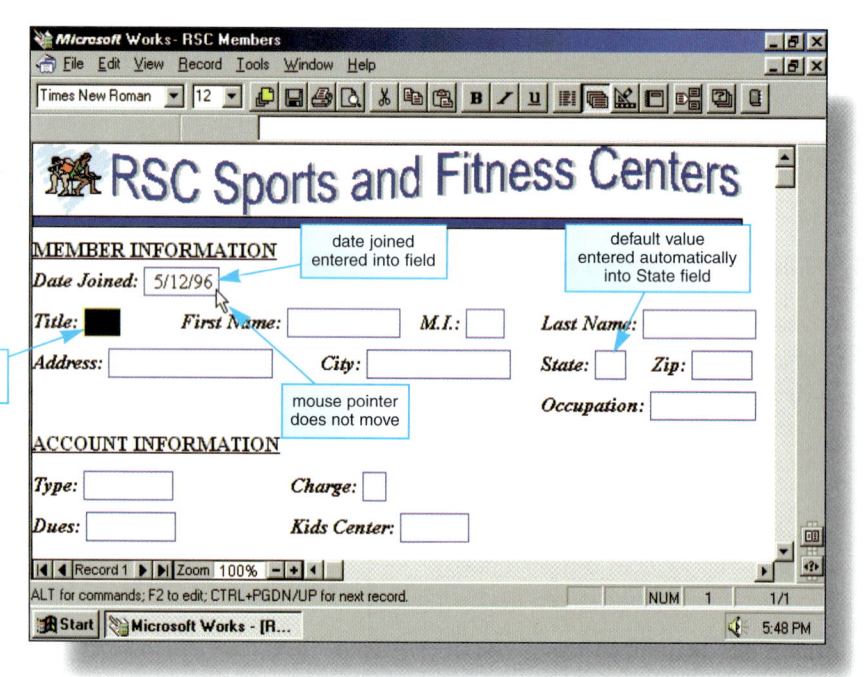

FIGURE 3-72

Microsoft **Works 4** *Windows 95*

Entering Data into the Database in Form View • **W 3.43**

3 **Type** Mr. **in the Title field and then press the TAB key.**

Works enters the title, Mr., into the Title field and highlights the next field, First Name (Figure 3-73).

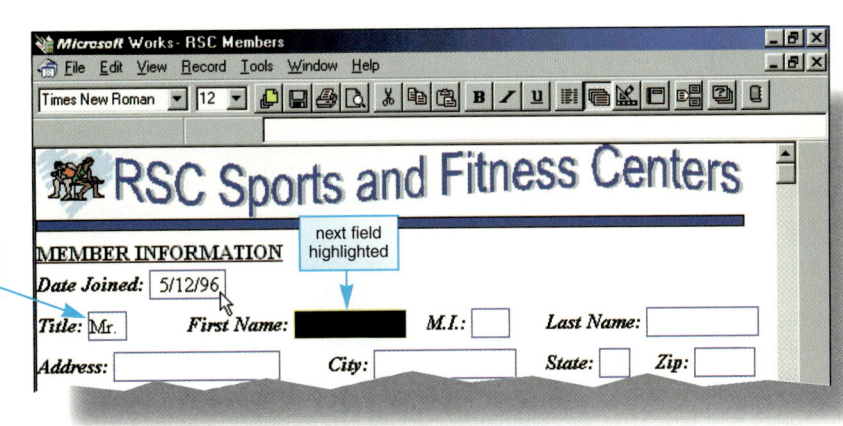

FIGURE 3-73

4 **Enter the remaining data for each of the fields in the first record. After entering the Kids Center value, press the ENTER key or click the Enter box.**

All the data for the first record is now entered (Figure 3-74). The Kids Center field is highlighted because you pressed the ENTER key or clicked the Enter box rather than pressing the TAB key. Pressing the TAB key would cause Works to highlight the Date Joined field in the second record.

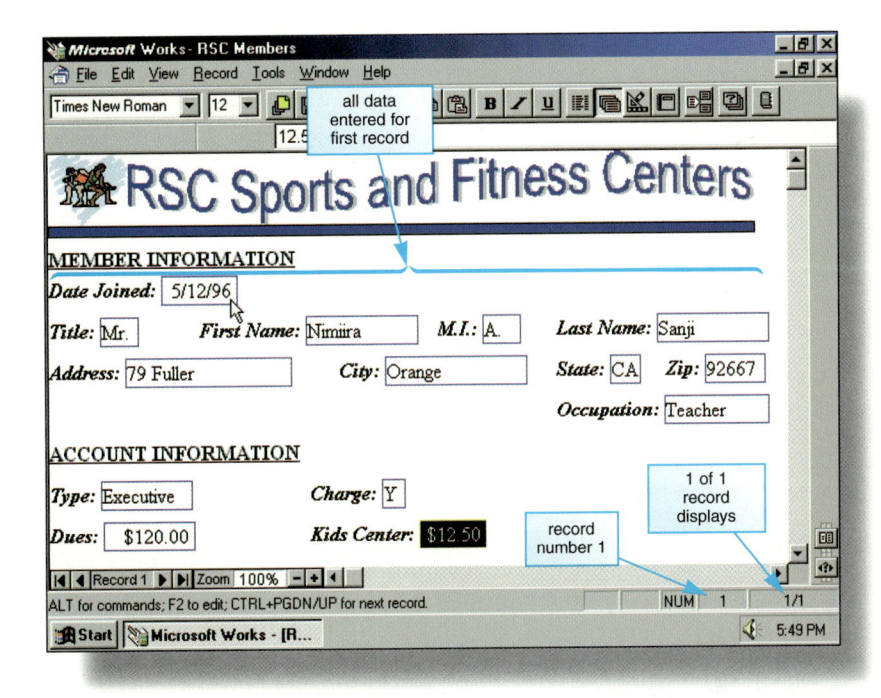

FIGURE 3-74

Notice several important items in the record shown in Figure 3-74. First, Works considers the Date Joined field to be numeric because the field was formatted as a date field. Thus, the date entered is right-aligned in the field. Dues and Kids Center fields also are numeric fields and data is right-aligned in the fields. Second, text fields, such as Title and First Name, are left-aligned in their fields.

If you accidentally enter erroneous data, you can correct the entry by highlighting the field containing the error and entering the correct data. Works will replace the erroneous data with the correct data.

To continue entering data into the database, you must display the form for record number 2 on the screen as shown in the step on the next page.

**More *About*
Tab Order**

In some database programs, when you rearrange the fields on the database form, the tab order, the order you move from field to field using the TAB key, does not change. This means when you press the TAB key to move from field to field, the highlight moves according to the original order of the fields, not in the order they currently appear on the screen. In Works, the tab order automatically changes when you rearrange fields. The tab order always goes from top to bottom, left to right. You can change this default tab order by clicking Tab Order on the Format menu in form design view.

W 3.44 • Project 3 • Using Form Design to Create a Database

Steps   To Display the Next Record in Form View

1 **Ensure the Kids Center field is highlighted and then press the TAB key.**

Works displays record number 2 (Figure 3-75). Notice that the Date Joined field is highlighted. When you press the TAB key, Works highlights the next field, even if the next field is in the next record in the database. The field names are formatted the same as in record number 1.

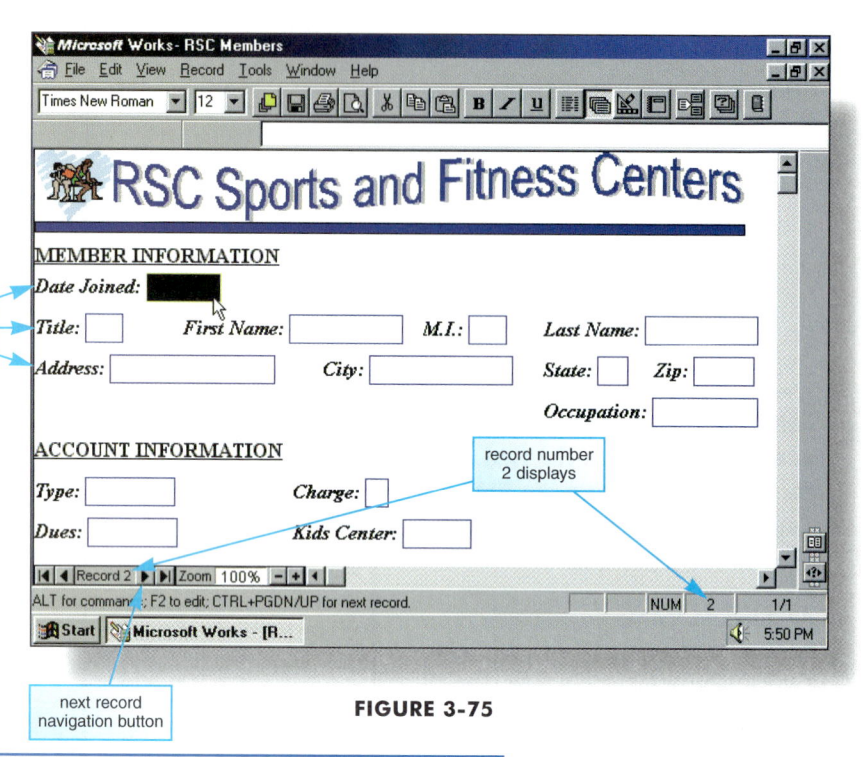

FIGURE 3-75

You also can move from one record to another using the navigation buttons on the scroll bar at the bottom of the screen (Figure 3-75). When record number 1 is displayed and you click the next record navigation button, Works will display record number 2. The field highlighted, however, is the same field as on record number 1. Therefore, in the sequence from Figure 3-74 on the previous page to Figure 3-76, if you click the next record navigation button, record number 2 will display on the screen with the Kids Center field highlighted. When you are entering data into the database, normally you want the first field in the next record highlighted. Therefore, pressing the TAB key is the preferred way to move from the last field in one record to the first field in the next record.

With record number 2 displayed, complete the steps on the next page to enter the data for record number 2 (Figure 3-76).

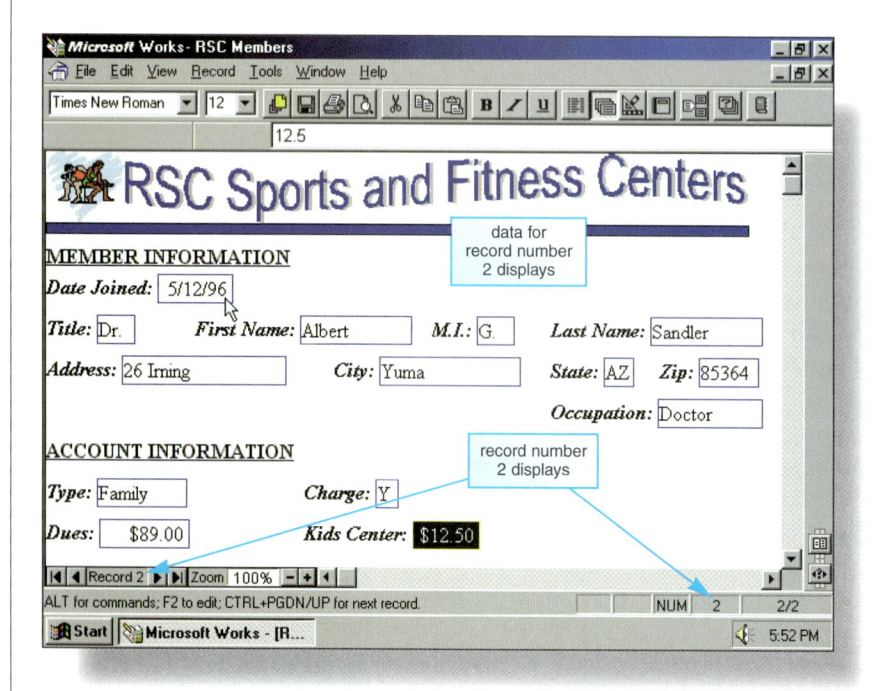

FIGURE 3-76

Entering Data into the Database in Form View • **W 3.45**

TO ENTER DATA FOR THE NEXT RECORD

Step 1: Type 5/12/96 in the Date Joined field and then press the TAB key.
Step 2: Type Dr. in the Title field and then press the TAB key.
Step 3: Complete the remainder of the record using the data shown in Figure 3-76. When you type 12.50 for the Kids Center, press the ENTER key or click the Enter box to enter the value in the field.

The screen after you enter this data is shown in Figure 3-76. Notice that even though the State field displayed CA after the date joined was entered, you can enter a different value in the field.

Continue entering the data for the remaining records in the database as specified in the following steps.

TO ENTER ALL DATA IN THE DATABASE

Step 1: With the Kids Center field in the second record highlighted, press the TAB key.
Step 2: Using the table in Figure 3-1 on page W 3.5 for data, enter the data for records 3 through 16. As you enter the data, you should save the database periodically so your work will not be lost in case of a power failure or other mishap. When you enter the data for the Kids Center field for record 16, press the ENTER key or click the Enter box.
Step 3: Click the Save button on the toolbar.

The database contains sixteen records. The sixteenth record is shown in Figure 3-77.

After you have entered all records, you may want to display the first record in the database. To accomplish this, perform the following steps.

Steps To Display the First Record in the Database

1 Point to the first record navigation button on the scroll bar (Figure 3-77).

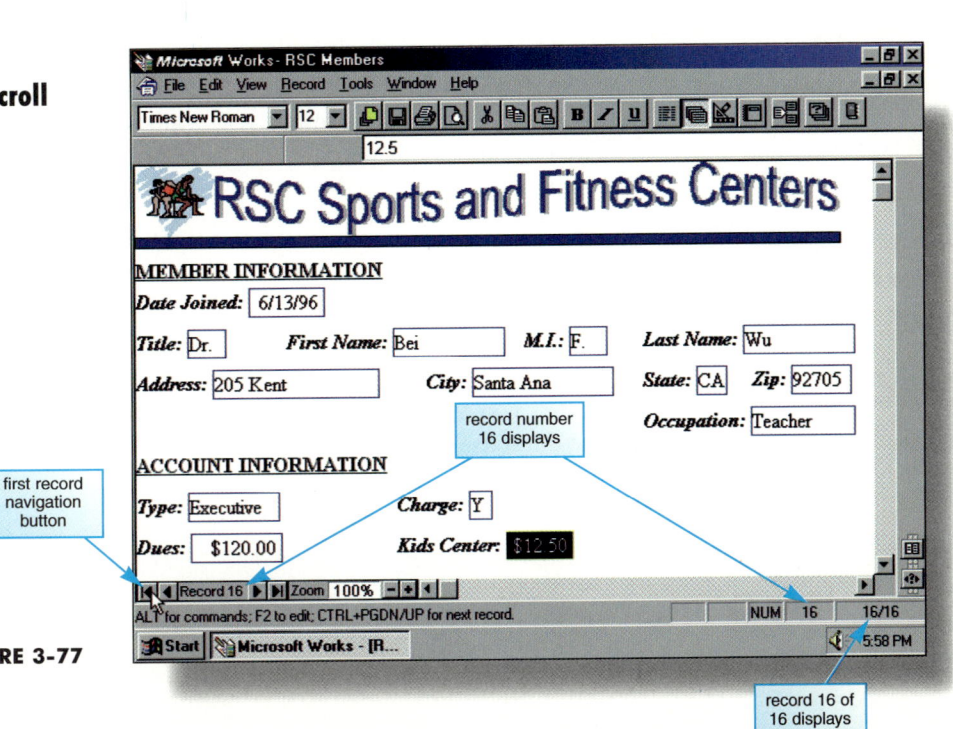

FIGURE 3-77

W 3.46 • Project 3 • Using Form Design to Create a Database

2 **Click the first record navigation button.**

Works displays the first record in the database (Figure 3-78).

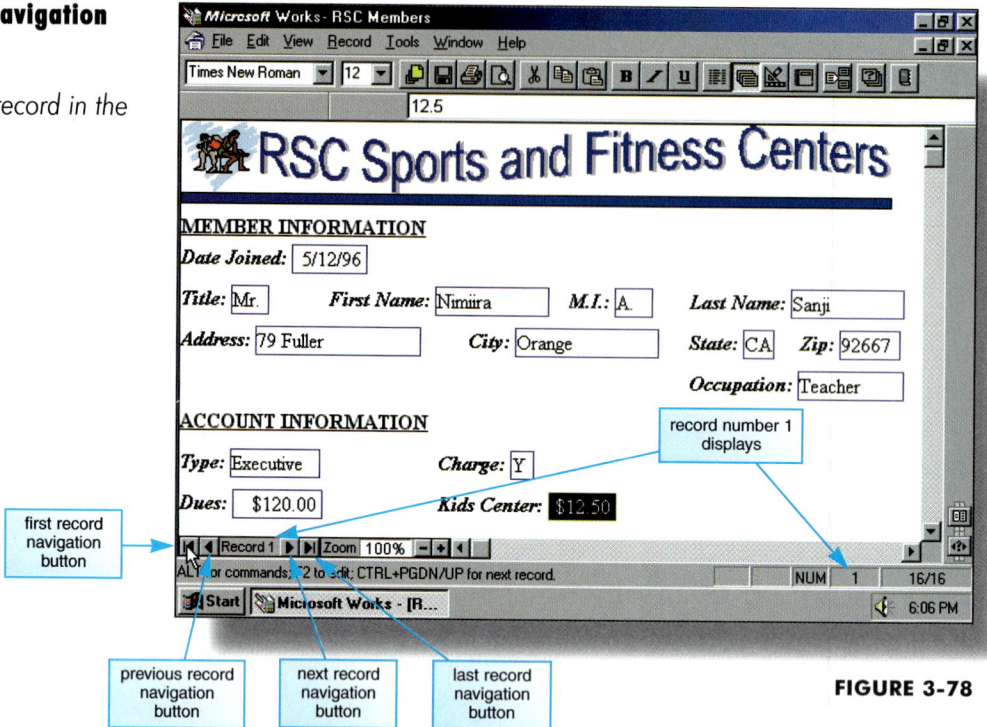

FIGURE 3-78

OtherWays

1. On Edit menu click Go To, type 1 in Go to text box, click OK button
2. Press CTRL+G, type 1 in Go to text box, click OK button
3. Press CTRL+HOME

To move from record to record in the database, you can use the **next record navigation button** or the **previous record navigation button** (Figure 3-78). To move to the last record in the database, click the **last record navigation button**. Works always displays the last record in the database as a blank record. For example, in the database for this project, sixteen records have been entered. If you click the last record navigation button, Works will display the seventeenth record, a blank record.

You also can move to a specific record in the database by clicking Edit on the menu bar and then clicking Go To. In the Go to text box in the Go To dialog box, type the record number you want to display and click the OK button. In the Go To dialog box, you also can select a desired field.

List View

More About List View

List view looks like a spreadsheet with records in rows and fields in vertical columns. In this view, you can enter data across one record at a time, or down one field at a time. Because you can see more than one record at a time, you can easily see whether you have duplicate records.

Thus far, you have created and formatted the database form in form design view and entered the data into the database one record at a time in form view. Works allows you to view multiple records at the same time using **list view**. To display the database in list view, perform the steps on the next two pages.

Microsoft **Works 4** Windows 95

List View • W 3.47

Steps To Display the Database in List View

1 **Highlight the Date Joined field. Point to the List View button on the toolbar (Figure 3-79).**

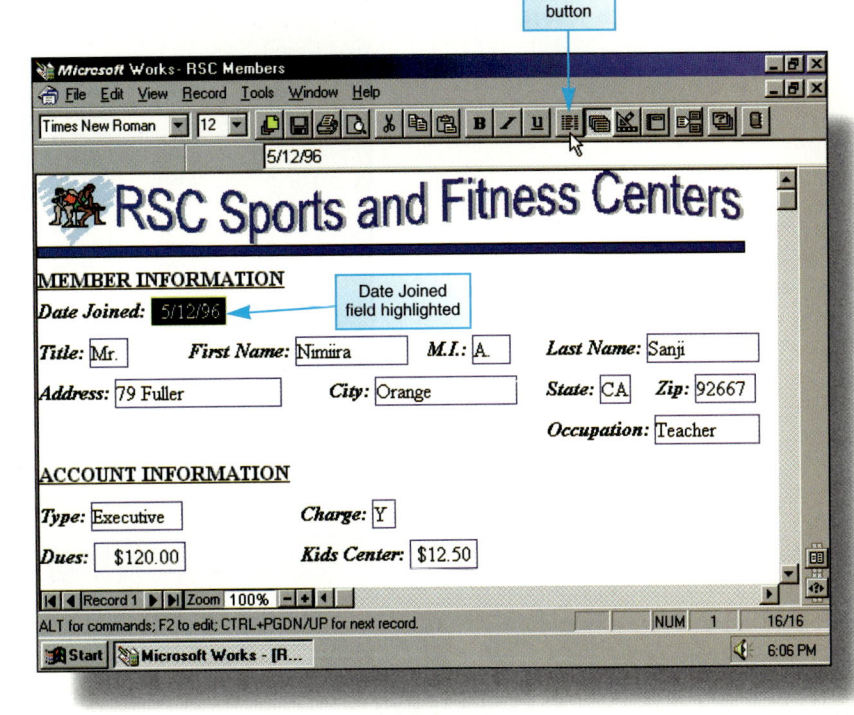

FIGURE 3-79

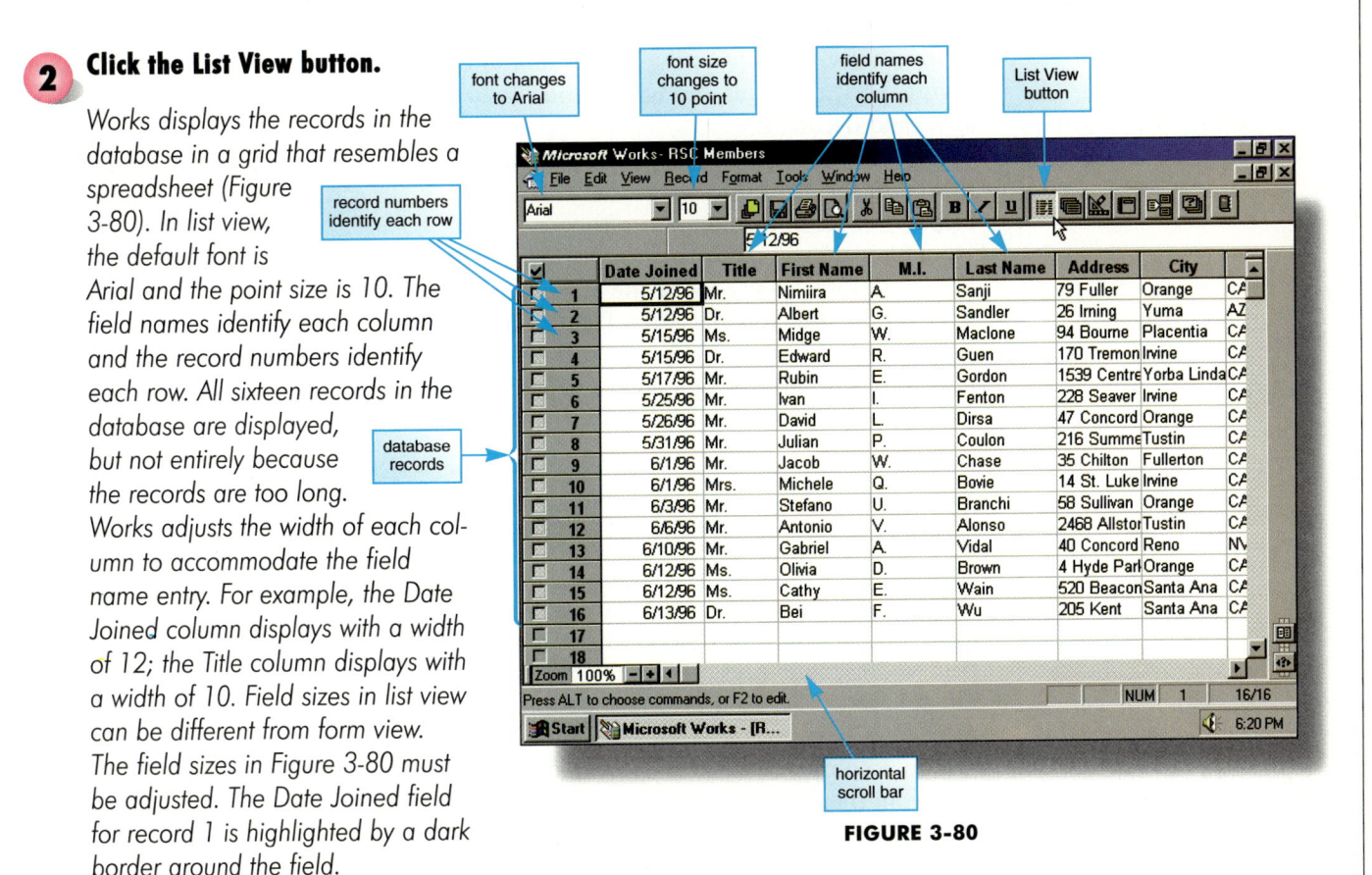

2 **Click the List View button.**

Works displays the records in the database in a grid that resembles a spreadsheet (Figure 3-80). In list view, the default font is Arial and the point size is 10. The field names identify each column and the record numbers identify each row. All sixteen records in the database are displayed, but not entirely because the records are too long. Works adjusts the width of each column to accommodate the field name entry. For example, the Date Joined column displays with a width of 12; the Title column displays with a width of 10. Field sizes in list view can be different from form view. The field sizes in Figure 3-80 must be adjusted. The Date Joined field for record 1 is highlighted by a dark border around the field.

FIGURE 3-80

W 3.48 • Project 3 • Using Form Design to Create a Database

3 **Click the horizontal scroll bar one time to display the remainder of each record.**

Works displays the rightmost fields in the database records (Figure 3-81).

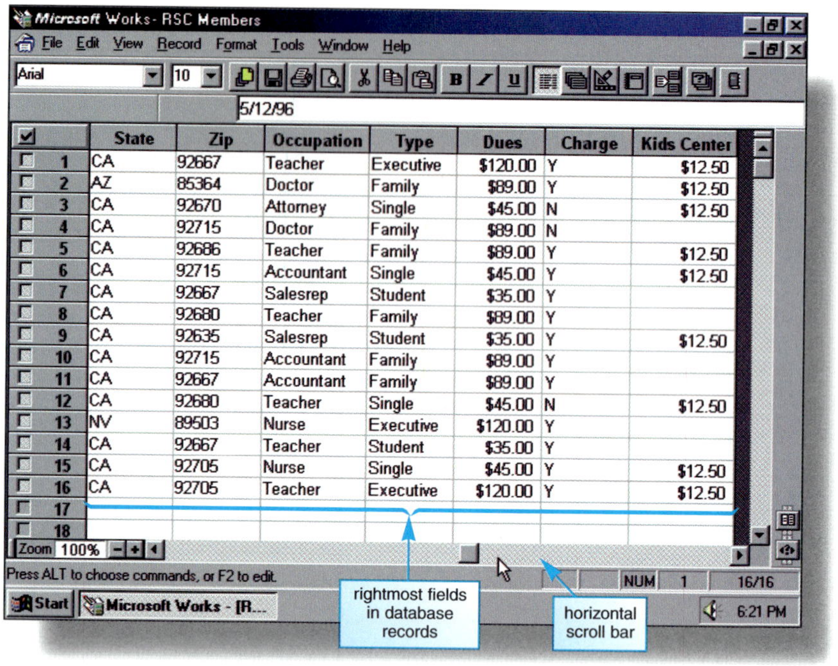

FIGURE 3-81

> **OtherWays**
> 1. On View menu click List
> 2. Press SHIFT+F9

Notice several important factors about the list view of the database. First, even though the field widths of the columns are not the same as the field widths in form view, the formatting of the data in each field is the same. For example, in Figure 3-81, the Dues and Kids Center field entries display the values with dollar signs and decimals.

Second, in Figure 3-81, when you clicked the scroll bar, the window display moved to the right one full window. If you click the scroll arrow, the window display moves one column at a time.

Third, when switching from form view to list view, the record and field highlighted in form view will be the record and field highlighted in list view. In Figure 3-79 on the previous page, the Date Joined field in record 1 is highlighted. When you change to list view (Figure 3-80 on the previous page), the Date Joined field in record 1 is still highlighted. This process works in the same manner when switching from list view to form view.

Formatting the Database in List View

When you format the database in list view, normally you will not change the field entry formats such as Text, Date, or Number. Instead, normally you change the field widths, font sizes, and other factors to accomplish two goals: (1) display all the data in the fields; and (2) if possible, size the list view so an entire record can print on a single page.

To accomplish these goals, you should proceed as follows: (1) change the font size from the default of 10 point to the smaller 8-point size; and (2) arrange the column widths to accomplish the goals. Complete the steps on the next page to format the database in list view.

Microsoft **Works 4** Windows 95

Formatting the Database in List View • **W 3.49**

Steps To Select the Entire Database and Change Font Size in List View

1 Click the horizontal scroll bar so the first fields in the database display. Click the selection box in the upper left corner of the grid above the row headings. Click the Font Size box arrow on the toolbar. Point to the number 8 in the Font Size drop-down list box (Figure 3-82).

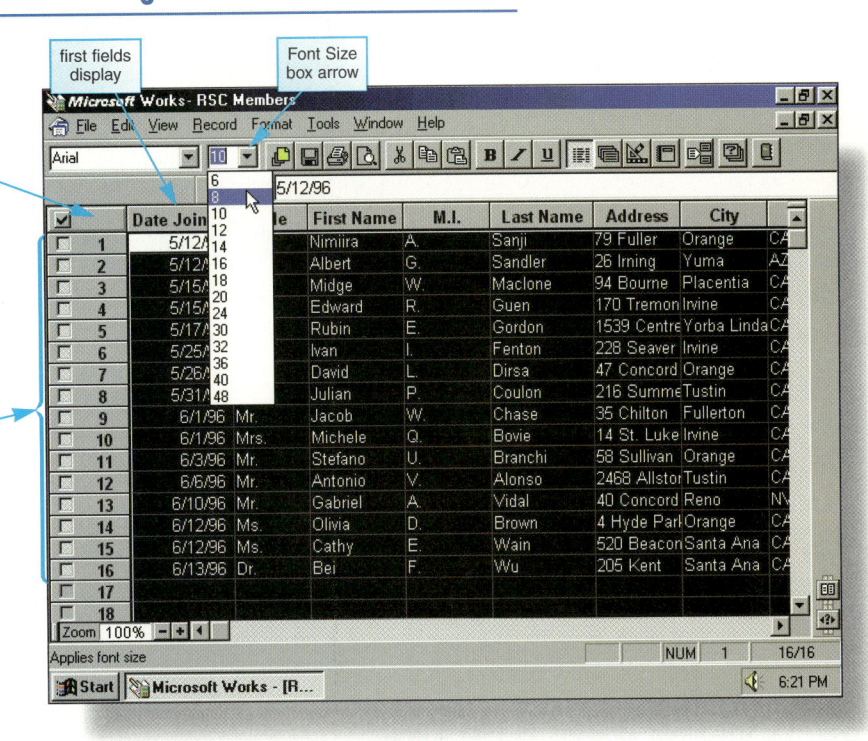

FIGURE 3-82

2 Click 8.

The entire database, including the field names, the record numbers, and the actual data in the database display in 8-point Arial font (Figure 3-83). A font size of 8 point is large enough to be readable but small enough to allow an entire record to print on one page in this project.

OtherWays

1. On Edit menu click Select All, on Format menu click Font and Style, click desired font size in Font Size drop-down list box, click OK button

2. Press CTRL+A, on Format menu click Font and Style, click desired font size in Font Size drop-down list box, click OK button

3. Press CTRL+SHIFT+F8

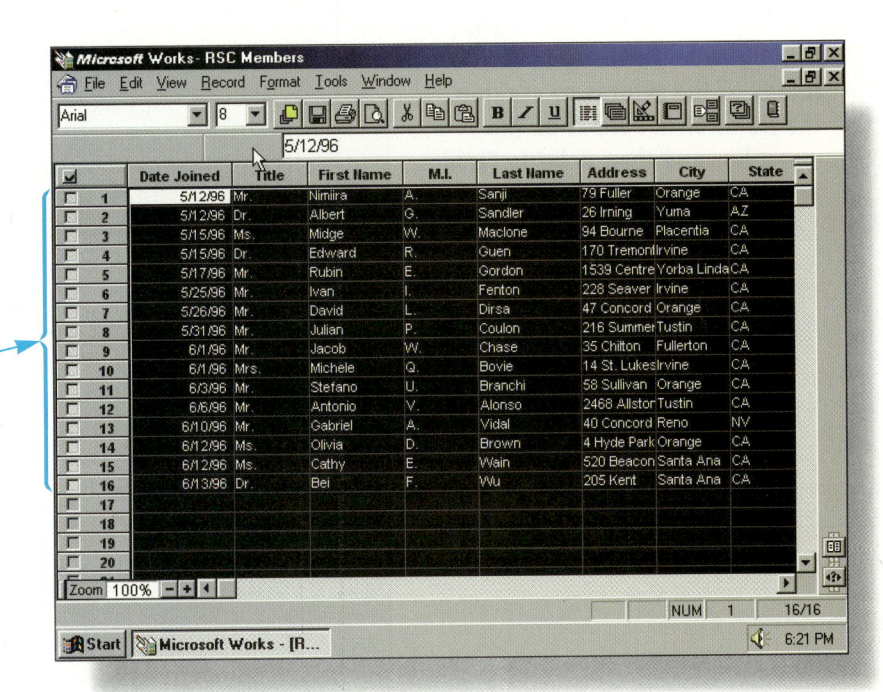

FIGURE 3-83

Setting Field Widths

The next step is to set the field widths for each of the fields in list view. Recall that the field widths set in list view will not necessarily be the same as those in form view, and changing the list view field widths will have no effect on the form view field widths.

TABLE 3-4

FIELD NAME	FIELD WIDTH	FIELD NAME	FIELD WIDTH
Date Joined	11	State	5
Title	5	Zip	6
First Name	10	Occupation	10
M.I.	3	Type	8
Last Name	10	Dues	8
Address	11	Charge	7
City	10	Kids Center	11

Setting field widths in list view may involve some experimentation to determine the proper widths to show the field names, show all data in all records, and yet keep the field widths to a minimum. Table 3-4 shows the field widths for the list view of the database.

Perform the following steps to set the field widths of the fields in list view.

Steps To Set Field Widths in List View

1 Highlight the Date Joined field in any of the records by clicking the field. Click Format on the menu bar and then point to Field Width (Figure 3-84).

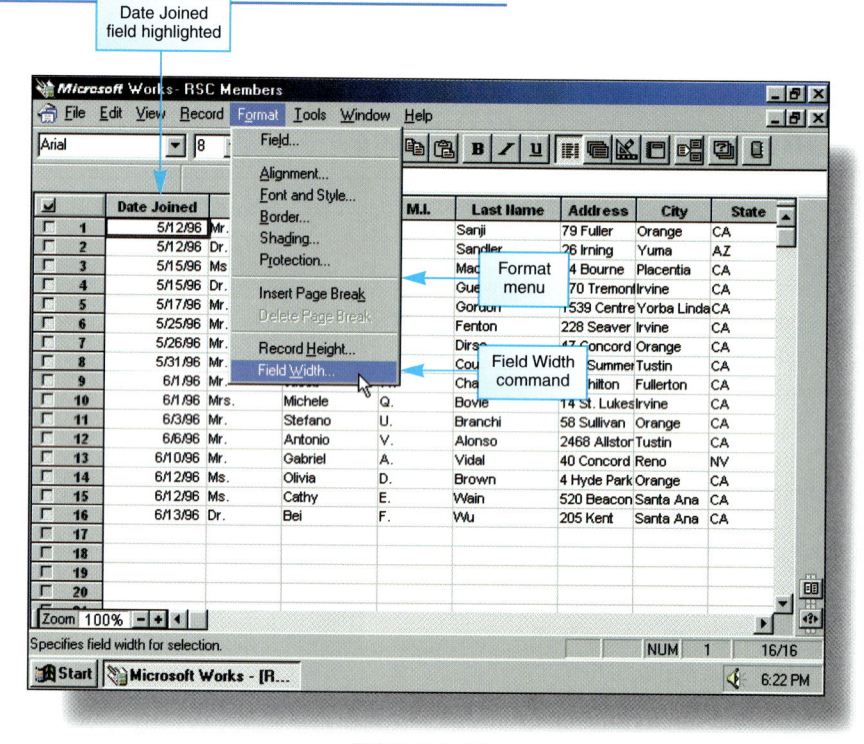

FIGURE 3-84

Formatting the Database in List View • W 3.51

2 **Click Field Width. Type 11 in the Column width text box and then point to the OK button.**

Works displays the Field Width dialog box (Figure 3-85). The number 11 displays in the Column width text box.

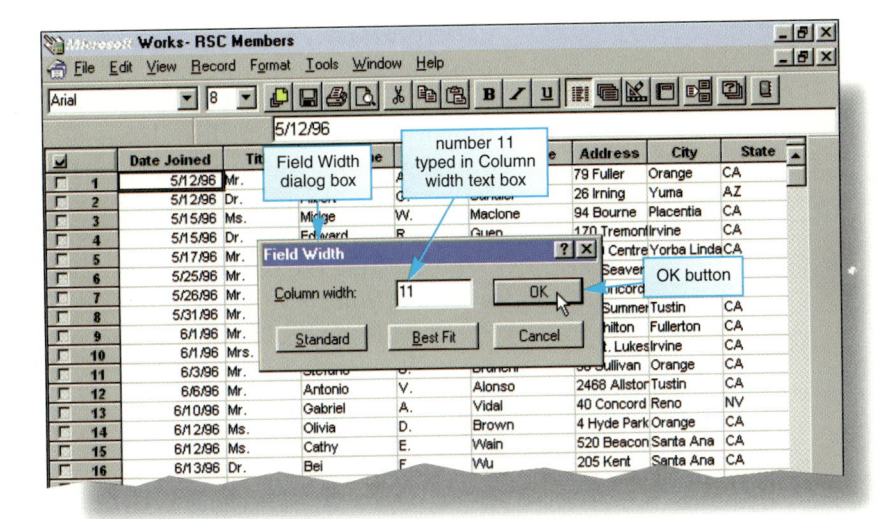

FIGURE 3-85

3 **Click the OK button.**

Works changes the width of the Date Joined field to 11 (Figure 3-86). All the values fit within the field.

FIGURE 3-86

4 **Use the techniques in Steps 1 through 3 to set the remainder of the field columns to their proper widths as specified in Table 3-4.**

After setting the field sizes, each of the fields is just wide enough to display both the field name and all the data in each field (Figure 3-87).

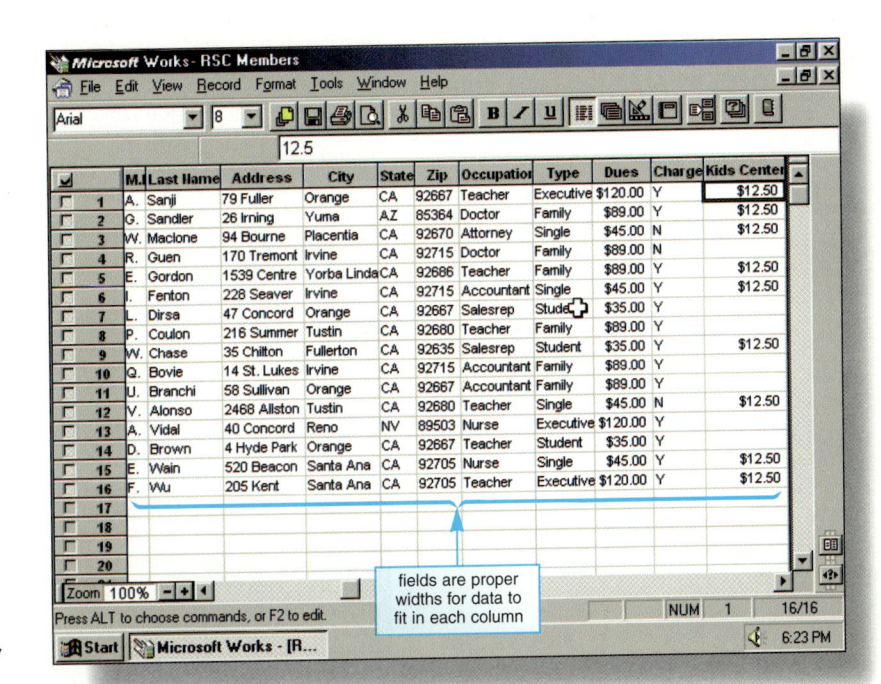

FIGURE 3-87

As previously stated, you also can drag the border to change the field width or use the Best Fit feature of Works. The method you choose when specifying the field width depends on your preference. Using the Field Width command from the Format menu is slower than dragging, but you can specify the exact field width. Dragging allows you to see the actual field width, but because Works does not display the field width on the screen, the only way to determine the exact width is by using the Field Width command on the Format menu.

Formatting the database in list view is now complete. Once the database is formatted, you should save it once again. To save the database on drive A using the same filename (RSC Members), click the Save button on the toolbar.

Printing the Database

The next step is to print the database. You can print the database from either form view or list view. When you print from form view, normally you will see one record per page, with the record appearing in the same format as it displays on the screen. When you print from list view, you can view up to twenty entire records per page, assuming the record is not too long to fit on one page. The next section of this project describes the steps to print the database from both form view and list view.

Printing the Database in Form View

To print in form view, first you must display the database in form view on the screen. Then, after setting some options for how the database should print, click the Print button on the toolbar. The steps to perform these tasks follow.

Steps: To Print the Database in Form View

1 If the database is displayed in list view, point to the Form View button on the toolbar (Figure 3-88).

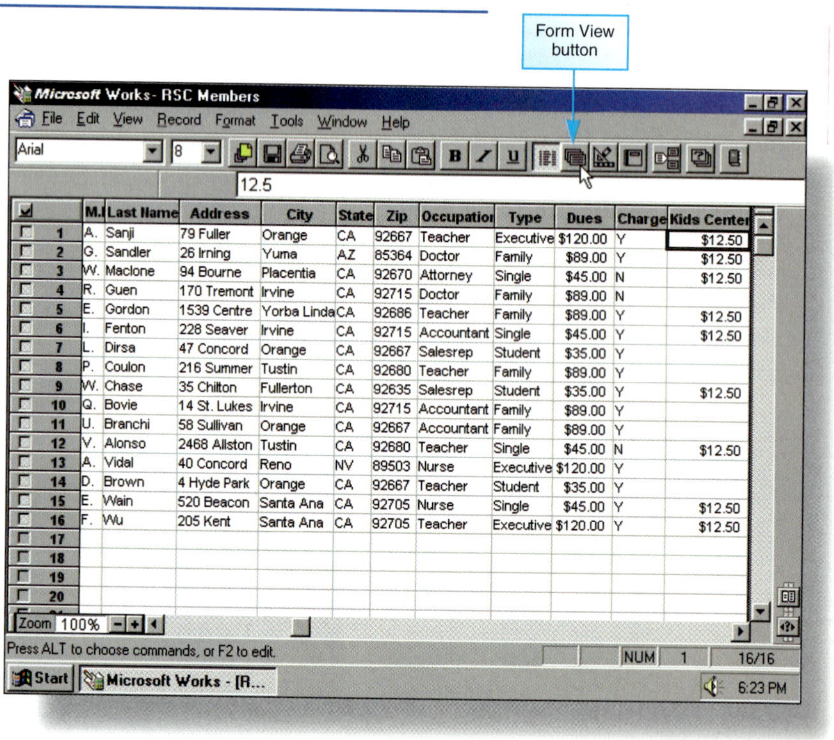

FIGURE 3-88

Microsoft **Works 4** Windows 95

Printing the Database • **W 3.53**

② Click the Form View button. Click File on the menu bar and then point to Print.

Works displays the database in form view, and the File menu displays (Figure 3-89). The record number displayed and the field highlighted will be the same as when the database was displayed in list view unless another field is selected.

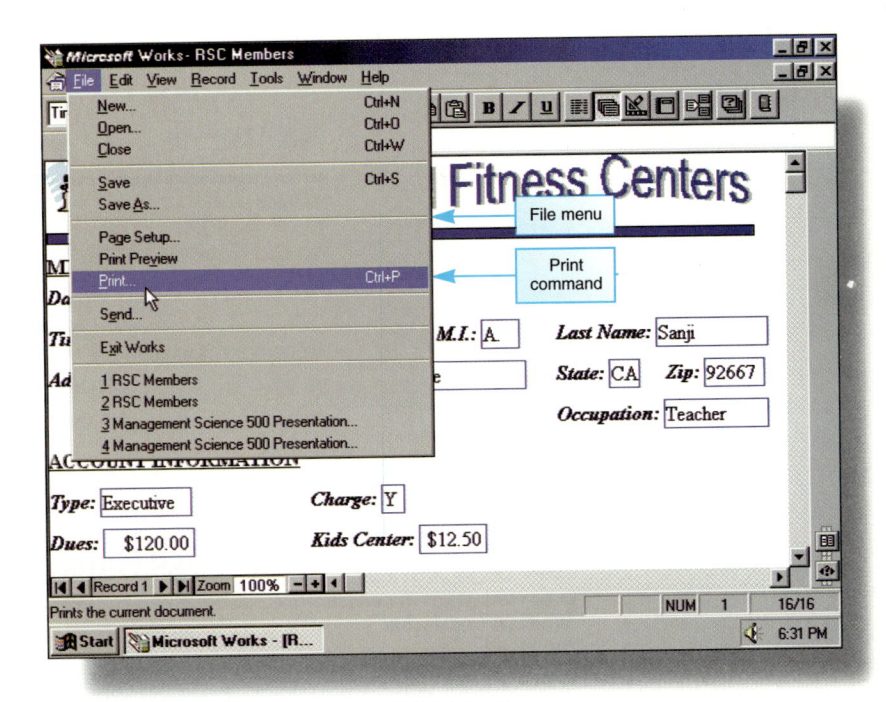

FIGURE 3-89

③ Click Print. Make the appropriate entries in the Print dialog box, and then point to the OK button.

Works displays the Print dialog box (Figure 3-90). Make sure the All records option button is selected.

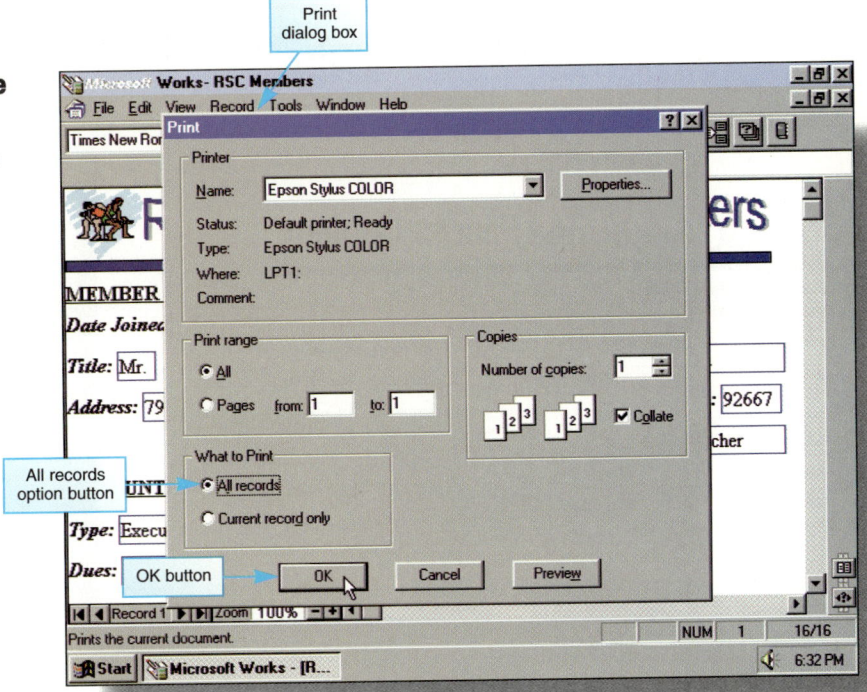

FIGURE 3-90

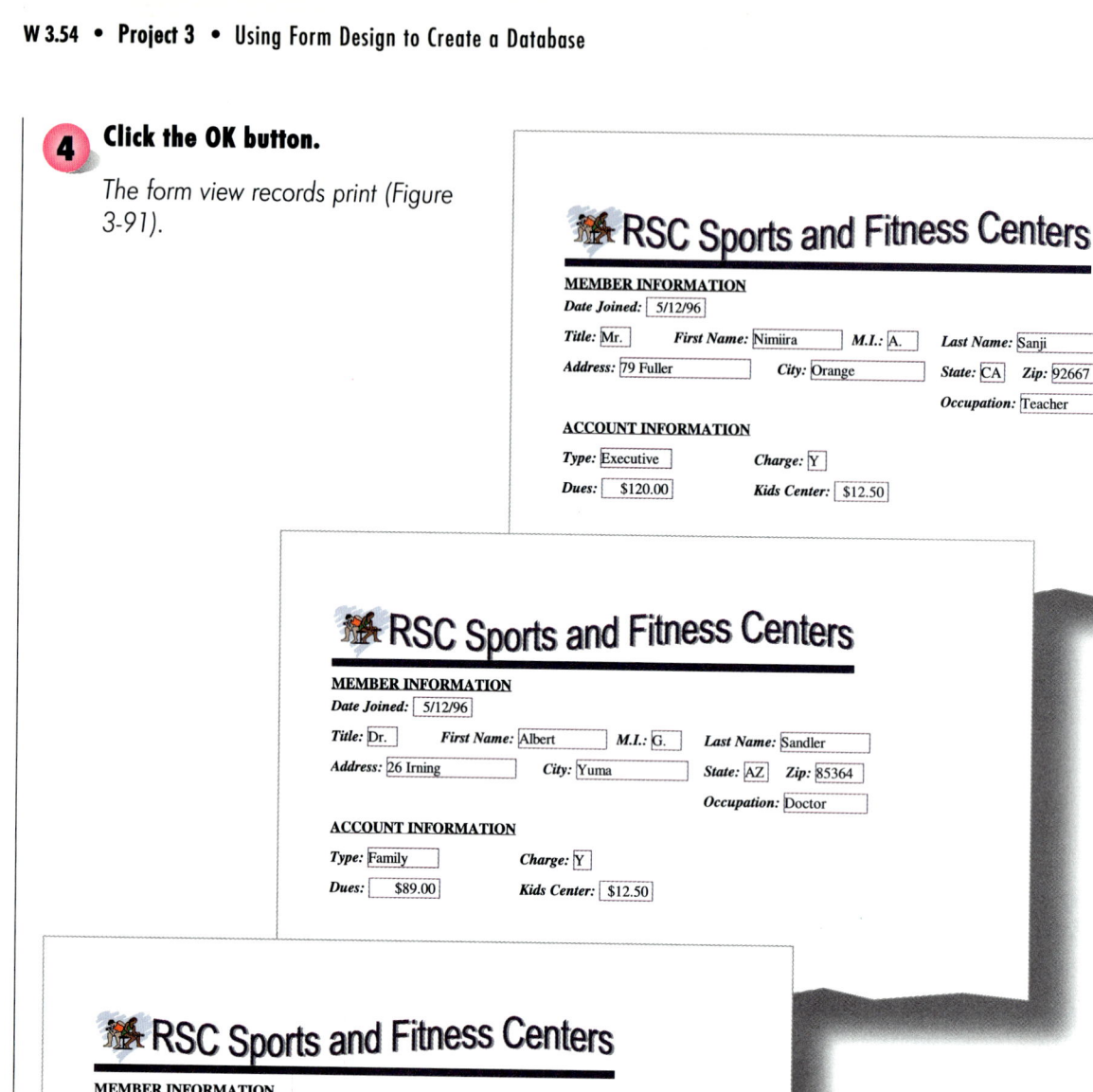

W 3.54 • Project 3 • Using Form Design to Create a Database

4 Click the OK button.

The form view records print (Figure 3-91).

RSC Sports and Fitness Centers

MEMBER INFORMATION
Date Joined: 5/12/96
Title: Mr.　First Name: Nimiira　M.I.: A.　Last Name: Sanji
Address: 79 Fuller　City: Orange　State: CA　Zip: 92667
Occupation: Teacher

ACCOUNT INFORMATION
Type: Executive　Charge: Y
Dues: $120.00　Kids Center: $12.50

RSC Sports and Fitness Centers

MEMBER INFORMATION
Date Joined: 5/12/96
Title: Dr.　First Name: Albert　M.I.: G.　Last Name: Sandler
Address: 26 Irning　City: Yuma　State: AZ　Zip: 85364
Occupation: Doctor

ACCOUNT INFORMATION
Type: Family　Charge: Y
Dues: $89.00　Kids Center: $12.50

RSC Sports and Fitness Centers

MEMBER INFORMATION
Date Joined: 5/15/96
Title: Ms.　First Name: Midge　M.I.: W.　Last Name: Maclone
Address: 94 Bourne　City: Placentia　State: CA　Zip: 92670
Occupation: Attorney

ACCOUNT INFORMATION
Type: Single　Charge: N
Dues: $45.00　Kids Center: $12.50

FIGURE 3-91

OtherWays
1. Click Print button on toolbar in form view
2. Press CTRL+P

More About Printing

When you click the Print button on the toolbar or click Print on the File menu in form design view, Works prints a blank form showing the field names and labels of the database form. You can use this blank form as a paper form to enter data manually.

Microsoft **Works 4** Windows 95

Printing the Database • W 3.55

Printing a Single Record in Form View

When working in form view, you may want to print a single record. To print a single record, such as record 10, perform the following steps.

Steps To Print a Single Record in Form View

1 **Click Edit on the menu bar and then point to Go To (Figure 3-92).**

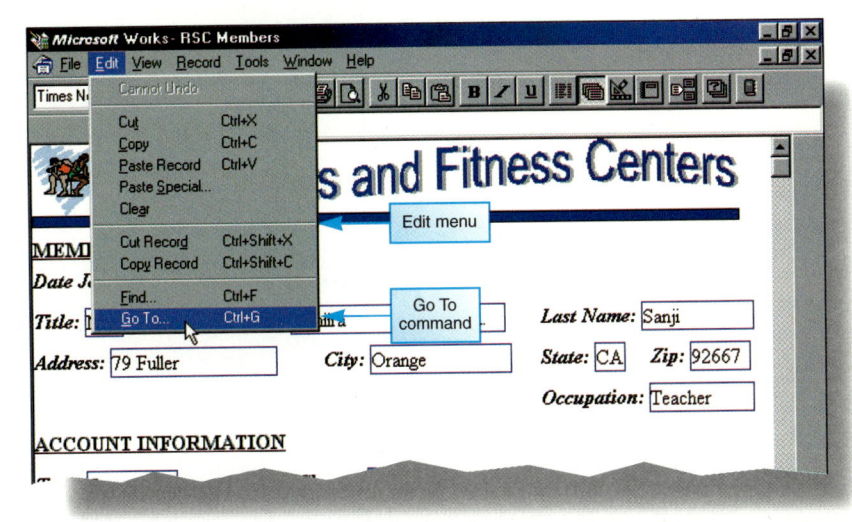

FIGURE 3-92

2 **Click Go To. When the Go To dialog box displays, type 10 in the Go to text box. Then, point to the OK button.**

The Go To dialog box displays (Figure 3-93). The number 10 displays in the Go to text box.

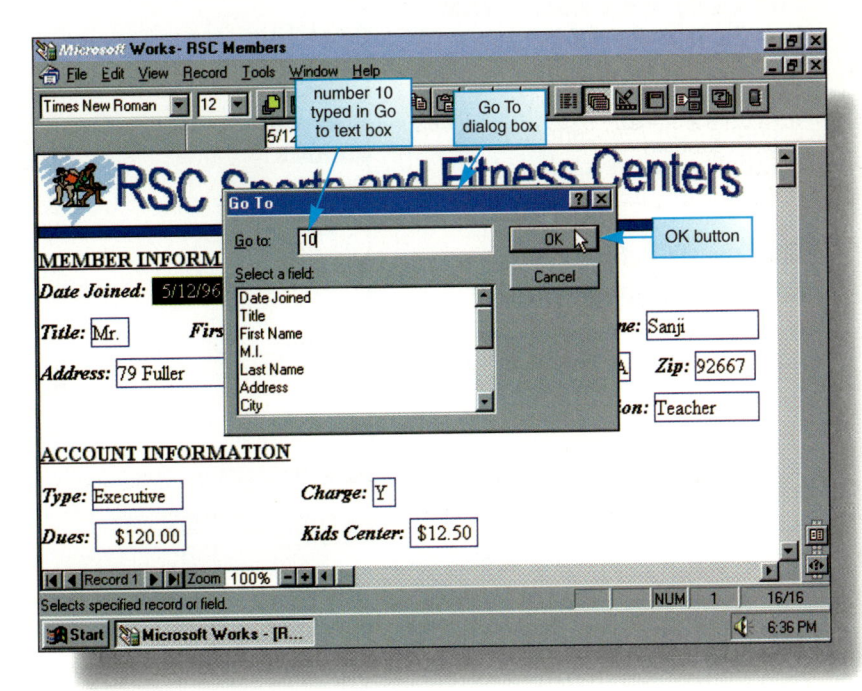

FIGURE 3-93

W 3.56 • Project 3 • Using Form Design to Create a Database

3 **Click the OK button. Click File on the menu bar and then point to Print.**

Works displays record 10 in form view, and the File menu displays (Figure 3-94).

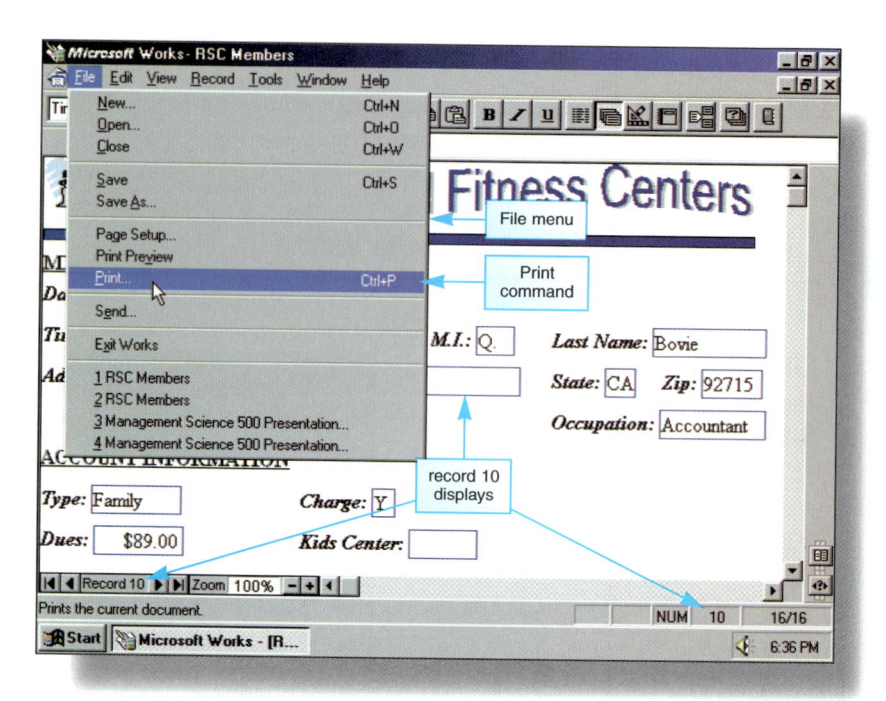

FIGURE 3-94

4 **Click Print. When the Print dialog box displays, click Current record only in the What to Print box. Point to the OK button.**

The Print dialog box displays (Figure 3-95). The Current record only option button is selected.

5 **Click the OK button.**

Record 10 in form view will print on the printer.

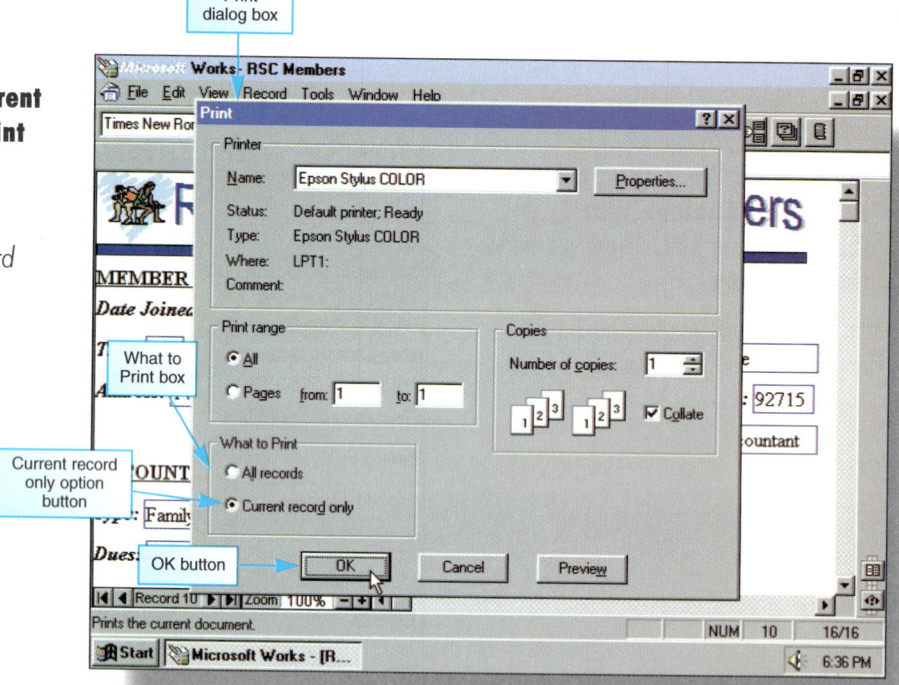

FIGURE 3-95

You have additional control over how form view records print by using the Page Setup command on the File menu. The dialog box that displays when using this command contains settings that allow you to control the printing of Field Lines and Field Entries. You also can control printing more than one record on a page.

It also is possible to print records in list view. The method to do this is explained in the following paragraphs.

Printing the Database in List View

Printing the database in list view allows you to print multiple records on one page. One of the concerns when printing in list view is to ensure the entire record fits on a single page. You can use the Print Preview feature of Works to determine if the record fits on one page. In this project, you must print the database using Landscape orientation in order to fit the entire record on a single page. To print using Landscape orientation, you must click Landscape in the Page Setup dialog box.

To use Print Preview and then print the list view of the database using Landscape orientation, perform the following steps.

Steps To Print the Database in List View

1 **If the database is not displayed in list view, display it in list view by clicking the List View button on the toolbar. Click File on the menu bar and then point to Page Setup.**

Works displays the database in list view, and the File menu displays (Figure 3-96).

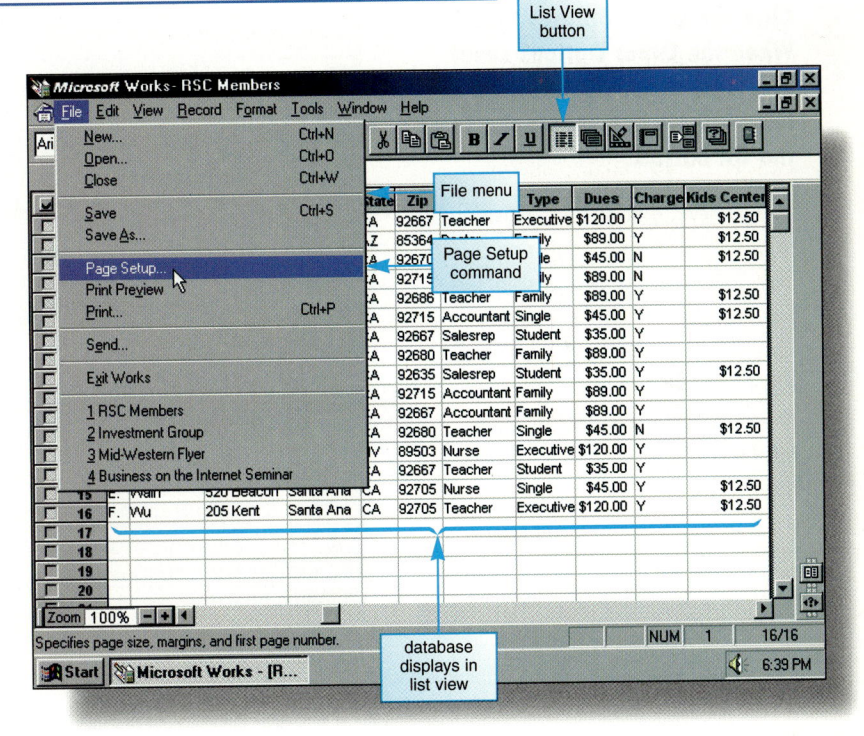

FIGURE 3-96

W 3.58 • Project 3 • Using Form Design to Create a Database

2 **Click Page Setup. When the Page Setup dialog box displays, click the Source, Size & Orientation tab. Click the Landscape option button in the Orientation box and then point to the Other Options tab.**

The Page Setup dialog box displays (Figure 3-97). Works automatically enters 11" in the Width text box and 8.5" in the Height text box when the Landscape option button is selected. The sample page illustrates Landscape orientation.

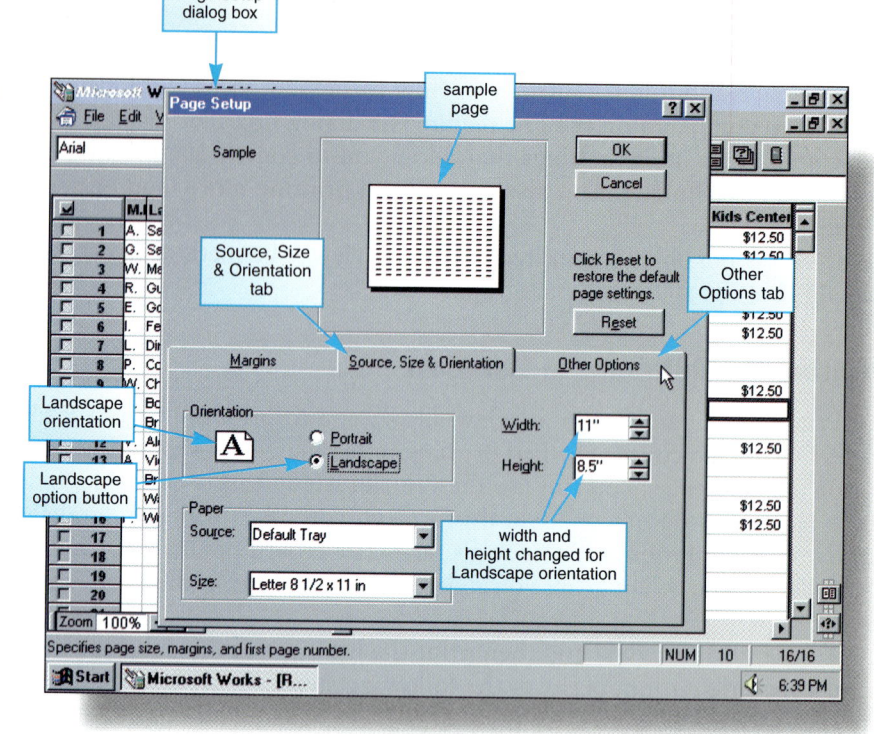

FIGURE 3-97

3 **Click the Other Options tab. When the Other Options sheet displays, click Print record and field labels, and then point to the OK button.**

The Other Options sheet displays (Figure 3-98). The Print record and field labels check box is selected, which means both the record numbers and the field labels will display on the report. If you leave this box unselected, only the field entries will appear on the report.

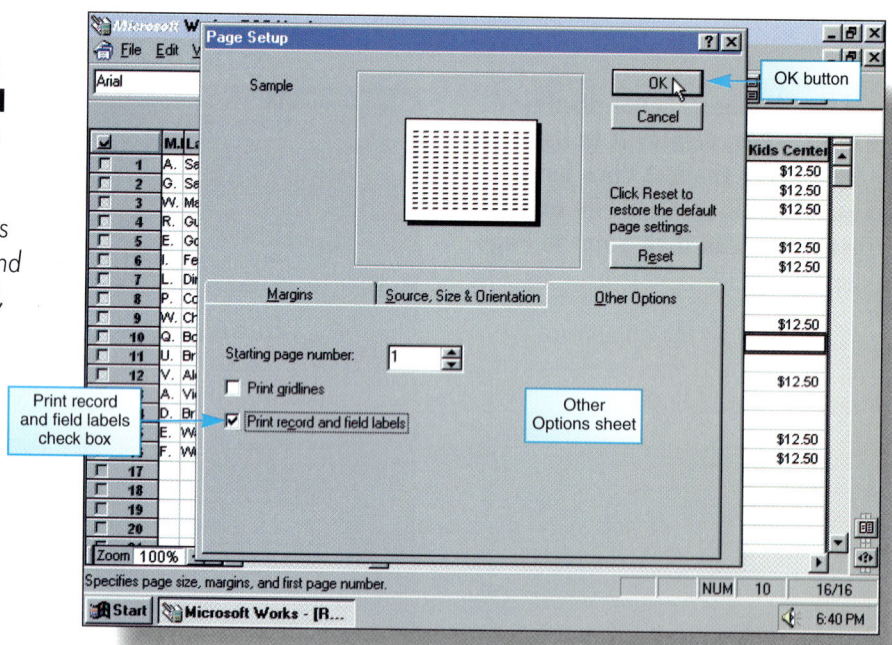

FIGURE 3-98

Microsoft **Works 4** Windows 95

Printing the Database • **W 3.59**

4 **Click the OK button. Point to the Print Preview button on the toolbar (Figure 3-99).**

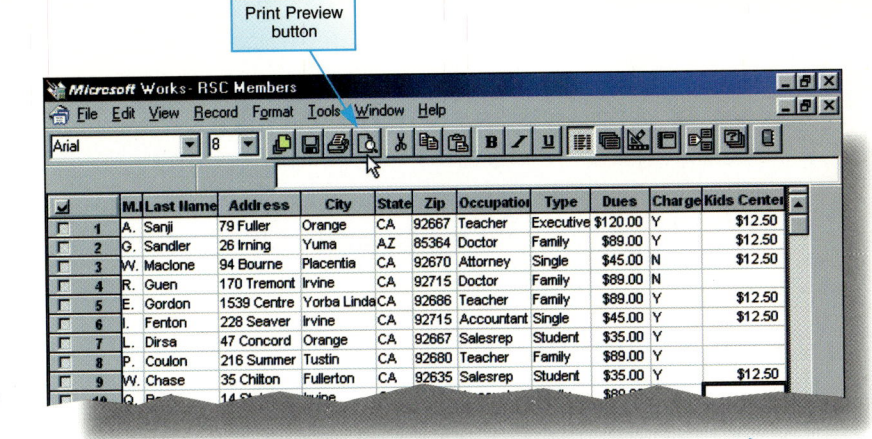

FIGURE 3-99

5 **Click the Print Preview button. When the Print Preview window displays, click the report twice to magnify the view of the database. Scroll left and right to ensure the database displays properly. Point to the Print button.**

Works magnifies the report to approximately the same size as the list view display (Figure 3-100). You can see the Kids Center field fits on the page. Because the Kids Center field is the rightmost field in the list view of the database and all the other fields are to the left, the entire record fits on one page.

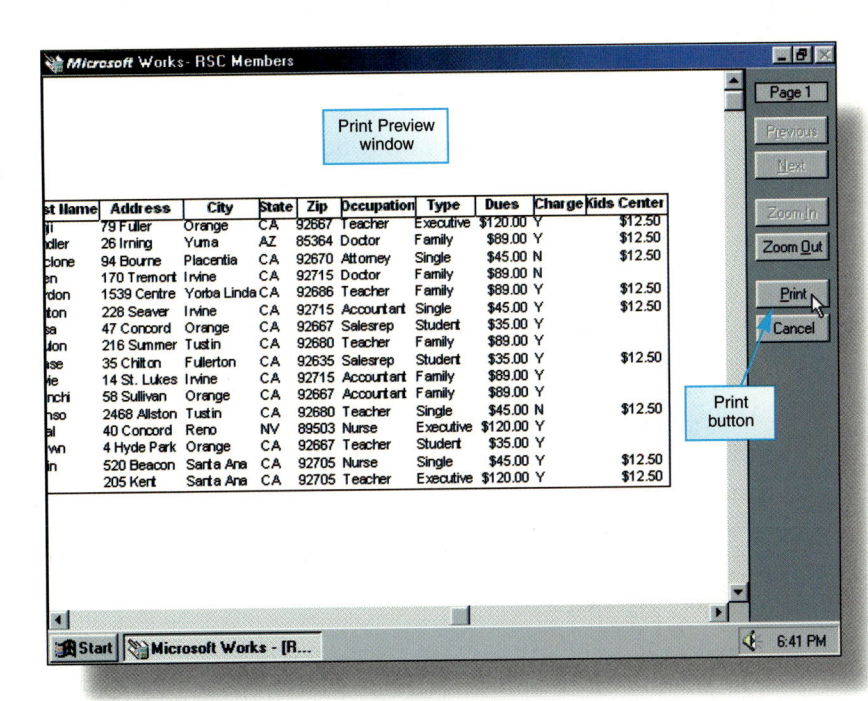

FIGURE 3-100

6 **Click the Print button.**

Works momentarily displays the Printing dialog box, and then prints the report (Figure 3-101). Notice the entire database fits on one page.

FIGURE 3-101

Exiting Works

After you have completed your work on the database, you can close the database file by clicking the Close button in the top right corner of the application window.

Project Summary

In this project, you learned to define the structure of a database using the Works Database tool. Connecting to the World Wide Web, you imported clip art from Microsoft Clip Gallery Live. Using WordArt, you entered the database title. In form design view, you moved the fields to an appropriate location, formatted the field names, inserted the clip art, inserted a title using WordArt, inserted a rectangle, and added color. Using the techniques you learned in an earlier project, you saved the database on disk. Then you entered data into the database in form view. Switching to the list view of the database, you specified the field widths for the fields. Finally, you printed the database using both form view and list view.

What You Should Know

Having completed this project, you should now be able to perform the following tasks:

- Add Color to the Rectangular Bar *(W 3.35)*
- Add Text Labels to the Database Form *(W 3.39)*
- Change the Margins on the Database Form *(W 3.16)*
- Change to Form View *(W 3.41)*
- Create a Database *(W 3.8)*
- Display the Database in Form Design View *(W 3.14)*
- Display the Database in List View *(W 3.47)*
- Display the First Record in the Database *(W 3.45)*
- Display the Next Record in Form View *(W 3.44)*
- Enter All Data in the Database *(W 3.45)*
- Enter and Format a Title Using WordArt *(W 3.29)*
- Enter Data for the Next Record *(W 3.45)*
- Enter Data into the Database *(W 3.42)*
- Format the Field Names *(W 3.36)*
- Insert a Rectangular Bar in the Title Area *(W 3.34)*
- Insert Clip Art from Microsoft Clip Gallery Live *(W 3.24)*
- Move Field Names as a Unit *(W 3.22)*
- Position Fields on the Form *(W 3.20)*
- Print a Single Record in Form View *(W 3.55)*
- Print the Database in Form View *(W 3.52)*
- Print the Database in List View *(W 3.57)*
- Quit a Web Session *(W 3.28)*
- Remove Field Lines and Add a Border on Fields *(W 3.37)*
- Save the Database *(W 3.12)*
- Select the Entire Database and Change Font Size in List View *(W 3.49)*
- Set Field Widths in Form Design View *(W 3.18)*
- Set Field Widths in List View *(W 3.50)*
- Start Microsoft Works *(W 3.7)*
- Underline and Apply Bold to Text Labels *(W 3.40)*

Test Your Knowledge

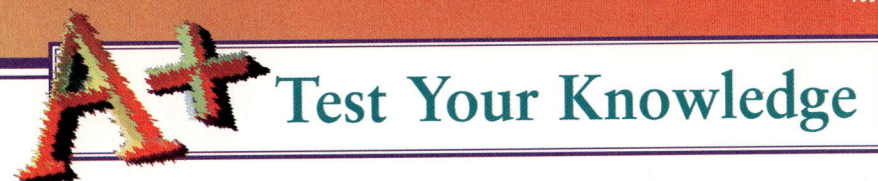

1 True/False

Instructions: Circle T if the statement is true or F if the statement is false.

T F 1. To create a new database, click the Database button in the Works Task Launcher dialog box.
T F 2. When you create a new database, you must enter a field name and a field format for each field in the database.
T F 3. Information in a database is divided into fields and characters.
T F 4. List view displays your database one record at a time on the screen.
T F 5. You use form view to position the fields and set field widths on the database form.
T F 6. You can specify a maximum of twenty-five fields in a database.
T F 7. In form view, dotted lines display around all elements, indicating you can select the elements for editing or changing their locations on the form.
T F 8. A text label is identifying information placed on a database form.
T F 9. You use form design view to enter data into a database.
T F 10. You can print a single record in form view.

2 Multiple Choice

Instructions: Circle the correct response.

1. Information in a database is divided into _____.
    a. form view and form design view
    b. characters and fields
    c. fields and records
    d. files and records
2. You can define up to _____ fields in a database.
    a. 25
    b. 256
    c. 32,000
    d. 1 million
3. To format the database form, use _____ view.
    a. form
    b. list
    c. form design
    d. print preview

(continued)

Test Your Knowledge

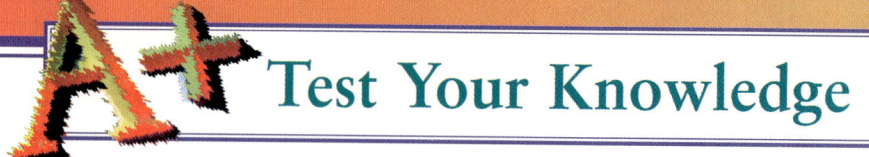

Multiple Choice *(continued)*

4. To move from one field to the next in form view of the database, _____.
   a. click the first record navigation button
   b. press the TAB key
   c. click the List View button on the toolbar
   d. press the SHIFT+TAB keys

5. To move from the last record in the form view of the database to the first record in the form view of the database, _____.
   a. click the first record navigation button
   b. click the last record navigation button
   c. press the TAB key
   d. click the List View button on the toolbar

6. Works displays multiple records at a time in _____.
   a. form view
   b. list view
   c. form design view
   d. print preview

7. If a field is formatted to receive numeric data in a database, Works will enter the data _____.
   a. left-aligned in the field
   b. right-aligned in the field
   c. center-aligned in the field
   d. evenly across the field

8. To set the field widths for a field in list view, click _____ on the Format menu.
   a. Field
   b. Border
   c. Field Width
   d. Field Size

9. When you print a database in form view, _____.
   a. you can print all records in the database on one page
   b. you can print only the record displayed on the screen
   c. you must print all records
   d. you can print all records or any single record

10. When you print a database in list view, _____.
    a. you can choose to print gridlines and record and field labels
    b. you can choose to print the records in Landscape orientation
    c. you can use Print Preview to ensure all fields in the database will print
    d. all of the above

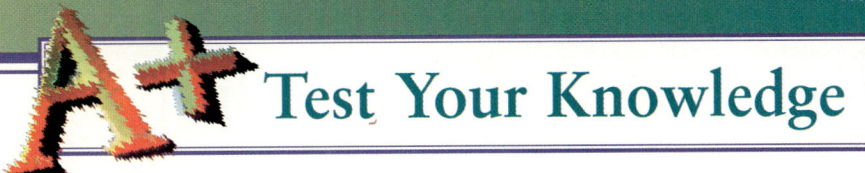

Microsoft **Works 4** Windows 95
Test Your Knowledge • W 3.63

A+ Test Your Knowledge

3 Understanding Form Design View

Instructions: In Figure 3-102, arrows point to the toolbar and major parts of a record displayed in form design view. Identify the elements in the spaces provided.

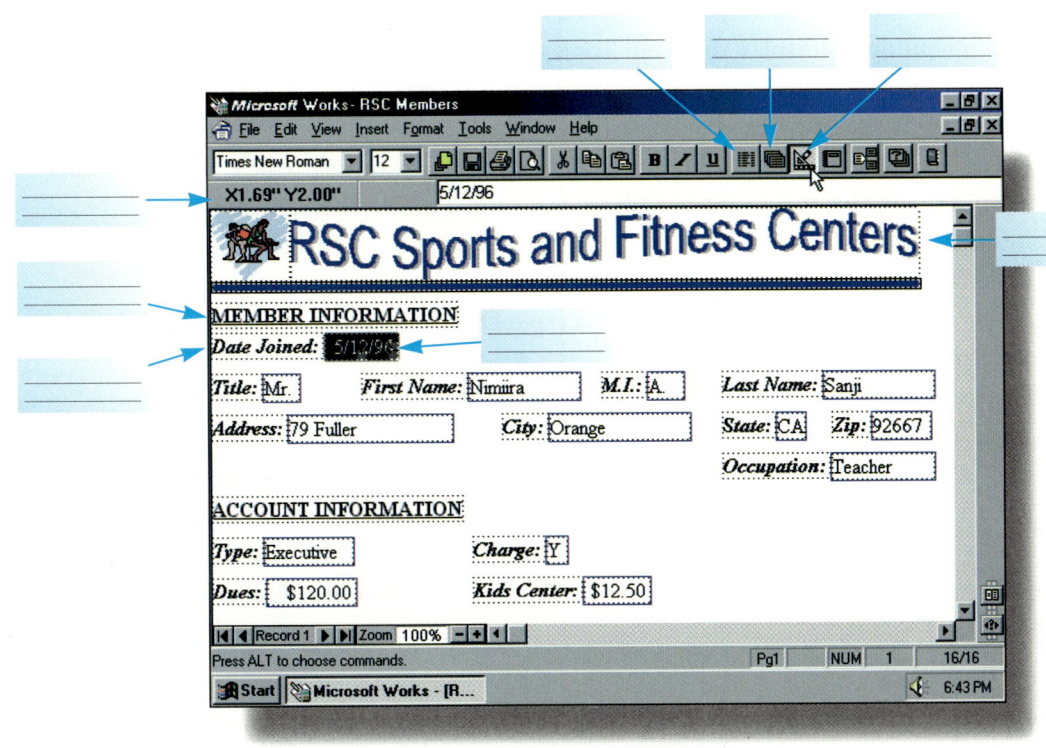

FIGURE 3-102

4 Working with Database Views

Instructions: Write the appropriate view in which to display a database to accomplish each task.

TASK	VIEW
Position fields on a database form	_____
View the X-Y coordinates of a field	_____
Insert clip art	_____
Insert text labels	_____
Insert a rectangle on a database form	_____
Enter data in a database	_____
Change the field width	_____
Print a single record in a database	_____
Print multiple records on one page	_____

W 3.64 • Project 3 • Using Form Design to Create a Database

Use Help

1 Reviewing Project Activities

Instructions: Use your computer to perform the following tasks to obtain experience using online Help.

1. Start Microsoft Works.
2. When the Works Task Launcher dialog box displays, click the Cancel button. Click the Index button in the Help window to display the Help Topics: Microsoft Works dialog box.
3. On the Index sheet, type `printing database forms` in the 1 Type a word for the action or item you want information about text box.
4. Click printing database forms in the 2 Click the Index entry you want list. Click To print a blank form DB. Read and then print the To print a blank form topic on the Step-by-Step sheet.
5. Click the More Info tab. Click the Overview button. Read and then print Printing database information. Click the Done button.
6. Click the topic, To print more than one record on a page DB. Read and then print the To print more than one record on a page topic.
7. Click the Close button in the application window to close Works.

2 Expanding on the Basics

Instructions: Use Works online Help to better understand the topics listed below. Answer the questions on a separate piece of paper.

1. Start Microsoft Works.
2. When the Works Task Launcher dialog box displays, click the Database button. When the Create Database dialog box displays, use the question mark button in the upper right corner to answer the questions.
   a. What are the rules for typing a field name in the Field name text box in the Create Database dialog box?
   b. What button changes names depending upon the status of the Create Database dialog box?
   c. What is the purpose of the Serialized option in the Format box?
   d. Explain the difference between the 1234.56 format with zero decimal places and the 01235 format in the Appearance list.
3. Click the Close button in the application window to close Works.

Apply Your Knowledge

1 Understanding Form Design View and Form Formatting

Instructions: Start Microsoft Works. Open the document, Pet Supplies, on the Student Floppy Disk that accompanies this book. This file contains the form design view of the database before positioning and formatting the fields. Format the form as illustrated in Figure 3-103. Use the Connect to Web for additional clips button in the Microsoft Clip Gallery 3.0 dialog box to download the clip art shown in Figure 3-103 (search using the keyword, rabbit). After formatting, print the form and turn in the form to your instructor.

FIGURE 3-103

In the Lab

1 Creating and Formatting an Alumni Database

Problem: Create a database that contains information regarding alumni donations given to the Alumni Scholarship Fund. The contents of the database are shown in Table 3-5.

TABLE 3-5

DONATION DATE	TITLE	FIRST NAME	M.I.	LAST NAME	SCHOLARSHIP	CLASSIFICATION	DONATION
10/16/97	Mr.	Wilson	B.	Haus	Business	Corporate	$1,500.00
10/17/97	Ms.	Anne	M.	Garcia	Music	Private	$100.00
10/22/97	Mr.	Donald	H.	Emerson	Science	Corporate	$700.00
10/31/97	Miss	Ealin	L.	Deras	Music	Private	$2,500.00
11/15/97	Mrs.	Melissa	R.	Deric	Science	Private	$500.00
11/22/97	Mr.	Donald	V.	Roy	Business	Corporate	$3,000.00
11/28/97	Mr.	Vincent	D.	Portofino	Business	Corporate	$5,000.00
12/3/97	Ms.	Lillian	J.	Henry	Fine Arts	Private	$850.00
12/15/97	Ms.	Ledy	R.	Mejia	Fine Arts	Private	$250.00
12/30/97	Mr.	Martin	V.	Lee	Business	Corporate	$400.00

(continued)

In the Lab

Creating and Formatting an Alumni Database *(continued)*

Instructions: Perform the following tasks:

1. Create the database in the format shown in Figure 3-104. Use the Connect to Web for additional clips button in the Microsoft Clip Gallery 3.0 dialog box to download the clip art shown in Figure 3-104 (search using the keyword, gold). Experiment with the clip art size, title size, text label, and field positions to obtain the desired format.
2. Format the field names as shown in Figure 3-104.
3. Enter the data from the table into the database.
4. Determine the proper field widths so that in list view the entire record in the database prints on a single page.
5. Save the database on a floppy disk. Use the filename, Alumni Scholarship Donations.
6. Print the database in both form view and list view.
7. Follow the directions from your instructor for turning in this assignment.

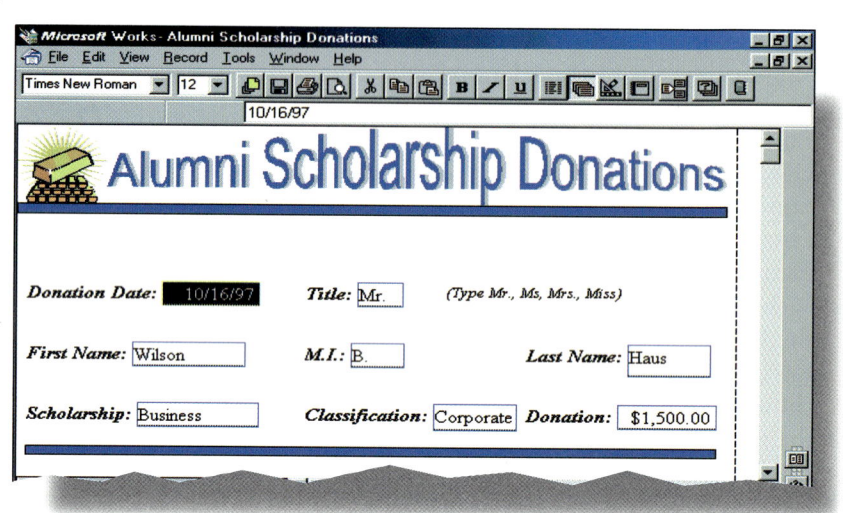

FIGURE 3-104

2 Creating and Formatting an Employee Database

Problem: Create a database that contains information regarding Custom Gifts, Intl employees. The contents of the database are shown in Table 3-6.

TABLE 3-6

EMPLOYEE ID	DATE HIRED	FIRST NAME	LAST NAME	HOURLY RATE	WEEKLY HOURS	STATUS	DEPARTMENT
50123	4/13/93	Abraham	Ackerman	$16.50	40	F	Accounting
20157	5/26/93	Aaron	Sikora	$15.25	40	F	Purchasing
50105	6/14/93	Denzal	Simes	$15.75	35	F	Accounting
20158	7/15/93	Ben	Ryu	$14.75	40	F	Purchasing
30135	9/23/94	Sandra	Perez	$12.50	32	F	Customer Service
30235	12/1/94	Philip	Ortiz	$13.25	40	F	Customer Service
30698	8/3/95	Joni	Echsner	$10.50	20	P	Customer Service
30812	9/24/95	Mihai	Ochoa	$12.75	40	F	Customer Service
20587	10/15/95	Michelle	Quon	$11.35	40	F	Purchasing
50642	12/3/95	Duc	Dinh	$10.00	25	P	Accounting

In the Lab

Instructions: Perform the following tasks:

1. Create the database in the format shown in Figure 3-105. Use the Connect to Web for additional clips button in the Microsoft Clip Gallery 3.0 dialog box to download the clip art shown in Figure 3-105 (search using the keyword, rabbit). Experiment with the clip art size, title size, and field positions to obtain the desired format.
2. Format the field names as shown in Figure 3-105.
3. Enter the data from the table into the database.
4. Determine the proper field widths so that in list view the entire record in the database prints on a single page.
5. Save the database on a floppy disk. Use the filename Custom Gifts, Intl.
6. Print the database in both form view and list view.
7. Follow the directions from your instructor for turning in this assignment.

FIGURE 3-105

3 Creating and Formatting an Investor Database

Problem: Create a database that contains information regarding investors in the Investment Group. The contents of the database are shown in Table 3-7.

TABLE 3-7

DATE	TITLE	FIRST NAME	LAST NAME	ADDRESS	CITY	STATE	ZIP	OCCUPATION	FUND	SHARES	SHARE PRICE
9/12/97	Dr.	Thomas	Messer	13272 Grand	Yorba	CA	92686	Dentist	Technology	750	$10.00
9/15/97	Mr.	Robert	Kranitz	1300 Adams	Fullerton	CA	92633	Attorney	International	200	$18.00
9/25/97	Dr.	Elaine	Hince	10821 Capital	Bellevue	WA	98005	Teacher	Technology	1,200	$11.00
9/26/97	Miss	Janette	Lewis	1707 Kingman	Brea	CA	92621	Teacher	Growth	250	$17.00
9/27/97	Ms.	Ester	Guitron	530 Escanada	Anaheim	CA	93834	Salesperson	Aggressive	400	$16.00
9/28/97	Mr.	Joe	Gruden	2424 Holiday	Cerritos	CA	90701	Teacher	International	550	$9.00
9/28/97	Mrs.	Susan	Drussler	989 Grove	Irvine	CA	92754	Attorney	Technology	2,500	$7.00
10/6/97	Mr.	Essey	Meshi	555 Shafer	Yorba	CA	92686	Salesperson	Growth	800	$12.00
10/7/97	Dr.	Warren	Bacani	267 Portola	Tustin	CA	92670	Doctor	Aggressive	100	$23.00
10/9/97	Ms.	Rosey	Zamora	396 Barranca	Irvine	CA	92754	Attorney	Growth	750	$25.00

(continued)

In the Lab

Creating and Formatting an Investor Database *(continued)*

Instructions: Perform the following tasks:

1. Create the database in the format shown in Figure 3-106. Use the Connect to Web for additional clips button in the Microsoft Clip Gallery 3.0 dialog box to download the clip art shown in Figure 3-106 (search using the keyword, hearts). Experiment with the clip art size, title sizes, and field positions to obtain the desired format.
2. Format the field names as shown in Figure 3-106.
3. Enter the data from the table into the database.
4. Determine the proper field widths so that in list view the entire record in the database prints on a single page.
5. Save the database on a floppy disk. Use the filename, Investment Group.
6. Print the database in both form view and list view.
7. Follow the directions from your instructor for turning in this assignment.

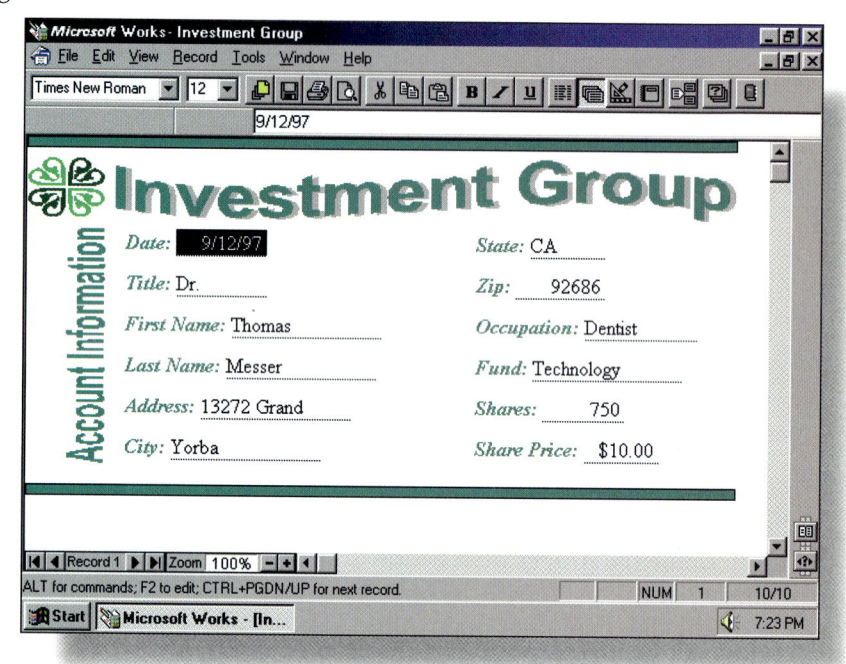

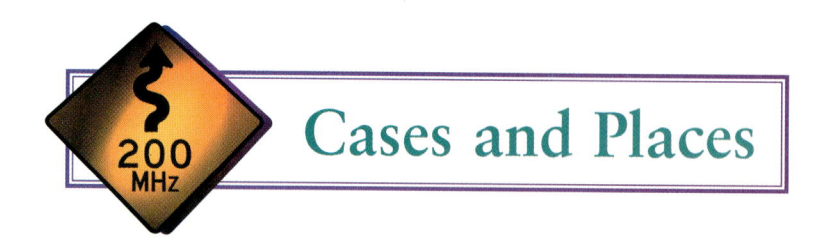

FIGURE 3-106

Cases and Places

The difficulty of these case studies varies:

▶ Case studies preceded by a single half moon are the least difficult. You are asked to create the required database based on information that has already been placed in an organized form.

▶▶ Case studies preceded by two half moons are more difficult. You must organize the information presented before using it to create the desired database.

▶▶▶ Case studies preceded by three half moons are the most difficult. You must choose a specific topic, then obtain and organize the necessary information before using it to create the required database.

Cases and Places

1 ▸ In the United States, 15 people out of 1,000 will suffer from pneumonia each year. In an effort to stay healthy, you investigate how these individuals get this disease. You learn that pneumonia is generally caused by various types of bacteria and viruses, as shown in Figure 3-107.

CAUSE	WHEN SYMPTOMS APPEAR	BODY TEMPERATURE (FAHRENHEIT)	SYMPTOMS
Cytomegalovirus	Within several days	101	Tiredness
Influenza virus	Within hours of infection	104	Blue lips and nails
Legionnaire's disease bacterium	2-10 days	104	Chills
Mycoplasma	3-4 days	101	Headache
Pneumococcus bacterium	Within hours of infection	104	Chills
Other viruses	4-5 days	101	Tiredness

FIGURE 3-107

Create a database that contains this information, and enter the data from Figure 3-107. Design the form using clip art from the Microsoft Clip Gallery Live Web site and WordArt.

2 ▸ Whale-watching expeditions have been growing in popularity. Now, you are considering planning such a trip to see the humpback or orca whales as a graduation present to yourself. After visiting several travel agencies and calling environmental organizations for details, you compile the information in Figure 3-108 to help you decide on a vacation destination.

DESTINATION	WHALE SPECIES	WATCHING SEASON	ACCESS
Antarctica	Humpback	Summer	Boat
Argentina	Orca	Summer/Fall	Boat
British Columbia	Orca	Summer	Boat/Shore
Dominican Republic	Humpback	Winter	Boat/Shore
Massachusetts	Humpback	Summer	Boat
Mexico	Humpback	All year	Boat/Shore
Norway	Orca	Summer	Boat
New Zealand	Orca	All year	Shore
South Africa	Orca	Fall	Shore

FIGURE 3-108

Create a database that contains these records, and enter the data from Figure 3-108. Design the form using the Microsoft Clip Gallery Live Web site, WordArt, and labels. Use rectangles to set off areas of the form.

Cases and Places

3 ▶▶ A potential employer has asked you to send him various materials, including a completed application, three letters of reference, your college transcripts, and several writing samples. You want him to receive this information the following day, so you call the post office and several overnight delivery companies for their rates. You learn that the post office offers Express Mail, which guarantees next day delivery by noon. The rates are $10.75 for up to eight ounces and $15 for up to two pounds. Airborne charges $14 for packages weighing up to eight ounces and $25 for packages weighing up to two pounds. Delivery on both is the following day before noon or before 5:00 p.m., depending on the package's destination. Federal Express separates its charges based on time of delivery. Packages weighing eight ounces or less cost $13 for priority delivery by 10:30 a.m. and $10 for standard delivery by 3:00 p.m. Packages weighing more than eight ounces and one pound or less cost $20 for priority delivery and $14 for standard delivery. Packages weighing more than one pound and two pounds or less cost $21.75 for priority delivery and $15 for standard delivery. Using this information, together with the techniques presented in this project, create a database showing the name of the delivery company, the rate for a package weighing eight ounces or less, the rate for a package weighing one pound or less, the rate for a package weighing two pounds or less, and delivery times.

4 ▶▶▶ You have managed to save $2,500 and want to invest this money in a six-month certificate of deposit (CD) to help save for next semester's tuition. Visit a local bank, credit union, and savings and loan association and make a list of the current interest rates, minimum investment amounts, total amounts earned in six months, penalties for early withdrawal, and other restrictions. Using this information, together with the techniques presented in this project, create a database showing the name of the financial institution, its address and telephone number, the interest rate, the total value of the CD in six months, the amount of interest earned, the amount you would be penalized if you withdrew the money in two months and in four months, and any other restrictions. Include a bar graph indicating the amount of interest you would earn and the total value of your investment.

5 ▶▶▶ You work for the classified ad section of your local newspaper. Your editors have decided to introduce a new service where readers can call the office and inquire if a particular car is being advertised. The editors have assigned this task to you. Begin by creating a database with fields for car manufacturer, model, year, price, transmission (automatic or manual), mileage, and engine size. Then enter data for 20 ads in today's newspaper. If any information is missing, enter the letters NA (not available). Test the project by performing queries to find records of cars from each of the past 10 years.

6 ▶▶▶ Food manufacturers claim that consumers can eat more nutritionally by purchasing specific items. For example, an ice cream manufacturer will label its products as low calorie (the product has 40 or fewer calories per serving), light calorie (1/3 fewer calories than the referenced product), or calorie free (fewer than 5 calories per serving). Visit a grocery store and examine the labels of five specific products claiming to be low, light, or calorie free. Then compare these five products to the referenced products. Using this information, together with the techniques presented in this project, create a database showing the name of the reduced-calorie product, the name of the referenced product, the serving size of each, and the number of calories per serving.